Mental Representation

Mental Representation

A Reader

Edited by

Stephen Stich
and
Ted A. Warfield

BLACKWELL
Oxford UK & Cambridge USA

Copyright © Basil Blackwell Ltd 1994

First published 1994
Reprinted 1995

Blackwell Publishers Inc.
238 Main Street
Cambridge, Massachusetts 02142
USA

Blackwell Publishers Ltd
108 Cowley Road
Oxford OX4 1JF
UK

Library of Congress Cataloging-in-Publication Data

Mental representation : a reader / edited by Stephen Stich and Ted A.
Warfield.
    p.   cm.
    Includes bibliographical references and index.
    ISBN 1-55786-476-4 (alk. paper). — ISBN 1-55786-477-2 (pbk. :
alk. paper)
    1. Mental representation.   2. Philosophy of mind.   I. Stich,
Stephen P.   II. Warfield, Ted A., 1969–   .
BF367.M46   1994
121'.4—dc20
                                                          93-31974
                                                               CIP

British Library Cataloguing in Publication Data

A CIP catalogue record for this book is available from the British Library.

Typeset in 10½ on 12 pt Ehrhardt
by Graphicraft Typesetters, Hong Kong
Printed in Great Britain by T.J. Press, Padstow, Cornwall

This book is printed on acid-free paper

Contents

Contributors

Fred Adams
Ken Aizawa
Ned Block
Robert Cummins
Daniel Dennett
Fred Dretske
Hartry Field
Jerry Fodor

Peter Godfrey-Smith
Terence Horgan
Ernest Lepore
Barry Loewer
Ruth Millikan
Lynne Rudder Baker
Stephen Stich
Ted A. Warfield

Part I

Introduction

1 Introduction

Ted A. Warfield and Stephen Stich

1 The Representational Theory of the Mind

Jessica believes that the flower is in the vase. Jeff wants to get a high mark on his philosophy exam. Jeff's desire and Jessica's belief are alike in that each has a *condition of satisfaction*. The satisfaction-condition of a belief is its truth-condition: Jessica's belief is true just in case the flower is in the vase. The satisfaction-condition of a desire is the condition under which it is fulfilled: Jeff's desire is fulfilled just in case he gets a high mark on his philosophy exam. Jessica's belief and Jeff's desire are also alike in that both states are about certain things and not about others. Jessica's belief is about the flower and the vase, and is not about the table on which the vase is sitting, though of course she may have beliefs about the table as well. Similarly, Jeff's desire is about his philosophy exam, not about the history exam on the following day.

Philosophers and cognitive scientists often use the term *propositional attitude* as a general label for those mental states that have conditions of satisfaction – states like believing, desiring, wishing and fearing. According to the most widely held theory in this area, what it is for a person to have a propositional attitude is for the person to stand in an appropriate sort of relation to a special kind of internal state – a *mental representation*. Thus, for example, for a person to believe that the flower is in the vase is for the person to stand in the relation constitutive of believing to a state of the person, a mental representation, which *means* that the flower is in the vase. This account of the nature of propositional attitudes raises lots of questions. Here are two:

(1) What is the nature of each particular propositional attitude relation (i.e., the belief relation, the desire relation, etc.)?[1]

(2) Why is it that a given mental representation has the meaning that it has, rather than some other meaning or none at all?

Question (1), though extremely interesting and important, is not the question that concerns us presently. We will therefore sidestep this question with the help of a useful metaphor introduced some time ago by Stephen Schiffer.[2] Let's pretend that there are little boxes in people's heads which correspond to each of the propositional attitudes. So we are pretending that there is a belief box, and a separate desire box, and additional boxes for such attitudes as hoping and fearing. Given this rather fanciful supposition, what it is for a person to have a belief is for a mental representation to be in that person's belief box. And what it is for a person to believe that the flower is in the vase is for a representation which means that the flower is in the vase to be in the person's belief box. Of course, the belief box metaphor does no real philosophical or explanatory work. We use the metaphor because it is employed by many philosophers who work in this area, and because it allows us to bracket question (1) and move on to other issues.

It is important to note that while question (1) is about relations such as believing and desiring, question (2) is about mental representations, and while "belief" and "desire" are ordinary terms, the term "mental representation" is not. Mental representations are theoretical postulates invoked by philosophers and cognitive scientists in an attempt to analyze or explain propositional attitudes, such as belief and desire, that play a central role in commonsense psychology. Both propositional attitudes and the mental representations invoked to explain them have *semantic* or *intentional* properties – they have satisfaction-conditions and they are about certain things. Theorists who adopt the approach to propositional attitudes that we have been sketching typically try to account for the semantic properties of propositional attitudes by appeal to the semantic properties of mental representations. On the simplest story, beliefs and other propositional attitudes simply inherit their semantic properties from the semantic properties of the associated mental representations.

Writing nearly ten years ago, in his now classic paper "Fodor's Guide to Mental Representation," Jerry Fodor observed that, "as things now stand," we have "no adequate account" of the "semanticity of mental representations." In light of this, he offered the following prediction:

> Which semantic theory to tell is . . . going to be *the* issue in mental representation theory for the foreseeable future.[3]

Fodor's prediction has, to put it mildly, come true. But not even Fodor could have predicted the fervor with which this topic was to be pursued.[4] In one guise or another, the project of providing a semantic theory for mental representations (or a "theory of content" as it is often called) has been center stage in the philosophy of mind for much of the past decade. Many writers now view it as the *central* project in the philosophy of mind. It is to this project that the present volume is dedicated.[5]

2   Some Constraints on Theories of Content

Though many philosophers and cognitive scientists think it is enormously important to develop an acceptable theory of content, it is far from clear what would *count* as an acceptable theory in this area. Indeed, in the last paper in this volume, Stich argues that there are actually many different projects being pursued by theorists who offer accounts of mental representation. In the remaining pages of this Introduction we will sketch some of the constraints on theories of mental representation that play a central role in the papers to follow. These constraints are general conditions that, on the view of many theorists, any theory of mental representation should meet. We offer this list of constraints as a sort of checklist that the reader can use to evaluate the various theories debated in the ensuing essays. However, the list must be used with care. For it is certainly not the case that each constraint on our list would be accepted as a requirement by everyone working in the area. It is our contention that the three constraints on our list have considerable *prima facie* plausibility. So if a theorist proposes an account of content that violates one or another of the constraints, the theorist should be able to provide some explanation of why he or she thinks the constraint can be ignored.

2.1   Naturalism

Perhaps the most common constraint placed on theories aimed at explaining the semantics of mental representations is the requirement that the theory be *naturalistic*. What exactly this "naturalism constraint" amounts to is a matter of considerable debate.[6] But the basic idea is that semantic properties are not part of the basic building blocks of the universe and thus semantic facts should not be viewed as primitive or unanalyzable. Rather, the naturalism constraint insists, a theory of mental representation must provide some account of how semantic properties arise out of more basic non-semantic properties. Fodor gives voice to this sentiment in a particularly vivid way.

> I suppose that sooner or later the physicists will complete the catalogue they've been compiling of the ultimate and irreducible properties of things. When they do, the likes of *spin*, *charm*, and *charge* will perhaps appear on the list. But *aboutness* surely won't; intentionality simply doesn't go that deep. It is hard to see, in face of this consideration, how one can be a Realist about intentionality without also being, to some extent, a Reductionist. If the semantic and the intentional are real properties of things, it must be in virtue of their identity with (or maybe of their supervenience on?) properties that are themselves *neither* intentional *nor* semantic. If aboutness is real, it must be really something else.[7]

There is a second reason for enforcing the requirement that theories of mental representation not appeal to any semantic notions: the constraint is imposed in an attempt to avoid circularity. Recall that the semantic properties of mental representations are typically invoked in order to explain the semantic properties of beliefs, desires and other propositional attitude states. And the semantic properties of propositional attitudes are often pressed into service to explain the semantic properties of linguistic entities like words and sentences. A theorist who adopts this strategy for explaining the semantic properties of propositional attitudes and linguistic entities cannot then appeal to the semantic properties of propositional attitudes or linguistic entities in explaining the semantic properties of mental representations. For to do so would be patently circular.

2.2   Misrepresentation

Another very general constraint on an account of mental representation is that the account should explain how *misrepresentation* is possible. Sometimes when Jessica believes that the flower is in the vase her belief will be true. But sometimes her belief will be false. Perhaps, unbeknown to Jessica, the flower has been removed. Or perhaps the flower is actually behind the vase, though from where Jessica is standing it looks like the flower is in the vase. According to the relation-to-representation account of belief, when Jessica mistakenly believes that the flower is in the vase there is, in her belief box, a mental representation which means that the flower is in the vase. And since the flower is not in the vase, that representation misrepresents the way the world actually is. So, if we accept the relation-to-representation account of propositional attitudes, it seems undeniable that mental representations sometimes represent what is not the case. Thus there is something deeply problematic about any account of the content of mental representations that makes this phenomenon mysterious or impossible.

It is important to note that not all cases of mental misrepresentation are cases in which an *error* has occurred. We often think about states of affairs that are not the case, and it does not follow that errors are occurring each time we do this. Perhaps the most obvious examples of this phenomenon are cases in which people imagine or hypothesize that certain things are the case, even though they know full well that what they are imagining or hypothesizing is false. The mental representations invoked in such instances of thinking, imagining and hypothesizing are misrepresentations, though these episodes do not involve any sort of error. The moral to draw here is that misrepresentation is a broad category, including, but not limited to, cases of error.

The problem of accounting for misrepresentation looms especially large for theorists such as Dretske and Stampe who seek to use the notion of a "natural sign" or various closely related notions as the foundation on which to build an account of mental representation. On Dretske's account, a natural sign is a *reliable indicator* of some state of affairs; if the indicated state of affairs had not occurred, then the sign would not be present. But obviously, if it is characterized in this way, a natural sign can't mis-indicate. Thus a central part of Dretske's project is to explain how misrepresentation is possible on an account of representation built upon the notion of a natural sign.

2.3   Fine-grained meanings

Propositional attitudes can often be remarkably specific. It seems perfectly possible for a person to want to visit Ben Franklin's birthplace, while having no desire at all to visit the birthplace of the inventor of bifocals. This is possible despite the fact that Franklin was the inventor of bifocals. Similarly, it seems entirely possible that a person might believe that the stuff in the glass she is holding is water, and not believe that the stuff is H_2O. It is even possible for a person to believe that the triangle he is looking at is equilateral, but not believe that it is equiangular. If propositional attitudes are relations to mental representations, and if they inherit their semantic properties from the mental representations, then any account of the semantics of mental representations is going to have to draw lots of very fine-grained distinctions. And, as the essays in this volume make all too clear, this requirement can pose some very daunting problems.

Many theorists attempt to explain the meaning of a mental representation by appealing to some sort of relation obtaining between the mental representation and the world. Dretske, for example, appeals to causal relations between mental representations and states of affairs. Fodor offers an account in which counterfactual relations play a central role. Both Field and Millikan appeal to historical relations, though the relations they exploit are very different. But for all of these authors the fine grainedness of meanings poses at least a *prima facie* problem. For, as we have seen, it looks like a theory of content will have to distinguish between mental representations that mean water and others that mean H_2O. The theory will also have to distinguish between mental representations that mean equilateral from others that mean equiangular. But water *is* H_2O, and all equilateral triangles are equiangular. So if a mental representation bears a relation, R, to water (or to equilateral triangles), then, it would seem, it must bear the relation R to H_2O (or to equiangular triangles) as well. A number of the authors represented in this volume offer sophisticated strategies to resolve this problem. Others argue that their theories need not account for the fine grainedness of meaning. Whether any of these efforts succeed is a question that we propose to leave for the reader to decide.

Notes

1 It would appear that ordinary language terms for propositional attitudes can encompass more than one relation. So, for example, a slight urge to drink a soda and an intense craving for a soda would both count as desire states. Because of this multi-faceted nature of "desire" it is unlikely that there will be a single relation constitutive of the relation. A similar point applies to most if not all of the other ordinary language propositional attitude terms.

2 Schiffer (1981).

3 Fodor (1985), p. 96.

4 The bibliography of this volume provides no more than a sampling of the enormous literature aimed at understanding the semantics of mental representations.

5 We should note that not all of the contributors to this volume accept the theory that propositional attitudes are best viewed as relations between a person and a mental representation. Cummins endorses no view about the propositional attitudes invoked in ordinary discourse. His focus is on the semantic properties of mental representations as they are invoked in various scientific theories. Dennett is a trenchant critic of the relation-to-mental-representation view of propositional attitudes. He offers a radically different account of the attitudes and their semantic properties in which his notion the "intentional stance" plays a central role.

6 See, for example, Stich and Laurence (1994).

7 Fodor (1987), p. 97. Perhaps the most influential writer to _reject_ the naturalism constraint is John Searle, who writes:

> You cannot reduce intentional content (or pains or "qualia") to something else, because if you could they would be something else, and they are not something else. The opposite of my view is stated very succinctly by Fodor: "If aboutness is real, it must really be something else." On the contrary, aboutness (i.e., intentionality) is real, and it is not something else. (Searle, 1992, p. 51)

2 Fodor's Guide to Mental Representation: The Intelligent Auntie's Vade-Mecum

Jerry Fodor

It rained for weeks and we were all *so* tired of ontology, but there didn't seem to be much else to do. Some of the children started to sulk and pull the cat's tail. It was going to be an *awful* afternoon until Uncle Wilifred thought of Mental Representations (which was a game that we hadn't played for *years*) and everybody got *very* excited and we jumped up and down and waved our hands and all talked at once and had a perfectly *lovely* romp. But Auntie said that she couldn't stand the noise and there would be tears before bedtime if we didn't please calm down.

Auntie rather disapproves of what is going on in the Playroom, and you can't entirely blame her. Ten or fifteen years of philosophical discussion of mental representation has produced a considerable appearance of disorder. Every conceivable position seems to have been occupied, along with some whose conceivability it is permissible to doubt. And every view that anyone has mooted, someone else has undertaken to refute. This does *not* strike Auntie as constructive play. She sighs for the days when well-brought-up philosophers of mind kept themselves occupied for hours on end analyzing their behavioral dispositions.

But the chaotic appearances are actually misleading. A rather surprising amount of agreement has emerged, if not about who's winning, at least about how the game has to be played. In fact, everybody involved concurs, pretty much, on what the options are. They differ in their hunches about which of the options it would be profitable to exercise. The resulting noise is of these intuitions clashing. In this paper, I want to make as much of the consensus as I can explicit, both by way of reassuring Auntie and in order to provide new participants with a quick guide to the game. Who's where and how did they get there? Since it's very nearly true that you can locate all the players by their answers to quite a small number of diagnostic questions, I shall organize the discussion along those lines. What follows is a short projective test of the sort that self-absorbed persons use to reveal their hitherto unrecognized proclivities. I hope for a great success in California.

First Question: How Do You Feel about Propositional Attitudes?

The contemporary discussion about mental representation is intimately and intricately involved with the question of Realism about propositional attitudes. Since a goal of this essay is to locate the issues about mental representation with respect to other questions in the philosophy of mind, we commence by setting out this relation in several of its aspects.

The natural home of the propositional attitudes is in "commonsense" (or "belief/desire") psychological explanation. If you ask the Man on the Clapham Omnibus what precisely he is doing there, he will tell you a story along the following lines: "I wanted to get home (to work, to Auntie's) and I have reason to believe that there – or somewhere near it – is where this omnibus is going." It is, in short, untendentious that people regularly account for their voluntary behavior by citing beliefs and desires that they entertain; and that, if their behavior is challenged, they regularly defend it by maintaining the rationality of the beliefs ("Because it *says* it's going to Clapham") and the probity of the desires ("Because it's *nice* visiting Auntie"). That, however, is probably as far as the Clapham Omnibus will take us. What comes next is a philosophical gloss – and, eventually, a philosophical theory.

First philosophical gloss

When the ordinary chap says that he's doing what he is because he has the beliefs and desires that he does, it is reasonable to read the "because" as a *causal* "because" – whatever, exactly, a causal "because" may be. At a minimum, common sense seems to require belief/desire explanations to support counterfactuals in ways that are familiar in causal explanation at large: if, for example, it is true that Psmith did A because he believed B and desired C, then it must be that Psmith would *not* have done A if either he had not believed B or he had not desired C. (Ceteris paribus, it goes without saying.) Common sense also probably takes it that, if Psmith did A because he believed B and desired C, then – ceteris paribus again – believing B and desiring C is causally sufficient for doing A. (However, common sense does get confused about this since – though believing B and desiring C was what caused Psmith to do A – still it is common sense that Psmith could have believed B and desired C and *not* done

A had he so decided. It is a question of some interest whether common sense can have it both ways.) Anyhow, to a first approximation the commonsense view is that there is mental causation, and that mental causes are subsumed by counterfactual – supporting generalizations of which the practical syllogism is perhaps the paradigm.

Closely connected is the following: Everyman's view seems to be that propositional attitudes cause (not only behavior but also) other propositional attitudes. Thoughts cause desires (so that thinking about visiting Auntie makes one want to) and – perhaps a little more tendentiously – the other way around as well (so that the wish is often father to the thought, according to the commonsense view of mental genealogy). In the paradigm mental process – viz. thinking – thoughts give rise to one another and eventuate in the fixation of beliefs. That is what Sherlock Holmes was supposed to be so good at.

Second philosophical gloss

Common sense has it that beliefs and desires are semantically evaluable, that they have *satisfaction-conditions*. Roughly, the satisfaction-condition for a belief is the state of affairs in virtue of which that belief is true or false and the satisfaction-condition for a desire is the state of affairs in virtue of which that desire is fulfilled or frustrated. Thus, "that it continues to rain" makes true the belief that it is raining and frustrates the desire that the rain should stop. This could stand a lot more sharpening, but it will do for the purposes at hand.

It will have occurred to the reader that there are other ways of glossing commonsense belief/desire psychology. And that, even if this way of glossing it is right, commonsense belief/desire psychology may be in need of emendation. Or cancellation. Quite so, but my purpose isn't to defend or criticize; I just want to establish a point of reference. I propose to say that someone is a *Realist* about propositional attitudes if (a) he holds that there are mental states whose occurrences and interactions cause behavior and do so, moreover, in ways that respect (at least to an approximation) the generalizations of commonsense belief/desire psychology; and (b) he holds that these same causally efficacious mental states are also semantically evaluable.

So much for commonsense psychological explanation. The connection with our topic is this: the full-blown Representational Theory of Mind (hereinafter RTM, about which a great deal presently) purports to explain how there *could be* states that have the semantical and causal properties that propositional attitudes are commonsensically supposed to have. In effect, RTM proposes an account of what the propositional attitudes *are*. So, the further you are from Realism about propositional attitudes, the dimmer the view of RTM that you are likely to take.

Quite a lot of the philosophical discussion that's relevant to RTM, therefore, concerns the status and prospects of commonsense intentional psychology. More, perhaps, than is generally realized. For example, we'll see presently that some of the philosophical worries about RTM derive from scepticism about the semantical properties of mental representations. Putnam, in particular, has been explicit in questioning whether coherent sense could be made of such properties. (See Putnam, 1986, 1983.) I have my doubts about the seriousness of these worries (see Fodor, 1986a); but the present point is that they are, in any event, misdirected as arguments against RTM. If there is something wrong with meaning, what that shows is something *very* radical, viz. that there is something wrong with propositional attitudes (a moral, by the way, that Quine, Davidson, and Stich, among others, have drawn explicitly). That, and *not* RTM, is surely the ground on which this action should be fought.

If, in short, you think that common sense is just plain *wrong* about the etiology of behavior – i.e., that there is *nothing* that has the causal and semantic properties that common sense attributes to the attitudes – then the questions that RTM purports to answer don't so much as arise for you. You won't care much what the attitudes are if you take the view that there aren't any. Many philosophers do take this view and are thus united in their indifference to RTM. Among these Anti-Realists there are, however, interesting differences in motivation and tone of voice. Here, then, are some ways of not being a Realist about beliefs and desires.

First anti-realist option

You could take an *instrumentalist* view of intentional explanation. You could hold that though there are, *strictly speaking*, no such things as belief and desires, still talking as though there were some often leads to confirmed behavioral predictions. Everyman is therefore licensed to talk that way – to adopt, as one says, the intentional stance – so long as he doesn't take the ontological commitments of belief/desire psychology literally. (Navigators talk geocentric astronomy for convenience, and nobody holds it against them; it gets them where they want to go.) The great virtue of instrumentalism – here as elsewhere – is that you get all the goodness and suffer none of the pain: you get to use propositional-attitude psychology to make behavioral predictions; you get to "accept" all the intentional explanations that it is convenient to accept; but you don't have to answer hard questions about what the attitudes *are*.

There is, however, a standard objection to instrumentalism (again, here as elsewhere): it's hard to explain why belief/desire psychology works so well if belief/desire psychology is, as a matter of fact, not true. I propose to steer clear, throughout this essay, of general issues in the philosophy of science; in particular of issues about the status of scientific theories at large. But – as Putnam, Boyd and others have emphasized – there is surely a presumptive inference from the predictive successes of a theory to its truth; still more so when (unlike geocentric astronomy) it is the *only* predictively successful theory in the field. It's not, to put it mildly, obvious why this presumption shouldn't militate in favor of a Realist – as against an instrumentalist – construal of belief/desire explanations.

The most extensively worked-out version of instrumentalism about the attitudes in the recent literature is surely owing to D. C. Dennett. (See the papers in Dennett, 1978a, especially the essay "Intentional Systems.") Dennett confronts the "if it isn't true, why does it work?" problem (Dennett, 1981c), but I find his position obscure. Here's how I *think* it goes: (a) belief/desire explanations rest on very comprehensive rationality assumptions; it's only fully rational systems that such explanations could be literally true of. These rationality assumptions are, however, generally contrary to fact; *that's* why intentional explanations can't be better than instrumental. On the other hand, (b) intentional explanations *work* because we apply them only to evolutionary successful (or other "designed") systems; and if the behavior of a system didn't at least *approximate* rationality it wouldn't *be* evolutionarily successful; what it would be is extinct.

There is a lot about this that's problematic. To begin with, it's unclear whether there really is a rationality assumption implicit in intentional explanation and whether, it there is, the rationality assumption that's required is so strong as to be certainly false. Dennett says in "Intentional Systems" (Dennett, 1978c) that, unless we assume rationality, we get no behavioral predictions out of belief/desire psychology since without rationality any behavior is compatible with any beliefs and desires. Clearly, however, you don't need to assume *much* rationality if all you want is *some* predictivity; perhaps you don't need to assume more rationality than organisms actually have.

Perhaps, in short, the rationality that Dennett says that natural selection guarantees is enough to support *literal* (not just instrumental) intentional ascription. At a minimum, there seems to be a clash between Dennett's principles (a) and (b) since, if it *follows from* evolutionary theory that successful organisms are pretty rational, then it's hard to see how attributions of rationality to successful organisms can be construed purely instrumentally (as merely a "stance" that we adopt towards systems whose behavior we seek to predict).

Finally, if you admit that it's a matter of fact that some agents are rational to some degree, then you have to face the hard question of how they *can* be. After all, not *everything* that's "designed" is rational even to a degree. Bricks aren't for example; they have the wrong kind of structure. The question what sort of structure is required for rationality does, therefore, rather suggest itself, and it's very unclear that that question can be answered without talking about structures of beliefs and desires; intentional psychology is the only candidate we have so far for a theory of how rationality is achieved. This suggests – what I think is true but won't argue for here – that the rational systems are a species of the intentional ones rather than the other way around. If that is so, then it is misguided to appeal to rationality in the analysis of intentionality since, in the order of explanation, the latter is the more fundamental notion. What with

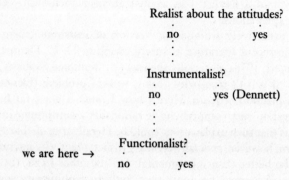

Realist about the attitudes?

no   yes

Instrumentalist?

no   yes (Dennett)

Functionalist?

we are here →

no   yes

Figure 2.1 Decision tree, stage 1

one thing and another, it does seem possible to doubt that a coherent instrumentalism about the attitudes is going to be forthcoming.

Second anti-realist option

You could take the view that belief/desire psychology is just plain false and skip the instrumentalist trimmings. On this way of telling the Anti-Realist story, belief/desire psychology is in competition with alternative accounts of the etiology of behavior and should be judged in the same way that the alternatives are: by its predictive successes, by the plausibility of its ontological commitments, and by its coherence with the rest of the scientific enterprise. No doubt the predictive successes of belief/desire explanations are pretty impressive − especially when they are allowed to make free use of ceteris paribus clauses. But when judged by the second and third criteria, commonsense psychology proves to be a *bad* theory; "stagnant science" is the preferred epithet (see Churchland, 1981; Stich, 1983). What we ought therefore to do is get rid of it and find something better.

There is, however, some disagreement as to what something better would be like. What matters here is how you feel about Functionalism. So let's have that be our next diagnostic question.

(Is everybody still with us? In case you're not, see the decision tree in figure 2.1 for the discussion so far. Auntie's motto: a place for every person; every person in his place.)

Second Question: How Do You Feel about Functionalism?

(This is a twice-told tale, so I'll be quick. For a longer review, see Fodor, 1981a; Fodor, 1981c.)

It looked, in the early 1960s, as though anybody who wanted psychology to be compatible with a physicalistic ontology had a choice between some or other kind of *behaviorism* and some or other kind of *property-identity theory*. For a variety of reasons neither of these options seemed very satisfactory (in fact, they still don't), so a small tempest brewed in the philosophical teapot.

What came of it was a new account of the type/token relation for psychological states: psychological-state tokens were to be assigned to psychological-state types *solely* by reference to their causal relations to proximal stimuli ("inputs"), to proximal responses ("outputs"), and to one another. The advertising claimed two notable virtues for this theory: first, it was *compatible* with physicalism in that it permitted tokenings of psychological states to be identical to tokenings of physical states (and thus to enjoy whatever causal properties physical states are supposed to have). Second, it permitted tokens of one and the same psychological-state type to differ arbitrarily in their physical kind. This comforted the emerging intuition that the natural domain for psychological theory might be physically heterogeneous, including a motley of people, animals, Martians (always, in the philosophical literature, assumed to be silicon based), and computing machines.

Functionalism, so construed, was greeted with audible joy by the new breed of "Cognitive Scientists" and has clearly become the received ontological doctrine in that discipline. For, if Functionalism is true, then there is plausibly a *level of explanation* between commonsense belief/desire psychology, on the one hand, and neurological (circuit-theoretic; generally "hard-science") explanation on the other. "Cognitive Scientists" could plausibly formulate their enterprise as the construction of theories pitched at that level. Moreover, it was possible to tell a reasonable and esthetically gratifying story about the relations *between* the levels: commonsense belief/desire explanations *reduce* to explanations articulated in terms of functional states (at least the true ones do) because, according to Functionalism, beliefs and desires *are* functional states. And, for each (true) psychological explanation, there will be a corresponding story, to be told in hard-science terms, about how the functional states that it postulates are "realized" in the system under study. Many different hard-science stories may correspond to one and the same functional explanation since, as we saw, the criteria for the tokening of functional states abstract from the physical character of the tokens. (The most careful and convincing Functionalist manifestos I know are Block, 1981c; and Cummins, 1983; q.v.)

Enthusiasm for Functionalism was (is) not, however, universal. For example, viewed from a neuroscientist's perspective (or from the perspective of a hard-line "type-physicalist") Functionalism may appear to be merely a rationale for making do with bad psychology. A picture many neuroscientists have is that, if there really are beliefs and desires (or memories, or percepts, or mental images or whatever else the psychologist may have in his grab bag), it ought to be possible to "find" them in the brain; where what *that* requires is that two tokens of the same *psychological* kind (today's desire to visit Auntie, say, and yesterday's) should correspond to two tokens of the same *neurological* kind (today's firing of neuron #535, say, and yesterday's). Patently, Functionalism relaxes that requirement – relaxes it, indeed, to the point of invisibility. Functionalism just *is* the doctrine that the psychologist's theoretical taxonomy doesn't need to look "natural" from the point of view of any lower-level science. This seems to some neuroscientists, and to some of their philosopher friends, like letting psychologists get away with murder. (See, for example, Churchland, 1981, which argues that Functionalism could have "saved" alchemy if only the alchemists had been devious enough to devise it.) There is, for once, something tangible at issue here: who has the right theoretical vocabulary for explaining behavior determines who should get the grants.

So much for Functionalism except to add that one can, of course, combine *accepting* the Functionalist ontology with *rejecting* the reduction of belief/ desire explanations to functional ones (for example, because you think that, though *some* Functionalist psychological explanations are true, no commonsense belief/desire psychological explanations are). Bearing this proviso in mind, we can put some more people in their places: if you are Anti-Realist (and anti-instrumentalist) about belief/desire psychology *and* you think there is no Functional level of explanation, then probably you think that behavioral science is (or, anyhow, ought to be) neuroscience.[1] (A fortiori, you will be no partisan of RTM, which is, of course, way over on the other side of the decision tree.) The Churchlands are the paradigm inhabitants of this niche. On the other hand, if you combine eliminativist sentiments about propositional attitudes with enthusiasm for the functional individuation of mental states, then you anticipate the eventual *replacement* of commonsense belief/desire explanations by theories couched in the vocabulary of a Functionalist psychology: replacement rather than *reduction*. You are thus led to write books with such titles as *From Folk Psychology to Cognitive Science* and are almost certainly identical to Stephen Stich.

One more word about Anti-Realism. It may strike you as odd that, whereas instrumentalists hold that belief/desire psychology works so well that we can't do anything without it, eliminativists hold that it works so badly ("stagnant science" and all that) that we can't do anything *with* it. Why, you may ask, don't these Anti-Realists get their acts together?

This is not, however, a real paradox. Instrumentalists can agree with eliminativists that *for the purposes of scientific/serious explanation* the attitudes have to be dispensed with. And eliminativists can agree with instrumentalists that, for *practical* purposes, the attitudes do seem quite indispensable. In fact – and here's the point I want to stress just now – what largely motivates Anti-Realism is something deeper than the empirical speculation that belief/desire explanations won't pan out as science; it's the sense that there is something intrinsically wrong with the intentional. This is so important that I propose to leave it to the very end.

Now for the other side of the decision tree. (Presently we'll get to RTM.)
If you are a Realist about propositional attitudes, then of course you think
that there are beliefs and desires. Now, on this side of the tree too you get to
decide whether to be a Functionalist or not. If you are not, then you are
probably John Searle, and you drop off the edge of this paper. My own view
is that RTM, construed as a species of Functionalist psychology, offers the
best Realist account of the attitudes that is currently available; but this view
is – to put it mildly –not universally shared. There are philosophers (many of
whom like Searle, Dreyfus, and Haugeland are more or less heavily invested in
Phenomenology) who are Hyper-Realist about the attitudes but deeply un-
enthusiastic about both Functionalism and RTM. It is not unusual for such
theorists to hold (a) that there *is* no currently available, satisfactory answer to
the question "how could there be things that satisfy the constraints that common sense places upon the attitudes?"; and (b) that finding an answer to this
question is, in any event, not the philosopher's job. (Maybe it is the psychologist's job, or the neuroscientist's. See Dreyfus, 1979; Haugeland, 1978; Searle,
1980.)

For how the decision tree looks now, see figure 2.2.

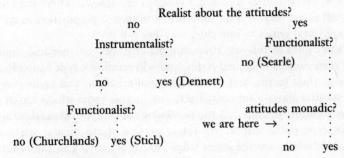

Figure 2.2 Decision tree, stage 2

If you think that there are beliefs and desires, and you think that they are
functional states, then you get to answer the following diagnostic question:

Third Question: Are Propositional Attitudes Monadic Functional States?

This may strike you as a *silly* question. For, you may say, since propositional
attitudes are by definition relations to propositions, it follows that propositional
attitudes are by definition not monadic. A propositional attitude is, to a first approximation, a *pair* of a proposition and a set of intentional systems, viz. the set
of intentional systems which bear that attitude to that proposition.

That would seem to be reasonable enough. But the current (Naturalistic) consensus is that if you've gone this far you will have to go further. Something has to be said about the place of the semantic and the intentional in the natural order; it won't do to have unexplicated "relations to propositions" at the foundations of the philosophy of mind.

Just *why* it won't do – precisely what physicalist or Naturalist scruples it would outrage – is, to be sure, not very clear. Presumably the issue isn't Nominalism, for why raise that issue *here*; if physicists have numbers to play with, why shouldn't psychologists have propositions? And it can't be worries about individuation since distinguishing propositions is surely no harder than distinguishing propositional attitudes and, for better or worse, we're committed to the latter on this side of the decision tree. A more plausible scruple – one I am inclined to take seriously – objects to unreduced *epistemic* relations like *grasping* propositions. One really doesn't want psychology to presuppose any of *those*; first because epistemic relations are preeminently what psychology is supposed to *explain*, and second for fear of "ontological danglers." It's not that there aren't propositions, and it's not that there aren't graspings of them; it's rather that graspings of propositions aren't plausible candidates for ultimate stuff. If they're real, they must be really something else.

Anyhow, one might as well sing the songs one knows. There *is* a reductive story to tell about *what it is* for an attitude to have a proposition as its object. So, metaphysical issues to one side, why not tell it?

The story goes as follows. Propositional attitudes are monadic, functional states of organisms. Functional states, you will recall, are type-individuated by reference to their (actual and potential) causal relations; you know everything that is essential about a functional state when you know which causal generalizations subsume it. Since, in the psychological case, the generalizations that count for type individuation are the ones that relate mental states to one another, a census of mental states would imply a network of causal interrelations. To specify such a network would be to constrain the nomologically possible mental histories of an organism; the network for a given organism would exhibit the possible patterns of causal interaction among its mental states (insofar, at least, as such patterns of interaction are relevant to the type individuation of the states). Of necessity, the actual life of the organism would appear as a path through this network.

Given the Functionalist assurance of individuation by causal role, we can assume that each mental state can be identified with a node in such a network: for each mental state there is a corresponding causal role and for each causal role there is a corresponding node. (To put the same point slightly differently, each mental state can be associated with a formula – e.g., a Ramsey sentence; see Block, 1981c – that uniquely determines its location in the network by specifying its potentialities for causal interaction with each of the other mental states.) Notice, however, that, while this gives a Functionalist sense to the individuation of propositional attitudes, it does not, in and of itself, say what it is for a propositional attitude to have the propositional content that it has. The present proposal is to remedy this defect by reducing the notion of propositional content to the notion of causal role.

So far, we have a network of mental states defined by their causal inter-relations. But notice that there is also a network generated by the *inferential* relations that hold among *propositions*; and it is plausible that its inferential relations are among the properties that each proposition has essentially. Thus, it is presumably a non-contingent property of the proposition that Auntie is shorter than Uncle Wilifred that it entails the proposition that Uncle Wilifred is taller than Auntie. And it is surely a non-contingent property of the proposition that $P \, \& \, Q$ that it entails the proposition that P and the proposition that Q. It may also be that there are evidential relations that are, in the relevant sense, non-contingent; for example, it may be constitutive of the proposition that many of the G's are F that it is, ceteris paribus, evidence for the proposition that all of the G's are F. If it be so, then so be it.

The basic idea is that, given the two networks – the causal and the inferential – we can establish partial isomorphisms between them. Under such an iso-morphism, *the causal role of a propositional attitude mirrors the semantic role of the proposition that is its object*. So, for example, there is the proposition that John left and Mary wept; and it is partially constitutive of this proposition that it has the following semantic relations: it entails the proposition that John left; it entails the proposition that Mary wept; it is entailed by the pair of propo-sitions {John left, Mary wept}; it entails the proposition that somebody did something; it entails the proposition that John did something; it entails the proposition that either it's raining or John left and Mary wept . . . and so forth. Likewise there are, among the potential episodes in an organism's mental life, states which we may wish to construe as: (S^1) having the belief that John left and Mary wept; (S^2) having the belief that John left; (S^3) having the belief that Mary wept; (S^4) having the belief that somebody did something; (S^5) having the belief that either it's raining or John left and Mary wept . . . and so forth. The crucial point is that it constrains the assignment of propositional contents to these mental states that the latter exhibit an appropriate pattern of causal relations. In particular, it must be true (if only under idealization) that being in S^1 tends to cause the organism to be in S^2 and S^3; that being in S^1 tends to cause the organism to be in S^4; that being (simultaneously) in states (S^2, S^3) tends – very strongly, one supposes – to cause the organism to be in state S^1; that being in state S^1 tends to cause the organism to be in state S^5 (as does being in state S^6, viz. the state of believing that it's raining). And so forth.

In short, we can make non-arbitrary assignments of propositions as the objects of propositional attitudes because there is this isomorphism between the network generated by the semantic relations among propositions and the network generated by the causal relations among mental states. The assignment is non-arbitrary precisely in that it is constrained to preserve the isomorphism. And because the isomorphism is perfectly objective (which is not, however, to say that it is perfectly unique; see below), knowing what proposition gets assigned to a mental state – what the object of an attitude is – is knowing something useful. For, within the limits of the operative idealization, *you can deduce the causal consequences of being in a mental state from the semantic relations of its propositional object.* To know that John thinks that Mary wept is to know that it's highly probable that he thinks that somebody wept. To know that Sam thinks that it is raining is to know that it's highly probable that he thinks that either it is raining or that John left and Mary wept. To know that Sam thinks that it's raining and that Sam thinks that if it's raining it is well to carry an umbrella is to be far along the way to predicting a piece of Sam's behavior.

It may be, according to the present story, that preserving isomorphism between the causal and the semantic networks is *all* that there is to the assignment of contents to mental states; that nothing constrains the attribution of propositional objects to propositional attitudes *except* the requirement that isomorphism be preserved. But one need not hold that that is so. On the contrary, many – perhaps most – philosophers who like the isomorphism story are attracted by so-called two-factor theories, according to which what determines the semantics of an attitude is not just its functional role but also its causal connections to objects "in the world." (This is, notice, still a species of Functionalism since it's still causal role alone that counts for the type individuation of mental states; but two-factor theories acknowledge as semantically relevant "external" causal relations between, for example, states of the organism and *distal* stimuli. It is these mind-to-world causal relations that are supposed to determine the denotational semantics of an attitude: what it's about and what its truth-conditions are.) There are serious issues in this area, but for our purposes – we are, after all, just sightseeing – we can group the two-factor theorists with the pure functional-role semanticists.

The story I've just told you is, I think, the standard current construal of Realism about propositional attitudes.[2] I propose, therefore, to call it Standard Realism (SR for convenience). As must be apparent, SR is a compound of two doctrines: a claim about the "internal" structure of attitudes (viz. that they are *monadic* functional states) and a claim about the source of their semantical properties (viz. that some or all of such properties arise from isomorphisms between the causal role of mental states and the implicational structure of propositions). Now, though they are usually held together, it seems clear that these claims are orthogonal. One could opt for monadic mental states without functional-role (FR) semantics; or one could opt for functional-role semantics together with some non-monadic account of the polyadicity of the attitudes. My own view is that SR should be rejected wholesale: that it is wrong about both the structure *and* the semantics of the attitudes. But – such is the confusion and perversity of my colleagues – this view is widely thought to be

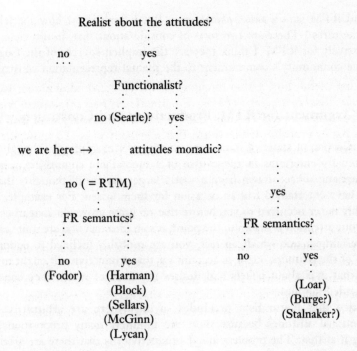

Realist about the attitudes?

no　　　　　yes

Functionalist?

no (Searle)?　yes

we are here →　attitudes monadic?

no (= RTM)

yes

FR semantics?　　　　　FR semantics?

no　　yes　　　　no　　yes
(Fodor)　(Harman)
　　　(Block)
　　　(Sellars)　　　　　　(Loar)
　　　(McGinn)　　　　　(Burge?)
　　　(Lycan)　　　　　(Stalnaker?)

Figure 2.3　Decision tree, stage 3

eccentric. The standard Realistic alternative to Standard Realism holds that SR is right about functional semantics but wrong about monadicity. I propose to divide these issues: monadicity first, semantics at the end.

If, in the present intellectual atmosphere, you are Realist and Functionalist about the attitudes, but you don't think that the attitudes are *monadic* functional states, then probably you think that to have a belief or a desire – or whatever – is to be related in a certain way to a Mental Representation. According to the Canonical formulation of this view: for any organism O and for any proposition P, there is a relation R and a mental representation MP such that: MP means that (expresses the proposition that) P; and O believes that P iff O bears R to MP. (And similarly, R desires that P iff O bears some *different* relation, R', to MP. And so forth. For elaboration, see Fodor, 1975, 1978; Field, 1978.) This is, of course, the doctrine I've been calling full-blown RTM. So we come, at last, to the bottom of the decision tree (see figure 2.3).

As compared with SR, RTM assumes the heavier burden of ontological commitment. It quantifies not just over such mental states as believing that P and desiring that Q but also over mental representations; symbols in a "language of thought." The burden of proof is thus on RTM. (Auntie holds that it doesn't matter who had the burden of proof because the choice between

SR and RTM isn't a *philosophical* issue. But I don't know how she tells. Or why she cares.) There are two sorts of considerations that, in my view, argue persuasively for RTM. I think they are the implicit sources of the Cognitive Science community's commitment to the mental representation construct.

First Argument for RTM: Productivity and Constituency

The collection of states of mind is productive: for example, the thoughts that one actually entertains in the course of a mental life comprise a relatively unsystematic subset drawn from a vastly larger variety of thoughts that one could have entertained had an occasion for them arisen. For example, it has probably never occurred to you before that no grass grows on kangaroos. But, once your attention is drawn to the point, it's an idea that you are quite capable of entertaining, one which, in fact, you are probably inclined to endorse. A theory of the attitudes ought to account for this productivity; it ought to make clear what it is about beliefs and desires in virtue of which they constitute open-ended families.

Notice that Naturalism precludes saying "there are arbitrarily many propositional attitudes because there are infinitely many propositions" and leaving it at that. The problem about productivity is that there are arbitrarily many propositional attitudes that one can *have*. Since relations between organisms and propositions aren't to be taken as primitive, one is going to have to say what it is about organic states like believing and desiring that allows them to be (roughly) as differentiated as the propositions are. If, for example, you think that attitudes are mapped to propositions in virtue of their causal roles (see above), then you have to say what it is about the attitudes that accounts for the productivity *of the set of causal roles*.

A natural suggestion is that the productivity of thoughts is like the productivity of natural languages, i.e., that there are indefinitely many thoughts to entertain for much the same reason that there are indefinitely many sentences to utter. Fine, but how do natural languages manage to be productive? Here the outlines of an answer are familiar. To a first approximation, each sentence can be identified with a certain sequence of subsentential constituents. Different sentences correspond to different ways of arranging these subsentential constituents; new sentences correspond to new ways of arranging them. And the meaning of a sentence – the proposition it expresses – is determined, in a regular way, by its constituent structure.

The constituents of sentences are, say, words and phrases. What are the constituents of propositional attitudes? A natural answer would be: other propositional attitudes. Since, for example, you can't believe that P and Q without believing that P and believing that Q, we could take the former state to be a complex of which the latter are the relatively (or perhaps absolutely) simple parts. But a moment's consideration makes it clear that this won't work with any generality: believing that *P* or *Q* doesn't require either believing that *P* or believing that *Q*, and neither does believing that if *P* then *Q*. It looks as though we want propositional attitudes to be built out of *something*, but not out of other propositional attitudes.

There's an interesting analogy to the case of speech-acts (one of many such; see Vendler, 1983). There are indefinitely many distinct assertions (i.e., there are indefinitely many propositions that one can assert); and though you can't assert that *P* and *Q* without asserting that *P* and asserting that *Q*, the disjunctive assertion, *P* or *Q*, does not imply the assertion of either of the disjuncts, and the hypothetical assertion, if *P* then *Q*, does not imply the assertion of its antecedent or its consequent. So how do you work the constituency relation for *assertions*?

Answer: you take advantage of the fact that making an assertion involves using symbols (typically it involves *uttering* symbols); the constituency relation is defined for the symbols that assertions are made by using. So, in particular, the standard (English-language) vehicle for making the assertion that either John left or Mary wept is the form of words "either John left or Mary wept"; and, notice, this complex linguistic expression *is*, literally, a construct out of the simpler linguistic expressions "John left" and "Mary wept." You can assert that *P* or *Q* without asserting that *P* or asserting that *Q*, but you can't utter the form of words "*P* or *Q*" without uttering the form of words "*P*" and the form of words "*Q*."

The moral for treatments of the attitudes would seem to be straightforward: solve the *productivity* problem for the attitudes by appealing to constituency. Solve the *constituency* problem for the attitudes in the same way that you solve it for speech-acts: tokening an attitude involves tokening a symbol, just as tokening an assertion does. What kind of symbol do you have to token to token an attitude? A mental representation, of course. Hence RTM. (Auntie says that it is crude and preposterous and *unbiological* to suppose that people have sentences in their heads. Auntie always talks like that when she hasn't got any arguments.)

Second Argument for RTM: Mental Processes

It is possible to doubt whether, as functional-role theories of meaning would have it, the propositional contents of mental states are reducible to, or determined by, or epiphenomena of, their causal roles. But what *can't* be doubted is this: the causal roles of mental states typically closely parallel the implicational structures of their propositional objects; and the predictive successes of propositional-attitude psychology routinely exploit the symmetries thus engendered. If we know that Psmith believes that $P \rightarrow Q$ and we know that he

believes that P, then we generally expect him to infer that Q and to act according to his inference. Why do we expect this? Well, because we believe the business about Psmith to be an instance of a true and counterfactual-supporting
generalization according to which believing P and believing $P \rightarrow Q$ is causally
sufficient for inferring Q, ceteris paribus. But then, *what is it about the
mechanisms of thinking in virtue of which such generalizations hold*? What, in particular, could believing and inferring be, such that thinking the premises of a
valid inference leads, so often and so reliably, to thinking its conclusion?

It was a scandal of midcentury Anglo-American philosophy of mind that
though it worried a lot about the nature of mental states (like the attitudes) it
quite generally didn't worry much about the nature of mental *processes* (like
thinking). This isn't, in retrospect, very surprising given the behaviorism that
was widely prevalent. Mental processes are causal sequences of mental states;
if you're eliminativist about the attitudes you're hardly likely to be Realist
about their causal consequences. In particular, you're hardly likely to be Realist about their *causal interactions*. It now seems clear enough, however, that our
theory of the structure of the attitudes *must* accommodate a theory of thinking;
and that it is a preeminent constraint on the latter that it provide a mechanism
for symmetry between the inferential roles of thoughts and their causal roles.

This isn't, by any means, all that easy for a theory of thinking to do. Notice,
for example, that the philosophy of mind assumed in traditional British Em-
piricism was Realist about the attitudes and accepted a form of RTM. (Very
roughly, the attitudes were construed as relations to mental images, the latter
being endowed with semantic properties in virtue of what they resembled
and with causal properties in virtue of their associations. Mental states were
productive because complex images can be constructed out of simple ones.)
But precisely because the mechanisms of mental causation were assumed to be
associationistic (and the conditions for association to involve preeminently
spatio-temporal propinquity), the Empiricists had no good way of connecting
the *contents* of a thought with the effects of entertaining it. They therefore
never got close to a plausible theory of thinking, and neither did the associationistic psychology that followed in their footsteps.

What associationism missed – to put it more exactly – was the similarity
between trains of thoughts and *arguments*. Here, for an example, is Sherlock
Holmes doing his thing at the end of "The Speckled Band":

> I instantly reconsidered my position when . . . it became clear to me that what-
> ever danger threatened an occupant of the room could not come either from the
> window or the door. My attention was speedily drawn, as I have already re-
> marked to you, to this ventilator, and to the bell-rope which hung down to the
> bed. The discovery that this was a dummy, and that the bed was clamped to the
> floor, instantly gave rise to the suspicion that the rope was there as a bridge for
> something passing through the hole, and coming to the bed. The idea of a snake
> instantly occurred to me, and when I coupled it with my knowledge that the

Doctor was furnished with a supply of the creatures from India I felt that I was probably on the right track . . .

The passage purports to be a bit of reconstructive psychology, a capsule history of the sequence of mental episodes which brought Holmes first to suspect, then to believe, that the Doctor did it with his pet snake. Now, back when Auntie was a girl and reasons weren't allowed to be causes, philosophers were unable to believe that such an etiology could be literally true. I assume, however, that liberation has set in by now; we have no philosophically impressive reason to doubt that Holmes's train of thoughts went pretty much the way that he says it did.

What is therefore interesting, for our purposes, is that Holmes's story isn't *just* reconstructive psyhology. It does a double duty since it also serves to assemble *premises* for a plausible inference to the *conclusion* that the Doctor did it with the snake. ("A snake could have crawled through the ventilator and slithered down the bell-rope," "the Doctor was known to keep a supply of snakes in his snuff box," and so forth.) Because this train of thoughts is tantamount to an argument, Holmes expects Watson to be *convinced* by the considerations that, when they occurred to him, caused Holmes's own conviction. (Compare the sort of mental history that goes, "Well, I went to bed and slept on it, and when I woke up in the morning I found that the problem had solved itself." Or the sort that goes, "Bell-ropes always make me think of snakes, and snakes make me think of snake oil, and snake oil makes me think of doctors; so when I saw the bell-rope it popped into my head that the Doctor and a snake might have done it between them." That's mental causation perhaps; but it's not *thinking*.)

What connects the causal-history aspect of Holmes's story with its plausible-inference aspect is precisely the parallelism between trains of thought and arguments: the thoughts that effect the fixation of the belief that P provide, often enough, good *grounds* for believing that P. (As Holmes puts it in another story, "one true inference invariably suggests others.") Were this not the case – were there not this general harmony between the semantical and the causal properties of thoughts – there wouldn't, after all, be much profit in thinking.

What you want to make thinking worth the while is that trains of thoughts should be generated by mechanisms that are generally truth-preserving (so that "a true inference [generally] suggests other inferences *that are also true*"). Argument is generally truth-preserving; that, surely, is the teleological basis of the similarity between trains of thoughts and arguments. The associationists noticed hardly any of this; and even if they had noticed it, they wouldn't have known what to do with it. In this respect, Conan Doyle was a far deeper psychologist – far closer to what is essential about the mental life – than, say, James Joyce (or William James, for that matter).

When, therefore, Rationalist critics (including, notably, Kant) pointed out that thought – like argument – involves judging and inferring, the cat was out of the bag. Associationism was the best available form of Realism about the attitudes, and associationism failed to produce a credible mechanism for thinking. Which is to say that it failed to produce a credible theory of the attitudes. No wonder everybody gave up and turned into a behaviorist.

Cognitive Science is the art of getting the cat back in. The trick is to abandon associationism and combine RTM with the "computer metaphor." In this respect I think there really has been something like an intellectual breakthrough. Technical details to one side, this is – in my view – the *only* respect in which contemporary Cognitive Science represents a major advance over the versions of RTM that were its eighteenth- and nineteenth-century predecessors.

Computers show us how to connect semantical with causal properties *for symbols*. So, if the tokening of an attitude involves the tokening of a symbol, then we can get some leverage on connecting semantical with causal properties *for thoughts*. Here, in roughest outline, is how the story is supposed to go.

You connect the causal properties of a symbol with its semantic properties via its syntax. The syntax of a symbol is one of its second-order physical properties. To a first approximation, we can think of its syntactic structure as an abstract feature of its (geometric or acoustic) *shape*. Because, to all intents and purposes, syntax reduces to shape, and because the shape of a symbol is a potential determinant of its causal role, it is fairly easy to see how there could be environments in which the causal role of a symbol correlates with its syntax. It's easy, that is to say, to imagine symbol tokens interacting causally *in virtue of* their syntactic structures. The syntax of a symbol might determine the causes and effects of its tokenings in much the way that the geometry of a key determines which locks it will open.

But, now, we know from formal logic that certain of the semantic relations among symbols can be, as it were, "mimicked" by their syntactic relations; that, when seen from a very great distance, is what proof-theory is about. So, within certain famous limits, the semantic relation that holds between two symbols when the proposition expressed by the one is implied by the proposition expressed by the other can be mimicked by syntactic relations in virtue of which one of the symbols is derivable from the other. We can therefore build machines which have, again within famous limits, the following property: the operations of such a machine consist entirely of transformations of symbols; in the course of performing these operations, the machine is sensitive solely to syntactic properties of the symbols; and the operations that the machine performs on the symbols are entirely confined to alterations of their shapes. Yet the machine is so devised that it will transform one symbol into another if and only if the symbols so transformed stand in certain *semantic* relations; e.g., the relation that the premises bear to the conclusion in a valid argument. Such machines – computers, of course – just *are* environments in which the causal role of a symbol token is made to parallel the inferential role of the proposition that it expresses.[3]

I expect it's clear how this is all supposed to provide an argument for quantifying over mental representations. Computers are a solution to the problem of mediating between the causal properties of symbols and their semantic properties. So *if* the mind is a sort of computer, we begin to see how you can have a theory of mental processes that succeeds where associationism (to say nothing of behaviorism) abjectly failed – a theory which explains how there could regularly be non-arbitrary content relations among causally related thoughts.

But, patently, there are going to have to be mental representations if this proposal is going to work. In computer design, causal role is brought into phase with content by exploiting parallelisms between the syntax of a symbol and its semantics. But that idea won't do the theory of *mind* any good unless there are *mental* symbols, mental particulars possessed of semantic *and syntactic* properties. There must be mental symbols because, in a nutshell, only symbols have syntax, and our best available theory of mental processes – indeed, the *only* available theory of mental processes that isn't *known* to be false – needs the picture of the mind as a syntax-driven machine.[4]

A brief addendum before we end this section: the question of the extent to which RTM must be committed to the "explicitness" of mental representation is one that keeps getting raised in the philosophical literature (and elsewhere; see Dennett, 1978b; Stabler, 1983). The issue becomes clear if we consider real computers as deployed in Artificial Intelligence research. So, to borrow an example of Dennett's, there are chess machines that play as though they "believe" that it's a good idea to get one's Queen out early. But there needn't be – in fact, there probably wouldn't be – anywhere in the system of heuristics that constitutes the program of such a machine a symbol that *means* "(try and) get your Queen out early"; rather the machine's obedience to that rule of play is, as it were, an epiphenomenon of its following many *other* rules, much more detailed, whose joint effect is that, ceteris paribus, the Queen gets out as soon as it can. The moral is supposed to be that, though the contents of *some* of the attitudes it would be natural to attribute to the machine *may* be explicitly represented, none of them *have* to be, *even assuming the sort of story about how computational processes work that is supposed to motivate RTM*. So, then, what exactly *is* RTM minimally committed to by way of explicit mental representation?

The answer should be clear in light of the previous discussion. According to RTM, mental processes are transformations of mental representations. The rules which determine the course of such transformations may, but needn't, be themselves explicitly represented. But the mental contents (the "thoughts," as it were) that get transformed *must be* explicitly represented or the theory is simply false. To put it another way: if the occurrence of a thought is an episode in a mental process, then RTM is committed to the explicit representation of the content of the thought. Or, to put it still a third way – the way they like to put it in AI – according to RTM, programs may be explicitly represented and data structures have to be.

For the sake of a simple example, let's pretend that associationism is true; we imagine that there is a principle of Association by Proximity in virtue of which thoughts of salt get associated with thoughts of pepper. The point is that, even on the assumption that it subsumes mental processes, the rule "associate by proximity" need not itself be explicitly represented; association by proximity may emerge from dynamical properties of ideas (as in Hume) or from dynamical properties of neural stuff (as in contemporary connectionism). But what *must* be explicit is the Ideas – of pepper and salt, as it might be – that get associated. For, according to the theory, mental processes are actually *causal sequences of tokenings of such Ideas*; so, no Ideas, no mental processes.

Similarly, mutatis mutandis, for the chess case. The rule "get it out early" may be emergent out of its own implementation; out of lower-level heuristics, that is, any one of which may or may not itself be explicitly represented. But the representation of the board – of actual or possible states of play – over which such heuristics are defined *must* be explicit or the representational theory of chess playing is simply false. The theory says that a train of chess thoughts is a causal sequence of tokenings of chess representations. If, therefore, there are trains of chess thoughts but no tokenings of chess representations, it *follows* that something is not well with the theory.

So much, then, for RTM and the polyadicity of the attitudes. What about their semanticity? We proceed to our final diagnostic question:

Fourth Question: How Do You Feel about Truth-Conditions?

I remarked above that the two characteristic tenets of SR – that the attitudes are monadic and that the semanticity of the attitudes arises from isomorphisms between the causal network of mental states and the inferential network of propositions – are mutually independent. Similarly for RTM; it's not mandatory, but you are at liberty to combine RTM with FR semantics if you choose. Thus, you could perfectly well say: "Believing, desiring, and so forth are relations between intentional systems and mental representations that get tokened (in their heads, as it might be). Tokening a mental representation has causal consequences. The totality of such consequences implies a network of causal interrelations among the attitudes . . ." and so on to an FR semantics. In any event, it's important to see that RTM needs *some* semantic story to tell if, as we have supposed, RTM is going to be Realist about the attitudes and the attitudes have their propositional objects essentially.

Which semantic story to tell is, in my view, going to be *the* issue in mental representation theory for the foreseeable future. The questions here are so difficult, and the answers so contentious, that they really fall outside the scope of this paper; I had advertised a tour of an intellectual landscape about whose topography there exists some working consensus. Still, I want to say a little about the semantic issues by way of closing. They are the piece of Cognitive Science where philosophers feel most at home; and they're where the "philosophy of psychology" (a discipline over which Auntie is disinclined to quantify) joins the philosophy of language (which, I notice, Auntie allows me to spell without quotes).

There are a number of reasons for doubting that an FR semantic theory of the sort that SR proposes is tenable. This fact is currently causing something of a crisis among people who would like to be Realists about the attitudes.

In the first place – almost, by now, too obvious to mention – FR theories make it seem that empirical constraints must underdetermine the semantics of the attitudes. What I've got in mind here isn't the collection of worries that cluster around the "indeterminacy of translation" thesis; if that sort of indeterminacy is to be taken seriously at all – which I doubt – then it is equally a problem for *every* Realist semantics. There are, however, certain sources of underdetermination that appear to be built into FR semantics as such; considerations which suggest either that there is no unique best mapping of the causal roles of mental states on to the inferential network of propositions or that, even if there is, such a mapping would nevertheless underdetermine assignments of contents to the attitudes. I'll mention two such considerations, but no doubt there are others; things are always worse than one supposes.

Idealization

The pattern of causal dispositions actually accruing to a given mental state must surely diverge very greatly from the pattern of inferences characteristic of its propositional object. We don't, for example, believe all the consequences of our beliefs; not just because we haven't got time to, and not just because everybody is at least a little irrational, but also because we surely have some false beliefs about what the consequences of our beliefs are. This amounts to saying that some substantial idealization is required if we're to get from the causal dispositions that mental states actually exhibit to the sort of causal network that we would like to have: a causal network whose structure is closely isomorphic to the inferential network of propositions. And now the problem is to provide a non-circular justification – one which does not itself appeal to semantical or intentional considerations – for preferring *that* idealization to an infinity or so of others that ingenuity might devise. (It won't do, of course, to say that we prefer that idealization because it's the one which allows mental states to be assigned the intuitively plausible propositional objects; for the present question is precisely whether anything besides prejudice underwrites our commonsense psychological intuitions.) Probably the idealization problem arises, in some form or other, for any account of the attitudes which proposes to reduce their semantic properties to their causal ones. That, alas, is no reason to assume that the problem can be solved.

Equivalence

Functionalism guarantees that mental states are individuated by their causal roles, hence by their position in the putative causal network. But *nothing* guarantees that *propositions* are individuated by their *inferential* roles. Prima facie, it surely seems that they are not, since equivalent propositions are ipso facto identical in their inferential liaisons. Are we therefore to say that equivalent propositions are identical? Not, at least, for the psychologist's purposes, since attitudes whose propositional objects are equivalent may nevertheless differ in their causal roles. We need to distinguish, as it might be, the belief that P from the belief that P and $(Q \vee -Q)$, hence we need to distinguish the *proposition* that P from the proposition that P and $(Q \vee -Q)$. But surely what distinguishes these propositions is not their inferential roles, assuming that the inferential role of a proposition is something like the set of propositions it entails and is entailed by. It seems to follow that propositions are not individuated by their position in the inferential network, hence that assignments of propositional objects to mental states, if constrained only to preserve isomorphism between the networks, ipso facto underdetermine the contents of such states. There are, perhaps, ways out of such equivalence problems; "situation semantics" (see Barwise and Perry, 1983) has recently been advertising some. But all the ways out that I've heard of violate the assumptions of FR semantics; specifically, they don't identify propositions with nodes in a network of inferential roles.

In the second place, FR semantics isn't, after all, much of a panacea for Naturalistic scruples. Though it has a Naturalistic story to tell about how mental states might be paired with their propositional objects, the semantic properties of the propositions themselves are assumed, not explained. It is, for example, an intrinsic property of the proposition that Psmith is seated that it is true or false in virtue of Psmith's posture. FR semantics simply takes this sort of fact for granted. From the Naturalist's point of view, therefore, it merely displaces the main worry from: "What's the connection between an attitude and its propositional object?" to "What's the connection between the propositional object of an attitude and whatever state of affairs it is that makes the proposition true or false?" Or, to put much the same point slightly differently, FR semantics has a lot to say about the mind-to-proposition problem but nothing at all to say about the mind-to-world problem. In effect FR semantics is content to hold that the attitudes inherit their satisfaction-conditions from their propositional objects and that propositions have *their* satisfaction-conditions *by stipulation*.

And, in the third place, to embrace FR semantics is to raise a variety of (approximately Quinean) issues about the individuation of the attitudes; and these, as Putnam and Stich have recently emphasized, when once conjured up are not easily put down. The argument goes like this: according to FR semantic theories, each attitude has its propositional object in virtue of its position in the causal network: "different objects iff different loci" holds to a first approximation. Since a propositional attitude has its propositional object essentially, this makes an attitude's identity depend on the identity of its causal role. The problem is, however, that we have no criteria for the individuation of causal roles.

The usual sceptical tactic at this point is to introduce some or other form of slippery-slope argument to show – or at least to suggest – that there *couldn't be* a criterion for the individuation of causal roles that is other than arbitrary. Stich, for example, has the case of an increasingly senile woman who eventually is able to remember about President McKinley only that he was assassinated. Given that she has no *other* beliefs about McKinley – given, let's suppose, that the *only* causal consequence of her believing that McKinley was assassinated is to prompt her to produce and assent to occasional utterances of "McKinley was assassinated" and immediate logical consequences thereof – is it clear that she in fact has *any* beliefs about McKinley at all? But if she *doesn't* have, *when, precisely, did she cease to do so?* How much causal role does the belief that McKinley was assassinated have to have to be the belief that McKinley was assassinated? And what reason is there to suppose that this question has an answer? (See Stich, 1983; and also Putnam, 1983.) Auntie considers slippery-slope arguments to be in dubious taste and there is much to be said for her view. Still, it looks as though FR semantics has brought us to the edge of a morass and I, for one, am not an enthusiast for wading in it.

Well then, to summarize: the syntactic theory of mental operations promises a reductive account of the *intelligence* of thought. We can now imagine – though, to be sure, only dimly and through a glass darkly – a psychology that exhibits quite complex cognitive processes as being constructed from elementary manipulations of symbols. This is what RTM, together with the computer metaphor, has brought us; and it is, in my view, no small matter. But a theory of the *intelligence* of thought does not, in and of itself, constitute a theory of thought's *intentionality*. (Compare such early papers as Dennett, 1978c, where these issues are more or less comprehensively run together, with such second thoughts as Fodor, 1982, and Cummins, 1983, where they more or less aren't.) If RTM is true, the problem of the intentionality of the mental is largely – perhaps exhaustively – the problem of the semanticity of mental representations. But of the semanticity of mental representations we have, as things now stand, no adequate account.

Here ends the tour. Beyond this point there be monsters. It may be that what one descries, just there on the farthest horizon, is a glimpse of a causal/teleological theory of meaning (Stampe 1977; Dretske, 1981; Fodor, 1984 and 1990c); and it may be that the development of such a theory would provide a way out of the current mess. At best, however, it's a long way off. I mention it only to encourage such of the passengers as may be feeling queasy.

"Are you finished playing now?"
"Yes, Auntie."
"Well, don't forget to put the toys away."
"No, Auntie."

Notes

"Fodor's Guide to Mental Representation: The Intelligent Auntie's Vade-Mecum" originally appeared in *Mind* 94 (1985), and is reprinted here by permission of Oxford University Press and the author.

1   Unless you are an eliminativist behaviorist (say, Watson), which puts you, for present purposes, beyond the pale.

While we're at it, it rather messes up my nice taxonomy that there are philosophers who accept a Functionalist view of psychological explanation and are Realist about belief/desire psychology, but who reject the reduction of the latter to the former. In particular, they do not accept the identification of any of the entities that Functionalist psychologists posit with the propositional attitudes that common sense holds dear. (A version of this view says that functional states "realize" propositional attitudes in much the way that the physical states are supposed to realize functional ones. See, for example, Matthews, 1984.)

2   This account of the attitudes seems to be in the air these days, and, as with most doctrines that are in the air, it's a little hard to be sure exactly who holds it. Far the most detailed version is in Loar (1981), though I have seen variants in unpublished papers by Tyler Burge, Robert Stalnaker, and Hartry Field.

3   Since the methods of computational psychology tend to be those of proof theory, its limitations tend to be those of formalization. Patently, this raises the well-known issues about completeness; less obviously, it connects the Cognitive Science enterprise with the Positivist program for the formalization of inductive (and, generally, nondemonstrative) styles of argument. On the second point, see Glymour (1987).

4   It is possible to combine enthusiasm for a syntactical account of mental processes with any degree of agnosticism about the attitudes – or, for that matter, about semantic evaluability itself. To claim that the mind is a "syntax-driven machine" is precisely to hold that the theory of mental processes can be set out in its entirety without reference to any of the semantical properties of mental states (see Fodor, 1981b), hence without assuming that mental states *have* any semantic properties. Stephen Stich is famous for having espoused this option (Stich, 1983). My way of laying out the field has put the big divide between Realism about the attitudes and

its denial. This seems to me justifiable, but admittedly it underestimates the substantial affinities between Stich and the RTM crowd. Stich's account of what a good science of behavior would look like is far closer to RTM than it is to, for example, the eliminative materialism of the Churchlands.

3   Mental Representation

Hartry H. Field

Any interesting version of materialism requires not only that there be no irreducibly mental *objects*, but also that there be no irreducibly mental *properties*: the idea that, although people and certain higher animals do not contain any immaterial substance, nonetheless they have certain mental properties that are completely unexplainable in physical terms, is an idea that very few people who regard themselves as materialists would find satisfying.[1] The unsatisfactoriness of postulating irreducibly mental properties is the source of the two main problems in the philosophy of mind. The first and more widely discussed problem is the problem raised by *experiential* properties, for instance the property of feeling pain: a materialist needs to provide a believable account of such properties according to which those properties are not irreducibly mental. The second problem, raised by Brentano,[2] is the problem of *intentionality*. Many mental properties – believing, desiring, and so forth – appear to be *relational* properties: more precisely, they appear to relate people to non-linguistic entities called *propositions*. So any materialist who takes believing and desiring at face value – any materialist who admits that belief and desire *are* relations between people and propositions – any such materialist must show that the relations in question are not irreducibly mental. Brentano felt that this could not be done; and since he saw no alternative to viewing belief and desire as relations to propositions, he concluded that materialism must be false.

The first half of this paper is an examination of Brentano's problem – that is, of the problem (which Brentano believed to be unsolvable) of giving a materialistically adequate account of believing, desiring, and so forth. Unlike Brentano, I take it as unquestionable (given what we know about the world) that materialism is true; I also take it as unquestioned for the purposes of this paper that people do believe and desire. These two assumptions together amount to the assumption that Brentano's problem *can* be solved; what I shall be interested in is the question of *how* it can be solved, that is, of *what the assumption that it can be solved shows about the nature of belief and desire*. I will be particularly concerned to show that one cannot solve Brentano's problem merely by adopting the kind of functionalist theory of belief and desire that

Robert Stalnaker and David Lewis have advocated.[3] In the second half of the paper I shall elaborate on the position suggested in the first half, and discuss some implications of my conclusions about intentionality for the theory of meaning.

I should say at the outset that my presupposition that people do in fact believe and desire is intended to be a presupposition that an instrumentalistic view of belief-talk and desire-talk is inappropriate. I am presupposing in other words that belief and desire ascriptions can be literally true, rather than being merely useful devices that we adopt for various purposes but for which talk of truth and falsity is inappropriate. It is clear that belief in materialism even together with the view that belief-talk and desire-talk are highly useful instruments is not sufficient to entail that Brentano's problem is solvable;[4] so the adoption of an instrumentalistic view of belief-talk and desire-talk is a possible way to save materialism and yet avoid having to solve Brentano's problem. To my mind, however, instrumentalism is unappealing: it seems to me that if a psychological theory that postulates beliefs and desires works well, and there is no available theory that works better, then, barring strong specific reasons to the contrary, we should regard that theory as literally true. That it should be so regarded is a working hypothesis under which I am operating in this paper.

1 The Basic Argument

One way to reply to Brentano's argument would be to develop a theory of belief, desire, etc., according to which the objects of belief and desire were not propositions, but something more "accessible," say sentences. If we construed belief and desire as relations between people and sentences, then – at least if we also demanded that the sentences a believer or desirer were related to were sentences in a language he was familiar with – it would presumably be possible to give an account of these relations in a materialistically impeccable way. I will have more to say about this method of dealing with Brentano's problem later on. For now I want to ignore it.

Suppose then that we accept the idea that belief and desire are relations between people and propositions; and suppose, for definiteness, that we follow Lewis and Stalnaker in taking propositions to be sets of possible worlds. The question arises, how can one give a materialistically acceptable account of a relation between a person and a proposition so construed?

The question is neither silly nor impossible to answer. One might think it were silly: "If you accept the ontology of propositions, plus a minimal amount of set theory, then a relation between people and propositions is merely a set of ordered pairs whose first members are people and whose second members are propositions. Or better – since the same person can be in the belief relation at one time but not at another – the belief relation is merely a function that assigns to each time a set of ordered pairs of people and propositions. A function assigning sets of ordered pairs is not a mental entity at all, let alone an irreducibly mental one, so what's the problem?" Needless to say, this misses the point. If this way of dismissing Brentano's question were legitimate, we could equally well dismiss any other *prima facie* difficulty for materialism without doing any substantive work, so that materialism would be a totally vacuous doctrine. For instance, if someone asked how to give a materialist account of pain, one could say, "What's the problem? Pain is simply a set of people, viz. those people that we say 'feel pain' or 'are in pain.' Or better – since the same person can feel pain at one time but not at others – pain is a function that assigns to each time the set of people who are in pain at that time. Such a function is a purely set-theoretic entity; it is not mental, let alone irreducibly mental, hence it carries no problem for materialism." I take it to be obvious that this set-theoretic approach to the theory of pain is totally unsatisfying. And I can't think of any reason why the set-theoretic approach to the theory of belief and desire should be thought to be any better.

Part of the explanation of why the set-theoretic account of pain is unsatisfying is that it treats pain as a set rather than a property. What is needed is an account of that property of people that "pain" stands for which is materialistically acceptable – we need to show that property is not irreducibly mental. What the set-theoretic account does is to ignore the question of the *property* altogether, and to focus instead on the *set of things that have that property*. (Or – since the same thing can have the property at one time but not another – it focusses on the function-in-extension mapping each time into the set of things that have the property at the time.) Obviously there is no substantive question of this set (or this function) being irreducibly mental; but that just shows that the interesting question concerns not the set but the property. This diagnosis extends to the case of belief: the interesting question about belief is a question about the relation that "belief" stands for, where by "relation" I mean not "set of ordered pairs" but "2-place property." What a materialist needs to show is that that property is not irreducibly mental.

But is there any hope of giving a materialistically acceptable account of the belief relation? In particular, is there any hope of doing this when we take belief to be a relation between people and propositions, and construe propositions in terms of possible worlds? It might be thought that the answer is "obviously no," and that this fact shows the untenability of treating belief as a relation between a person and a set of possible worlds. I believe, however, that such a dismissal of the possible-worlds view of belief would be too quick: for I believe, that it *is* possible to give a materialistically adequate account of the belief relation, even if that relation is construed as a relation to sets of possible worlds. I will now sketch a possible such account. We will see later that the main elements of this account can be preserved even if we abandon the assumption that belief is a relation between people and sets of possible worlds.

The account involves the assumption that the belief relation is a composite of two other relations: first, a relation between a person and a *sentence* that the person understands; second, a relation between the sentence and a set of possible worlds. This will be refined shortly, but unrefined, the claim is this:

(1) X believes that p if and only if there is a sentence S such that X believes* S and S means that p.

Here *believes** is a relation between a person and a sentence in his own language: I believe* the English sentence "Snow is white" but not the sentence "Snow is green," and no one ignorant of English believes* either of these sentences.[5] The effect of adopting (1) is to divide the problem of giving a materialistically adequate account of the belief relation into two subproblems:

subproblem (a): the problem of explaining what it is for a person to believe* a sentence (of his or her own language).

subproblem (b): the problem of explaining what it is for a sentence to mean that p.

(The problem of giving a materialistically adequate account of the desire relation would be split into two subproblems in the analogous way, by introducing a notion of desiring*.)

The rough idea of how to give an account of (a) should be clear enough: I believe* a sentence of my language if and only if I am disposed to employ that sentence in a certain way in reasoning, deliberating, and so on. This is very vague of course, but providing that the vagueness can be eliminated and providing that a physical basis can be found for the dispositions invoked, then believing* will not be a relation that poses any problems for the materialist. Later on in this section I will state a more precise version of a dispositional account of believing*, one which will make it pretty clear what a physical basis for the disposition invoked would have to be like. But I hope that even the vague remarks above are enough to predispose the reader to think that believing* is not a relation that should be a particular worry to a materialist (even a materialist impressed by Brentano's problem). On the other hand, anyone impressed with Brentano's problem *is* likely to be impressed with subproblem (b), for, unlike (a), (b) invokes a *semantic* relation (of *meaning that*).

Before looking into the question of whether it is reasonable to expect that a materialistically acceptable account of (b) could be given, let me note two auxiliary advantages of adhering to (1), and then go on to consider a necessary refinement in what I have said. The first auxiliary advantage of approaching the problem of explaining what it is to believe that p via (1) is that with this approach we need not assume from the outset the controversial assumption that the objects of belief are propositions. That is, if we later come up with a way to explain what it is to mean that p which does not make *meaning that* a relation between sentences and propositions, then if we also adopted (1) we would have an account of *believing that* according to which it was not a relation between people and propositions either. In fact, one can adhere to (1) without assuming that the occurrences of "*p*" in it are occurrences of a quantifiable variable; they can be taken to be just instances of a schematic letter, so that talk of the objects of belief (as such talk has heretofore been construed) makes no literal sense. Such a possibility will be discussed in Section III; for now, however, I will continue to adopt Lewis's and Stalnaker's assumption that "*p*" is a quantifiable variable and stands for entities that are to be explained in terms of possible worlds.

A second auxiliary advantage of (1), for possible-worlds theorists, is that it would give them a plausible way to make distinctions of belief which are intuitively there but which cannot be made on the possible-worlds account as it stands. Consider any set theorist (who believes the axiom of choice) who has never heard of the Banach-Tarski theorem; if someone now formulates the theorem for him (without telling him that it is a theorem), he will almost surely not believe it to be true. (In fact, he is almost sure to believe it false;[6] to believe it true in the circumstances described would be a more likely sign of irrationality than to believe it false.) There is a big difference, then, between believing set theory and believing set theory plus the Banach-Tarski theorem; yet set theory and set-theory-plus-Banach-Tarski are logically equivalent, hence must be represented by the same set of possible worlds. Now, David Lewis has pointed out that a possible-worlds theorist need not say that the conjunction of the axioms of set theory[7] *means the same as* the conjunction of those axioms plus the Banach-Tarski theorem: he can recognize finer grades of *meaning* than sets of possible worlds.[8] A set of possible worlds can be called a *coarse-grained proposition*; a *fine-grained proposition* is a certain complicated kind of function defined out of possible worlds, but which has coded into it, so to speak, the structure of a specific sentence. What a sentence *means*, on Lewis's account, is fine-grained; but what a person *believes* is coarse-grained, so believing set theory and believing set-theory-plus-Banach-Tarski are precisely the same thing.

Now formally speaking, it would be possible simply to take these fine-grained propositions and use them in a way that Lewis does not, as the objects of belief. But is is quite implausible to do so unless we think of beliefs as being represented in the head by sentences or something like sentences, for fine-grained propositions have the structure of specific sentences coded right into them. Consequently, Lewis and Stalnaker accept the idea that to believe set theory and to believe set-theory-plus-Banach-Tarski are the same things. Stalnaker has tried to explain away our strong feelings to the contrary as follows:

There are only two mathematically true propositions, the necessarily true one and the necessarily false one, and we all know that the first is true and the second false. But the functions that determine which of the two propositions is expressed by a given mathematical statement are just the kind that are sufficiently complex to give rise to reasonable doubt about which proposition is expressed by a statement. *Hence it seems reasonable to take the objects of belief and doubt in mathematics to be propositions about the relations between statements and what they say* (Stalnaker, 1976, p. 88; italics mine).

But this will not do. Let "the Banach-Tarski conditional" stand for the conditional whose antecedent is the conjunction of the axioms of set theory (including choice) and whose consequent is the Banach-Tarski theorem. Consider a person who doubts or disbelieves the Banach-Tarski result, *but who knows the semantic rules that relate sentences in the language of set theory to propositions*. According to Stalnaker, such a person doesn't really doubt or disbelieve the proposition expressed by the Banach-Tarski conditional, since that is a logical truth; what he does doubt or disbelieve is the proposition expressed by

(i)   the semantic rules for the language of set theory relate the Banach-Tarski conditional to the necessary truth.

But since the person knows what the semantic rules for the language of set theory are, the only way he can doubt or disbelieve the proposition expressed by (i) would be to doubt or disbelieve the proposition expressed by

(ii)   the semantic rules ＿＿＿ relate the Banach-Tarski conditional to the necessary truth,

where in the blank goes a statement of the semantic rules for the language of set theory. Unfortunately for Stalnaker, however, the proposition expressed by (ii) is itself a necessary truth, and hence on Stalnaker's coarse-grained possible-worlds view there is no way that anyone could doubt or disbelieve it. The ascent from mathematical propositions to metalinguistic propositions has gained nothing.

I take it, then, that it is clearly desirable to be able to divide propositions more finely than sets of possible worlds: and Lewis's analysis shows us how to do this, *if we can accept the idea that believing a proposition involves an attitude toward sentences.* To believe set theory is very roughly to believe* the conjunction of the axioms; to believe set-theory-plus-Banach-Tarski is very roughly to believe* the conjunction of those axioms plus the Banach-Tarski theorem. The sentences believed* have different fine-grained meanings, on Lewis's analysis; hence (1) assigns different fine-grained propositions to the two believers.

It might be thought, however, that this sentential approach induces *too* fine-grained a distinction among beliefs; it makes the belief that either Russell was hairless or snow is white differ from the belief that if Russell was not hairless then snow is white; how then can we confidently pass from the claim that someone has the first belief to the claim that he has the second? These are two possible lines of answer. The first, which I believe to be rather *ad hoc* and artificial, is to introduce a slight coarsening of the fine-grained propositions, by taking equivalence classes under a suitable equivalence relation. The second and more satisfactory is to grant that the beliefs are indeed distinct, but to explain why someone who has one belief will nearly always have the other. Such an explanation is easy enough to give: it involves the idea that belief* is dispositional. I will now elaborate on the dispositional nature of belief* (thus returning to subproblem (a)); in the course of doing so, it will become clear why someone who has one of the two beliefs about Russell will nearly always have the other.

The crudest approach to the problem of giving a materialistic account of belief* would be wholly non-dispositional: this approach would involve the assumption that a person could believe* a sentence only if the sentence were explicitly stored in the person's head. (Similarly for desire*. If we adhere to this non-dispositional approach we must suppose that there are at least two kinds of storage, storage-as-belief and storage-as-desire. The precise details of *how* sentences are stored-as-beliefs or stored-as-desires is of course not a matter that can be settled without detailed neuro-physiological investigation.) A defect of this approach is that people apparently believe infinitely many propositions; if so, then if we adopt (1) (and assume that the relation of *meaning that* is not one-many), it follows that people believe* infinitely many sentences. But there is no way that infinitely many sentences can be explicitly stored in a finite head, so the idea that a sentence must be explicitly stored to be believed* is false.

This argument suggests that some kind of dispositional approach to belief* is required. (This conclusion can in fact be argued for without the assumption that we have infinitely many beliefs.) The simplest kind of dispositional account (suggested by Dennett)[9] is that an organism has stored within it certain explicitly represented beliefs, which Dennett calls *core beliefs*; and what we say a person *believes* are just *the obvious consequences of* his core beliefs. [Not: the obvious consequences of his *beliefs*; for then we could show recursively that even very unobvious consequences of beliefs had also to be beliefs (since unobvious inferences can be broken down into a large number of obvious ones).] If the core belief approach is correct, then it may be the notion of core belief rather than the notion of belief that would enter into any detailed psychological theory. But even if this is so, it is the notion of belief rather than the notion of core belief which is more useful to us in everyday life, for it is much easier to know what a person believes than what he core-believes. The reason is clear: when the proposition A is an obvious enough consequence of one's core beliefs, one is almost sure to add A to one's belief core whenever any question as to the truth of A arises; behaviorally, then, it will be hard to distinguish this case from the case where A was present in one's belief core all along. But there are many cases where it is perfectly clear that a belief is not part of one's belief core. For instance, suppose I tell you that no one dug a tunnel from here to China through the center of the earth in 1953. I'm sure that by telling you this I'm not telling you something you didn't already believe, but I'm equally sure that it was not part of your belief core – i.e., not one of your explicitly represented beliefs – before I told it to you.

This idea of core belief gives us a very natural proposal for solving subproblem (a). The idea is simply to say that one believes* a sentence if and only if that sentence is an obvious consequence of sentences that are explicitly stored (in that manner of storage appropriate to beliefs as opposed to, say, desires).[10] This kind of account would make clear why someone who believes that either Russell was hairless or snow is white would almost certainly also believe that if Russell was not hairless then snow is white: almost any stock of core beliefs from which the former was an obvious consequence would also be a stock of core beliefs from which the latter was an obvious consequence.[11] (This solves the problem from which we began.) The account also makes clear why there is a certain vagueness or indeterminacy in ascriptions of belief that are far removed from the core (e.g., of why, when a philosopher's beliefs show a deep inconsistency, there is no clear point to asking whether he believes or disbelieves a proposition about which he has expressed no opinion but which is both provable and refutable by equally unobvious reasoning from things that he has committed himself to). The indeterminacy comes in because of the use of the notion of obviousness in defining belief from core belief.[12] It is a striking advantage of the core-belief proposal that it explains these facts.

I think then that the core-belief approach to subproblem (a) is quite attractive. However, I do not want to insist on it: conceivably it is possible to develop a more subtle kind of dispositional approach to belief* – perhaps an approach which would require fewer sentences to be explicitly stored. (It seems quite unlikely, however, that one could do without stored sentences altogether.) I take no stand on whether an alternative to the core-belief approach would be preferable, for I think I have said enough to make it plausible that in some way or other sub-problem (a) could be solved.

Before turning to subproblem (b) – the problem of giving a materialistically adequate account of the relation of *meaning that* (which we are temporarily assuming to relate sentences to sets of possible worlds) – I should mention the long-promised refinement that is needed in (1). The need of the refinement arises from the fact that dogs, chimpanzees, and young children presumably have beliefs but have no language. One could of course simply insist that beliefs and desires are not to be attributed to these or any other languageless creatures. To do so, however, does not seem very plausible. After all, we do often explain the behavior of languageless creatures by postulating beliefs and desires; and while in some such cases the explanations are clearly anthropomorphic and the behavior can be explained in simpler ways, there are many cases involving psychologically complicated organisms where these are the only sorts of explanation available. It seems rather rash to conclude that all such explanations are false, and therefore we must modify (1). Fortunately only a minor modification is needed, if we accept the widely held view[13] that, though a dog has no language, he does have some kind of system of internal representation, and that it is only *because* he has some system of internal representation that he can represent to himself, and believe, any proposition. Let us then modify (1) by abandoning the requirement that the entities which are believed* be literally *sentences*; let us require instead only that they be either sentences or *sentence-analogs* – where by a sentence analog I simply mean some psychological entity which represents propositions (or, more neutrally, which has the kind of meaning or content which sentences have). (1) should be replaced, then, by

(1′) X believes that p if and only if there is a sentence or sentence-analog S such that X believes* S and S means that p.

This shift has an independent virtue in connection with adult humans that do have a language: it allows for the possibility that they might have beliefs that go somewhat beyond the expressive capacity of their languages.

Many philosophers are hostile to postulating systems of internal representation in languageless organisms; I will try to remove some of that hostility later on in the paper. But perhaps I can undercut some of the hostility in advance by noting that, on my view, the system of internal representation in which a chimpanzee believes and desires would presumably have a much simpler structure than human languages have – its "sentence-analogs" would be much simpler syntactically than English sentences are, and by calling them "sentence-analogs" I do not mean to be denying the existence of these structural disanalogies. How simple could an animal's "system of internal representation" be and still count as a system of representation? This seems to me an uninteresting question of terminology. If you like, you could even allow that an animal's "system of internal representation" consisted of five sentences, each of them syntactically unstructured. However, I don't think that there is much *point* in saying that an animal believes or desires things unless one attributes a reasonably complex system of beliefs and desires to it; and (according to (1′)) a reasonably complex system of beliefs and desires will require a reasonably complex system of representation. So there is no point in attributing a system of internal representation at all unless one attributes a reasonably complex one. But there is no need to draw a precise line and say "something must be at least this complicated to count as a system of internal representation"; where such a line would go is merely a matter of how widely one wants to extend the term "belief." My claim is independent of such terminological issues: it is that *organisms which are sufficiently complicated for the notions of belief and desire to be clearly applicable have systems of internal representation in which the sentence-analogs have significant grammatical structure.*

Couldn't we avoid introducing systems of internal representation, by an alternative modification of (1)? The alternative revision would be to give up the requirement that an organism believe* a sentence only if he understands it: we could then say that dogs believe* sentences of human languages like English and Serbo-Croatian. There are three problems with this approach:

(A) The approach is not very useful as a step toward solving Brentano's problem: on this approach, believes* would become a *semantic* relation – it would be a relation between organisms and sentences of English (or Serbo-Croatian) which holds in virtue of the meanings of those sentences. Consequently, the proposed alternative to (1) would divide the original belief relation between organisms and propositions into *two* semantic relations (since *means that* is also semantic); and since semantic relations are just the sorts of relations that Brentano thought were inexplicable, this would appear to be a doubling of our original problem.

(B) The second problem with the suggestion is that the whole point of the notions of belief and desire is to aid us in explaining behavior. It seems rather bizarre to explain a chimpanzee's behavior via his relation to sentences in a human language that he doesn't understand; facts about English sentences have nothing whatever to do with why the chimpanzee behaves as he does. So it is important to leave English sentences out of the account of belief and desire for chimpanzees.

The third problem with the suggestion is mentioned in Section III. Because of these difficulties, I think that (1′) is the only reasonable modification of (1).

Let us turn, finally, to subproblem (b), which because of the shift from (1) to (1′) is the problem of giving a materialistically acceptable account of what it is for a sentence or a sentence-analog in a system of internal representation to mean that *p*. Recall that we are temporarily construing *means that* as relating sentences (and sentence-analogs) to sets of possible worlds (or to slightly more structured entities built up out of functions defined on possible worlds; but for simplicity let us ignore this more complicated account – it raises no new difficulties of principle for a materialist theory of belief). What set of possible worlds does a sentence (or sentence-analog) mean? It means the set of possible worlds at which the sentence is true. If then we can give a materialistically acceptable account of the relation between sentences and worlds of *being true at*, then we will have a materialistically acceptable account of (b).

Now, in another paper[14] I have argued that it *is* possible to give a materialistically adequate account of *truth* (i.e., of truth *at the actual world*). The idea of how this is done is simplest for the very simple languages that logicians usually discuss; there it involves giving a Tarski-type truth-definition. Such a truth-definition explains what it is for a sentence to be true (at the actual world) in terms of what it is for a name to denote an object (at the actual world), what it is for a predicate to have a certain extension (at the actual world), and so forth. In other words, such a truth-definition reduces the problem of what it is for a sentence to be true (at the actual world) to what it is for the one-word components of the sentence to stand (at the actual world) for certain entities or sets of entities. I argued that we have every reason to think that the relations of *standing for* (i.e., the relations of *denoting, having as an extension*, etc.) are explainable in a materialistically acceptable way, and so the truth definition gives us derivatively a materialistically acceptable account of truth (at the actual world). The above remarks hold for sentences of the simple languages to which Tarski's methods apply directly; but following Davidson[15] and many other philosophers, I believe that such methods are generalizable to natural languages, so that for sentences in natural languages too we can say that truth can be explained in a materialistically acceptable way. And the same should be true for sentence-analogs, if we suppose that they are sufficiently like the sentences in natural languages.

I have claimed that we can give a materialistically adequate account of *truth*, i.e., truth *at the actual world*. But what we need, if we are to explain what it is to mean a Stalnaker-type proposition, is a materialistically adequate account of *truth at w* for an arbitrary possible world *w*. And this, it may seem, is much harder to come by: for if we relativize Tarskian semantics to an arbitrary possible world *w*, we find that it explains what it is for a sentence to be true at *w* in terms of *what it is for a name to refer to an entity at w and what it is for a predicate to have a set of entities as its extension at w*. That is, we need to invoke relations of words (in the actual world) standing for entities or sets of entities *in the possible world w*; and it is difficult to see how to explain such trans-world relations in a materialistically acceptable way.

This, however, is a very misleading way of looking at the matter: for in actual fact one can define truth at *w* purely in terms of relations between words (in the actual world) and entities *in the actual world*. For instance, for a sentence of form $\ulcorner P(b) \urcorner$ where P is a predicate and b a name, the definition will read

$\ulcorner P(b) \urcorner$ is true at *w* if and only if there is an object *x* that *b* denotes (in the actual world) and a property *Z* that *P* stands for (in the actual world), and *w* is a world in which *x* exists and has *Z*.

For example, "Bertrand Russell is hairless" is true at any possible world *w* in which Bertrand Russell (i.e., the person denoted *in the actual world* by the name "Bertrand Russell") exists and is hairless (i.e., has the property that the word "hairless" stands for *in the actual world*). So truth at *w* is definable in terms of the relation of denotation for names together with the relation of standing for predicates, where it is now to be understood that a predicate stands not for a set (its extension) but for a *property* that exists in the actual world.[16]

So the problem of giving a materialistically adequate account of truth at *w* reduces to (i) the problem of giving a materialistically adequate account of actual-world-denotation for names, and (ii) the problem of giving a materialistically adequate account of actual-world-standing-for for predicates, where as I've said predicates are now to be construed as standing for properties rather than sets. But (i) is a problem that arose even in the account of truth in the actual world; I'm assuming (since I've argued it in the aforementioned article) that we have good reason to believe that that problem is solvable. With (ii) the situation is a bit different. What we need in any account of truth-in-the-actual-world is a materialistically adequate account of the relation between predicates and their actual world *extensions*; let us then assume that that problem is solvable. But (ii) requires something that is formally stronger; it requires a materialistically adequate account of the relation between predicates and *properties*; and since these properties determine but are not determined by the extensions of the predicates, what we need is formally stronger than what actual-world semantics would have to give us. A little reflection will show, however, that actual-world semantics is bound to give the formally stronger thing as well. For what could a materialistically adequate account of the relation "is the extension of" be like? Such an account would have to tell us the kinds of facts about the way we use words in virtue of which the set of hairless things is the extension of the word "hairless." How could it do that? One possibility is that it would be a causal theory of reference: it would state that some kind of causal connection between hairless individuals and our use of the word "hairless" is responsible for our word having the set of hairless individuals as its extension. But surely we have not come into causal contact with *all* members of the extension of "hairless" – after all, there are hairless things on remote planets, there are hairless things that exist only in the distant future, and so forth. How could causal contact with certain hairless individuals help in solving the problem of what makes our word "hairless" have as its extension a set which includes such future hairless creatures (and which excludes the future hairy ones)? The only possible answer, I think, is that the extension of the term "hairless" is determined by a property. What is *directly* associated with the predicate is not its *extension*, but a certain *property*. Perhaps the property of hairlessness is associated with the term "hairless" by causal connection with a number of hairless individuals, as a causal theory of reference would have it; or perhaps there is some non-causal theory of reference which determines how the property of hairlessness is associated with the word. But however *that* association is made, the association of an extension with the word "hairless" is a derivative one: the extension of "hairless" is simply the set of objects (in the actual world) which have that property which in the actual world is associated with the word "hairless." If it were impossible to give a materialistically adequate account of how properties were associated with predicates, then it would be impossible to give a materialistically adequate account of how sets are associated with predicates, and so it would be impossible to give a materialistically adequate account of actual-world truth. So *the problem of giving a materialistically adequate account of truth-at-a-possible-world is no more difficult than the task of giving a materialistically adequate account of truth-in-the-actual-world; fundamentally, these apparently distinct problems are one and the same.*

I now have all the pieces: let me put them in place. The task with which I have been occupied for most of Section I has been to explain one *possible* approach to giving a materialistically adequate account of belief; and I have been assuming for the time being that belief is to be construed as a relation between people and sets of possible worlds. The "other-worldly" character of the assumed objects of belief might appear to rule out the possibility of a materialistic account of the belief relation, but, I have argued, that appearance is illusory. For we can say that a person believes a set p of possible worlds if and only if he believes* some sentence (or sentence-analog) S, and p is the set of possible worlds at which S is true. And (given the ontology of possible worlds) defining truth at a possible world requires no more resources than are required for defining genuine truth, i.e., truth at the actual world: both of these tasks require us to explain what makes the names in S denote whatever items in the actual world they do denote, and what makes the predicates in S stand for whatever properties in the actual world they do stand for,[17] and that is doubtless a difficult task; but I know of no reason to believe that the task is hopeless, and in fact (as I've argued in the aforementioned article) I think there is good reason to think it can be solved.

The account of believing that has just been elaborated has only been put forward as a *possible* account. It is in fact an account that I will want to revise in certain respects later on – e.g., by dropping all reference to propositions and possible worlds. But I will not revise the two central features of the account given so far: the idea that belief involves a relation to sentences or to something very much like sentences, and the idea that these sentences must be given a Tarski-like semantics (including a theory of reference for the primitives). To a large extent, my adherence to these two ideas is based on an inability to conceive of what a solution to Brentano's problem that did *not* rely on these ideas would be like. I do not claim to have proved that there *could be* no alternative account of belief that solved Brentano's problem but did not have the two features mentioned above. However, I have never seen even a *clear sketch* of what such an alternative account would be like. The fact that the kind of account that I have sketched above would solve Brentano's problem, and that no alternative solutions to the problem are known, seems to me to provide a very strong reason for tentatively accepting the kind of account sketched.[18]

At this point the reader may feel that there is a well-known alternative account of belief that will either solve Brentano's problem, or show it to be a pseudo-problem. That alternative account (according to my hypothetical reader) is the account that Lewis and Stalnaker actually advocate: it is the functionalist alternative. In the next section I will examine the question of whether functionalism does indeed solve or dissolve Brentano's problem.

II Functionalism

The Lewis-Stalnaker approach to belief involves the idea that believing is a functional state. Putting the view very roughly, a state of an organism is a state of believing that p if that state plays an appropriate role in the organism's psychology: that is, if it is causally connected to inputs and outputs and to other psychological states in the right sort of way. Now it certainly seems at first as if such a functional theory of belief allows for the possibility of beliefs independent of language or of inner representations: that is, why couldn't it be the case that an organism is in a state which is causally connected to inputs and outputs and to other states in the right sort of way for that state to satisfy the functional conditions for being a belief that p, even though that state does not involve a relation to any sentence or to any sentence-like item in any system of inner representation? Stalnaker has put the point as follows:

> It is conceivable (whether or not it is true) that there are rational creatures who have beliefs and desires, but who do not use language, and who have no internal representations of their attitudes which have a linguistic form. I think this is true of many animals – even some rather stupid ones – but there might be clearer cases. Imagine that we discovered living creatures – perhaps on some other planet – who did not communicate, but whose behavior was predictable, for the most part, on the hypothesis that they engaged in highly sophisticated theoretical deliberation. Imagine further that we had this indirect evidence supporting our hypothesis: that the beliefs that our hypothesis attributed to these creatures could be causally explained, in many cases, in terms of their sensory inputs; and that the desires attributed to them by the hypothesis were correlated appropriately, for the most part, with the physical requirements for their survival. Finally, imagine that we test the hypothesis by manipulating the environments of these creatures, say by feeding them misleading "evidence" and by satisfying or frustrating some of their alleged desires. If they continued to behave as predicted, I think we would be tempted to attribute to these creatures not just belief and desire analogues, but beliefs and desires themselves. We would not, however, have any reason to hypothesize that they thought in a mental language, or in any language at all (Stalnaker, 1976, p. 82).

Is Stalnaker right about this?

In order to evaluate Stalnaker's claims, we need to make the idea of a functional theory of belief much clearer than my crude description above makes it. According to the crude description above, a state of an organism is a state of believing that p if the state is causally connected to inputs and outputs and to other psychological states in the right sort of way; but until we know what the other psychological states are that it must be causally connected to, and what is "the right sort of way" for it to be connected to them, we are in no position to determine whether such a functional theory of belief requires a system of inner representation. (E.g., why couldn't one of the other states to which a state of belief that p must be causally connected be a state of having an inner representation of the proposition p?) This fact must be borne in mind in considering Stalnaker's story about the creatures on another planet. It is perfectly clear that, in the situation Stalnaker describes, we could not be absolutely certain that the creatures thought in any internal system of representation. But it is also perfectly clear that we could not be absolutely certain that they had beliefs and desires. We couldn't be certain of this because (a) we have not observed all of their actual behavior, let alone all of their possible behavior, and (b) because, even if we had, a claim about beliefs and desires is not simply a claim about behavior, it is a claim about how that behavior is produced. Of course, we do not need to have *detailed* knowledge of how that behavior is produced to know whether the organism has beliefs and desires – the whole point of functionalism is to provide a fairly abstract representation of an organism's inner states, so that *certain kinds* of information about the organism's inner states will be irrelevant to the question of whether it has beliefs and desires. But we do need *some* knowledge about how that behavior is produced in order to know that it has beliefs and desires: a functionalist's claims about an organism's inner states is a claim *about that organism's inner states*, and is not reducible to any claims about the organism's actual and possible behavior. (That fact is, I hope, common knowledge. It comes out very clearly in Lewis's precise explication of the functionalist claim, which I will give shortly.) Consequently, when we conclude of the creatures on the other planet that they have beliefs and desires, we do so because that is the best explanation we can find of their behavior. But now, if we can know that the creatures have beliefs and desires because belief-and-desire theory is the best available explanation of their behavior, why couldn't we also know that the creatures have a system of inner representation, by the same means? Whether the first inference has better inductive warrant than the second is not something that can be settled by a casual appeal to intuitions: it depends on whether it is possible to come up with an adequate functional account of belief and desire according to which belief and desire do not require internal representation. So the last sentence of the quotation from Stalnaker (or, if you like, the conjunction of the last two sentences) simply begs the question at issue. Perhaps its conclusion is correct, but we can show this only by a detailed examination of what a functional theory of belief would be like.

A full discussion of this topic would be two-fold. Part of such a discussion would involve the question of whether any adequate theory of belief would have to have assumptions about internal representation *explicitly built into it*. I am strongly inclined to think it would, and I think my remarks about core beliefs in Section I and the remarks about propositions in Section III provide *some* support for this claim; but the ultimate proof of the claims lies in the detailed development of psychological theory. In this section I will not deal with these matters, but will undertake a more modest task: I want to show that the functionalist approach to theories of believing and desiring does not provide an *alternative* to the idea that belief requires some system of representation.

In saying this I mean to be saying much more than that functionalism is compatible with there being some system of inner representation (involving sentences of natural language and/or sentence-analogs): that point is certainly not one that either Lewis or Stalnaker would deny. Both of them would certainly agree that if we opened up a person's head and found a blackboard inside on which various English sentences were written, and if we also found that the occurrence of those sentences on that blackboard entered in the right way into that person's behavior, then that would be strong reason to suppose that (for that person anyway) belief involved inner representation. This would of course not conflict with functionalism, for what we would be discovering is simply that the state which (in that person) is causally connected in the right sort of ways to inputs and outputs and to other states happens to be a state which involves inner representations. It is uncontroversial, then, that functionalism is compatible with the inner representation hypothesis. But I want to argue for a much stronger claim, one which I *suspect* Lewis and Stalnaker would deny (though I infer this more from the general tone of their discussions than from anything they explicitly say). What I suspect Lewis and Stalnaker hold is that, without opening up people's heads, we can have little or no reason to *think* that believing anything involves a system of inner representation; the hypothesis that belief does involve a system of inner representation, then, is simply *unfounded neurophysiological speculation*. Now, in Section I I have given a *prima facie* argument that it was not just unfounded neurophysiological speculation: the inner representation hypothesis, I claimed, was *the only known possibility* for solving Brentano's problem, and this in itself provides good reason for tentatively accepting it. But in arguing that, I ignored the possibility of the functionalist approach. What we must investigate now, then, is whether the functionalist approach alters the conclusion. My claim is that it does not, and *that* is what I mean when I say that functionalism provides no alternative to the view that belief *requires* some system of representation.

To put my claim in a sentence, then, it is that *functionalism does not provide a solution to Brentano's problem, nor does it in any way dissolve the problem.* That is the claim to be argued in this section.

The whole point of functionalism in psychology is to provide a fairly abstract representation of psychological properties, a representation that is not tied too closely to the details of the physical structure of particular organisms; in fact, a functional theory guarantees that if two organisms are, in a suitable sense, psychologically isomorphic, then they have precisely the same psychological properties, however different they may be in those aspects of physical structure that are not relevant to establishing the psychological isomorphism. A functionalist does not say that the physical structure of an organism is *irrelevant* to its psychological properties: nearly all functionalists are materialists, that is, they believe that all psychological properties require a *physical realization*.[19] This means for instance that, for any organism X and any time t, X can have a 1-place psychological property F at t only if X has at t some physical property $R(F)$ which *realizes* F (in a sense soon to be made precise). But different physical properties can realize the same psychological properties in different organisms (or in the same organisms at different times); so organisms of very different structure can have the same psychological properties. It is because the functionalist allows the possibility of *different* realizations – *not* because he gives up the requirement of a realization altogether – that he achieves the goal of abstracting from the physical structure of particular organisms.[20]

It will be important in what follows to have a clear idea of what a realization of a psychological property is, and of what a psychological property itself is. The following account is David Lewis's,[21] except for a few minor divergences (mentioned in footnotes) which make no difference to the argument at hand.

Suppose that H is a psychological theory that is intended to apply at any time t to all organisms which are of type K at t. (H might for instance be a theory intended to apply to all adult humans, or to all organisms capable of feeling pain, or to all rational beings.)[22] For simplicity, let us suppose that H is finitely axiomatized; then we can represent it as a single formula which I abbreviate as $A(x, t)$, where x is a variable ranging over organisms and t a variable ranging over times. [Then the theory is true of all the organisms in its intended range if and only if the following claim holds:

> For any t and any x, if x is of type K
> at t then $A(x, t)$.

It is this last claim, rather than H, that is properly speaking true or false, so you might prefer to use the term "theory" for the last claim rather than for H.] In giving crude formulations of psychological theories we often omit the variables (and initial quantifiers), but they must be understood as implicit: we say "pain has such and such a causal role" when what we really mean is "For any t and any x of type K at t, pain has such and such a causal role in x at t." If we do not write the theory in this way, we cannot properly define the notion of a realization.[23]

Suppose that the specifically psychological[24] primitives in H are $T_1, \ldots, T_n$; then we can write H as $A(T_1, \ldots, T_n; x, t)$. For simplicity, I will assume that $T_1, \ldots, T_n$ are all predicates.[25] Let us say that an n-tuple $[P_1, \ldots, P_n]$ of properties *realizes H in organism X at time t* if and only if the formula $A(Y_1, \ldots,$

Y_n; x, t) is true of $[P_1, \ldots, P_n, X, t]$; and that such an n-tuple *uniquely realizes* H in X at t if it and no other n-tuple realizes H in X at t.

Now if H is a psychological theory with n primitive psychological predicates we can use it to define *n functional properties*. Suppose for instance that T_j is a predicate that stands for a 1-place property of organisms, the kind of property (like pain) of which it makes sense to say that the organism has it at one time but not at another. (Lewis calls properties of this sort "states,"[26] but I prefer to reserve this term for a different use.) If T_j is a predicate of this sort, then *the jth functional property associated with H* is the property F defined as follows:

(2) X has F at t if and only if there is some 1-place physical[27] property P such that

   (i) P is the jth component of a unique[28] realization of H in X at t

   (ii) X has P at t.

If F is the jth functional property associated with H, we can then say that a *realization of F* in X at t is simply the jth component of a unique realization of H in X at t. From this and (2) we derive

(2′) X has F at t if and only if there is some 1-place physical property P such that

   (i) P realizes F in X at t, and

   (ii) X had P at t.

This machinery enables us to give a precise sense to the general remarks of five paragraphs back. What functionalism about pain claims is that *the property of pain*[29] *is a functional property associated with some theory* H_p *by* (2) (or by the analog of (2) with the word "physical" replaced by "non-functional" – see note 27). By taking functionalism in this way we can make precise sense of various vague notions appealed to in the general remarks (e.g., the notion of psychological isomorphism), and we can also verify the really important claim that, if materialism is true, then for an organism to have the psychological property of pain it must have some physical property that realizes that psychological property in the organism.

Now let us apply this machinery to the case of believing, where we assume as before that belief is a relation between an organism and a proposition. Belief, then, will be a functional relation associated with some theory H_b in which the term "believes" occurs, say as the jth psychological term. We cannot of course apply the schema (2) to define such a functional property, since (2) made sense only in defining properties that correspond to *1-place* predicates, but it is clear enough how to generalize it to entities of another kind:

(3) X bears F to p at t if and only if there is some 2-place physical property R such that

(i)   *R* is the *j*th component of a unique realization of *H* in *X* at *t*

(ii)   *X* bears *R* to *p* at *t*.

No other generalization of (2) to the case of 2-place functional properties is possible.

Now the important thing to note about this is that it existentially quantifies over physical relations between people and propositions. If there is no physical relation of an appropriate sort between a person and a proposition, then according to (3) the person cannot stand in the functional relation *F* to the proposition. The functional relation *F* is not itself a physical relation; but if *F* is to relate an organism to a proposition at a time, there must be some physical relation *R(F)* which realizes *F* and which relates the organism to the proposition. Thus even if we take belief to be a functional relation, we have to solve Brentano's problem: we have to show that there *are* physical (non-functional) relations between people and propositions. That is what I meant when I said earlier that *functionalism does not either solve or dissolve Brentano's problem. The only thing it says of relevance to that problem is something that probably no one ever doubted anyway*: that the physical relation that relates me now to the propositions I believe can differ from the one that relates dogs to the propositions they believe; and even from the one that relates other people to the propositions they believe, and from the one that related me twenty years ago to the propositions I believed then. In other words: *it is indeed legitimate to solve Brentano's problem in different ways for different organisms; but this does not remove the need for solving the problem within an organism.* I don't mean to downgrade the importance of the observation that we don't need to solve Brentano's problem in the same way in different organisms: that fact is crucial to the plausibility of the model of believing put forth in Section I, for no one could plausibly claim that the relation of believing* is physically the same across different species. All I am saying is that to admit the allowability and importance of such variation across organisms does not in any way diminish the force of the tentative argument for the model of believing put forth in Section I. It remains true that if no other model can be given of what a physical relation between people and propositions would be like, then we should tentatively accept the model there proposed.

The argument I have just given is I think an extremely obvious one: one would expect it to be obvious to anyone who thought about functionalism for a moment. Yet I have found in conversation that the conclusion of the argument is one that nearly all functionalists oppose: nearly all of them are convinced that functionalism somehow undermines the argument of Section I. One reason, I suspect, is a tendency to slip from functionalism to an extreme behaviorism according to which nothing inside an organism is relevant to determining its psychological properties. Another reason is perhaps a Leibnizian tendency to regard relations as less real than 1-place properties – not out of conscious doctrine but merely because of the fact that the word "relation," unlike the word "property," doubles as a word for a certain kind of set. But there is a third source of error that I now want to consider. It is equally crude, but I think that there are deep and subtle confusions that lead people implicitly to make it.

The third source of error is that even among people who explicitly advocate the view that belief is a relation between people and propositions, there seems to be a tendency sometimes to fall into the "orthographic accident" view: the view that an adequate theory of belief could treat "X believes that Russell was hairless," "X believes that either Russell was hairless or snow is white," etc., as primitive 1-place predicates, and do without the 2-place predicate "X believes that p" entirely. (The fact that the term "believes that" occurs in both 1-place predicates would then be, from a theoretical view, of no significance, a mere orthographic accident; that fact that both contain "Russell was hairless" would likewise be an orthographic accident). It is not easy to take such a view seriously. But let us suppose it were true: what would follow? Well, the account would clearly obviate the need for a physical relation between people and propositions: since it didn't talk of a *psychological* relation between people and propositions, it is clear that no *physical* relation between people and propositions would be needed in a realization. But this of course does not refute the point I was making in this section, which is that if you *do* construe belief relationally, you need a physical realization of the belief relation.

In spite of the crudity of this mistake, I think that it is an easy one to make implicitly. In fact, in the opening paragraph of this section, when I tried to motivate the view that functionalism obviated the need of a system of representation, I found myself talking in a way that strongly suggested the orthographic accident view: I said "a state of an organism is a state of believing that p if that state plays the appropriate role in the organism's psychology." Now, for this to make any sense, the letter "p" here must be understood as abbreviating a specific sentence – say "Either Russell was hairless or snow is white." Now, what is "the appropriate role" of the state of believing that either Russell was hairless or snow is white? I do not say that no sense can be made of such talk: if we give a functional account of the relation of believing which holds between organisms and propositions, such an account will certainly have *implications* about the state of believing the particular proposition that Russell was hairless or snow is white. I think, however, that talk of "the appropriate role" of the state of believing this particular proposition *strongly suggests* that we can give a direct functional definition of *this particular state*. And *that* strongly suggests that the kind of procedure used for "pain" can be applied to "believes that either Russell was hairless or snow is white": in other words, it suggests that *believing that either Russell was hairless or snow is white* can be regarded as a functional 1-place property defined by schema (2). That, however, is the orthographic accident view, for it presupposes that the theory H

from which *believing that either Russell was hairless or snow is white* is to be functionally defined contains a primitive term that represents this property. The moral is that if you want to avoid the orthographic accident view, you should not regard "X believes that p_0" for specific sentences p_0 as functionally definable in the way that "X is in pain" is: you should regard them as defined non-functionally from a relational predicate "X believes that p" which is functionally defined by (3). And that means that we must invoke physical relations between organisms and sets of possible worlds.

I believe that there is a deeper source of the tendency to slip into the orthographic accident view; it has to do with functional theories that invoke psychological *states*, where "state" is not used in Lewis's sense (cf. note 26) but in the sense of "type of inner occurrence." There is nothing wrong with such functional theories, but they must be treated with care, as I will now explain. The reader may, however, wish to skip the explanation and move directly to Section III.

Let us first consider the case of pain. Linguistic usage suggests the following view:

> (4) X feels pain at t if and only if there is an internal occurrence o such that
> (i) X feels o at t, and
> (ii) o is a pain.

Now suppose that we give a theory H'_p of the sortal property *being a pain* which was used in clause (ii) of (4). It is easy to see that the proper way to functionally define *being a pain* from such a theory is this:

> (5) o is a pain if and only if there is some physical property P of inner occurrences such that
> (i) P is the jth component of a unique realization of H'_p in X at t, and
> (ii) o has the property P.

(Here t is the time of occurrence of o and X is the organism in which o occurred.) Putting this together with (4), we get

> (6) X feels pain at t if and only if there is an internal occurrence o and a physical property P such that
> (i) X feels o at t
> (ii) o has the property P, and
> (iii) P is the jth component of a unique realization of H'_p in X at t.

Now suppose we introduce the word "state" for physical properties of inner occurrences. (That is, let us use it for *state-types*; if P is a state-type then the state-*tokens* are the inner occurrences that *have* P.) If we also introduce the expression "is in P at t" for "feels at t some internal occurrence of type P (i.e., with the property P)," then we can rewrite (6) as

(7) X feels pain at t if and only if there is a physical state P such that
  (i) X is in P at t, and
  (ii) P is the jth component of a unique realization of H'_p in X at t.

The problem of finding a realization of pain-theory of this kind in X at t, then, is the problem of finding a *physical state* of pain in X at t; physical state in the sense of state-type, that is, in the sense of property of inner occurrences.

Now the same thing done here for pain can be done for belief. The analog of (4) is

(4′) X believes that p at t if and only if there is an inner occurrence o such that
  (i) o occurs in X at t, and
  (ii) o is a belief that p.

Functionally defining the relation *is a belief that*, analogously to (5) above, and combining the result with (4′), we get (in analogy to (6) above)

(6′) X believes that p at t if and only if there is an internal occurrence o and a physical relation R between internal occurrences and propositions such that
  (i) o occurs in X at t,
  (ii) o bears R to p, and
  (iii) R is the jth component of a unique realization of H'_b in X at t.

So far so good: the result makes clear that, in using a psychological theory of belief of this sort, we need to find physical realizations of a relation between internal occurrences and propositions. Now suppose we want to introduce the term "state" for a 1-place property of inner occurrences. There is no objection to doing so: for each sentence p_0, there is a 1-place property of bearing R to p_0, and we can call this a state (meaning of course a state-type). And we can go on to define what it is for an organism to be in such a state: X is in the state Q_0 at t if and only if there occurs in X at t some inner occurrence of the type Q_0 (i.e., with the property Q_0). But now if we try to reformulate (6′) in terms of state-types, we find that we get the following:

(7′) X believes that p_0 at t if and only if there is a physical state Q_0 such that
  (i) X is in Q_0 at t, and
  (ii)   *the relational component* of Q_0 is the jth component of a unique realization of H'_b in X at t.

(Q_0 is the property of bearing R to the specific sentence p_0; by the relational component of Q_0 I mean the relation R.) This is the *correct* way to introduce talk of state-types into a functional theory of belief.

But, I suspect, many people do not bother to think the matter through. Seeing functionalism for pain formulated as (7), they immediately jump to the conclusion that belief-theory formulated in terms of states should read as

> (7*) X believes that p_0 at t if and only if there is a physical state Q_0 such that
> (i) X is in Q_0 at t, and
> (ii) Q_0 is the jth component of a unique realization of H_b' in X at t.

Formulated in this way, H_b' has to be construed as a theory in which a term for being a state of believing p_0 (for the specific sentence p_0) appears as a primitive. And that of course is the orthographic-accident view.

The moral of all this is that the view that functionalism either solves or dissolves Brentano's problem results from confusion: the confusion of a relational theory of belief with an orthographic-accident theory of belief according to which belief is not a relation at all. I am sure that any functionalist would emphatically reject the idea that psychological theories of belief should have the orthographic-accident format; but if one thinks of states of believing as having functional roles not derivative on the functional role of the belief relation, then one is implicitly adhering to an orthographic-accident account.

III   Dispensing with Propositions

At the beginning of Section II, I quoted an argument of Stalnaker's which suggested that a functional theory of belief would obviate the need for a system of internal representation. I remarked that, in order fully to evaluate the argument, it was necessary to get clear on what a functional account of belief would be like. I have done that only in a very minimal sense: I have looked only at those features of a functional account of belief which follow from the nature of functionalism together with the (supposed) fact that belief involves a relation between people and propositions. But much more than this is involved in getting clear about what a functional account of belief would be like. For we have seen that, on any functional account of belief, the relation of believing is a functional relation *associated with a certain theory H_b*. Part of what's involved in getting clear on what a functional account of belief would be like, then, is getting clear on what H_b would be like. I am strongly inclined to think that any adequate H_b would have to explicitly postulate a system of representation, and that this provides a reason to believe the internal representation hypothesis *independently of any considerations about Brentano's problem*. I will not, however, try to argue this claim here. Instead I will merely note a converse: that since (as I've argued) we appear to need a system of representation in order to solve Brentano's problem, we shouldn't have too much reluctance about explicitly incorporating such a system into our psychological theory H_b if doing so seems helpful.

One advantage of explicitly incorporating a system of representation into one's psychological theory is that it enables us to obtain most of the advantages of regarding belief and desire as relations between people and propositions, without the attendant liabilities. Suppose that for some reason or other we do not want to quantify over propositions; in that case, then apparently we will be unable to say things like

(8)   There are many things she believes about him, and none of them are at all complimentary;

or

(9)   No one can perceive an object without coming to believe various things about it;

for apparently the "things" quantified over in (8) and (9) are propositions. However, I know of no reason why our purposes in uttering (8) and (9) wouldn't be equally well served by quantifying over objects of belief* rather than of belief: e.g., "No one can perceive an object without coming to believe* various things about it"; here the "things" quantified over are not propositions, but sentences in an internal system of representation. Of course, we could accept this reformulated version of (9) in our psychological theory only if we incorporated the inner representation hypothesis explicitly into the theory.

I think that by now the asterisks have become tiresome: so let us introduce the terminological convention that the word "believes" is to be used in the way that I have heretofore used "believes*." On this way of talking, the objects of belief are sentences or sentence-analogs, and these sentences or sentence-analogs have content or meaning. Contrary to the suggestion in the first paragraph of Section I, this way of talking does not really remove Brentano's problem: that problem rearises as the problem of giving a materialistic account of *having content*. Unless such an account of content can be given, much of what we say about belief (e.g., that certain beliefs are *about Caesar*, that certain beliefs are *true*, and so forth) makes no sense at all. I have, however, suggested, at the end of Section I, that the problem of giving a materialistic account of content seems manageable: one way to manage it is to give a Tarski-like account of truth, supplemented by theory of reference.

My use of the word "believes" to mean "believes*" does not accord very well with the use of the term "believes" in English: in English "believes" is pretty much synonymous with "believes that," and we can say even of organisms who know no English that they believe that snow is white. Let us then introduce a new technical term, "believes that," which will serve the purposes that "believe" and "believe that" serve in English: let us say that a person "believes that *p*" (where "*p*" abbreviates an English sentence *S*) if that person believes some sentence in his system of internal representation whose translation into English is *S*. In effect then "believes that" is to be used for a relation between organisms and English sentences. It must be realized that the notion of translation employed in the definition of "believes that" is a loose and sloppy one. For even those of us who are hostile to Quine's radical indeterminacy thesis are bound to recognize that translation *between languages of very different structure or expressive power* is highly indeterminate. (Part of the reason is that a sentence in language L_1 need not have exactly the same meaning as any sentence in language L_2, so that a translator of L_1 into L_2 has to settle for approximate sameness of meaning; and which approximation one picks depends on complicated pragmatic considerations.) Since the notion of *believing that* is to be applied to organisms whose system of internal representation is doubtless quite different from ours – e.g., chimpanzees, Martians, and (if Whorff is right) humans *whose spoken and written language* differs significantly from ours – then it would be absurd not to recognize that the translation involved in the definition of "believes that" is highly indeterminate. For this reason the notion of "believing that" defined above is itself a highly indeterminate notion, and consequently it is a notion that we ought to avoid in our psychological theorizing.[30] Instead, we should use the notion of believing (i.e., believing*), together perhaps with various semantic notions applied to the sentences believed. (Another reason for avoiding use of "believing that" (as defined above) in our psychological theories has already been mentioned in Section I – cf. (B).

I have introduced conventions about the use of "believes" and "believes that" according to which the first term relates organisms to sentences in their own system of representation and the second relates organisms to sentences in English. These terminological conventions are not intended to rule out the possibility that we need propositions in the analysis of belief and desire: it may be that we need propositions in our account of meaning for the sentences that are believed and desired. My own view, however, is

(a)   that talk of propositions is best avoided (except as a dispensable manner of speaking) unless it can be shown to serve purposes that cannot be served otherwise; and it is doubtful that this condition is met;

(b)   that such talk commits us to semantic theses which (independently of ontological scruples) may well be false.

Let's take (a) first. That one should not posit entities needlessly is, I take it, uncontroversial: to do so would be to indulge in "unfounded ontological speculation." And that there is no particular need to introduce propositions – at least, no need to introduce propositions construed in terms of possible worlds – was implicit in my discussion at the end of Section I. There I argued that, if one wanted to use the idea of possible worlds, and if one construed a proposition as a set of possible worlds, then the correlation of a particular proposition with a sentence posed no problem as long as we had an adequate truth-theoretic semantics for the language. Another way of putting this point is that talk of propositions adds nothing of semantic interest; everything that is semantically of interest is already there in the truth-theoretic semantics. (I'm speaking of course of a truth-theoretic semantics that assigns properties rather than sets to predicates.) In other words, instead of saying that a person is related to the set of possible worlds in which Russell was hairless (or to some fine-grained proposition constructed out of possible worlds), why not say instead that he is related to a sentence that consists of a name that stands for Russell copulated with a predicate that stands for hairlessness?[31]

One might try to respond to this question by holding (implausibly, I think) that names are non-rigid designators. But this response, while adequate to the question just asked, does not undercut the point I am trying to make (as has in effect been observed already, in note 16). For if "Russell" is non-rigid, then to believe that Russell was hairless is to believe some sentence that contains a definite description, some sentence of the form "G(the x such that Fx)" in which "F" is an individuating description of Russell and "G" stands for hairlessness. A truth-theoretic analysis of *this* sentence contains all the semantic information that is contained in a possible world analysis; so why bring in possible worlds? Again, they seem to be excess ontological baggage serving no semantic role.

Under (b) there are two points to be made. The first is that if one talks of propositions and also assumes that propositions must be explicable in terms of possible worlds, then one will be driven to postulate that proper names and theoretical terms like "temperature" are non-rigid designators; and this postulate is controversial at best. The second point is that, whether or not one adheres to the possible-worlds approach, talk of propositions commits one to a general relation of synonymy, and it is not at all obvious that there is any such general relation. I will develop these points, especially the second one, in Section VI. Their upshot is that the postulate of propositions involves not only unfounded ontological speculation but highly controversial semantic speculation as well. To me both the ontological and the semantic claims that underlie the postulate of propositions seem far more dubious than the postulate of a system of internal representation, especially since this last postulate appears to be a necessary one for the solution of Brentano's problem.

Let us say then that belief and desire are not attitudes toward propositions, but toward meaningful sentences in a system of internal representation. Presumably part of any adequate account of meaning for a system of internal representation is a truth-theoretic semantics; I will suggest in Section VI that there is another aspect of meaning as well. But first I would like to try to clarify the idea of a system of internal representation.

IV   Remarks on the Inner Representation Hypothesis

I have spoken of belief and desire as involving a system of *internal* representation; but I have allowed that, in the case of organisms that have a genuine
language, the system of internal representation might either be the language or
include the language as a part.[32] This combination of claims may seem puzzl-
ing: if the only representation is in natural language, why call it internal
representation? If there is internal representation, what sense does it make to
say that the representation is in a natural language?

The answer to these questions lies in the distinction between types and
tokens. I have talked of an organism as believing (i.e., believing*) sentence-
types. But I said in Section I that (neglecting the complication about core
beliefs) a person believes a sentence-type if and only if he employs that sentence-type in an appropriate way in reasoning, deliberating, etc.; and the only
way to employ a sentence-type is to employ some of its tokens. Now, it is clear
that in order to believe (or core believe) a sentence I can't be required to
employ *spoken or written* tokens of it: no one writes down all of his beliefs (or
all of his core beliefs). Consequently, if I believe sentences of my language,
what I employ has to include *internal* tokens of those sentences. That explains
why, even if all representation is in natural languages, we have to speak of
internal representation: some of the tokens are certainly internal.

This brings us to the second question: does it make sense to speak of
internal representation as representation *in natural language*? It makes sense if,
and only if, it makes sense to speak of internal tokens as being of the same type
as spoken or written tokens. One might argue that any claim of type-identity
between internal tokens and spoken or written tokens is highly implausible:
after all, it seems pretty absurd to suppose that there is much of a physical
resemblance between internal tokens on the one hand and spoken or written
tokens on the other. But this of course would be a very bad argument: after all,
a spoken token can be said to be of the same type as a written token, and yet
spoken and written tokens bear little physical resemblance to each other.

My own view is that the issue of whether we speak of internal tokens
as type-identical to spoken or written tokens is partly a verbal issue, but that
there are interesting empirical questions that underlie it, of which the most
important is the extent to which (and the manner in which) linguistic development involves conceptual development. To put the point very vaguely: if (as
seems to me quite likely) learning a first language involves *extending* an initial
representational system to include an isomorphic copy of the language being
learned, then I think it is quite natural to view the isomorphism as establishing
a criterion of type-identity between internal tokens and spoken or written
tokens. However, the issues here are pretty complicated. (See Harman, 1970,
for an interesting discussion which more or less supports the pro-type-identity

position, and Fodor, 1975, ch. 2, for an interesting discussion in support of the other side.) My sympathies are much more with Harman than with Fodor on this matter, but I will try to remain neutral on the question in the rest of the paper.[33]

But there are other questions that need to be considered. First, I have talked of "internal tokens." What kinds of entities are these? Presumably they are inner occurrences of some kind, but *what* kind? Second, although I have begged off the question of what it is for an internal token to be of the same type as a spoken or written token, there is also the question of what it is for two internal tokens to be of the same type as each other; and since a psychological theory will clearly need to use the notion of type-identity between different tokens, this question cannot very well be ignored. Third, there is the question of syntactically characterizing internal tokens – what is it for an internal token to belong to a given syntactic category (e.g., what is it for it to be a sentence token)? Again, we will need to appeal to syntactic characterizations of inner tokens in developing the psychological theory, so this question is a fairly pressing one.

There are two possible strategies in dealing with such questions. The first strategy, which I think is the wrong one, is to try to answer the above questions prior to developing the psychological theory. Such a strategy is a bad one because it is hard to see how to carry it out without doing a great deal of neurophysiological speculation: e.g., we would apparently have to specify two neurophysiological properties P_1 and P_2 and a neurophysiological relation R, and say that an inner occurrence is an expression-token if and only if it has P_1, and is a sentence-token if in addition it has P_2, and that two inner occurrences with property P_1 are of the same type if one bears R to the other. The task of specifying P_1, P_2 and R is certainly not a task we are equipped for in our current state of knowledge, and I don't see how we could even become equipped for it *prior* to the development of psychological theory.

The second strategy, which is the one I advocate, is to develop the syntax of the system of representations as part of the psychological theory: *we can then use the psychological theory to give a functionalist answer to the questions raised above*. That this is the right way to proceed seems completely obvious: it is simply an instance of the general rule that psychological theories ought to be construed functionally.

Let me be a bit more explicit about what is involved in this functionalist approach. If one were to write out in detail a theory H that postulates a system of inner representation, such predicates as "x is an expression-token," "x is a sentence-token," and "x and y are expression-tokens of the same type" would either appear as primitives or be explicitly definable (within set theory or higher order logic) from other such syntactic primitives. *Such syntactic primitives are to be included among the psychological primitives when we "functionalize" H:* that is, a *realization* of H is to be an n-tuple consisting of properties and relations corresponding to the syntactic predicates of the theory as well as to the more straightforwardly psychological predicates. If we "functionalize" the theory in this way then the answers to the questions raised above can be read right off of the theory H.[34] For instance, suppose for simplicity that "x and y are tokens of the same type" is a primitive of H. If we want to know what it is for two internal occurrences in an organism X at a time t to be tokens of the same type, the answer is simple: c and d are tokens of the same type if and only if there is a physical relation R which is the appropriate component of a unique realization of H in X at t, and c bears R to d.[35, 35a] (If "x and y are tokens of the same type" is a defined term rather than a primitive, the answer is slightly more complicated; but again, it can be read right off of the theory.) The upshot is that there is no need in developing psychological theory to specify what R is; we can leave that to future neurophysiology. (Moreover, we can allow that there are different physical type-identity relations in different organisms.) The fact that we leave the question to future neurophysiology does not imply any unclarity in our theory: *in some sense, the theory implicitly specifies what it is for two inner tokens in a system of representation to be tokens of the same type.*

There is one final point to be made about theories that postulate a system of internal representation. I have said that the *syntax* of a system of internal representation should be explicitly stated in a psychological theory of belief and desire. Should the *semantics* of the system of internal representation *also* be stated as part of the psychological theory? That depends on what we want psychological theory for. If the task of psychology is to state

(i)   the laws by which an organism's beliefs and desires evolve as he is subjected to sensory stimulations, and

(ii) the laws by which those beliefs and desires affect his bodily movements,

then I think that it is clear we do not need to use the semantics of the system of representation in stating the psychological laws: the sentences in the system of internal representation might as well be meaningless as far as the psychology is concerned.[36] This is not the only way to view a psychological theory – a broader conception of a belief-desire psychology will be suggested in the next section, and in it semantic notions would play a genuine role. But it is worth stressing the narrow kind of psychology at least momentarily. For we have seen that the syntax and type-identity conditions for a system of internal representation should be regarded as functionally characterized by a psychological theory in which they appear; and we can take that theory to be narrow psychology, that is, the kind of psychology that does not employ any semantic characterizations of the sentences in a system of representation. This is important, for it means that the syntax and conditions of type-identity for the system of representation could in principle be determined independently of any considerations about what the sentences in the system mean.

V   Truth

What would a theory of meaning for system of internal representation be like? In Sections I and III I have hinted at one aspect of my views on this question: a theory of meaning for a system of internal representation must consist in part of a truth-theoretic semantics of a more-or-less Tarskian kind. If we do not give a theory of truth for the system of internal representation, we cannot make sense of the idea that some of our beliefs are true and others are false; and I think we do want to be able to make sense of this idea (for reasons to be sketched shortly). Moreover, the only kind of theory of truth that I have ever heard of which is not obviously deficient is the Tarskian kind. The upshot, then, is that we need to give a Tarski-type semantic theory for the system of internal representation. In a recent article to which I am in most respects very sympathetic, Gilbert Harman has questioned this:

> . . . no reason has been given for a compositional theory of meaning for whatever system of representation we think in, be it Mentalese or English. (Harman, 1975, p. 286)

Presumably, however, if the notion of truth makes any sense, then truth and meaning must be related in the following way: the truth of the sentence "Caesar crossed the Rubicon" should follow from the meaning of the sentence together with the fact that Caesar crossed the Rubicon. *In this sense* a theory of meaning must include a theory of truth-conditions. And as far as I can see, the theory of truth-conditions has to be a compositional theory of roughly the type that Tarski made famous.

Harman's critique of compositional semantics is based on an important insight. He points out in the article that there is a serious problem for those philosophers, like Davidson, who regard *knowledge of* truth-conditions as what is essential in semantics:

> Davidson would (presumably) say that the speaker understands [the sentence "Snow is white"] by virtue of the fact that he knows it is true if and only if snow is white. The difficulty . . . is that [for the speaker to know any such thing he] needs some way to represent to himself snow's being white. If the relevant speaker uses the words "snow is white' to represent in the relevant way that snow is white, . . . Davidson's [theory] would be circular. And, if speakers have available a form of Mentalese in which they can represent that snow is white, so that the [theory avoids] circularity, there is still the problem of meaning of Mentalese. (p. 286)

But the moral to be drawn is that *knowledge* of truth-conditions is not what is important to the semantics of a system of internal representation. The theory must ascribe *truth-conditions*, not *knowledge of truth-conditions*, to the sentences of English or Mentalese; for if it doesn't ascribe truth-conditions to these sentences it will not have given sense to talk of our beliefs as being true or false.

I have assumed that we do want to make sense of the idea that some of our beliefs are true and others are false; I would also assume that we want to make sense of the idea that some of our beliefs are about Julius Caesar and that other of our beliefs are about quarks. It seems to me, however, that there is a serious question as to why we *should* want to make sense of these ideas. Is our desire to do so based on anything other than a naive metaphysics that has no place in a properly scientific account of the world?

That this question is not a silly one can be seen from a fact noted at the end of the previous section. If the task of psychology is to state.

    (i)   the laws by which an organism's beliefs and desires evolve as he is subjected to sensory stimulations, and

    (ii)   the laws by which those beliefs and desires affect his bodily movements,

then semantic characterizations of beliefs and desires are irrelevant to psychology: one can state the laws without saying anything at all about what the believed and desired sentences mean, or what their truth-conditions are or what their subject matter is. For instance, we might imagine a super-crude psychology that contained laws like the following:

there is some connective "$\longrightarrow$" in the system of internal representation such that, for all sentences S_1 and S_2 in the system, whenever a person believes $\ulcorner S_1 \longrightarrow S_2 \urcorner$ and desires S_2 then he also desires S_1.

[*Editor's note*: In this anthology, "$\longrightarrow$" is used instead of the horseshoe and the arrow as the material conditional ("if . . . then").] The connective "$\longrightarrow$" that satisfied this law might mean "only if," that is, it might obey the truth-table for the conditional; but the fact that it obeys this truth-table is not something we need to say in stating the psychological law.[37] The psychology, since we are imagining it to be super-crude, might also contain laws like this:

there is a privileged class of sentences in the system of representation, called the class of *observation sentences*, with the property that each sentence in the class has associated with it a particular type of sensory stimulation. Whenever a sensory stimulation of the appropriate type occurs, the organism believes the observation sentence.

Intuitively, we might expect that if a particular observation sentence is associated in this way with the class of retinal stimulations that are characteristically caused by nearby rabbits, then the observation sentence means something like "there are rabbits nearby"; but even if this is true, the psychological theory need not say that it is true. Why then do we need to semantically characterize the sentences in the system of inner representation? Why not simply say that belief and desire are relations between people and meaningless sentences? Saying this would preclude us from speaking of beliefs as being true or as being about rabbits, but would anything of scientific value be lost?

Here is one answer to this question – not the whole story, I think, but the part of the story that is emphasized in the writings of such philosophers as Quine, Davidson, and Harman (and perhaps Lewis in 1974). Imagine that we find ourselves with a foreigner whose language we do not understand. A rabbit scurries by, in the foreigner's line of sight, and the foreigner raises his gun in its direction – by now we have rather overwhelming grounds for thinking that he believes that there is a rabbit nearby. But can we say so in the vocabulary of the narrow psychology considered heretofore? We can't say "He believes the sentence . . ." (giving the name of the sentence); for we don't know his language. How about if we say instead "He believes some sentence which is an observation sentence associated with sensory stimulations of type . . . (and which serves as evidence for syntactically related sentences according to laws . . ., and so forth)." The difficulty is clear: only someone with a great deal of very detailed information about the psychology of our foreigner could fill in the blanks. A third possibility is much better:

> He believes some sentence of his language which plays approximately the role in his psychology that the sentence "There's a rabbit nearby" plays in mine.

But this, it might be claimed, really involves a semantic notion! For isn't it really just a long-winded way of saying

> He believes some sentence of his language that *translates* into my language as "There's a rabbit nearby"?

And isn't translation a semantic notion?

This answer does not satisfy me, for though it does definitely motivate the introduction of a notion of translation, it does not motivate the introduction of any non-translational semantic notions; that is, it motivates the introduction of a more-or-less[38] semantic notion about the relation of one language to another, but it does not motivate the introduction of any semantic notions like "true" or "refers" which relate language to the world. No reason has been offered, it seems to me, for regarding another person as having beliefs that are *true* or *about rabbits*. The Quinean reply, I would imagine, is that we need such notions as truth in connection with our own language (e.g., to state generalizations like "Every sentence of the form 'p or not p' is true");[39] and that we can then use the notion of translation that we have motivated on other grounds to carry over the truth concept to foreign languages. I do not want to discuss this Quinean reply here; but it seems to me rather weak, and I would like to do better.

I think that the reason why we need to be able to apply semantic notions like truth and reference to the sentences that people believe and desire is that we hold the theory that people's beliefs are, in many circumstances, reliable indicators about the world; and the only way to state this theory is to use the notion of truth (and probably the notion of reference as well). *Moreover, this theory is not a piece of gratuitous metaphysics that could easily be dispensed with*: it is central to our getting information about the world, for we are constantly using our opinions about other people's beliefs in forming opinions about the world. The fact that a child believes that he has done something I won't like (a fact that can often be inferred from his behavior) gives good reason to think he *has* done something I won't like; the fact that most physicists believe that there are gravitational waves (a fact that can be inferred from reading a few physics books) is good reason for me to believe that there *are* gravitational waves; and so forth. These inferences evidently proceed by means of certain *reliability principles*, principles that say under what conditions a person's beliefs about certain things are likely to be true. The principles we need are not easy to state: after all, the fact that a child believes in Santa Claus is not good reason for me to believe in Santa Claus, and the fact that most members of a certain religious cult believe that flying saucers will land on a certain farm in Arizona next month is not good enough reason for me to believe that flying saucers will land there. (I don't think that the failure of these inferences is due entirely to independent evidence as to the falsity of the conclusion.) We do evidently have a stock of reliability principles, though we can not explicitly formulate them; and one can imagine that they will someday be systematized into an explicit theory. In a suitably broad sense, we might even regard this "reliability theory" as part of psychology.

What such a reliability theory would look like I do not know. My guess is that it would have to include not only the notion of truth but the notion of reference: for we want to be able to say in the theory that some people have very reliable beliefs *about physics* but very unreliable beliefs *about the state of the economy*, and so forth. We might imagine then that "true," "refers," etc., are primitives of the theory. If we do that – and if we imagine that the reliability theory is elaborated with such detail and precision that it is uniquely realized in each of the organisms to which the theory is intended to apply – then we could use this theory to give a functional account of truth and reference for systems of internal representation. Such a functional account would of course be desirable, for the reason that functional accounts are always desirable: it would allow for the possibility that the reference relation is realized by different physical relations in different organisms.[40]

VI   More on the Semantics of Internal Representation

Is there more to the semantics of a system of internal representation than is given by truth-theoretic semantics? I think that there is; and I think that this casts considerable doubt on the possible-worlds analysis of propositions, even independently of ontological considerations. In fact, I think it casts some doubt (independent of ontological considerations) on whether *any* notion of proposition is possible. In explaining these matters, I will begin by discussing the semantics of spoken and written languages, since I want to discuss some points that Quine has made in the context of them; but what I say will carry over to systems of internal representation.

Many years ago Quine made the following observation:

A lexicographer may be concerned with synonymy between forms in one language and forms in another or . . . he may be concerned with synonymy between forms in the same language. It is an open question how satisfactorily the two cases can be subsumed under a single general formulation of the synonymy concept . . . (Quine, 1963, p. 56).

The point that Quine is making here is very relevant to the question of propositions: if one postulates propositions one is assuming a positive answer to Quine's "open question." For if sentences mean propositions, then apparently two sentences are synonymous if they mean the same proposition; and this would be a general concept of synonymy, it would apply both intralinguistically and interlinguistically.

Is Quine's "open question" really open? Well, at least this much is true: intralinguistic synonymy seems a lot easier to define than interlinguistic synonymy. (Similarly, intraspeaker synonymy is easier to define than interspeaker synonymy, suggesting that there might be still further divergence in the synonymy concept.) That intralinguistic synonymy is easier to define than interlinguistic synonymy *at least for what Quine calls occasion sentences* is a point that Quine argues in Sections 9 and 11 of (1960): he points out that the difference in meaning between "Everest" and "Gaurisanker" (construed as one-word sentences) for a certain speaker is revealed by the fact that different sensory stimulations would prompt him to assent to one than to the other; and that the difference in meaning of these one-word sentences in a given linguistic community is revealed by the fact that these sentences are intrasubjectively non-synonymous for most members of that community. Now, it seems to me that this talk of "prompting to assent" is much too behavioristic, and leads Quine into unnecessary worries, e.g., about "stimulations of second intention" (verbal stimulations like "Assent to one-word sentences that begin with 'E' or I'll beat your brains out") – cf. (1960), pp. 48–9. Nevertheless, it seems to me that Quine's general point is correct: *we can explain intralinguistic differences of meaning by evidential considerations.* I have developed this point elsewhere,[41] using a non-behavioristic (but, I admit, idealized) conception of evidence; and in addition to solving such humdrum difficulties with Quine's approach as the second-intention problem, it also obviates the need for restricting the account to occasion sentences. What is interesting about this approach I think is that it gives you differences of meaning where you would intuitively expect them, but where you do not get them on the possible-worlds approach (without adopting implausible assumptions about non-rigid designation). For instance, the following pair of sentences come out equivalent in meaning on the possible-worlds approach:

(10)   Everest is Gaurisanker

comes out equivalent to

(11)   Everest is Everest;

and

(12)   Temperature is mean molecular energy

comes out equivalent to[42]

(13)   Temperature is temperature.

But is should be pretty clear, even without looking up the details of my account, that these equivalences will not hold on any sufficiently sophisticated evidential criterion of intraspeaker synonymy, even for speakers who believe the sentences (10) and (12).

Such evidential considerations (coupled with truth-theoretic considerations if the latter are not redundant)[43] seem to me to provide a very natural account of intraspeaker synonymy. For interspeaker synonymy, however, the situation is quite different, for here it is very hard to formulate any evidential criteria for two words differing in meaning. The source of the difficulty is clear: you and I may disagree about what counts as evidence for a certain sentence, not because that sentence means something different to you than it means to me, but because of differences in the rest of our beliefs. One might try to find some rule of the form "If there is an evidential difference of such and such a kind between your sentence and mine, then they differ in meaning"; this is the task that Quine refers to as "trying to strip away the effects of collateral information." Quine has cast considerable doubts on the possibility of carrying out this task (1960, section 9), and I think that if you look at the question in terms of my formal model in Field (1977) you will find that Quine's doubts are reinforced.

It seems to me that the criteria of interlinguistic synonymy we actually employ are, *almost* exclusively, the criteria provided by truth-theoretic semantics.[44] This is not quite true; when there are two sentences S_1 and S_2 in one language that are equivalent from the point of view of truth-theoretic (or possible-world) semantics, but which differ evidentially, and when there is a sentence S_3 in another language that is truth-theoretically equivalent to both S_1 and S_2 but is much more similar evidentially to S_1 than to S_2, then we regard it as definitely a mistake to translate S_3 as S_2 – the translation S_1 seems required. But except in such cases, little if any intersubjective sameness of evidential role is required; if the Martians have singled out Everest i.e., Gaurisanker, by their powerful telescopes and have named it "Schrdlu," we would translate their name "Schrdlu" by "Everest" or by "Gaurisanker" indifferently, however much we might want to say that "Everest" and "Gaurisanker" differ in meaning for us. One might object to this argument by saying that translation is a loose and pragmatic notion: the true situation (one might say) is that "Schrdlu" differs in meaning *both* from "Everest" *and* from "Gaurisanker"; we translate the name indifferently by "Everest" or by "Gaurisanker" because these approximate "Schrdlu" about equally well. I sympathize with this response, except for one thing: it assumes that there is *some* clear notion of interlinguistic difference in meaning between words that refer to the same thing, and that is what I think needs to be established.

My view then is that truth-theoretic semantics – i.e., possible-world semantics without the possible worlds – is almost enough, but that there are certain very fine-grained distinctions of meaning that it cannot explain. These fine-grained distinctions of meaning seem to be clearly drawable only intra-linguistically, and that fact appears to make the notion of proposition suspect.

It should be clear that these remarks about synonymy between sentences in public languages apply also to synonymy between sentences in systems of internal representation. It should also be clear that, to define the evidential differences between sentences in the same system of internal representation, one does not need to employ any concepts that go outside psychology in the narrow sense. Consequently there seems to be no special problem in motivating the introduction of such evidential considerations into a semantic theory for the system of inner representation, in a way that there did seem to be a special problem of motivating the introduction of truth-theoretic concepts.

I want to conclude this paper by raising what I regard as an open question: what connections are there between a theory of meaning for a system of internal representation and a theory of meaning for a spoken or written language?[45] According to one influential approach[46] to the theory of meaning for spoken and written languages, the meaning of a sentence in such languages is to be explained in terms of beliefs (or desires, etc.) that are conventionally correlated with the sentence. Roughly, to know the meaning of "Caesar was egotistical" is to know that this sentence is conventionally correlated with the belief that Caesar was egotistical; and similarly for every other sentence in one's public language. (The conventional correlation must be spelled out recursively, of course.) This approach presupposes that one can explain what it is to believe that Caesar was egotistical *without relying at any point on the semantic features of the sentence "Caesar was egotistical" in one's spoken or written language*: for if one relied on the semantic features of the spoken or written sentence in one's account of the belief, then to explain the meaning of the sentence in terms of the belief would involve a circularity. So a crucial question is whether that presupposition is correct.

Putting the presupposition in terms of internal representation, it is this: that one can explain what it is for a sentence in the internal system of representation to mean that Caesar was egotistical without relying in one's explanation on the fact that certain words and phrases in the public language stand for Caesar or that certain other words and phrases in the public language stand for the property of being egotistical. *If this presupposition is correct*, then the above approach to the theory of meaning is quite attractive: if worked out, it would reduce all questions about the semantics of the spoken or written language to the corresponding questions about the semantics of the system of internal representation; and those questions could then be answered without further reference to language. I am inclined to doubt, however, that the presupposition is true. My *guess* is that, in a typical case, *part of* what makes a symbol in my system of internal representation a symbol that stands for Ceasar is that this symbol acquired its role in my system of representation as a result of my acquisition of a name that stands for Caesar in the public language. If something of this sort is true, it would appear to defeat[47] the above approach to a theory of meaning for a public language. I believe, however, that the issues here are quite complicated, and deserve a great deal of further study.

An opposite approach to the theory of meaning would be to try to reduce the semantics of the system of internal representation to the semantics for public language. To do this would be to assume that although dogs, chimpanzees, etc. might have systems of internal representation which played an important role in the explanation of their behavior, these systems of representation would not be ones to which notions like meaning and truth applied: such semantic notions could be applicable only to the representational systems of organisms with a spoken or written language. To me, such a conclusion seems very implausible. It may nevertheless be that there is *something* to this approach, for it may be that *certain aspects* of meaning can be explained more directly for public language than for systems of internal representation. The suggestion is not that these aspects of meaning can be explained without reference to beliefs and desires, for two reasons. In the first place, in explaining the fact that the public word "Caesar" referred to Caesar one could appeal freely to certain sorts of beliefs and desires, e.g., those beliefs and desires that a languageless organism could possess; for we have granted that such beliefs and desires can be accounted for in a language-independent way. In the second place, there is an important sense in which one could appeal to other beliefs and desires as well in our semantic theory for public language; we could appeal to beliefs and desires *construed as attitudes towards internal sentences* all we liked; the only restriction would be on which semantic features of those internal sentences we appealed to.

I do not want to draw any very definite conclusions from this last discussion. I merely want to say that it may well be necessary to develop the semantic theory for internal languages and the semantic theory for public languages together rather than developing one kind of semantics independently of the other and reducing the other kind to it. The reductionist strategy (particularly the strategy that tries to reduce public semantics to internal semantics) is worth pursuing, but alternative strategies are worth pursuing as well.[48]

Notes

"Mental Representation" first appeared in *Erkenntnis*, 13, 1 (1978), 9–61. Copyright 1978 by D. Reidel Company. Reprinted by permission of Kluwer Academic Publishers.

1   See for instance Armstrong (1968), ch. 3, and Putnam (1975b).
2   Brentano's problem is discussed by Chisholm (1957), ch. 11; references to Brentano can be found there.
3   See Stalnaker (1976). Lewis's remarks on functionalism are scattered throughout various writings; see Lewis (1970), (1971), (1972b), (1974), and (1975).
4   See Quine (1960), section 45.
5   *Believing** is thus different from *believing true*: a foreign speaker can believe an English sentence true while having no idea what it means, e.g., if he sees a headline in the *N.Y. Times*. To believe a sentence *S* true (i.e., to believe that *S* is true) is, if (1) is right, to believe* a sentence *S** which means *that S is true*. Believing true involves the concept of truth; believing* does not.
6   The Banach-Tarski theorem says roughly that a solid sphere can be decomposed into a finite number of disjoint "pieces" in such a way that the "pieces" can then be put back together again to form two solid spheres the same size as the original one. (For a more precise statement (and a proof) see Jech, 1973, pp. 3–6.)
7   For pedants: I'm speaking of von Neumann set theory including the axiom of choice; it is finitely axiomatized.
8   Lewis (1972a), pp. 182ff.
9   Dennett (1975b), p. 410. Dennett seems to regard the introduction of the notion of core-believing as an *ad hoc* device to save stored-sentence approaches from the absurdity of requiring infinitely many sentences to be stored: but the following discussion will show I think that the notion can be given strong independent motivation.
10 To spell this out more fully, we'd need first to spell out the characteristic role of beliefs (as opposed to, say, desires) in reasoning deliberating, and so on – call this characteristic role Role B. Then the materialistic view of believing* that I am suggesting is roughly that in each believer there is some kind of physical storage of sentences such that the things stored in that way and their obvious consequences are the things that have Role B.
11 The "almost" appears to be needed here because of the non-transitivity of "is an obvious consequence of." I doubt that there are any *clear cases* of believing that either Russell was hairless or snow is white but not believing that if Russell was not hairless then snow is white; but I regard this as more or less analogous to the fact that there are no clear cases of numbers *n* such that some individuals with fewer than *n* hairs are bald but no individual with *n* or greater hairs is bald. I

would not want to assert that because there are no *clear* cases of such numbers, there are no such numbers, because that would led to a Sorites paradox. Similarly, I would not want to assert that because there are no *clear* class of believing p and not believing an obviously equivalent proposition q, there are no such cases; for that would lead by Sorites-like reasoning to the conclusion that one can't believe p and yet not believe the unobviously equivalent claim r.

12   The acceptance of indeterminacies of the kind mentioned here is a minor concession to an instrumentalistic view of ordinary belief-talk, but only a minor one; for even if it does not always make sense to ask whether a belief-ascription is true or false, we have seen no reason to deny that a core-belief ascription is always true or false: and that is close enough. (Another minor concession to an instrumentalistic view of our ordinary) belief-talk will be made in Section III.)

13   See for instance Fodor (1975) and Harman (1973), ch. 4, section 2.

14   Field (1972).

15   Davidson (1967).

16   I have assumed in this paragraph that proper names are always rigid designators. Some people, however, deny this: they believe that when we use the name "Bertrand Russell" we associate with this name a property H which we think picks out Russell uniquely: and that when we say "Bertrand Russell is hairless," what we say is true at a world w if and only if there is exactly one thing in w with property H in w, and that thing is hairless in w. (The thing with H in w need not be the thing with H in the actual world, i.e., it need not be Russell.) I find this doctrine that names can denote non-rigidly quite implausible; but the point I am making in the paper could be generalized so as to allow for names to be non-rigid designators for anyone who finds that desirable. To see this, reflect on how we would associate a property H with a name. The only way I can see to do that is to associate with that name some expression (in a natural language or in a system of internal representation) which stands for that property. What the advocate of non-rigid designation is saying, then, is that, when we utter the sentence "Bertrand Russell is hairless," that sentence merely serves to abbreviate the sentence (or sentence-analog) that we really mean, which is something of the form "There is exactly one thing x such that $F(x)$, and x is hairless." Truth-at-a-possible-world can then be defined for the sentences (or sentence-analogs) *that we really mean*, by the process described in the text; and we can say that, derivatively, a sentence S containing the name "Bertrand Russell" is true at w if and only if the associated sentence (or sentence-analog) *that we really mean when we utter S* is true at w.

17   I don't really mean to be assuming that the primitive symbols in the sentence-analogs are names or predicates; who knows what they are? All that the account I am suggesting assumes is that *whatever* problems of (actual world) reference such symbols raise are soluble in a materialistically acceptable manner.

18   I should add that the difficulty of constructing an alternative account of a relation between people and propositions is especially acute if one takes propositions to be fine-grained.

19   Lewis certainly believes this, and I suspect that Stalnaker does too.

20   This is true even of non-materialist functionalists; they too require realizations of psychological properties, they merely allow that the realizations be non-physical.

(Only an instrumentalistic functionalist would deny the requirement of realizations entirely.)

21 Lewis (1970), (1971), and (1972b).

22 I do not impose Lewis's requirement that *H* be a *commonsense* psychological theory. But if you want to add that (to my mind unnecessary) requirement, you may: the argument of this section of the paper will not be affected.

The restriction to commonsense psychological theories *might* interfere with a proposal to be made later on: that we explicitly build the postulate of a system of internal representation into *H*. At first blush this would seem to conflict with letting *H* be a common sense theory, since common sense would not appear to be committed to systems of internal representation. However, Lewis is rather generous in what he regards common sense as committed to: he does not regard the fact that a theory postulates possible worlds other than our own as going against the requirement that it say only what is common sense. I believe that systems of internal representation are at least as close to being postulates of common sense as are possible worlds.

I have said that I think that the requirement that *H* be a commonsense theory is unnecessary. I also think that it is harmful. For one thing, it is not at all clear that any of the commonsense theories of belief are (or even come close to being) *uniquely* realized; the only way to get anything like *unique* realization may be to invoke non-commonsense suppositions. It may well be for instance that only a theory of belief that explicitly postulates a system of internal representation can come anywhere near to being uniquely realized. But I do not want to press this point here: the argument of this section goes through even if *H* itself does not postulate a system of internal representation or in any other way (apart from propositions!) strain the bounds of common sense.

23 Lewis's own account of what realizations are is strictly speaking inaccurate because he does not take the precaution I've recommended: as his account stands, something can serve as a realization of pain only if it realizes pain in *all* organisms at *all* times, thus depriving functionalism of its point (cf. Harman, 1973, ch. 3, section 4). But it is clear that what I have suggested (which is equivalent to what Harman suggests) is what Lewis really had in mind.

24 Here I oversimplify: we might imagine that $T_1, \ldots, T_n$ include non-psychological terms that are needed in the theory; and we might also imagine that some psychological terms needed in the theory are not included among $T_1, \ldots, T_n$, because their reference is fixed independently of *H*.

25 For reasons not relevant to the present paper, Lewis finds it convenient to imagine that the theory has been rewritten so that all the psychological terms are names. I have chosen not to do this, and the features of the next paragraph that do not look quite like anything explicitly in Lewis result from this fact. The conclusion I will derive, however, would have been forthcoming on his procedure as well.

26 "I take states to be attributes of a special kind: attributes of things at times" (1971, p. 165). When Lewis says that "pain" refers to a state he does not of course mean that it refers to what might be called a *state-token*, that is, an individual inner occurrence (an occurrence of the type that the organism feels

when it "feels pain"). Nor does he mean what might be called a *state type*: a sortal property of such inner occurrences, a property that might be expressed by the predicate "is a pain." Rather, pain is taken to be an attribute *of organisms*, the attribute that is expressed by "feels pain" (cf. 1971, footnote 1). I think myself that the word "state" is best reserved for what I've called state-tokens and state-types; for Lewis's use of the term helps foster a confusion between states in his sense and state-types in mine, and this can lead to a disastrous confusion to be noted later in this section. (Lewis himself does not fall into the confusion, as footnote 13 of (1972) shows, but I think his terminology has led others to make it.)

27   Strictly speaking, it might be better to leave out the word "physical" here: that way if materialism is only *contingently* true, then we can allow organisms in those possible worlds in which H is realized by irreducibly mental properties to have functional properties. This change in the definition of functional property would in no way affect the application of functional properties to organisms in those worlds where materialism is true; in particular, it would not affect the application of functional properties in the actual world, if as I am assuming materialism is indeed true. Since my own interest lies wholly in the actual world, my addition of the word "physical" does no harm.

I chose to put in the word "physical" partly to remind the reader of the materialist premise, and partly as a convenient way to introduce distinctions of *order*. For the method of defining properties used in (2) to make sense, the functional property being defined cannot be one of the properties in the range of property-quantifier. If we use the notion of "physical property" narrowly, so that functional properties like those defined in (2) do not themselves count as physical, then this condition is met. On this narrow use of the term physical, the materialist thesis is that all non-functional properties are physical.

28   The uniqueness requirement is Lewis's. I think that it must be taken with a grain of salt, but I do not have the space here to explain my reservations or to develop the machinery needed to avoid it. (The word "unique" in (2) cannot merely be dropped.)

29   According to Lewis, "the property of being in pain" and "pain" refer to different properties: "the property of being in pain" refers to a functional property, and "pain" refers (in the context of discussing a specific organism X at a specific time t) to the non-functional property which realizes the functional property in X at t. I have tried to remain neutral on the question of whether "pain" refers to the functional property or refers (in a context-dependent way) to a realization of it.

30   This is not intended as an argument against using a notion of *believing that* which relates people to propositions, but only as an argument against using a notion which relates people to English sentences (or to utterances of English sentences). A theory involving propositions is exempt from the criticism, since if there are propositions at all then presumably there are propositions not expressible in English. (However, even if "believes that" relates people to propositions, it is not clear that sentences attributing *particular* beliefs to organisms very unlike us could ever be literally true.)

31   Some people may feel that there is no ontological gain in quantifying over properties rather than over propositions. Such a person should read Putnam

(1975b). Putnam makes a good case (a) that quantification over properties is needed in science, and (b) that properties are quite distinct from meanings, in that two predicates like "x has temperature 210° C" and "x has mean molecular energy 10^{-20} joules" can turn out to stand for the same property even though they clearly differ in meaning.

32   I have allowed this by allowing for the possibility that the sentences which are believed be genuine sentences in a genuine language, rather than sentence-analogs.

33   Where neutrality of formulation is difficult to achieve without verbosity, I have frequently sacrificed the neutrality; but even in these cases it is not difficult to rephrase what I say so as to accord with the position that I am temporarily excluding.

34   This assumes that the syntactic theory is formulated in such a way that all syntactic predicates are predicates of tokens. To assume this is not to assume that the syntax can be given nominalistically, i.e., without quantifying over abstract entities like sets, or even like sequences which can be intuitively regarded as having more or less the role of expression-types. Once this is realized, the task of formulating the syntactic theory in the way required presents no difficulty.

   Incidentally, I should remark that the syntactic theory can be formulated in such a way as to allow wide diversity in the grammars of the systems of representation of organisms to which the theory is intended to apply. (One way in which it might do this is to postulate a general system of syntactic categories. Different subsets of this general system could be instantiated in different organisms to which the theory applies, and in this way a wide syntactic diversity in systems of representation would be compatible with the general theory. See Lewis (1972a) for an illustration of the kind of general syntax I have in mind.)

35   Incidentally, R could perfectly well be a disjunctive relation, say of the form "Either x and y are both occurrences in the left hemisphere of the brain and x bears R_1 to y, or x and y are occurrences in the right hemisphere and x bears R_2 to y, or one is an occurrence in the left and the other in the right and the one in the left bears R_3 to the one in the right." Disjunctive realizations are needed for other functional theories – e.g., it is perfectly possible that pain is realized in a given organism at a given time by a disjunctive property like "is a stimulation of the C-fibers or a firing of the X-neurons" – and there is no reason to rule out the same flexibility in the theory of belief and desire. I make this point because I think that a main reason why many philosophers resist the inner representation hypothesis is that they tend to exaggerate its neurophysiological commitments.

35a This only defines what it is for two tokens *in the same organism* to be of the same type; but the notion of type-identity between tokens in one organism and tokens in the other is not needed for psychological theory, and can be regarded as a meaningless notion.

36   I will elaborate on this point in the next section.

37   The proposed "law" involving "$+$" is of course *exceptionally* crude: to get anything that looks at all plausible, one probably has to bring in something like *degrees* of belief and *degrees* of desirability. But the point I am making is unaffected: the degrees of belief and degrees of desirability can be regarded as attaching to sentences, and laws can be given relating the degrees of belief and

desirability of a sentence of the form $\ulcorner S_1 \longrightarrow S_2 \urcorner$ to the degrees of belief and desirability of the component sentences S_1 and S_2 and of other compound sentences containing S_1 and S_2. (E.g., if B is degree of belief, one law might be that

$B(S_1 \longrightarrow S_2)$ is greater than or equal to max $[B(S_2), 1 - B(S_1)]$).

At no point do the meanings of the component sentences or of the logical connectives need to be mentioned.

38   I think that there is some question as to whether the notion of translation, used in the very loose and pragmatic way just explained, ought to count as a genuinely semantic notion; hence the "more or less."

39   Cf. Quine (1970), p. 11.

40   Without a functional account, we can in a sense recognize this: we can let "refers" stand for a certain physical relation in connection with organisms of one kind (say, organisms that speak some language of a certain general type), and also let "refers" stand for a different physical relation in connection with organisms of another type; but without a functional account we do not have the means to explain what these two uses of "refers" have in common. (Similarly for "true.")

41   Field (1977).

42   Strictly, this equivalence holds only on the coarse-grained possible-worlds approach. But we could imagine that a one-word phrase "glub" had been introduced into the language by the stipulation that it was to denote (rigidly) the property of mean molecular energy; then "Temperature is glub" would be equivalent to (13) even on the fine-grained possible-worlds approach, but they would clearly be non-synonymous.

43   Whether they are redundant depends on whether one treats evidential considerations in a fine-grained or a coarse-grained manner; see Field (1977), pp. 396–7.

44   Our criteria for interspeaker but intralinguistic synonymy are less clear: sometimes we treat this case like the interlinguistic case, and sometimes we use the common language to extend considerations of intraspeaker synonymy across different speakers.

45   Here I am concerned primarily with the truth-theoretic aspects of meaning. Also, the question I am asking does not really presuppose what the formulation in the text suggests, that a person's system of internal representation is distinct from his public language. If we adopt the opposite presupposition, we can phrase the question as follows: in what ways if any does one need to bring in the fact that a system of internal representation is also used publicly, in giving a complete theory of truth-conditions for the system of internal representation; and in what ways does one need to bring in the fact that a public language is used for thinking, in giving a complete theory of meaning for it.

46   See Schiffer (1972). Lewis's approach in (1975) is quite similar. Harman's suggestion in (1968) that the "level 2 theory of meaning" presupposes the "level 1 theory of meaning" but not conversely seems to involve a similar idea.

47   It might not defeat it, if as suggested at the end of Section V we give a functional account of reference: for then we could grant that we need to specify the use of the word "Caesar" in public language in order to specify a *realization* for the reference-relation as applied to the system of internal representation, but hold that we do not need to mention it *in the functional theory itself*. However, it does

not seem to me at all *obvious* that we do not need to mention the public use of words in a satisfactory functional theory of truth-conditions for systems of internal representation; it seems to me that no one has developed any such theory in anywhere near enough detail for us to tell. It may well be for instance that a fairly detailed causal account of reference has to be explicitly built into reliability theory (or whatever other kind of broad psychological theory it is in which the notion of reference or of truth-conditions appears), and that such a detailed causal theory will have to explicitly mention acquisition of a public word that refers to something as one of the mechanisms by which people can become causally related to an object in the way that is relevant to having beliefs about the object.

48   I have greatly benefited from discussion on these issues with David Lewis, Janet Levin, Brian Loar, and Stephen Schiffer. The latter two especially, by their relentless criticism of the way I expressed my ideas in conversation, have forced me to write a very much better paper than I would otherwise have written. I am also grateful to Ned Block, Tyler Burge, Michael Devitt, Keith Donellan, and David Hills for helpful comments on an earlier version.

Part II

The Theories

4 Advertisement for a Semantics for Psychology

Ned Block

Meaning is notoriously vague. So, it should not be surprising that semanticists (those who study meaning) have had somewhat different purposes in mind, and thus have sharpened the ordinary concept of meaning in somewhat different ways. It is a curious and unfortunate fact that semanticists typically tell us little about what aspects of meaning they are and are not attempting to deal with. One is given little guidance as to what extent "rival" research programs actually disagree.

My purpose here is to advocate an approach to semantics relevant to the foundations of psychology, or, rather, one approach to one branch of psychology, namely cognitive science. I shall be talking in terms of some of the leading ideas of cognitive science, most importantly the representational theory of mind, aspects of which will be sketched as they become relevant.[1] The representalist doctrine that my argument depends on is that thoughts are structured entities. I know this will be a sticking point for some readers, so I will say a bit more about what this comes to, and I will compare my position with related positions that reject it.

My strategy will be to begin with some desiderata. These desiderata vary along many dimensions: how central they are to meaning, how psychologically oriented they are, how controversial they are. I will argue that one approach to semantics (not to keep you in suspense – conceptual role semantics) promises to handle such desiderata better than the others that I know about. Though I think my desiderata yield a coherent picture of a psychologically relevant semantics, they are not intended to be pretheoretically obvious; rather, they were chosen to flatter the theory I have in mind. I will *not* be arguing that semantic theories that fail to satisfy these desiderata are thereby defective; there are distinct – and equally legitimate – questions about meaning that a semantic theory can seek to answer.

The view that I am advertising is a variant on the functionalism familiar in the philosophy of mind. However, I will not be attempting to counter the objections that have been raised to that view (except briefly, and in passing). My bet is that looking at functionalism from the point of view of meaning (rather than mentality) and with an eye to its fertility and power rather than its weaknesses will provide a rationale for working on its problems.

Desiderata

Desideratum 1: Explain the relation between meaning and reference/truth. This is the least psychological of all my desiderata. The details of what I have in mind will be discussed when I say how conceptual role semantics promises to explain the relation between meaning and truth.

Desideratum 2: Explain what makes meaningful expressions meaningful. What is it about "cat" in virtue of which it has the meaning it has? What is the difference between "cat" and "glurg" in virtue of which the former has meaning and the latter does not? (And so on, for types of expressions other than words.)

Desideratum 3: Explain the relativity of meaning to representational system. This desideratum is arguably just a special case of the preceding one, but I think it is worth mentioning and discussing separately. As we all know, one linguistic item – for example, a sound or linguistic expression – can have different meanings in different languages. For example, many vocabulary items have different meanings in the dialects of English spoken in North America and England, as in "trailer" and "bathroom."

But the significance of this relativity of meaning to system of representation goes deeper than such examples suggest. One way to see this is to note that whole semantic (and syntactic) *categories* are relative to system of representation. Ink marks that function as a picture in your tribe may function as a word in mine. Further, within the category of pictures, representations are understood differently in different cultures.[2] Finally, syntactic category is relative in the same way. Handwriting, for example, differs in different school systems. Perhaps the ink marks that are regarded as an "A" in Edinburgh are regarded as an "H" in Chicago. Is there some common explanation of the relativity to representational system of both semantic and syntactic categories?

Desideratum 4: Explain compositionality. The meaning of a sentence is in some sense a function of the meanings of the words in it (plus the syntax of the sentence). What, exactly, is the relation between the semantic values of sentences and words? Is one more basic than the other? Another question arises once we have fixed on an answer to these questions – namely, why is it that the semantic value of a sentence has whatever relation it has to the semantic values of its parts?

Desideratum 5: Fit in with an account of the relation between meaning and mind/brain. Why should one expect (or at least hope for) a *semantic* theory to fit into an account of the relation between meaning and mind or brain? Because it would be surprising if the nature of meaning (what meaning *is*) were utterly irrelevant to explaining what it is to grasp or understand meanings, and how grasping meanings can have physical effects. At least, one can imagine differences between x and y that make for a difference between what it is to grasp x and y. For example, understanding x may require skills or recognitional abilities, whereas understanding y may require only propositional knowledge.

I said "mind *or* brain," but in fact I will focus on the brain. And in discussing this matter, I will simply adopt a form of materialism (the "token" identity thesis – that each particular mental occurrence is a physical occurrence).

What is supposed to be in need of explanation about the relation of meaning to the brain? Well, one obvious question is: what is for the brain to grasp meanings, and how is it that the brain's grasp of meanings has effects on the world? Meanings are (at least apparently) non-physical abstract objects. And the relation between a brain and the meanings it grasps does not seem to be like the relation between a metal bar and the number of degrees Celsius that is its temperature – a case in which there are proposals about how a change in the value of the temperature can cause, say, expansion of the bar (see Field, 1980). Yet the difference between a brain that grasps a certain meaning and a brain that does not makes for a difference in the causal properties of that brain. A brain that grasps the meaning of "transmogrify" can win a quiz show for its owner, transporting the two of them to a hotel in the Catskills. We need an account of how such a relation between a brain and a meaning can make a causal difference.

Desideratum 6: Illuminate the relation between autonomous and inherited meaning. If there are representations in the brain, as the representational theory of the mind contends, then there is an obvious distinction to be made between them and other representations – for instance, representations on this page (Searle, 1980; Haugeland, 1980). The representations on the page must be read or heard to be understood, but not so for the representations in the brain. The representations on the page require for their understanding *translation*, or at least *transliteration* into the language of thought; the representations in the brain (some of them, at any rate) require no such translation or transliteration. Let us say that the representations that require no translation or transliteration have *antonomous* meaning, whereas the ones that do require translation or transliteration have *inherited* meaning.

Different views of meaning have quite different consequences for the issue of what a semantic theory could hope to say about either type of meaning. On Searle's view, for example, the most a semantic theory could say about this matter is to give an account of how inherited meaning (*observer-relative* meaning, in his terminology) is inherited from autonomous meaning (*intrinsic meaning*, in his terminology). Explaining autonomous meaning itself, in his view, is simply outside the scope of semantics. The most we can say by way of giving an account of autonomous meaning, according to Searle, is that it arises from the causal powers of the human brain and would arise from any other object (e.g., a machine) that has "equivalent causal powers."

Despite the panoply of views on this matter, there are a few questions whose interest should be agreed on by all who accept the distinction between autonomous and inherited meaning to begin with. The main questions are: What are autonomous and inherited meaning? What is the relation between autonomous and inherited meaning? For example, are they just two different types of meaning, neither of which is derivative from or reducible to the other?[3]

A related question is how a representation with autonomous meaning can mean the same as a representation with inherited meaning. Many philosophers would disparage such a question because of skepticism about synonomy. But it is not clear that those who accept it are caught in the Quinean quicksand. That depends on whether the notion of meaning used in cognitive science must carry with it commitment to *truths* of meaning, and hence commitment to a priori truth.[4]

Desideratum 7: Explain the connections between knowing, learning, and using an expression, and the expression's meaning. Obviously, there is a close connection between *the meaning of a word*, on the one hand, and *what we know when we know or understand a word* and *what we learn when we learn a word*, on the other hand. Indeed, it is intuitively plausible that these italicized descriptions have the same referent (though it would be a mistake to adhere dogmatically to this pretheoretic intuition).

Further, one who has learned an expression (and therefore knows it automatically has a capacity to use it correctly; also, evidence of correct usage is evidence for knowing the meaning. A psychologically relevant theory of meaning ought to illuminate the connections between knowing/understanding/learning and usage, on the one hand, and meaning on the other.

Desideratum 8: Explain why different aspects of meaning are relevant in different ways to the determination of reference and to psychological explanation. One can distinguish between two aspects of meaning that are relevant to psychological explanation in quite different ways. One type of case involves indexicals, for example:

(1) I am in danger of being run over.
(2) Ned Block is in danger of being run over.

Consider the difference between the beliefs I would express by uttering (1), as compared with (2). Believing (2) cannot be guaranteed to have the same life-saving effect on my behavior as believing (1), since I may not know I am Ned Block (I may think I am Napoleon).[5] So there is an important difference between (1) and (2) with respect to causation (and therefore causal explanation) of behavior.

This observation is one motivation for a familiar way of thinking about meaning and belief content in which, when you and I have beliefs expressed by our (respective) utterances of (1), we have beliefs with the same content. This is the way of individuating in which two lunatics who say "I am Napoleon" have the *same delusion*. Corresponding to this way of individuating belief content, we have a way of individuating meanings in which the meanings of the two lunatics' sentence-tokens are the same. This is the way of individuating meanings of tokens that is geared toward sentence-types, and thus seems most natural for linguistics – since it makes the meaning of a sentence a function of the meanings of the words in the sentence (plus syntax). Notice that on this way of individuating, utterances of (1) and (2) by me have *different* meanings and standardly express beliefs with *different* contents. Again, this way of individuating is natural for linguistics, since no reasonable dictionary would give "I" and "Ned Block" the same entry.

Nonetheless, (1), said by me, and (2) express the same proposition, according to a familiar way of individuating propositions. In a familiar sense of "meaning" in which two sentence-tokens have the same meaning just in case they express the same proposition, (1), said by me, and (2) have the same meaning. If we individuate contents of beliefs as we individuate the propositions believed, the belief I express by (1) would have the same content as the belief I express by (2). Further, the belief I express by (1) would have different content from the belief you express by (1); similarly, the meaning of my utterance of (1) would be different from your utterance of (1).

Call the former scheme of individuation *narrow* individuation and the latter *wide* individuation (cf. Kaplan's different distinction between character and content). Wide individuation groups token sentences together if they attribute the same properties to the same individuals, whereas narrow individuation groups sentence-tokens together if they attribute the same properties using the same descriptions of individuals – irrespective of whether the individuals referred to are the same. In other words, narrow individuation abstracts from the question of (i.e., ignores) whether the same individuals are involved and depends instead on how the individuals are referred to.[6] (Note that the question of how individuals are referred to is quite different from the question of how the referrer thinks of the referent. For example, two uses of (1) have the same narrow meaning (in my sense of the phrase) even if one user thinks he's Napoleon while the other thinks he's Wittgenstein.)

One can think of narrow and wide individuation as specifying different aspects of meaning, narrow and wide meaning. (I am not saying that narrow and wide meaning are *kinds* of meaning, but only aspects or perhaps only *determinants* of meaning.) Narrow meaning is "in the head," in the sense of this phrase in which it indicates supervenience on physical constitution,[7] and narrow meaning captures the semantic aspect of what is in common to utterances of (e.g.) (1) by different people. Wide meaning, by contrast, depends on what individuals outside the head are referred to, so wide meaning is not "in the head." The type of individuation that gives rise to the concept of narrow meaning also gives rise to a corresponding concept of narrow belief content.

Two utterances have the same narrow meaning just in case the beliefs they express have the same narrow content.

Note that, despite the misleading terminology, wide meaning does not *include* narrow meaning. Utterances of (1) (by me) and (2) have the same wide meaning but not the same narrow meaning.[8]

Narrow meaning/content and wide meaning/content are relevant to psychological explanation in quite different ways. For one thing, the narrow meaning of a sentence believed is more informative about the mental state of the believer. Thus narrow meaning (and narrow content) is better suited to predicting and explaining what someone decides or does, so long as information about the external world is ignored. Thus, if you and I both have a belief we would express with (1), one can explain and predict our sudden glances at nearby vehicles and our (respective) decisions to leap to the side. Wide meanings are less suited to this type of prediction and explanation, because they "leave out" information about the way one refers to oneself. Since the wide meaning of (1) said by me and (2) are the same, if you are told I believe a sentence with this wide meaning (i.e., the wide meaning common to my [1] and [2]), you know that I believe that something – me, as it happens, but you aren't told that I know it's me – is in danger of being run over. Thus, information is omitted, since you aren't told how I conceive of the thing in danger. On the other hand, you do know that I believe that something is in danger, so you do have *some* information about my mental state.

From what I have just said, it would seem that narrow meaning includes everything relevant to psychological explanation that wide meaning does, and more. But wide meaning may be more useful for predicting in one respect: to the extent that there are nomological relations between the world and what people think and do, wide meaning will allow predicting what they think and do without information about how they see things. Suppose, for example, that people tend to avoid wide open spaces, no matter how they describe these spaces to themselves. Then knowing that Fred is choosing whether to go via an open space or a city street, one would be in a position to predict Fred's choice, even though one does not know whether Fred describes the open space to himself as "that," or as "Copley Square."

Narrow meaning has another kind of theoretical import: it determines a function from expressions and contexts of utterance onto referents and truth values.[9] When you and I utter "I" in (1), there is something we share, some semantic aspect of the word "I" that in your context maps your token onto you and in my context maps my token onto me.

Let me guard against some misunderstandings. First, as I already indicated, the narrow meaning of "I" does not include one's conception of oneself. Second, although I have said that there is a shared semantic aspect of "I" relevant to explaining behavior and a shared semantic aspect relevant to determining a function from context to referent, I do not suggest that these shared semantic aspects are exactly the same. It is an open question whether they are the same, and hence whether "narrow meaning," as I am using the term, picks out a single thing. On the theory I will be arguing for, the semantic aspect that determines the function from context to referent (and truth value) turns out to be a *part* of the semantic aspect that plays a part in explaining behavior. Thus the latter semantic aspect does *both* jobs. Hence, I will use "narrow meaning/ content" as uniquely referring to the more inclusive semantic aspect. I do want to note, though, that this way of talking carries a strong theoretical commitment. Finally, the narrow/wide distinction as I have described it so far applies to tokens, not types. However, there is an obvious extension to (non-indexical) types.

I will now pause to say what the considerations raised in this section so far have to do with a semantics for psychology. First, a semantics for psychology should have something to say about what the distinction between narrow and wide meaning comes to and, ideally, should give accounts of what the two aspects of meaning are. Second, the theory ought to say why it is that narrow and wide meanings are distinctively relevant to the explanation and prediction of psychological facts (including behavior). Third, the theory ought to give an account of narrow meaning that explains how it is that it determines a function from the context of utterance to reference and truth value.

I have been talking so far about the meaning of sentences with indexicals, but the points I have been making can be extended to names and, more controversially, to natural kind terms. Consider Teen (of Earth) and her twin on Twin Earth, Teen$_{te}$. The two are particle-for-particle duplicates who have had exactly the same histories of surface stimulations. In various different versions of the story, we are to imagine various differences in their worlds outside the sphere of what has impinged on them. For now, let us suppose their environments are exactly the same, except, of course, that the individuals on the two worlds are distinct – Teen's hero is Michael Jackson, whereas Teen$_{te}$'s hero is a distinct but indistinguishable (except spatiotemporally) personage. Teen and Teen$_{te}$ each have the thought they would express with:

(3)   Michael Jackson struts.

Once again, we can distinguish between two ways of individuating thought contents, and also the meanings of the sentences thought. On one, the narrow scheme, we can talk of Teen and Teen$_{te}$ as having the same thought, and we can talk of them as uttering sentences with the same meaning. If they would both sincerely say "Michael Jackson has supernatural powers," they share the same delusion. This is narrow meaning and narrow content. Alternatively, we can regard the meanings and thought contents as distinct simply in virtue of the fact that Teen is referring to Michael Jackson and Teen$_{te}$ is referring to Michael Jackson$_{te}$. This is wide meaning and content.

This illustrates same narrow/different wide meaning and content. The case of same wide/different narrow meaning (the case analogous to [1] and [2] above uttered by the same person) is illustrated by "Cicero orates" and "Tully orates." The principles of individuation in these name cases are the same as in the indexical cases, though their motivation is in one respect weaker because it is controversial whether names even *have* meanings. Also, the nomological connection between names and behavior is not as simple as that between "I" and behavior.

There are two basic facts on which the narrow/wide distinction is based. One is that how you represent something that you refer to can affect your psychological states and behavior. So if you know that Cicero orates and you don't know that Cicero = Tully, you are not in a position to make use of the fact that Tully orates. The second basic fact is that there is more to semantics than what is "in the head." The contents of the head of a person who asserts (3), together with the fact that Michael Jackson struts, are *not enough to determine whether (3) is true or false*, since the truth value depends as well on who "Michael Jackson" refers to. Imagine that, though Michael Jackson is an excellent strutter, his twin cannot strut; the strutting ascribed to his twin by Twin Earth teenagers is actually done by a stuntman. Then utterances of (3) on Twin Earth differ in truth value from utterances of (3) on Earth, despite no relevant differences between teenage heads on the two planets, and despite it being just as much a fact on Twin Earth as on Earth that Michael Jackson struts. (If this seems mysterious to you, note that, in the last sentence, I used "Michael Jackson" as it is used in my language community – Should I talk someone else's language? – and the language community on Twin Earth uses the same expression to refer to a different person.) *Since the truth value of a sentence is determined by the totality of semantic facts, plus the relevant facts about the world, there is more to the totality of semantic facts about the sentence than is in the speaker's head. The "extra" semantic facts are about what the referring terms in the sentence refer to.*[10] But even though there are semantic differences between Teen's and Teen$_{te}$'s utterance of and thinking of (3), there are important similarities as well – and this is the main point of this section – that give rise to notions of aspects of content and meaning (narrow content and meaning) *that are shared by Teen and Teen$_{te}$* and that explain similarities in their (for example) fantasy life and ticket-buying behavior and that determine the function from their different contexts to their different referents.

As in the indexical case, wide meaning and content are not well suited to explaining change of mental state and behavior. The wide meaning of "Water is wet" (in English – not Twin English) is the same as that of "H_2O is wet," despite the potentially different effects of believing these sentences on mental states and on behavior. Further, as Kripke's Pierre example reveals (Kripke, 1979), if one's conception of translation is overly referential (allowing "London" to translate "Londres" inside belief contexts), one is faced with situations in which one is forced to ascribe contradictory beliefs that are no fault of the believer.[11] In addition, what is shared by Teen and Teen$_{te}$ also determines that one is referring to Michael Jackson, whereas the other is referring to Michael Jackson's twin. What is shared determines a function from context to reference. Had Teen been raised on Twin Earth, she would have been molecule for molecule the same as she actually is (ignoring quantum indeterminacy), but her token of "Michael Jackson" would have referred to Michael Jackson's twin.[12]

The reader may wonder why I have gone on about this desideratum (on the narrow/wide distinction) at such length. (And I'm not finished yet!) The version of conceptual role semantics that I will be defending characterizes *narrow* meaning in terms of conceptual role. There is another version (Harman, 1982) that has no truck with narrow content or meaning. Harman's conceptual roles involve perceptual and behavioral interactions with what is seen and manipulated, that is, objects in the world, whereas my conceptual roles stop at the skin. (So if you don't like all this narrow this and narrow that, you can still appreciate the previous desiderata as motivating a Harmanian version of conceptual role semantics.) I prefer my version, and I am trying to spell out part of the motivation for it.[13] (I will say more about Harman's alternative shortly.)

Consider Putnam's original Twin Earth story. My doppelgänger (again, a physical duplicate)[14] uses "water" to refer to XYZ. Suppose, along with Putnam, that XYZ is *not* a type of water. Further, we may add into the story ideas developed by Burge (Burge, 1979) that show the differences in how our different language communities use words can determine differences in the meanings of our words, even when they do not result in differences in stimuli impinging on our surfaces. Suppose my twin and I both say to ourselves:

> My pants are on fire. But luckily I am standing in front of a swimming pool filled with water. Water, thank God, puts out fires.

If Burge and Putnam are right (and I am inclined to agree with them), there are substantial semantic differences between my twin's and my meanings and thought contents because of the differences in physical and social environment. Nonetheless – and here, again, is the crucial idea behind my advocacy of narrow meaning and content – *there is some aspect of meaning in common to what he says and what I say (or at least a common partial determinant of meaning), and this common semantic aspect of what we say provides part of a common explanation of why we both jump into our respective pools.* And if current ideas about the representational theory of mind are right, narrow meaning and content will be usable to state nomological generalizations relating thought, decision, and action.

Further, had my twin grown up in my context, his token of "water" would refer to H_2O rather than XYZ. Thus, as before, it seems that there is some common semantic aspect of our terms that operates in my case to map my context onto H_2O, and in his case to map his context onto XYZ.

The reader may have noticed my shift to the natural extension I described of the narrow/wide distinction from tokens to types. Since "Cicero" and "Tully" are standardly used to refer to the same person, we can regard the sentence types "Cicero orates" and "Tully orates" a having the same wide meaning. Likewise for "water" (as used in English as opposed to Twin English) and "H_2O."

Let us say that a propositional attitude or meaning ascription is individualistic if it is supervenient on the physical state of the individual's body, where physical state is specified non-intentionally and independently of physical and social conditions obtaining outside the body.[15] I believe that there is an important individualistic scheme of individuation of beliefs, belief contents, and the meanings of the sentences believed. There is a strong element of individualistic individuation in ordinary thought, but its main home lies in scientific thinking about the mind, especially in contemporary cognitive science. I also agree with Burge and Putnam that there is an important non-individualistic scheme of individuation in ordinary thought. No incompatability yet.

But Putnam, Burge, and others have also argued against individualistic individuation. Putnam's conclusion (1983) is based on an argument that it is impossible to come up with identity conditions on content or meaning, individualistically considered. I don't have identity conditions to offer, but I am inclined to regard this not as an insurmountable obstacle but as an issue to be dissolved by theory construction. My guess is that a scientific conception of meaning should do away with the crude dichotomy of same/different meaning in favour of a multidimensional gradient of similarity of meaning.[16] After all, substitution of a continuum for a dichotomy is how Bayesian decision theory avoids a host of difficulties – for example, the paradox of the preface – by moving from the crude pigeonholes of *believes/doesn't believe* to degrees of belief.[17]

Burge (1986) is arguing mainly against "pan-individualism," the claim that *all* propositional-attitude individuation in psychology is individualistic. However, I am not advocating this doctrine but only the more limited claim that there is an important strain of individualistic individuation in psychology (and in commonsense discourse). Burge has doubts about this too, but the matter can only be settled by a detailed discussion of psychological practice.

Let me mention only one consideration. Psychology is often concerned with explaining psychological differences. The measure of these differences is *variance*.[18] For example, variance in intelligence and other mental attributes and states is ascribed to differences in genes and environment (and interactions of various sorts between these causal factors). Suppose we fill a tour bus with travelers, half from Twin Earth and half from Earth. The Earthlings believe that water is wet and prefer drinking water to gasoline, whereas the Twin Earthlings do not have these propositional attitudes (because when they think about what they call "water," they are not thinking about water – they have no term that refers to water). Suppose that the Earthlings and Twin Earthlings do not differ in relevant ways in genes or in the surface stimulation that has impinged on their bodies over their whole lives. Hence, in this population, differences in propositional attitudes cannot be attributed to environment (in the sense of surface stimulation) and genes (and their interactions): the differences in water attitudes are due to something that has nothing to do with differences in the genes or surface stimulations that have affected these people. An analysis of variance would have to attribute a large component of variance to differences in a factor that does not cause any differences in proteins, synaptic connections, or any other physicochemical feature of the body as do differences in genes and surface stimulations. This would amount to a kind of action at a distance, and this would clearly go counter to the methodology of attribution of variance. (Note that this point could have been formulated in terms of Burge's point about the social nature of meaning rather than Twin Earth.)

I just argued for individualistic individuation of propositional attitude states – for example, beliefs. But there is a gap between individuating beliefs individualistically and individuating belief *contents* individualistically. One might hold that, when you individuate belief individualistically, you still have belief of some strange sort; but that content, individualistically individuated, is like a president who is deposed – no longer a president (cf. Stich, 1983). I propose to fill the gap as follows.

Where we have a relation, in certain types of cases we have individualistic properties of the related entities that could be said to ground the relation. If *x* hits *y*, *y* has some sort of consequent change in a bodily surface, perhaps a flattened nose, and *x* has the property of, say, moving his fist forward. Of course, the same individualistic property can underlie many different relational properties, and some relations notoriously don't depend on individualistic properties – for example, "to the left of." When content is *non*-individualistically individuated, it is individuated with respect to relations to the world (as in the Twin Earth case) and social practice (as in Burge's arthritis example).[19] There is a non-relational aspect of propositional attitude content, the aspect "inside the head," that corresponds to content in the way that moving the fist corresponds to hitting. This non-relational aspect of content is what I am calling narrow content. But is narrow content really content?[20]

I find much hostility among philosophers to the ideas of narrow content and narrow meaning. There are many reasons for this resistance that I accept as points of genuine controversy, and about which I am not at all confident about my position. But the worry just mentioned seems to me misplaced, at least as a criticism of conceptual role semantics. The criticism is that I have wrongly assumed that the aspect of meaning or content that is inside the head is something genuinely *semantic*. Jerry Fodor once accused me of a "fallacy of subtraction," that is, of assuming that, if you take meaning or content and *subtract* its relation to the world and its social aspect, what you have left is something semantic.

There *is* such a thing as a fallacy of subtraction, of course. If you subtract the property of being coloured from redness, you do not get colorless redness. But the issue with respect to conceptual role semantics is merely verbal. Nothing in my position requires me to regard narrow meaning and narrow content as (respectively) *kinds* of meaning and content. As mentioned earlier, I regard them as aspects of or as *determinants* of meaning and content. All that is required for my position is that what I am calling narrow meaning is a distinct feature of language, a characterization of which has something important to contribute to a total theory of meaning (e.g., as indicated in my desiderata). Similarly for narrow content.

Am I conceding that conceptual role semantics isn't really part of *semantics*? The first thing to be said about this question is that it is of very minor intellectual importance. It is a dispute about the border between disciplines; like so many of these disputes, it can be resolved only by a kind of ordinary language philosophy applied to technical terms like "semantics" (or, worse, by university administrations). Ordinary language philosophy has its place in analyses of concepts that play a central role in ordinary human thought; but application of these techniques to technical terms, where stipulation is the order of the day, is not very illuminating. Nonetheless, I am as willing to quibble as the next person. The correct application of disciplinary terms depends in large part on developments in the disciplines. Often the pretheoretic ideas about the domain of the discipline are left far behind. If meaning indeed decomposes into two factors, then the study of the nature of these two factors belongs in the domain of semantics, even if one or both of them are quite different from meaning in any ordinary sense of the term. To appeal to ordinary ideas about meaning to argue for excluding narrow meaning from the domain of semantics is like excluding electrons from the domain of the study of matter on the ground that they aren't "solid" and diffract like light.

Further, the role of narrow meaning in determining the function from context to reference and truth value seems especially deserving of the appellation "semantic." (I will argue in discussing Desideratum 1 below that narrow meaning – as specified by conceptual role semantics – does indeed determine this function.)

I will continue to talk, as I have, of narrow meaning and narrow content; but I won't mind if the reader prefers to reformulate, using phrases like "narrow determinant of meaning."

Conceptual Role Semantics and Two-Factor Theory

Conceptual role semantics is not among the more popular approaches, but it has the distinction of being the only approach (to my knowledge, at any rate) that has the potential to satisfy all these desiderata. The approach I have in mind has been suggested, independently, by both philosophers and cognitive scientists: by the former under the title "conceptual role semantics" and by the latter under the title "procedural semantics." (Oddly, these two groups do not refer to one another.) The doctrine has its roots in positivism and pragmatism and in the Wittgensteinian idea of meaning as use. Among philosophers, its recent revival is due mainly to Harman (following Sellars)[21] and Field.[22] Churchland, Loar, Lycan, McGinn, and Schiffer have also advocated versions of the view.[23] In cognitive science, the chief proponent has been Woods,[24] though Miller's and Johnson-Laird's[25] versions have been of interest. The version I like is a "two-factor theory" something like the one advocated by Field,[26] McGinn (1982), and Loar (1982). (See also Lycan, 1981.)

The idea of the two-factor version is that there are two components to meaning, a conceptual role component that is entirely "in the head" (this is narrow meaning)[27] and an external component that has to do with the relations between the representations in the head (with their internal conceptual roles) and the referents and/or truth-conditions of these representations in the world. This two-factor approach derives from Putnam's argument (1975a, 1979) that meaning could not both be "in the head" and also determine reference. It also takes heart from the Perry-Kaplan points about indexicals mentioned earlier (character and content are two "factors"). The two-factor approach can be regarded as making a conjunctive claim for each sentence: what its conceptual role is, and what its (say) truth conditions are.[28] I will refer to the *two-factor version* of conceptual role semantics as CRS, though perhaps it should be TFCRS to remind the reader of the two-factor nature of the theory.

For present purposes, the exact nature of the external factor does not matter. Those who are so inclined could suppose it to be elucidated by a causal theory of reference or by a theory of truth-conditions. The internal factor, conceptual role, is a matter of the causal role of the expression in reasoning and deliberation and, in general, in the way the expression combines and interacts with other expressions so as to mediate between sensory inputs and behavioral outputs. A crucial component of a sentence's conceptual role is a matter of how it participates in inductive and deductive inferences. A word's conceptual role is a matter of its contribution to the role of sentences.[29]

For example, consider what would be involved for a symbol in the internal representational system, "$\rightarrow$," to express the material conditional. The "$\rightarrow$" in "FELIX IS A CAT $\rightarrow$ FELIX IS AN ANIMAL"[30] expresses the material conditional if, for example, when the just quoted sentence interacts appropriately with:

> "FELIX IS A CAT," the result is a tendency to inscribe "FELIX IS AN ANIMAL" (other things equal, of course).
> "FELIX IS NOT AN ANIMAL," the result is a tendency to prevent the inscription of "FELIX IS A CAT," and a tendency to inscribe "FELIX IS NOT A CAT."
> "IS FELIX AN ANIMAL?," the result is a tendency to initiate a search for "FELIX IS A CAT."

Conceptual role is *total causal role*, abstractly described. Consider, by way of analogy, the causal role of herring. They affect what they eat, what eats them, what sees them and runs away, and, of course, they causally interact with one another. Now abstract away from the total causal role of herring to their culinary role, by which I mean the causal relations involving them that have an effect on or are affected by human dining. Presumably, some of what affects herring and what they affect will not be part of their culinary role: for example, perhaps herring occasionally amuse penguins, and this activity has no culinary causes or effects. Similarly, elements of language have a total causal role, including, say, the effect of newsprint on whatever people wrap in it. Conceptual role abstracts away from all causal relations except the ones that mediate inferences, inductive or deductive, decision making, and the like.

A crucial question for CRS (*the* crucial question) is what counts as identity and difference of conceptual role. Clearly, there are many differences in reasoning that we do not want to count as relevant to meaning. For example, if you take longer than I do in reasoning from x to y, we do not necessarily want to see this as revealing a difference between your meanings of x and/or y and mine. Our reasoning processes may be the same in all inferentially important respects.

Further, CRS must face the familiar "collateral information" problem. Suppose you are prepared to infer from "TIGER" to "DANGEROUS," whereas I am not. Do our "TIGER"s have the same conceptual role or not? More significantly, what if we differ in inferring from "TIGER" to "ANIMAL"? Does the first difference differ in kind from the second?

CRS has less room to maneuver here than, say, Katzian semantics, since CRS cannot make use of an analytic/synthetic distinction. The problem is that, if we make the inferences that define "cat" just the putatively analytic ones (excluding, for example, the inference from "cat" to "is probably capable of purring"), we get a meaning for "cat" that is the same as for "dog." (One could try to distinguish them by making use of the difference between the words themselves [e.g., the fact that "is a cat" entails "is not a dog"], but that would at best allow intrapersonal synonymy, not interpersonal synonymy. See Field, 1978.) This is not a problem *within* Katzian semantics because Katzians appeal to primitive (undefined) elements of language in terms of which other elements are defined. (See Katz, 1972.) The Katzian picture is that you can distinguish the meaning of "dog" from "cat" by appealing to the analytic truths that cats are feline (and not canine) and dogs are canine (and not feline), where "feline" and "canine" are primitive terms. This move is not available for CRS, since it has no truck with primitive terms: conceptual role is supposed to determine narrow meaning completely. (One qualification: it *is* possible to take conceptual role as a *part* of a theory of the narrow meaning of *part* of the language – the non-primitive part – while appealing to some other conception of meaning of primitives; procedural semanticists sometimes sound as if they want to take *phenomenal* terms as primitives whose meaning is given by their "sensory content," while taking other terms as getting their meanings via their computational relations to one another and to the phenomenal terms as well [perhaps they see the phenomenal terms as "grounding" the functional structures]. It should be clear that this is a "mixed" conceptual role/phenomenalist theory and not a pure conceptual role theory.)

Without an analytic/synthetic distinction, we would, as I mentioned earlier, have to move to a scientific conception of meaning that does away with the crude dichotomy of same/different meaning in favor of a multidimensional gradient of similarity of meaning (hoping for results as good as those achieved by decision theory in moving from an all-or-nothing notion of belief to a graded notion).

If CRS is to be developed to the point where it can be evaluated seriously, definite proposals for individuating conceptual roles must be framed and investigated. One of the purposes of this paper is to try to make it plausible that CRS is worth pursuing.

What about the social dimension of meaning demonstrated in Burge (1979)? Two-factor theory *can* try to capture such phenomena in the referential factor. For example, perhaps the causal chain determining the reference of my use of "arthritis" is mediated by the activities of people who know more about arthritis than I do. (See Boyd, 1979, for an indication of how to knit the social aspect of meaning together with a causal theory of reference.) Alternatively, two-factor theory may have to expand to three-factor theory, allowing a distinct social factor to meaning. Since my mission is to compare the broad outlines of the view I am espousing with alternative points of view, I will not pursue the matter further (though later on I will take up the question of how the conceptual role factor is related to the referential factor).

It should be becoming clear that CRS as I am conceiving of it is so undeveloped as to be more of a framework for a theory than a theory. Why bother thinking about such a sketchy theory? I think that the current status of CRS is reminiscent of the "causal theory of reference." The root idea of causal theories of reference seems clearly relevant to central phenomena of reference, such as how one person can acquire the ability to refer to Napoleon from another person, even without acquiring many beliefs about Napoleon, and even if most of what he believes is false. Detailed versions of causal theories (Devitt, 1981) have not commanded widespread agreement; nonetheless, since the only alternative theories of reference (e.g., the description theory) seem hopeless as accounts of the phenomena just mentioned, we are justified in supposing that the central ideas of the causal theory of reference will have to play a part in some way in any successful theory of reference. I intend the desiderata I've discussed to provide a similar rationale for supposing that the central ideas of CRS must somehow fit into our overall semantic picture.

I should mention that (as with the causal theory of reference) a two-factor conceptual role semantics has been set out in one precise version – that of Field (1977). Though Field's account is very suggestive, I will not adopt it, for a number of reasons. For one thing, Field's account is not quite a conceptual role account in the sense in which I have defined it, since his conceptual roles are not quite causal. Field defines conceptual role in terms of conditional probability. Two sentences have the same conceptual role if and only if they have the same conditional probability with respect to every other sentence. Though Field is not explicit about this, he obviously intends some kind of causal account in terms of the causal consequences of new evidence on degrees of belief. Harman (1982) criticizes Field's account on the ground that it does not allow for revision of belief. Harman's argument, apparently, is that Bayesians merely change their degree of belief rather than changing their mind. That is, Bayesians do not treat new evidence as dictating that they should reject claims they formerly accepted (or conversely), but rather that they should move from a .67 degree of belief in a claim to a .52 degree of belief. I don't find Harman's objection very persuasive; what corresponds to change of mind in the Bayesian perspective just *is* change of degree of belief. The Bayesians reject change of mind in favor of change of degree of belief; this is a theoretical disagreement that is not settled by insisting. However, a version of Harman's conclusion seems quite likely right, but for another reason: in seeing change of mind entirely in terms of change in degree of belief via conditionalization (or generalized conditionalization), the Bayesian perspective (like the logical empiricist views that are concerned with justification rather than discovery) cannot model the kind of change of mind that involves the generation of new hypotheses (this point is most convincing with regard to new hypotheses that involve new ideas). It's not that the Bayesian perspective is in any way incompatible with the generation of new hypotheses, but rather that, on the Bayesian account of reasoning, new hypotheses must be treated as "given" via some non-Bayesian process, and so the Bayesian account is importantly incomplete. Conceptual role includes the kind of reasoning in which one infers from evidence against one's hypothesis to an obvious variant deploying a revised version of an old idea, and this cannot be captured wholly within a Bayesian framework.

Even ignoring this matter, Field's account highlights a choice that must be made by CRS theorists, one that has had no discussion (as far as I know): namely, should conceptual role be understood in ideal or normative terms, or should it be tied to what people actually do? As Harman (1987) points out (in another context), accounts of reasoning that involve change of degree of belief by conditionalizing on evidence require keeping track of astronomical numbers of conditional probabilities. (Harman calculates that a billion are needed for thirty evidence propositions.) So any Bayesian account would have to be very far removed from actual reasoning. However, if we opt against such idealization, must we stick so close to actual practice as to include in conceptual role well-known fallacious reasoning strategies, such as the gamblers' fallacy?[31]

I prefer not to comment on this matter, in part because I'm not sure what to say and in part because I am trying to stay away from controversies *within* conceptual role semantics, because the points I want to make can be made on the basis of a version of the doctrine that contains very little in the way of details.

Calling the causal roles CRS appeals to "conceptual" or "inferential" shouldn't mislead anyone into supposing that the theory's description of them can appeal to their meanings – that would defeat the point of reductionist theories. The project of giving a nonsemantic (and non-intentional) description of these roles is certainly daunting, but the reader would do well to note that it is no more daunting than the programs of various popular philosophical theories. For example, the causal theory of reference, taken as a reductionist proposal (as in Devitt's but not in Kripke's versions), has the same sort of charge. And a rather similar charge falls on "traditional" non-representational functionalism (e.g., as in Lewis's or Putnam's versions), where the causal roles of propositional attitude states are to be described in non-intentional and non-semantic terms.

Representationalists differ in how important they think the role of English expressions are in reasoning, deliberation, and so forth. At one end of the spectrum, we have the view that English is *the* language of thought (for English speakers). Near the other end, we have those who, more influenced by cognitive psychology, have tended to see reasoning in English as the tip of an iceberg whose main mass is computation in an internal language common to speakers of English and Walburi.[32] On the latter view, the narrow meaning of expressions is derivative from the narrow meanings of expressions in the internal language. (The dependency would, however, be the other way around for the referential component of meaning, since it is English expressions that are more directly related to the world.) I will not be concerned with this and a number of other disputes that can occur *within* the framework of conceptual role semantics.

In what follows, I shall be quite relaxed about this issue of the role of English in thinking. Sometimes, I will take English to be the language of thought. However, when it is convenient, I will assume that English is used only for communication and that *all* thought is in a language that does not overlap with English, Mentalese. When on this latter tack, I will also assume that mechanisms of language production and language understanding establish a *standard association* between English and Mentalese expressions. When a speaker formulates a message using "CAT," language – production mechanisms map "CAT" onto "cat"; and when the hearer understands "cat," the language – understanding mechanisms map it onto "CAT."

This standard-association notion can be used to construct a way of individuating conceptual roles in which English expressions have the conceptual roles of the Mentalese expressions with which they are standardly associated. Suppose I am told that Felix is a cat and am asked about Felix's weight. I answer "Felix weighs more than .01 grams." I suggest we start with the following simple mechanistic picture. When I hear "Felix is a cat," language-understanding mechanisms produce "FELIX IS A CAT." Reasoning mechanisms produce "FELIX WEIGHS MORE THAN .01 GRAMS," and language-production mechanisms result in the utterance of "Felix weighs more than .01 grams." Now an English sentence and its internal standard associate certainly have different causal properties. For example, one is visible or audible (normally) without neurophysiological techniques. But we can individuate conceptual roles so as to give them the *same* conceptual roles, simply by (1) taking the relevant causal properties of English expression as the ones that are mediated by their causal interactions with their standard associates and (2) abstracting away from the mechanisms that effect the standard association. Then any cause or effect of "cat" will, for purposes of individuation of conceptual roles, be regarded as the same as a cause or an effect of "CAT."

An analogy: Consider a computer in which numbers are entered and displayed in ordinary decimal notation, but in which all computation is actually done in binary notation. The way the computer works is that there are mechanisms that transform the "3 + 4" you enter on the keyboard into an internal expression we can represent as "+ (11,100)." This is a translation, of course, but we can talk about it without describing it as such, by describing it in terms of the mechanism that computes the function. Internal computational mechanisms operate on this expression, yielding another expression, "111," which is transformed by the translation mechanisms into a "7" displayed on the screen. Now the process by which "3 + 4" yields "7" is exactly the same as the process by which "+ (11,100)" yields "111," except for the two translation steps. So if we (1) ignore causes and effects of decimal digits other than those mediated by their interactions with binary digits in the innards of the machine and (2) abstract away from the translation steps, we can regard the decimal and corresponding binary expressions as having the same computational roles.

Thus, one can speak of the conceptual roles of English expressions, even when adopting the view that internal computation is entirely in Mentalese. This will seem strange if your picture of English tokens is inert expressions in dusty books, as compared with the dynamic properties of the internal representations in which all thought is actually conducted. So remember that I am adverting to what the English expressions do when seen or heard.

Let me try to clarify what I am trying to do with the notion of standard association by mentioning some caveats.

(1) The English language is of course a social object. In speaking of the conceptual roles of English expressions, I do not intend a theory of that social object. Conceptual role, you will recall, is meant to capture narrow meaning. Indeed, since causal roles differ from person to person, CRS deals with *idiolect* narrow meaning rather than public language narrow meaning.

(2) The existence of the mechanisms that effect the standard association is an empirical question (though, as Stich, 1983, p. 80, argues, something like this idea seems to be part of commonsense psychology). I appeal to empirical work on the "language module" – see Fodor (1983b). Were the empirical assumption to turn out false, a conceptual role theory of (the narrow meaning of) external language could still be given (in terms of the causal interactions between external and internal language), but what would be lost would be the plausibility of a conceptual role theory in which, for almost any external expression, one could expect an internal expression with the same narrow meaning. So as to have my empirical eggs in one basket, let me include the assumption of a language module under the rubric of "representationalism."

(3) In order for the notion of standard association to be usable to define conceptual roles, it must be characterizable non-semantically and non-intentionally. But doesn't this idea founder on obvious facts about the devious road from thought to language, for example, that people lie? The point of my appeal to the language module is that it works (once engaged) without the intervention of any intentional states. Of course, it is used by us in a variety of ways, since we have many purposes in using language. The language module works the same in lying and truth telling; the difference is to be found in the Mentalese message. Perhaps confusion would be avoided if one focuses on the use of language, not in communication, but in thinking out loud or in internal soliloquies.

(4) Language production may have to bear more of the burden in characterizing standard association than language perception, since the latter encounters complications with indexicals and the like. When one hears "I'm sick," one doesn't represent it the way one would represent one's own first person thought.

(5) Despite the convention I've adopted of writing Mentalese as English in capitals, nothing in the CRS position requires that a sentence spoken have the same meaning as that sentence thought. One can make sense of the idea that in speech one uses the English word "chase" to mean what one means in thought by the English work "CHAIR." Imagine yourself moving to a place where they speak a dialect of English that differs from yours in exchanging the

meanings of these two words. If you continue to think in your old dialect but talk in the new one, you would be in the described situation. Consider two quite different scenarios. In one, the new situation never effects a change in your language production/perception module. In communicating, you consciously adjust your words, but in thinking out loud, you talk as before. In the other scenario, the module changes so as to adjust to the external shift. In the former case, standard association will be normal. In the latter, "chair" will be standardly associated with "CHASE," and the conceptual role of "chair" will derive from "CHASE'" – thoughts (involving trying to catch rather than sitting). "Chair" will have the same conceptual role as "CHASE." Neither scenario provides any problem for the view of conceptual role of external language that I sketched. Schiffer and Loar have emphasized that, if there is an internal language, a sentence spoken need not have the same meaning as the same sentence thought, but they have been led to conclude that, if a language of thought hypothesis is true, it is reasonable to deploy two quite different types of theories of meaning – one for internal language, one for external language. Their concern with external language is with meaning in public language, whereas mine is with narrow meaning in idiolect, so there is no direct conflict. Still, I want to emphasize that a conclusion analogous to theirs for idiolect narrow meaning is mistaken. (See Loar, 1981; Schiffer, 1981.) This matter will come up again in the section below on what makes meaningful expressions meaningful.

One final point of clarification: though I am advocating CRS, I am far from a true believer. My position is that CRS can do enough for us (as indicated by the desiderata it satisfies) to motivate working it out in detail and searching for solutions to its problems.

Perhaps this is the place to mention why I am willing to advocate a version of functionalism despite my arguments against functionalism in Block (1978). First, I am impressed by the questions this particular version of functionalism (apparently) can answer. Second, I am now willing to settle for (and I think there is some value in) a theory that is chauvinist in the sense that it does not characterize meaning or intentionality in general, but only *human* meaning or intentionality. Third, the arguments I gave for the conclusion that functionalism is liberal (in the sense that it overascribes mental properties, e.g., to groups of people organized appropriately) were strongest against functionalist theories of *experiential* mental states. I am now inclined to regard intentional mental states as a natural kind for which a functionalist theory may be OK, even though it is not acceptable for experiential states. Indeed, if the domain of CRS is a natural kind, then so is the domain of intentional mental phenomena.

Ironically, this concession to functionalism may make my position harder to defend against thoroughgoing functionalists, since it may commit me to the possibility of intentionality – even intentional states with the same sort of intentional content as ours – without experience. Perhaps I would be committed to the possibility of "zombies," whose beliefs are the same as ours (including beliefs to the effect that they are in pain), but who have no real pains (only "ersatz" pains that are functionally like pain but lack qualitative content). Then I would have to confront the arguments against this possibility in Shoemaker (1984, chaps. 9 and 14). (On my view, pain, for example, is actually a composite state consisting of a non-functional qualitative state together with a functional state. Since the qualitative state can be neurophysiologically – but not functionally – characterized, I regard the full account of the mental as part functional, part physiological.) Finally, I believe many of the other arguments that have been advanced against functionalism in its various forms to be defective (see my argument below against Searle).

Two factors or one factor?

The version of CRS I have been talking about is a "two-factor" version, in which the conceptual role factor is meant to capture the aspect (or determinant) of meaning "inside the head," whereas the other is meant to capture the referential and social dimensions of meaning.

As I mentioned earlier, Gilbert Harman has been advocating a different version of conceptual role semantics. Harman's version makes do with *one* factor, namely, conceptual role. How does he do without the referential and social factors? By making his one factor reach out into the world of referents and into the practices of the linguistic community. I have been talking about conceptual roles along lines common in functionalist writing in philosophy of mind. These conceptual roles stop roughly at the skin. Outputs are conceived of in terms of bodily movements or, according to the more scientifically minded, in terms of outputs of, say, the motor cortex (allowing for thoughts in disembodied brains). Inputs are conceived of in terms of the proximal stimuli or in terms of outputs of sensory transducers. By contrast, here is Harman on the subject.

> Conceptual role semantics does not involve a "solipsistic" theory of the content of thoughts. There is no suggestion that content depends only on functional relations among thoughts and concepts, such as the role a particular concept plays in inference. (Field, 1977, misses this point.) Also relevant are functional relations to the external world in connection with perception, on the one hand, and action on the other. What makes something the concept red is in part the way in which the concept is involved in the perception of red objects in the external world. What makes something the concept of danger is in part the way in which the concept is involved in thoughts that affect action in certain ways.[33]

One might speak of Harman's conceptual role as "long-armed," as opposed to the "short-armed" conceptual roles of the two-factor theorist.

My objection to Harman, in brief, is that I don't see how he can handle the phenomena one would ordinarily think of as being in the purview of a theory of reference without extending his account to the point where it is equivalent to the two-factor account.

The point emerges as one looks at Harman's responses to problems that are dealt with by familiar theories of reference. Consider a resident of Earth who travels to Twin Earth in a space ship. He lands in a body of XYZ; but, ignorant of the difference between Twin Earth and Earth, he radios home the message "Surrounded by water." At first glance, one would think that the Harmanian conceptual role of the traveler's word "water" would at that moment involve a connection to XYZ, since that is what his perception and action is at that moment connected with. Then Harman would be committed to saying the traveler's message is true – in contrast with the Putnamian claim that his message is false because he is not surrounded by water (but rather twin water). Since Harman accepts the Putnam line, he deploys a notion of "normal context" (Harman, 1973), the idea being that the traveler's conceptual role for "water" is to be thought of as involving the substance he normally refers to using that word.

Another case Harman discusses is Putnam's elm/beech case. (You will recall that the question is how I can use "elm" to refer to elms when what I know about elms is exactly the same as what I know about beeches (except for the names). Harman's solution is to include in *my* conceptual role for "elm" its role in the minds of experts who actually know the difference.

It begins to look as if Harman is building into his long-arm conceptual roles devices that have usually been placed in the theory of reference. The point can be strengthened by a look at other phenomena that have concerned theories of reference, such as borrowed reference to things that do not now exist but did exist in the past. I can refer to Aristotle on the basis of overhearing your conversation about him, even if most of what I believe about Aristotle is false, because I misunderstood what you said. Will Harman deal with this by making his conceptual roles reach from one person to another, into the past, that is, making a causal relation between Aristotle and me – mediated by you, and your source of the word, and your source's source, etc. – part of the conceptual role of my use of "Aristotle"? If not, how can Harman handle borrowed reference? If so, Harman certainly owes us a reason for thinking that the outside-the-body part of his long-arm conceptual roles differs from the referential factor of two-factor theory.[34] The burden of proof on Harman is especially pressing, given that it appears that one could easily transform a theory of the sort he advocates into a theory of the sort I have been advocating. If you take Harman's long-arm conceptual roles and "chop off" the portion of these roles outside the skin, you are left with my short-arm conceptual roles. If the outside-the-body part that is chopped off amounts to some familiar sort of theory of reference, then the difference between Harman's one-factor theory and two-factor theory is merely verbal.

Conceptual role semantics is often treated with derision because of failure to appreciate the option of a two-factor version, a failure that is as common among the proponents of the view as the opponents. Consider Fodor's critique (1978) of Johnson-Laird's version of conceptual role semantics. Johnson-Laird's version tended in his original article towards verificationism; that is, the roles of words he focused on were their roles in one specific kind of reasoning, namely verifying. Fodor correctly criticizes this verificationism.[35] But I want to focus on a different matter. Fodor objected that the meaning of "Napoleon won the Battle of Waterloo" could not possibly consist in any sort of a set of procedures for manipulating internal symbols. That idea, he argued, embodies a use/mention fallacy.

> Suppose somebody said: "Breakthrough! The semantic interpretation of 'Did Napoleon win at Waterloo?' is: *find out whether the sentence 'Napoleon won at Waterloo?' occurs in the volume with Dewey decimal number XXX, XXX in the 42nd St. Branch of the New York City Public Library.*" . . . "'But,' giggled Granny, 'if that was what "Did Napoleon win at Waterloo?" meant, it wouldn't even be a question about *Napoleon*.' 'Aw, shucks,' replied Tom Swift."[36]

Fodor's objection is that, if meaning is identified with the causal interactions of elements of language, sentences would be about *language*, not the world.

My defence of Johnson-Laird should be obvious by now. Take the procedures that manipulate "Napoleon," etc. (or, better, the whole conceptual roles of these words) as specifying *narrow* meaning. Fodor's argument would only be damaging to a theory that took conceptual role to specify what language is *about*. But if conceptual role specifies only narrow meaning, not reference or truth conditions, then Fodor's criticism misses the mark. Were Johnson-Laird to adopt a two-factor theory of the sort I have been advocating, he could answer Fodor by pointing out that the job of saying what language is about is to be handled by the referential component of the theory, not the narrow-meaning component.

A similar point applies to Dretske's rather colorful criticism of remarks by Churchland and Churchland (1983).

> It sounds like magic: signifying something by multiplying sound and fury. Unless you put cream in you won't get ice cream out no matter how fast you turn the crank or how sophisticated the "processing." The cream, in the case of a cognitive system, is the *representational* role of those elements over which computations are performed. And the representational role of a structure is, I submit, a matter of how the elements of the system are related, not to one another, but to the external situations they "express."[37]

But the cream, according to two-factor theory, is conceptual role *together with* Dretske's representational role. Since CRS puts in Dretske's cream, plus *more*, there is no mystery about how you get ice cream out of it.

The same sort of point applies against criticisms of CRS that take the conceptual role component to task for not providing a *full* theory of meaning.

Our judgments of sameness of meaning are controlled by a complex mix of conceptual role and referential (and perhaps other) considerations.[38]

Fodor (1986a) points out that the concept of water can be shared by me and Blind Me. He says this presents problems for theories like CRS. He goes on to say:

> The obvious reply is that the properties of causal relation that make for sameness and difference of functional roles are very abstract indeed. Well, maybe; but there is an alternative proposal that seems a lot less strained. Namely that if Blind Me can share my concept of water, that's not because we both have mental representations with abstractly identical causal roles; rather, it's because we both have mental representations that are appropriately connected (causally, say) to *water.*[39]

But the two replies he gives aren't *incompatible alternatives*; CRS can adopt them both – though I think Fodor is right that the fact that the reference by me and Blind Me is to the same stuff is probably the main thing here. The point is that one cannot criticize a two-factor theory for not doing it all with one factor.

Overview

The rest of the paper is mainly concerned with showing how CRS satisfies the desiderata and with comparing CRS with other semantic theories in this regard. I will be talking about two quite different (but compatible kinds of semantic theories: reductionist and non-reductionist. A reductionist semantic theory is one that characterizes the semantic in non-semantic terms. A non-reductionist semantic theory is not one that is *anti*reductionist, but only one that does not have reductionist aims. These theories are mainly concerned with issues about constructions in particular languages, for example, why "The temperature is rising" and "The temperature is 70°" do not entail "70° is rising." The non-reductionist theories I will mention are possible-worlds semantics, the model-theoretic aspect of situation semantics, Davidsonian semantics, and Katzian semantics. The reductionist theories are CRS; Gricean theories, by which I mean theories that explain the semantic in terms of the mental; and what I call "indicator" theories, those whose metaphor for the semantic is the relation between a thermometer and the temperature it indicates, or the relation between the number of rings on the stump and the age of the tree when cut down. These theories regard the nomological relation between the indicator and what it indicates as the prime semantic relation. In this camp I include views of Dretske, Stampe, Fodor, and one aspect of Barwise and Perry's position.

The reductionist/non-reductionist distinction as I have drawn it does not do justice to Davidson's views. The problem is *not* that Davidson's work on, for example, the logical form of action sentences makes him a non-reductionist, whereas his view about what meaning is makes him a reductionist. As I pointed out, the reductionist and non-reductionist enterprises are compatible, and there is nothing at all odd about one person contributing to both. The problem, rather, is that Davidson has views about what meaning is, thereby making it seem (misleadingly) that he is a reducationist; however, his views of what meaning is are clearly *not* reductionist. (See Davidson, 1984, p. xiv, where he describes his project as explaining meaning in terms of truth.) A finer-grained classification would distinguish between (1a) reductionist and (1b) non-reductionist theories about what meaning is and distinguish both types of views of what meaning is from (2) the project of model-theoretic semantics, Davidson's work on action sentences, and the like. In labeling (1a) as reductionist and everything else as non-reductionist, I've unhappily lumped together (1b) and (2), but this is unimportant for my purposes, since I am ignoring (1b) theories.

Being reductionist in intent, CRS should not really be regarded as competing with the non-reductionist theories. Nonetheless, I shall be comparing CRS with these non-reductionist theories as regards the desiderata I have listed. To prevent misunderstanding, I want to emphasize that I am not attempting to criticize these non-reductionist theories. Rather, my purpose is to make it clear that they should not be seen as pursuing the same goals as the reductionist theories.

I will also be comparing CRS with the reductionist theories. These theories are in the same ball park as CRS, but most are not genuine competitors. Since CRS in the version I am promoting is a two-factor theory, it requires the partnership of a reductionist truth-conditional theory. Indicator semantics is a candidate. Another candidate that is both truth-conditional and reductionist is Field's interpretation (1972) of Tarski. I won't be discussing it because I know of no claims on its behalf that it is a full theory of meaning – indeed, Field views it as a candidate for the truth-conditional factor of a two-factor theory (see Field, 1977). Though I do not regard indicator semantics as a real competitor, I will mention serious problems with the view.

The only circumstance in which the reductionist truth-conditional theories would be genuine competitors to CRS would be if one of them could satisfy a range of desiderata of the sort I've mentioned. I consider it no problem if they can contribute to *some* such desiderata, since there is often more than one way of explaining something. But if some truth-conditional reductionist theory could satisfy *all of them*, the need for the conceptual role component would be brought into question.

The only approach that remains as a genuine competitor is the Gricean approach. I shall not attempt to refute this approach (for one thing, as will appear, it has considerable similarity to mine). I mainly aim to block an argument that anyone who favors a functionalist approach to meaning should adopt some sort of Gricean view rather than CRS.

A brief guide to the semantic theories I will be mentioning: I lump the truth-conditional theories minus indicator semantics plus Katzian semantics together as non-reductionist. Gricean and indicator theories, by contrast, are reductionist.

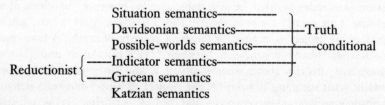

As you can see, four of the six theories I will be contrasting with CRS are classifiable as truth-conditional. While CRS in the version I am adopting has a truth-conditional component, it will play little role in satisfying the desiderata. Thus it may seem that I am taking truth-conditional theories to task for not doing something that they were never intended to do. The rationale for the contrasts I will be making is that radical disagreement is so common with regard to matters semantic that there is little consensus about which semantic theories have which purposes. For each of the truth-conditional theories I will mention, claims have been made on its behalf in the direction of satisfying desiderata of the sort I've listed.

Representationalism

Before I go on to discuss how CRS satisfies the desiderata, I want to make sure my representationalism is not misunderstood. I am committed to complex reasoning being a process that involves the manipulation of symbolic structures. I am not committed to the idea that these symbolic structures are *independent* of representational states of mind, mental objects that are viewed by an inner eye. It is convenient to talk in terms of internal representations as if they were literally sentences in the brain (and I do talk this way), but this talk is, of course, metaphorical. My commitment will be satisfied if the representational states themselves constitute a combinatorial system; that is, if they are structured in a way that allows parts corresponding to words to be combined so as to constitute representational states corresponding to sentences.[40]

I am not committed to the manipulation of symbol structures being involved in *all* reasoning, since I want to allow for "primitive" reasonings out of which complex reasonings are built. (E.g., in some computers, multiplication is a symbolic process in that a multiplication problem is "decomposed" into a series of addition problems; but addition itself is not "decomposed" into another type of problem, but rather accomplished by a hardware device, a primitive processor, that contains no internal representations. If you ask how the computer multiplies, you get a representational answer; if you ask how it adds, you do not.) I am not committed to rules for reasoning being themselves represented. Such an assumption involves notorious paradoxes, and in computers we have examples of symbol manipulators many of whose symbol-manipulating "rules" are implicit in the way the hardware works (see Block, 1983). I am not committed to any detailed thesis as to what the internal computations are like. For example, I am not committed to any such idea as that in computing "99 + 99 = 198" there is any internal analog of carrying a "1," or any such symbol manipulation of the sort a person might carry out in doing such a sum.

Further, the claim that we are symbol manipulators is intended as empirical and contingent. I find the idea perfectly intelligible and possible that we are "analog" computers whose internal activities involve no symbol manipulation at all. I make the representationalist assumption for two reasons: the most promising line of research in cognitive science is massively committed to representationalism, and it seems to be paying off; and I believe that there are an astronomical number of thoughts that people are capable of having. I would argue that the number of thinkable sentences thirty words long is greater than the number of particles in the universe. Consider the set of entertainable sentences of the following form: $n \times m = q$, where n and m are in the hundreds of billions range familiar from the national budget (twelve figures), and q is twice as long. Many of these sentences are not believable (e.g., nine hundred billion times itself $= 0$), but each is certainly thinkable. The number of distinct entertainable propositions of the form mentioned is on the order of forty-six digits long. An instructive comparison: the number of seconds since the beginning of time is only about eighteen digits long. I don't see what the mechanism could be by which a person can think any one of such a vast variety of thoughts without some sort of combinatorial system being involved. My representationalist assumption is in the spirit of Smart's claim that pain is a brain state: an empirically based thesis about what reasoning most likely is.

Of the semantic theories I will be contrasting with CRS, only Fodor's version of indicator semantics has a comparable representationalist asssumption; nonetheless, I do not think that my representationalism ought to be seen as the key difference between the theory I am advocating and most of the other theories. For one thing, a denotational theory like Fodor's could be framed in terms of assent to English sentences instead of computational relations to internal sentences. Fodor is a sententialist in that he believes that propositional attitude states are relations to internal sentences. But the internal sentences have no privileged *semantic* role in his account. Also, there are non-representationalist avenues towards the type of functionalist-based semantics I am advocating – for example, Loar's and Schiffer's version of the Gricean program. If CRS in the form in which I am advocating it were to meet serious empirical problems because of its representationalism, I would pursue a non-representationalist version.

Question: If my basic commitment is to a functionalist theory of meaning, why don't I *now* adopt a non-representationalist version of functionalism (e.g., the Loar-Schiffer program) instead of pursuing a program based on a risky empirical assumption (representationalism)? Answer: As I shall point out later, even if the Loar-Schiffer program works for natural language, if there is a language of thought not identical to natural language, their theory won't work for *it*. So *both* theories are subject to empirical risk. Theirs is inadequate if representationalism is true, whereas mine is wrong if representationalism is false.

Satisfying the Desiderata

In the rest of the paper, I shall be mainly concerned with showing how CRS satisfies the desiderata I sketched above and contrasting CRS's treatment with treatments possible for other approaches.

What is the relation between meaning and reference/ truth?

From the CRS perspective, what this question comes to is: what is the relation between the two factors? Are the two factors independent? Do they fit together in a coherent way?

I think the conceptual role factor is *primary* in that it determines the nature of the referential factor, but not vice versa. Suppose, for illustration, that one of the familiar versions of the causal theory of reference is true. What makes it true? Facts about how our language works – specifically, how it applies to counterfactual circumstances. Kripke convinces us that it is possible that Moses did not do any of the things the Bible said he did, but rather was an itinerant Egyptian fig merchant who spread stories about how he was found in the bulrushes, saw the burning bush, and so on. Kripke is convincing because we use names such as "Moses" to refer to the person who bears the right causal relations to our uses of the name, even if he does not fit the descriptions we associate with the name. This is a fact about the conceptual role of names, one that can be ascertained in the armchair, just by thinking about intuitions about counterfactual circumstances.

Of course, our names could have functioned differently; for example, they could have functioned as the competing "cluster of descriptions" theory dictates. If that had been how names functioned, it too could have been ascertained by thinking of the right thought experiments, since it would be a fact purely about the internal conceptual role of names. For example, if "Moses" functioned according to the cluster of descriptions theory, the intuition about Kripke's story dictated by the way names function would be "Oh, in that case Moses doesn't exist – there never was a Moses." What makes the cluster theory wrong is that that just isn't the intuition dictated by the function of our terms – the intuition, rather, is given by: "In that case, Moses wouldn't have done the things the Bible ascribes to him."

(Note that one cannot *identify* the intuition dictated by the function of names with the intuitions we actually have about cases, since there are all sorts of other factors that influence those intuitions. In the early days of the mind-body identity theory, many philosophers voiced the intuition that there was something semantically wrong with "I just drank a glass of H_2O." Presumably, they were influenced by the "oddity" of mixing scientific terms with mundane terms. Using intuitions to isolate facts about the function of names is not a simple matter.)

In short, what theory of reference is true is a fact about how referring terms function in our thought processes. This is an aspect of conceptual role. So it is the conceptual role of referring expressions that determines what theory of reference is true. Conclusion: the conceptual role factor determines the nature of the referential factor.

Note the crucial difference between saying that the conceptual role factor determines the nature of the referential factor and saying that the conceptual role factor determines reference. I hold the former, but not the latter. The two-factor theory is compatible with a variety of different mappings from a single conceptual role onto aspects of worlds. For example, a word with the conceptual role of our "water" could map onto one substance here, another on Twin Earth, and another on Triplet Earth. What is in the head – conceptual role – determines the nature of reference without determining reference itself.

If what I've just argued is right, it is easy to see that conceptual role determines the function from context to reference and truth value. It is the referential factor (as described in a theory of reference) that determines that "water'" picks out H_2O on Earth, but XYZ on Twin Earth. For example, on a causal theory of reference, this will be held to be a matter of the causal relation to different liquids in the two contexts. But since the referential factor must take context into account in this way in order to dictate reference, it will determine the function from context to reference.

What is the connection between the meaning of an expression and knowing or learning its meaning?

CRS says meaning is conceptual role. If someone uses a word (or a word functions in her brain) that has the conceptual role of "dog," then the word in question means the same as "dog." If a person's brain changes so as to cause a word to be used (by her or her brain) so as to have the conceptual role in question, then she has acquired the concept of a dog (unless she already has it); if the word in question is "dog" itself or a Mentalese standard associate of "dog," and if the brain change is a case of learning, then she has learned the meaning of "dog." Also, CRS allows us to see why evidence for proper use of "dog" is evidence for knowing the meaning of "dog." For a word to have proper use is for it to function in a certain way; hence someone whose word "dog" functions appropriately thereby knows the meaning of dog; hence evidence of function can be evidence of knowing the word. Finally, CRS allows us to see how knowing meaning is related to our ability to use language. To know the meaning of an English word is for it to function in a certain way, and the obtaining of this function, together with certain psychological facts (e.g., about motivation) explains correct external usage.

The non-reductionist theories should not be regarded as aimed at answering the questions just discussed, but should non-reductionists disagree, they could give a kind of answer (in the metatheory, of course). A theory that postulates a type of semantic value V (e.g., truth-conditions, situations, sets of possible worlds, markerese structures) can say that what it is to know or acquire the meaning of a sentence is to know or learn or acquire its V. But saying this only shifts the question to what it is to know or acquire V's. Consider the project of producing an account of what it is for "cat" to acquire its semantic value in the child. If the semantic value is conceptual role, we can at least picture how the project would go. But what would the project be like – if not the same as the one we just picture – for semantic values like truth-conditions, situations, sets of possible worlds, or markerese structures (rather, senses expressed by these structures)? Davidsonians say that to know the meaning of "Snow is white" is just to know that it is true iff snow is white. But, as Harman has pointed out, saying this just raises the issue of how one represents to oneself that snow is white. If one uses some sort of symbol structure (and how else is one supposed to do it?), the Davidsonian has only pushed the question back a step, for now we want a theory of the meaning of the symbol structure itself.

Further, there is an open question, on these non-reductionist semantic theories, as to how knowing a word's or a sentence's V could explain our ability to use the word or sentence appropriately. For example, suppose knowing the meaning of "The balloon burst" is knowing what situation it denotes. But how can knowledge of the denoted situation explain how we use the sentence appropriately?[41] Not that these questions could not be answered by the non-reductionist – for example, they could *adopt CRS*. The point is that the non-reductionist semantic theories I mentioned have no account of their own. (Of course, as I keep saying, this is not a *defect* of these theories.)

Another matter that distinguishes CRS from the non-reductionist theories (and the non-Gricean reductionist theories) is that CRS promises to give a semantic explanation of certain "principles of charity." Many philosophers of language imagine a "radical translation" or "radical interpretation" situation, in which one is trying to interpret utterances (typically, the problem is introduced with an anthropological situation, and then it is observed that the same issues arise in justifying the homophonic translation). As many philosophers have stressed, one must consider one's hypotheses about what the foreign terms mean together with hypotheses about the speakers' beliefs (and other pro-positional attitudes). It is the "simplicity" of the *total* theory that counts. Now it is often said that it is the *truth* of the alien beliefs that counts (Davidson sometimes says this); but this seems clearly wrong, in the absence of reason to believe that the alien has got things right. A better approach to principles of charity emphasizes coherence. Attribution of irrational belief cannot go on without limit; eventually, one loses one's grip on the content of what one has attributed. But this kind of charity can be explained by CRS. To understand the alien's beliefs, one has to appreciate their inferential roles (or rather, the inferential roles of the symbol structures that express them). If the mismatch between the alien's inferential roles and our own is too great, there will be no way for us to translate what he says (cf. Loar, 1982).

Further, to the extent that inferential role is normative (an issue within CRS, and therefore one I have avoided), there will be rationality constraints on what can sensibly be attributed. These rationality constraints are in no way a by-product of considerations about translation or about a mismatch of conceptual roles; rather, they are a matter of constraints on the conceptual roles that can possibly express concepts.

Let us return to the familiar claim that to know the meaning of a sentence is to know its truth-conditions. In any sense in which this claim has substantial content, it is not at all obvious. For example, it is possible to imagine someone knowing the entire set of possible worlds in which a sentence is true without knowing what the sentence means. For the *way the person represents the set of possible worlds* may not capture its meaning. Perhaps it is possible to develop a canonical notation for representing possible worlds. In terms of such a nota-tion, one could develop an ordering of possible worlds, and thus one might be able to exhibit a set of possible worlds via an arithmetical predicate that picks out the right numbers. But if one knows, say, that the prime-numbered possible worlds are the ones in which a sentence is true, does one thereby know its meaning? Further, even if no such ordering exists, one can imagine repre-senting the possible worlds in which a sentence is true in a way that makes use of a motley of devices, different devices for different classes of worlds. Such a representation needn't capture what the worlds have in common in virtue of which they are the ones in which the sentence is true.[42]

Though it is not at all obvious that knowing truth conditions guarantees knowing meaning, the converse claim is more plausible. And, as Harman has pointed out,[43] CRS can explain this in the following way: normal users of language understand certain metalinguistic ideas, such as the disquotational use of "true," and this is what gives them knowledge of truth conditions. The conceptual roles of "true" and non-semantic terms yield knowledge of bi-conditionals like " 'Snow is white' is true iff snow is white." But even if know-ing meaning involves knowing truth-conditions, one can hardly jump to the conclusion that knowing meaning *is* knowing truth-conditions.

The fertility of the CRS account of learning can be illustrated by its solution to what might be tendentiously called Fodor's Paradox. Fodor's Paradox is posed by the following argument (Fodor, 1975):

(1)   Learning the meaning of a word is a matter of hypothesis formation and testing.

(2)   When we learn a new English term (e.g., "chase"), we can do so only by hypothesizing definitions in terms already known (including terms of the language of thought).

(3)   The history of attempts to define English terms "decompositionally" (e.g., "try to catch") has been a dismal failure, and there are familiar Quinean considerations that explain why. This suggests that most English terms cannot be so defined.

(4)   Therefore, when a term like "chase" is learned, it must be learned by hypothesizing a definition in terms of a *single* term of the language of thought, "CHASE," which has the same meaning as "chase." In other words, the typical word-learning hypothesis has the form: "chase" means "CHASE."

(5)   Therefore, for most terms of English, we grasp them only because they correspond to (indeed, are standardly associated with) innate terms of Mentalese.

I call the argument a paradox because the conclusion is obviously unacceptable; the issue is which premise to give up. Why is the conclusion unacceptable? Could scientific concepts like "meson" and "enzyme," as well as technological ideas such as "monitor," "zipper," and "transistor," be *individually* innate? If so, either evolution mysteriously foresaw the concepts needed for science and technology, or else progress in science and technology is possible only with respect to a highly arbitrary, accidentally prefigured vocabulary. Were this the case, one could expect that some accidental modification of some current technological device would produce a new and utterly unintelligible device that we could use the way a two-year-old uses a telephone while confused about whether it is a game in which daddy is somehow hiding inside the phone.

So what premise must go? The first premise is empirically plausible, justified, for example, by appeal to the type of errors children make. Also, hypothesis formation and testing is the only model of learning we have.

Much ink has been shed over the third premise. No doubt readers have made up their minds on the issue, and what I could say in a brief space here would be of no use at all. I shall confine myself to the remark that *if* it has been shown that there aren't many analytic decompositional definitions in natural languages,[44] that doesn't *show* that there aren't many decompositional definitions of natural-language terms in Mentalese; but the burden of proof is on those who think Mentalese differs from English in this respect.

The premise CRS militates against is 2. According to CRS, the way we learn a new English term needn't be a matter of definition at all. Rather, the CRS picture is that the term (or its newly formed Mentalese standard associate) comes to have a certain function. To the extent that hypotheses are involved, they are hypotheses about how the term functions in thought, reasoning, problem solving, and so forth.

One way to see what the CRS proposal comes to is to reflect on how one learned the concepts of elementary physics, or anyway, how I did. When I took my first physics course, I was confronted with quite a bit of new terminology all at once: "energy," "momentum," "acceleration," "mass," and the like. As should be no surprise to anyone who noted the failure of positivists to define theoretical terms in observation language, I never learned any definitions of these new terms in terms I already knew. Rather, what I learned was how to *use* the new terminology – I learned certain relations among the new terms themselves (e.g., the relation between force and mass, neither of which can be defined in old terms), some relations between the new terms and old terms, and, most importantly, how to generate the right numbers in answers to questions posed in the new terminology. This is just the sort of story a proponent of CRS should expect.[45]

Note that CRS is not a psychological theory. In particular, though it can tell us that Fodor's second premise *needn't* be true, it is compatible with its actually being true. For it is compatible with the CRS account that the way one learns to use a new term correctly is by linking it to a term one already has that functions appropriately.

Let me now raise a bogeyman that will come up repeatedly: psychologism. Am I just making the verbal maneuver of using "semantics" to mean the study of the psychology of meaning, rather than the study of meaning proper? As pointed out in connection with the question of whether narrow meaning is genuine meaning, this question is a quibble. However, my answer is that, although knowing is a mental state and learning is a mental process, it is not psychologism to suppose that a theory of what meaning *is* ought to be in some way relevant to what it is to know or learn meaning. For example, one can imagine quite different ideas of what good taste is (ranging from a form of knowing how to a form of knowing that) that would engender quite different ideas of what it is to learn good taste. Closer to home, consider the view that philosophy is conceptual analysis contrasted with the view that philosophy is a kind of history (in which heavy emphasis is placed on knowing the texts). These conceptions would lead to different ideas of what it is to learn philosophy.

But how is the idea that meaning is, say, truth-conditions, supposed to be in any way relevant to what it is to learn or know meaning? (Unless truth-conditions are identified with *verification conditions*, in which case we have a rather unattractive *special case of* CRS in which conceptual role is role in verifying.) The issue of what it is to learn or know truth-conditions, or situation denoted, or associated semantic marker, or function from possible worlds to truth-values is just as much in need of illumination from a theory like CRS as what it is to learn or know meaning.

I chose the desideratum about learning as the place to bring up the psychologism bogeyman first because this desideratum is perhaps the most psychological of the ones I mentioned; so it is this desideratum for which, if I am just changing the subject, it should be most apparent. My hope is that exposing the weakness of the psychologism charge here will allow me to pay less attention to it with regard to later desiderata.

What makes meaningful expressions meaningful?

I will use this section to lay out the basic ideas of the comparisons with the alternative theories, especially the reductionist competitors. So this will be a long section. According to CRS, what makes an expression meaningful is that it has a conceptual role of a certain type, one that we may call "appropriate." The difference between "cat" and "glurg" is that "cat" has an appropriate conceptual role, whereas "glurg" does not. What gives "cat" the particular meaning that it has is its particular conceptual role. The difference between meaningful expressions with different meanings ("cat" and "dog") is a conceptual role difference *within* the category of appropriate conceptual roles.[46]

The dominant perspectives in semantics – possible-worlds semantics, situation semantics, and the approaches of Davidson and of Katz, can be used to give responses to my questions that look just as good at first glance. Suppose they say, for example, that what makes a meaningful sentence meaningful is that it has truth-conditions, or a set of truth-values in possible worlds, or an associated (sense expressed by a) markerese structure, or a denoted situation. But such answers just *put off* the semantic issue. For now we want to know what it is that makes for the difference – what it is in virtue of which there *is* a difference – between sentences that *have* and sentences that *lack* truth-conditions, truth-values in possible worlds, associated markerese structures, or denoted situations, and to these questions these non-reductionist perspectives have no answers.[47]

Of course, one can also ask of CRS what the difference is between sentences that have and sentences that lack conceptual roles. But CRS has an answer: certain causal properties. And if the questioner wants to know why sentences has the causal properties they do, again there are answers, at least in principle, to be sought, of the same sort that one would give to "Why do genes have the causal properties they have?"

What the difference comes down to is that CRS aims for a reductionist account, indeed, a naturalistic-reductionist account, in proposing to explain a semantic property in terms of a naturalistic, non-semantic property: causation.

CRS's reductionism and naturalism allow it to promise an answer to "What makes a meaningful expression meaningful?" The semantic approaches mentioned in the paragraph before last, being non-reductionist, cannot answer this question.

Although the dominant views in semantics should be regarded (in my view) as just not directed towards the sort of question typified by this desideratum it should be noted that they often seem to be responding to much the same motivation that lies behind a naturalistic-reductionistic account. For instance, Davidsonians, though not reductionists, make much of the claim that a theory of the sort they favor will allow a deduction from a finite non-semantic base of a specification of truth-conditions for any indicative sentence.

On the whole, most of the standard approaches have been primarily concerned with the *relations* among meanings, not the nature of meaning itself. For example, the standard approaches have been concerned with an aspect of compositionality: how the meanings of larger elements such as sentences are related to the meanings of smaller elements such as words. Another sort of issue motivating the standard theories is what we can tell about the logical form of "Sam ate with a fork" from the fact that, if it is true, so is "Sam ate." Another issue (one that has been a stumbling block for possible-worlds semantics and one that situation semantics hopes to make progress on) is what the relation is between the semantic value of "Grass is green" and "John believes that grass is green." But these questions can be and have been discussed without ever broaching the issue of what it is in virtue of which expressions have their meanings in the first place.

The main aim of most of the standard approaches to semantics has been to *correlate* meanings with certain objects, so that relations among meanings are mirrored by formal relations among the corresponding objects. These approaches have often been concerned with a purely *descriptive* project, a kind of "curve-fitting," not with explaining the nature of meaning.

The major tradition within this conception of semantics is well described in Barwise and Perry (1984).[48]

> We have intuitions about the logical behavior of a certain class of sentences. With attitudes reports, these are largely intuitions about the phenomenon of "opacity": reluctance to substitute co-referential terms and the like. We codify these intuitions in a set of logical principles, and then semantics consists of finding a collection of plausible set-theoretic models that makes the logical principles come out correct. I think this is the traditional conception in semantics, and it is the setting for Montague Grammar, but it is what I would now call the thin conception of semantics.

As suggested earlier, the Barwise and Perry effort to produce a semantics that satisfies a richer, "thicker" conception of semantics can be seen as moving on two fronts: one involves model-theoretic ideas (e.g., the idea of a partial model), the other a kind of indicator semantics (discussed later in this section). Another aspect of the thickness that Barwise and Perry seek is to make semantics compatible with commonsense psychology, for example, to avoid the possible-worlds semantics problem that one would seem to believe everything logically equivalent to what one believes.[49]

Now Barwise and Perry (1984) have advocated a functionalist theory of propositional attitudes. Perhaps they (and some Davidsonians, Katzians, and possible-worlds semanticists) envision a two-stage process of semantic theorizing: first, a non-reductive account of meanings, and second a reductive account aimed at desiderata something like the ones I have mentioned. Theorists in these traditions have not, however, put forward second-stage theories. I know of only two types of reductionist approaches to semantics other than CRS (and the causal theory of reference, which I am not discussing in any detail); after considering an objection, I shall sketch these approaches and their relation to CRS.

It may be objected that I have confused:

(i)   In virtue of what is a particular token/ches/-noise an utterance of the English word "chase" meaning, of course, "try to catch")?

(ii) In virtue of what does the English word type "chase" mean "try to catch"?[50]

It may be said that (ii) has no non-trivial answer – it is part of what it *is* to be the English word "chase" to mean what it does.[51] Asking (ii), on this view, is like asking what makes the number two even. If it weren't, it wouldn't be the number two. (Or: "Two is even" is analytic.)

On the objector's view, the problem I raise does not *disappear*, but is rather transformed. Instead of asking what it is in virtue of which "chase" means what it does, I must ask what it is in virtue of which a token is of the type *"chase" in English*, with the meaning that that word necessarily (?) has. Since the problem survives, I suppose that the real objection here is that the question I raise (being about a token) is really pragmatic rather than semantic.

Perhaps some perspective can be gained by contrasting the question about language with the question of why, in the American system of government, cabinet officers are approved by the Senate but presidential advisors are not? Here there seems little utility to seeing the American system of government as an abstract object that has this property necessarily (or analytically). It is not helpful to see the question as one about whether a certain token system is a token of the type "the American system of government." But is language more like a political institution or more like mathematics? This question won't get us very far. What issues belong in pragmatics as opposed to semantics is a matter to be settled by finding out which way of dividing up issues makes the most theoretical sense, not by consulting intuitions about whether language is more social than mathematical.

The important point against the objection is that it is a mistake to see the contrast the objector raises as hinging on the type/token distinction. This becomes especially obvious when one is reminded that the English language is in constant flux. "Yuppie" has no meaning in English-1982, but it has a meaning in English-1985. And "chase" may mean something different in English-1988 from what it does in English-1985. If a word's meaning is a necessary – though language-relative – property of the word, then (1) we must regard different dialects and language stages as, in the relevant sense, different languages; and (2) we must recognize a sense of "word type" in which word types are language specific. So we cannot speak of one word's different meanings in different dialects. But this is just a peculiar way of talking. As we have seen, there is a natural use of the notion of a word type in which we *can* speak of one word as having different meanings in different dialects (as is the case with "yuppie"). So, deploying the notion of word type in the latter way, the question of why the word type "chase" means "try to catch" in English-1985 is not trivial.

The reductionist alternatives

There are two competing families of approaches to semantics that *are* reductionist,[52] and hence that *do* have genuine answers to the questions posed in the desiderata I've been talking about. One of them is the approach of reducing meaning to *mental content*. Call this type of approach "Gricean." The Gricean approach as developed by Grice himself, and later Schiffer, reduces speaker meaning to the content of speaker's intentions. For the speaker to mean such and such by what he says is for him to intend his utterance to affect the propositional attitudes of hearers in certain ways. Sentence meaning, on this theory, can be reduced to speaker meaning via a conventional correlation between sentences in the language and communicative intentions. This conventional correlation makes it practicable for a speaker to use certain sentences to produce certain effects in hearers.[53]

Searle has an approach that is Gricean in my sense, in which the intention isn't communicative but rather an intention to produce an object with certain "satisfaction conditions" (Searle, 1983a). A rather different sort of Gricean approach was taken by Ramsey, who attempted to reduce the meaning of an item of language to the beliefs that would be expressed by that item.

Gricean approaches have been enveloped in controversies, none of which will be discussed here. Nor is this the place for a full-dress comparison between Gricean and conceptual role accounts. However, there are a few points of comparison that can be made rather briefly. Although I do not want to belittle the Gricean accomplishment, without a naturalistic account of the mental, the Gricean approach has little to contribute to the project I am discussing. One who is concerned with the questions I have been asking about meaning will be equally concerned with corresponding questions about intentional content. Consider, for example, the three questions involved in the desideratum currently being discussed:

(1)   What is it about a meaningful expression that makes it meaningful?
(2)   What is responsible for an expression's having the particular meaning it has?
(3)   What is the difference between expressions with different meanings in virtue of which they have different meanings?

The Gricean faces corresponding questions about intentional content, viz.:

(1')   What is it about a contentful state that makes it contentful?
(2')   What is responsible for a state's having the particular intentional content it has?
(3')   What is the difference between states with different intentional contents in virtue of which they have their different contents?

In the light of this problem, Griceans have a number of options. First, they could simply regard intentional content as primitive – in other words, regard questions like (1'), (2'), and (3') as having no answers. For Griceans to take this line would be to give up on satisfying the desiderata I've been talking about. This is the non-naturalistic option I mentioned. Another line would be to pursue some non-functionalist reductionist strategy, such as physiological reductionism. This is an unpromising tack (see Fodor, 1974), and it is especially unattractive if one is interested in a semantics that might apply to the language use of an intelligent computer or computerlike machine, if we ever construct one.[54]

Another option is Searle's reduction of intentionality to *the brain or whatever has "equivalent causal powers."* The wild card of "equivalent causal powers" allows Searle to avoid the usual drawbacks of physiological reduction. For example, the theory is not chauvinist because it allows for the possibility that the control systems of intelligent machines can have causal powers equivalent to ours. However, the other side of the coin is that the theory is far from naturalistic. To say a machine has causal powers equivalent to those of the human brain is only to say that the machine has causal properties that result in intentionality. So Searle must either (1) regard intentionality as primitive, in which case he has not answered the questions I am talking about, or (2) he must give some non-intentional analysis of "equivalent causal powers." It is clear that Searle takes option (1). That is, he has no intention of giving a reductionist theory of intentionality, though he takes physicochemical properties of *each being* that has intentional states to cause that being's intentional states. (See Searle, 1984.)

Searle repeatedly *says* that it is an empirical question whether a given machine has equivalent causal powers, but the careful reader discerns that it is an empirical question only in that the machine itself *will know* if it does indeed have equivalent causal powers.[55] The crux of the disagreement between Searle and me is not about whether a sapient and sentient machine will have to have innards with causal powers equivalent to those in us (we agree on this); the crux rather is whether some sort of functionalist thesis is true of us. For if intentionality can be characterized functionally, then *the way to make a machine with intentional states is to make a machine functionally equivalent to us – the equivalent causal powers of the machine's brain will come along for free.* Searle's argument against functionalism is his "Chinese room" argument, to be discussed briefly later in this paper.

There is one final "methodological" point to be made against Searle. One should not adopt his view without proper exploration of the alternatives, since if Searle's account is true, the sciences of mind and meaning would seem to be severely limited. In particular, it is hard to see how science (or philosophy) could ever tell us anything substantive about what the source of autonomous meaning or intentionality is.

Another Gricean option is that championed by Schiffer and Loar (and perhaps Grice): they couple the reduction of meaning to the mental with a functionalist reduction of the mental. A major difference between the functionalism-based Gricean theory and CRS is that the Gricean theory is not committed to any sort of representationalism, even of the weak sort that CRS is committed to (viz. that thoughts have recombinable ingredients). This difference between the Loar-Schiffer account and the CRS account is a disagreement about the empirical facts about how the mind works (or about how much philosophical ice such empirical facts cut), not about the functional source of meaning.[56] In sum, in one version Gricean theory is not a competitor to CRS; in another version, it is a competitor but has drawbacks; and in another version, it differs with respect to representationalism and, of course, the details of the Gricean reduction in terms of intentions, as well as the focus on public language meaning as opposed to idiolect narrow meaning.

I shall now turn to an argument by Loar (1981, chap. 9; 1983) against the sort of view I am advocating. As I understand it, Loar's argument is that a theory of meaning should not depend on a speculative psychological claim such as representationalism. So Loar advocates the Gricean reduction of external language to mentality (coupled with a functionalist reduction of the mental). If representationalism happens to be true, Loar favors what amounts to a conceptual role semantics theory of the internal language (though not external language). My objection is simple: if representationalism is false, CRS is certainly false. But if representationalism is true, Loar is stuck with an intention-based semantics for external language plus a conceptual role semantics for internal language – whereas CRS makes do with the latter type of semantics for *both* types of language. (Of course, Loar is concerned with public meaning rather than narrow idiolect meaning, but this fact does not play any direct role in his argument.) So, if representationalism is true, the Loar–Schiffer account seems at a disadvantage.

Is there some way in which the Gricean account could be extended to internal language? Computation in internal symbol systems appears to be of a rather "automatic" sort which gains efficiency through unflexibility.[57] For example, if one memorizes a list of six letters, say "UEKNMG," and one is asked whether "E" is on the list, one does an "exhaustive" serial search, looking at all six letters, one by one, even if "E" is the first letter in the list.[58] (This is one of the better tested results in all of cognitive psychology.) Is it at all plausible that one forms an *intention* to look at all the items, or to do an exhaustive serial search? Further, even if the uses of the internal system are intentional in some sense, surely the intentions are not intentions to *communicate*, as in the standard Gricean theories.

But what if the internal symbol system *is* English (that is, the same as whatever external language is spoken)? Can the Gricean then avoid the problem of the last paragraph by giving a theory of meaning for English, and simply postulating that sentences in the language of thought have the same meaning as in English? First, it is not at all obvious that the meaning of English as used in thought (if it is used in thought) is somehow derivative from its use in communication. Why not the other way around? Second, and more importantly, I have talked as if it is perfectly possible that English is the language of thought, but this is simply *not* in the cards. For one thing, external language is radically ambiguous, both syntactically and semantically. If there is no confusion in *thought* as between financial banks and river banks, then one word in the internal system presumably does not carry both meanings. And if someone says "I tire of visiting relatives," knowing full well whether relatives are visiting her or whether she is the visitor, then it is doubtful that the English sentence could be the vehicle of the thought. (But see Block and Bromberger, 1980.) From what I've said thus far, one might suppose that the language of thought might be a kind of regimented English (e.g., syntactic trees with English terminal nodes, as suggested for part of the language of thought in Harman, 1970). But, at most, some sort of regimented English could be *part* of the language of thought. (Indeed, although there is controversy over whether English is part of the language of thought, there is none over whether English is the *whole* of the language of thought.) For example there is enormous evidence for representations in mental imagery (see Block, 1983, for discussion and references to the literature); and it is quite out of the question that these representations are in English (none of the defenders of the view that the representations of imagery are languagelike have suggested such a thing). When one looks in any detail at what a languagelike representation would have to be to play the role of representations of imagery, this is obvious. Nor would any such suggestion be remotely sensible for the representations of early vision (see Marr, 1982).

If English is part of the language of thought, it would seem especially peculiar to treat the semantics of that part of the language of thought so differently from the semantics of external English.

In sum, the Griceans cannot claim that their account is to be preferred to CRS on the ground that their account has no empirical vulnerability, since both accounts have an element of empirical vulnerability. Nonetheless, the choice between the two approaches seems mainly a matter of philosophical metatheory. If one wishes to insulate one's semantics from experimental falsification, while being willing to tolerate ad hoc addition of components to handle experimental discoveries, the Loar-Schiffer perspective is better. If one is interested in a semantics based on the best empirical theories extant, CRS is better.

There is a second family of reductionist approaches to semantics that could be claimed to satisfy my desiderata: what I called "indicator semantics." Dretske (1981) and Stampe (1977) have similar versions, which I believe have been refuted by Fodor (1984), who has his own version of the view (Fodor, 1984, 1987). Barwise and Perry (1983) have a view that has affinities to that of Dretske and Stampe, which I will not be able to discuss in detail here.

Dretske and Stampe say what it is for a sentence S to have the content that T in terms of tokens of S carrying information about T; carrying information, in turn, is cashed in terms of a nomological relation between S's and T's (roughly, an S nomologically requires a T).[59] Fodor objects that, if error is possible, then a non-T can cause a tokening of S; but then why should we regard T as the state of affairs with which S is nomologically correlated when S has a *better* correlation with the disjunctive state of affairs whose disjuncts are T and the non-T state that causes S? So it seems that, on the Dretske/Stampe view, error is not possible.

Barwise uses the type/token distinction to deal with this problem. Suppose Ed "says 'It is 4 p.m.' at 4:30. While we can truly report that *Ed means what he says*, we can also truly report that *Ed's statement does not mean that it is 4 p.m.*"[60] Barwise's claim is that "means" is ambiguous: there is one sense appropriate to tokens, another to types. A false token does not convey the information (this is the sense of meaning appropriate to tokens) conventionally associated with the corresponding type. (What about false sentence-types? According to Barwise and Perry, it is only tokens [e.g., utterances] of sentences that have truth-values, not sentence-types.)

But I don't see how Barwise and Perry propose to avoid Fodor's objection in giving an informational account of sentence-type meaning. One often gets the impression that their theory is that the meaning of a sentence-type is the information *normally conveyed* by tokens of it. But what could "normally" come to here? This cannot be shorthand for information converted by *true uses*, since that would ruin any attempt to give an account of the semantic in non-semantic terms. If "normal" is some sort of appeal to what is usual, however, Fodor's problem stands in the way. The correlation between tokens of S and the disjunction of T and pseudo-T states of affairs (ones that mislead people into false assertions of S) will inevitably be better than the correlation between S and T itself. Indeed, it is not hard to think of sentences whose assertions are more often false than true (e.g., famous last words). If "normal" is some sort of appeal to the conventional, Barwise and Perry owe us an account of how that is supposed to connect with information conveyed and how they expect to avoid an analysis of conventionality in terms of intentional notions (as in Lewis's analysis). If it is a teleological notion, my guess is that their account will succumb to the kind of criticism now to be raised against Fodor's own account. (I've been assuming that Barwise and Perry do aim for an account of meaning in non-semantic and non-intentional terms. This conception seems to me to permeate Barwise and Perry (1983), though it is never explicitly announced. In recent conversations with Barwise and Perry, I gather that they do not take themselves to be aiming for an account of meaning that is reductionist in this sense.)

Fodor's own view attempts to capitalize on the very fact that torpedoes the Dretske-Stampe approach. The basic idea is that, in a sense, error is not possible. The aim of Fodor's theory is to give a naturalistic account of what it is in virtue of which a sentence has the truth condition it has – what *makes* a sentence have the truth-condition that it has. Some examples of theories that are in the same ball park: (1) the British empiricist theory that what gives a mental representation its truth-condition is *resemblance* between the representation and the state of affairs; (2) the Skinnerian theory that what makes T the truth condition of S is that T is the discriminative stimulus of S. These are both false doctrines, for well-known reasons, but they are nonetheless naturalistic.

Fodor's task is one that many writers have seen the need for. As Field (1972) pointed out, the Tarskian approach, on one construal, yields the truth-conditions of sentences only by means of *lists* of the referents of singular terms and the denotations of predicates. ("Boston swelters" is shown to be true only because the object that is listed as the referent of "Boston" is in the set that is listed as the denotation of "swelters.") However, serious suggestions for solving this problem are thin on the ground. The only remotely plausible views I know of are the indicator semantics approach (common to Fodor, Dretske/Stampe, and Barwise and Perry), and Tarski's approach, construed as in Field (1972), together with a naturalistic theory of reference such as the causal theory. (Field's construal of Tarski is as giving a way of reducing truth to primitive denotation.)

The heart of the theory is an account of the truth conditions for mental sentences.[61] The account makes use of the claim that believing is a computational relation between a person and a mental sentence. (This computational relation is described below as the sentence being in the "belief box.") The claim is that what it is for T to be the truth condition for a mental sentence M is:

(1) If the cognitive system is functioning as it is *supposed* to; and
(2) idealizing away from epistemic limitations, then *M is in the "belief box"* ↔ *T*.

There are two "wheels" that drive this account: the teleological wheel, indicated by the "supposed" in condition (1), and the epistemic idealization wheel. The idea behind Fodor's account is that there are cognitive mechanisms that are designed to put sentences in the belief box if and only if they are true. Error results when these mechanisms fail, or when epistemic conditions are less than ideal. Thus, if one can spell out the teleological notion and say what epistemically ideal conditions are in a naturalistic way, one will have a naturalistic theory of truth conditions.

There are serious problems with each of two "wheels." Let us begin with the epistemic idealization. One sees how it is supposed to go for cases of things that are to small to see, or happened too far away or too long ago. In these cases, what Fodor imagines we idealize away from is how big we are, where we are, or when we are. The idea is that if epistemically ideal conditions held, one's nose *would be rubbed in the truth*; then mechanisms whose function it is to make one see the truth would take over, and one would indeed see the truth.

But what about statements to the effect that space is Riemannian, or that some quarks have charm, or even that one is in the presence of a magnetic field? Here, it is not enough to suppose one's nose is rubbed in the truth, for it's no use having your nose rubbed in the facts – you have to come up with the right theory, too, and you have to know that it is the right theory. Imagine that in the long run the evidence converges on a Riemannian geometry for the universe. The ideal scientific community will only believe in this claim if someone *thinks* of it. After all, it is quite intuitive to suppose that there is exactly one parallel to a given line at a given point, as Euclidean geometry tells us. No *series of measurements* can guarantee that anyone thinks of (or takes seriously, even if they think of) claiming that the Euclidean parallel postulate is false. To make a long story short, I don't see how such theoretical statements can be handled without in one way or another abandoning naturalism – for example, appealing to some sort of magical machinery or smuggling something semantic into the specification of the epistemic idealization. Suppose that whenever a "theoretical" property of the sort I just mentioned is raised, the Fodorean constructs an idealization in which humans have a perceptual detector that detects this property. Nothing semantic need be smuggled in with the description of these detectors: they say "*p*" if and only if *p*. With such detectors, if your nose is rubbed in a fact, you will perceive it to obtain. But this response abandons naturalism. We have no idea how such detectors would work or even whether they are possible. Appealing to them is like saying: "Aha, what makes *T* the truth condition for *M* is that an omniscient wizard (i.e., one who believed '*p*' if and only if *p*) would believe *M* if and only if *T*."

You don't get a naturalistic account of truth-conditions by appealing to the imaginary behavior of an imaginary being.

Idealizing often starts with something familiar and envisions a systematic change. So, in the last paragraph, we started with normal perceptual detectors and imagined them getting better and better (or, alternatively, more and more numerous). Another idea is to try envisioning systematic change in our theorizing mechanisms. Of course, we need a non-semantic characterization of the ideal theorizing mechanisms. It won't do to say they find the *right* theory, since that is a semantic notion. Perhaps we can simply envision mechanisms that construct all possible theories and choose the simplest of them that is compatible with the data. The problems here are complex, and I can only hint at them. I would argue that, on any formal notion of simplicity (e.g., one that involves counting symbols), it just is not true that the simplest theory is true. And even if the simplest theory were true, this assumption – which, of course, is a semantic assumption – would be part of the account. So, the account would not be naturalistic.[62] On the other hand, a *semantic* conception of simplicity (e.g., one that involves the concept of truth) won't be naturalistic either.

The second wheel driving Fodor's account is the idea that the cognitive system is *supposed* to function in a certain way. How is this teleological talk supposed to be understood? (Anyone who has read the current literature on teleology knows that promising suggestions are hard to find.)[63] Sometimes Fodor talks in terms of a notion of teleology provided by evolutionary theory. The cognitive system is supposed to function a certain way in that is what evolution designed it to do.

One problem is that one cannot rely on evolution in such a simple way, since one can imagine a molecule-for-molecule duplicate of a baby who comes into being by chance and grows up in the normal way. Such a person would have language with the normal semantic properties, but no evolutionary "design."

Quite a different type of problem comes in through evolutionary theory itself. I think it is now quite generally accepted among evolutionary biologists that one cannot suppose that every phenotypic (i.e., actual) characteristic of an organism is an optimal design feature (in any non-trivial sense), given the environment.[64] To take a rather extreme case, for purposes of illustration, consider the phenomenon of "meiotic drive." Normally, each of a pair of genes has an equal chance of ending up in an offspring: if you have one blue-eye gene and one brown-eye gene, the chance that your child will get one of these from you is equal to the chance that it will get the other. But there are some known cases of genes – the mouse t-allele, for example – that beat out whatever gene they are paired to, thus propelling themselves into the next generation. Any such gene that does not have lethal effects on the phenotype is likely to spread in a population very quickly, even if it has suboptimal pheonotypic effects. The upshot is that there are known mechanisms (of which this is only one of many examples) that could have the effect of producing cognitive mechanisms that aim, to some extent, at properties of beliefs other than truth.[65]

One final point about Fodor's account. One peculiar fact about it is that it does not exploit the compositional structure of the language at all. (This is especially odd in view of the fact that Fodor's representationalism gives him objects in the belief box ripe for compositional exploitation.) In this respect, it is markedly inferior to Field's proposal (mentioned above), in which the truth conditions for sentences are built up out of naturalistic analyses of reference and denotation. This feature of Fodor's theory renders it vulnerable to the following problem (I am indebted here to Michael Bratman): If S and S' are nomologically correlated states of affairs, then, on Fodor's analysis, any sentence that is mapped onto one of them will be mapped onto the other. Consider, for example, the correlated properties of electrical and thermal conductivity (whose correlation is expressed in the Wiedemann-Franz Law). Let us agree with Fodor that it is the function of the cognitive mechanisms to put "The electrical conductivity is rising" in the belief box (in ideal epistemological circumstances) iff the electrical conductivity is rising. But since the right-hand side of this biconditional is true iff the thermal conductivity is rising, the left-hand side will be true iff the thermal conductivity is rising. So Fodor's theory will not distinguish between the semantic values of "The thermal conductivity is rising" and "The electrical conductivity is rising." I don't see how such a problem can be dealt with without going to a compositional story (e.g., by adding a conceptual role component to the theory).[66]

Let me summarize. I've mentioned two types of reductionist theories – indicator semantics and Gricean semantics. (I've also mentioned the causal theory of reference, but I haven't compared it with CRS since it is not normally thought of as full a semantic theory. It – like indicator semantics – is a candidate for the referential-truth-conditional factor of a two-factor theory.) I've mentioned and endorsed Fodor's reason for thinking one version of indicator semantics won't work, and I've given some reasons to be dissatisfied with Fodor's theory. I've mentioned a few versions of Gricean theory, arguing that Searle's version isn't naturalistic (and so isn't a competitor to CRS); and I have countered an argument that the Grice-Schiffer-Loar version should be preferred to CRS because the former, unlike the latter, does not depend on what psychologists find out about mental representation.

Before I go on the next desideratum, I shall very briefly consider an objection to the whole enterprise: I have been comparing a conceptual role theory of *narrow meaning* with theories that have conceptions of meaning that are quite different from narrow meaning (and also from one another's conceptions of meaning). Isn't this comparing apples, oranges, and mangoes?

Reply: (1) It would not change my points were I to switch from talk of narrow meaning to talk of meaning. Since meaning, on my view, is a pair of factors – the narrow meaning factor and the referential factor – to talk in terms of meaning would be to talk in terms of both factors of the two-factor account of meaning rather than just one of the factors (narrow meaning). After all, I chose the desiderata to exhibit strengths of the conceptual role factor of the two-factor theory, and I will be exercising the two-factor theory's right to introduce the referential factor where relevant. (2) It is true that different semantic theories differ in their conceptions of meaning, but that does not make comparison illegitimate. Vienna and New Delhi differ in their conception of dessert, but that won't stop me from preferring strudel to gulabja.

Why is meaning relative to representational system?

The CRS explanation of this relativity is simple. The conceptual role of a symbol is a matter of how it *functions* in a representational system (for this reason, conceptual role is sometimes called "functional role"). How a representation functions in a system depends, of course, on the system. If meaning is function, as CRS dictates, then meaning is system relative.

The non-reductionist semantic theories can, of course, be used to handle this phenomenon (in a non-explanatory way) by assigning different semantic values to an expression when it manifestly has different semantic properties. Thus a sentence with "trailer" in it would be assigned different situations, or truth-conditions, or extensions in possible worlds or markerese representations, depending on whether the dialect is American English or English English. Once again, this is accommodation, not explanation. The difference between CRS and the non-reductionist theories is that conceptual roles are, by their nature, system relative because they are functional entities and the semantic values of the non-reductionist theories are not.

It is worth emphasizing how important a matter this is. It is a banal feature of languages that the shape or sound of a word does not determine its meaning. Indeed, this point is sometimes described as "trivial semantic conventionalism," to distinguish it from more interesting claims. If no semantic theory could explain such a fact, semantics would be in trouble.

Perhaps it is worth mentioning the psychologism allegation again. Am I just demanding that semantics answer a question that belongs in the domain of, say, the psychology of language? Pretheoretically, the fact that one linguistic element can have different meanings in different languages would seem to be a clearly semantic phenomenon. I would think that the burden of argument would be on anyone who wanted to argue otherwise.

So CRS can explain the general fact that meaning is relative to representational system. Also, as pointed out in the last section, it promises to explain *particular* meaning differences. Since the difference in meaning of "trailer" in English English (in which it means: movie preview) and American English is a matter differences in the causal properties of the term, it is in principle possible, according to CRS, to specify the factors that cause the difference in causal properties. By contrast, think of how a possible-worlds semanticist or a Katzian would go about explaining the difference. Nothing in such non-reductionist semantic theories would help.

The relativity of meaning to system of use is more fundamental to cognitive science than attention to examples such as "trailer" indicates. Functional differences determine differences in the semantic (and syntactic) *categories* of representations – for example, the difference between the representational properties of *languagelike* and *picturelike* representations. This is especially important because there is reason to believe that many of our mental representations may actually be pictorial. None of the other semantic theories has a chance to explain the difference between the semantics of languagelike and picturelike representations.

Moreover, recall that syntactic category is as relative to system as semantic category. The relativity of syntactic category has the same explanation as the relativity of semantic category: syntax is functional too. If this isn't obvious, consider two processors that read English text: one reads odd-numbered characters, whereas the other reads even-numbered characters. One would read "CDAOTG" as "CAT," the other as "DOG." CRS allows a common explanation of an interesting fact – that both syntactic and semantic category are relative to system.

Further, CRS is important for avoiding misconceptions about concepts that are widespread in the psychological literature. The word "concept" is used in psychology to denote a mental or physiological entity that expresses or represents a concept in the philosopher's sense of the term (in which concepts are abstract entities). The concept of a cat (in the psychologist's sense of the term) is a mental or physiological entity that expresses or represents cathood (much as the word "cat" expresses or represents cathood). It is widely supposed in developmental psychology that mental images are probably children's concepts but that they could not be adult concepts. Piaget says:[67]

> The preconcepts of this level can be considered to be still half-way between the symbol and the concept proper. . . . [T]he preconcept involves the image and is partially determined by it, whereas the concept, precisely because of its generality, breaks away from the image. . . .

Another example: Premack (1983) argues that, whereas the concepts of many lower animals are pictorial, the concepts of primates must be in part languagelike because pictorial concepts cannot express certain abstract ideas. For example, chimps can "match to sample" not only in cases where the sample is red and the correct multiple choice item is red, but also where the sample is AA and the choices are AB, BC, and BB. Here the correct choice is BB, and the common property is being a pair whose members are identical. According to Premack, this requires a non-imagistic concept because the sample and target do not "resemble" one another. Another issue where this mistake (Which mistake? See the next paragraph) sometimes comes in is the issue of whether there is a "third code" more abstract than either languagelike or picturelike codes. The mistaken reasoning is that we have a non-languagelike code but that it could not be pictorial because pictorial representations could not have the kind of generality required of a concept.[68]

The doctrine that picturelike representations won't do for general or adult or primate concepts involves a conceptual error, one for which CRS is a corrective. CRS tells us that to be a concept of, say, dog, a mental representation must function in a certain way. Obviously, you can't tell how a certain representation functions by confining your attention to the representation alone, or to its "resemblances" to things in the world. You must know something about how the processors that act on it treat it. Thus a pictorial representation can express quite an abstract property, so long as the processors that act on it ignore the right specificities. To take a venerable example, a picture of an equilateral triangle can serve to represent triangles in general so long as the processors that act on it ignore the equality of the sides and angles. Similarly, a picture of a set of twins *could* represent or express the concept of a pair whose members are identical.

Note that I am not just pointing out that Piaget and Premack are the victims of "resemblance" theories of pictorial representation. The error I am pointing to is more fundamental in the sense that it includes the resemblance-theory error, plus a failure to see the shape of a positive doctrine – namely, that how or what a representation represents is a matter of more than the intrinsic properties of the representation or simple relational properties like "resemblance"; in particular, it is a matter of a complex relational property: how the representation functions.

What is the relation between meaning and mind/brain?

How does the brain confer meaning on its representations?[69] Answer: by conferring the right causal roles on the representations. What is it for a person to grasp the meaning of a word? Answer: for a person to grasp the meaning of a word is for the word (or its standard Mentalese associate) to have a certain causal role in his or her brain. How can it be that a person grasping an abstract object can propel the person (and his or her brain) to Hawaii? Answer: the difference between grasping a meaning and not grasping it is a difference in the causal role of entities in the person's brain, and differences in such causal roles can make for differences in behavior and the rewards that are contingent on behavior.

As before, the non-reductionist semantic theories can give superficial answers to the desideratum question. How does the brain grasp meanings? By grasping truth-conditions or a denoted situation or a markerese structure. But the question of how the brain grasps truth-conditions or denoted situations or markerese structures is just as pressing as the original question.[70]

What is the relation between autonomous and inherited meaning?

Recall the distinction (made in Desideratum 6) between autonomous and inherited meaning. Inherited meanings, like those of the linguistic expressions on this page, require translation or transliteration into the language of thought of a reader or hearer for their understanding. Autonomous meaning, the kind of meaning of the elements of the language of thought itself, requires no reading or hearing and thus no translation or transliteration in order to be understood. The questions I raised were: What is autonomous meaning? What is inherited meaning? What is the relation between autonomous and inherited meaning? For example, is one reducible to the other? Or are they both manifestations of a single type of meaning? Or are they unrelated phenomena with only a superficial resemblance?

The CRS answers to the first two questions are simple: autonomous meaning is conceptual role – and so is inherited meaning. (You will recall that, using the notion of standard association, one can individuate conceptual roles of English as their standard associates in the internal system.) Further the conceptual roles of external language are inherited from those of internal language. So inherited meaning is (surprise!) inherited from autonomous meaning.

The non-reductionist semantic theories, by contrast, have little to say about these matters. They *can* say that "cat" and "CAT" have the same semantic values; but, as far as I can see, none of them have conceptual resources adequate to spell out any reasonable characterizations of autonomous and inherited meaning or say anything about whether one is reducible to the other.

Psychologism again: is CRS supposed to be better for the purposes of psychology simply because it *contains* some psychological claims? Autonomous and inherited meaning are two categories of meaning (maybe even basic categories). It would be a surprise – *which itself would need explaining* – if no good theory of the nature of meaning could illuminate the issues I have been discussing about the relation between these two categories.

Indeed, once one sees the distinction between autonomous and inherited meaning, it is reasonable to ask of any theory of meaning *which* type of meaning it is intended to speak to. CRS speaks to both. Indeed, CRS explicates the difference between autonomous and inherited meaning without giving up a *unified* account of the two types of meaning. English inscriptions and utterances affect one another (via their effects on internal language) so as to give English expressions conceptual roles; and these conceptual roles are (at least on the simplified model I discussed) dependent on the conceptual roles of internal expressions.

Thus far, I have said little about causal theories of reference. Such theories, if they can be made to work, potentially have more to say about the relation between autonomous and inherited meaning than non-reductionist theories such as possible-worlds semantics, situation semantics, Davidsonian semantics, and Katzian semantics, because they can say something about the similarities and differences between the causal chains leading to "cat" and "CAT" that explains the differences and similarities between the two representations. But causal theories of reference cannot capture the aspect of meaning inside the head.[71] For example, they cannot capture the aspect of sameness in meanings of the sentences of me and my twin on Twin Earth (despite the difference in our causal chains outside our heads). From the point of view of a causal theory of reference, "Hesperus = Hesperus" and "Hesperus = Phosphorus" have the same semantic value.[72] Further, the theory that I am promoting can appropriate whatever successes causal theories of reference may have. Recall that CRS in the version I favor is part of a two-factor theory, the external factor of which can adopt aspects of a causal theory of reference account. In sum, causal theories of reference cannot accomplish the task I have set; and whatever they can accomplish can be appropriated by the two-factor version of CRS.

One final advantage of the CRS approach to the distinction between autonomous and inherited meaning is that it allows a theoretical approach to Searle's "Chinese Room" argument. With apologies to those who have heard this too many times: we are to imagine a monolingual English speaker who is placed in a room in a robot's head. He has a large library of instructions in English (the program) that tells him to push certain buttons (controlling outputs of the body) or write certain notes to himself (thus changing the "internal state" of the system) depending on what input lights are on and what notes he has written to himself earlier. The man never understands any Chinese, but nonetheless the robot he controls "speaks" excellent Chinese. Searle argues that since the man never understands Chinese, and since the robot paraphernalia adds no understanding, what we have is a Chinese simulator with no genuine Chinese understanding.

The most penetrating criticisms have focused on what Searle – anticipating the challenge – calls the systems reply. The systems reply says that since the system as a whole – man + library + room + robot body and control system – has the information processing characteristic of an intelligent Chinese speaker, we should take the whole system as understanding Chinese, even though the homunculus inside does not. The critics insist that the whole system does understand Chinese. (See Dennett, 1983a.) Searle has a clever reply. He tells the critics to just imagine the paraphernalia of the "system" *internalized*, as follows. First, instead of having the homunculus consult a library (the program), let him *memorize* the whole library. Second, let him memorize his notes instead of writing them down. Finally, instead of having the homunculus inhabit a robot body, let him *use his own body*. That is, what we are to imagine in the new version is that the homunculus manipulates his own body in just the way he manipulated the robot body in the previous version. When he seems to be asking for the salt in Chinese, what he is really doing is thinking *in English* about what noises and gestures the program dictates that he should produce next.[73]

At this point, the issue seems to come down just to a matter of conflicting intuitions. The opponents say the man following the instructions does understand Chinese, Searle says he does not.[74] This is where CRS comes in. The trouble with the systems reply as so far discussed is that it contains no theoretical perspective on what it would be for the system's Chinese symbols to be meaningful for it in the way the symbols in the head of a normal Chinese speaker are meaningful for that person – it contains no perspective on autonomous meaning. CRS has an answer: what would give the symbols autonomous meaning is the right conceptual role. There is a complication that makes this point harder to see. Namely, there is a crucial ambiguity in Searle's statement of his examples. Is the robot system (and the later case in which the homunculus internalizes the program) supposed to be one in which the information processing of a normal Chinese speaker is *simulated*? Or is the information processing of a normal Chinese speaker actually *instantiated* or *emulated* in the system?[75] (I can simulate an Aristotelian physicist's information processing by figuring out what someone would think if, like Aristotle, he didn't distinguish average from instantaneous velocity; but I cannot instantiate or emulate this information processing – that is, have this type of information actually go on in me – because I cannot avoid seeing the distinction.) In the case of mere simulation, the information-processing point of view does not dictate that the system *does* understand anything. But in the emulation case – the one in which Chinese symbols are processed so that they have the same conceptual roles they have in a normal Chinese speaker[76] – CRS dictates that the robot does indeed understand Chinese. I think that what makes Searle's argument sound so convincing is that it is difficult to imagine a version of Searle's example that is a genuine instantiation or emulation rather than a mere simulation.[77] In sum, CRS allows one to see an important distinction that is not respected in the debate, and it gives those who are inclined toward functionalism a positive view about autonomous meaning so they can steer away from mere intuition-mongering.

What's the difference between Searle's argument and my argument in Block (1978)? To make a long story short, though our examples were similar, Searle's argument has a wider target, the symbol-manipulating view of the mind common in cognitive science. This view entails functionalism but is not entailed by it. My aim, by contrast, was mainly to argue that functional definitions constructed from commonsense psychology (by a Ramsification procedure) carried a burden of proof. I argued that nothing of any substance had been said in their favor, and there was some reason to doubt them. Desiderata like the ones mentioned in this paper can be used to satisfy this burden of proof – for intentional states but not experiential states.

Compositionality

The points to be made about compositionality are very similar to points already made, so I will be brief.

According to CRS, it is sentences (and perhaps larger chunks of discourse) that embody hypotheses, claims, arguments, and the like, not subsentential elements. So, according to CRS, the semantic values of words and other subsentential elements are a matter of their contributions to the conceptual roles of sentences and supersentential elements. The conceptual role of "and," for example, derives from such facts as that a commitment to rejecting "p" (in the absence of a commitment to accept "p and q") can lead (in certain circumstances) to a commitment to rejecting "p and q." In this way, CRS explains why words have the conceptual roles they do by appeal to conceptual roles of sentences; thus the semantic values of words are seen to be a matter of their causal properties.

The non-reductionist theories do not and should not be regarded as aimed at this type of issue. They are concerned with what the relations among meanings of, say, words and sentences are, not with the issue of why those relations obtain.

What about indicator semantics and Gricean semantics? They, like CRS, take sentential and perhaps supersentential chunks as the basic semantic unit. And, like CRS, they can regard the meanings of words as their contributions to the semantic values of sentences. CRS has no advantage in this matter.

Narrow meaning, twin earth, the explanation of behavior, and the function from context to reference and truth conditions

The hard work of this section was done (or at any rate, attempted) in the desideratum on narrow meaning. I can be brief here, concentrating on objections and extensions.

What is narrow meaning? (Recall that CRS can do without the claim that narrow meaning is genuinely a kind of meaning, rather than a determinant of meaning.) Here, the comparison with the other theories looks quite different than with the other desiderata. CRS does have an answer – namely, conceptual role – and the other theories have no answer. But the other theories I've been mentioning are not *about* narrow meaning.

Why is narrow meaning relevant to the explanation of behavior, and why is it relevant in the same way for me and my twin? Taking the second question first: since my twin and I are physically identical, all of our representations have exactly the same internal causal roles, and hence the same narrow meanings.

But why is narrow meaning relevant to the explanation of behavior in the first place? To have an internal representation with a certain narrow meaning is to have a representation with certain likely inferential antecedents and consequents. Hence, to ascribe a narrow meaning is to ascribe a syndrome of causes and effects, including, in some cases, behavioral effects (or at least impulses in motor-output neurons). The reason my twin and I both jump is that we have representations with conceptual roles that have, as part of their syndrome of effects, jumping behavior. The reason that wide meaning is not as relevant to the explanation of behavior as is narrow meaning is that differences in wide meaning that do not involve differences in narrow meaning (e.g., the difference between me and my twin) do not cause behavioral differences.[78]

The CRS explanation of behavior may seem circular, hence trivial. How can I characterize a meaning functionally, in part in terms of a tendency for representations that have it to cause jumping, and then turn around and explain jumping by appeal to a representation's having this meaning? This is an objection of a well-known sort to explanation in terms of functionally individuated entities, and it has a familiar sort of rebuttal. "Gene" is defined functionally in Mendelian genetics, in part in terms of effects on, for instance, hair color. "Reinforcement" is defined in operant-conditioning circles in part in terms of effects on, for instance, bar-pressing. How, then can one turn around and explain blonde hair in terms of genes, or bar-pressing in terms of history of reinforcement? Part of the answer is that one is not talking about a *single* effect, postulated ad hoc, but rather a complex web of interacting effects. A sickle-cell gene yields sickle-cell anemia in one circumstance (when paired with another sickle-cell gene) but resistance to malaria in another. When one postulates a gene on the basis of one effect, one can obtain converging evidence for it from other effects; and these effects enrich the functional characterization. If you give a rat Burpee Rat Chow (at 80 per cent body weight)[79] contingent on bar-pressing, the rat's bar-pressing response normally increases in strength (on a variety of measures). So it is said that the Burpee Rat Chow is a reinforcer. Part of what makes this a non-empty claim is that one can get the rat to do all sorts of other things using Burpee Rat Chow or other reinforcers.

Second, and more importantly, a functionally individuated entity can, in principle, be identified by independent (usually physicalistic) means and the mechanism of its causal connection to the effects described. For example, a gene identified functionally via the methods of Mendelian genetics can be identified as a clump of DNA via the methods of molecular genetics. And the mechanism by which the gene produces phenotypic characteristics can be described biochemically. Similarly, the mechanism by which Burpee Rat Chow affects behavior can (presumably) be characterized biologically, or perhaps even psychologically (in terms of the rat's information processing).

The application of the first point to CRS is obvious, but the application of the second is more problematic. The problem has to do with the type-token relation for mental representations. The hope is that there will be a stable physical realization (at least over short stretches of time) of, say, the representation "CAT," which of course will be identifiable only by its functional role. Then, in principle, one could trace the causal links between this representation and behavior, just as the biochemist can in principle trace the mechanism by which a gene affects the phenotype.[80]

Let us now turn briefly to the matter of the essential indexical. "I am in the path of danger" and "Ned Block is in the path of danger" can have systematically different conceptual roles, depending on whether I know I am Ned Block (rather than, say, Napoleon). "I," used by a speaker, differs systematically from the speaker's own name in its conceptual role, even though they refer to the same thing. Hence CRS assigns them different narrow meanings. Thus the thought I express with "I" (or its internal associate) is different in narrow content from the thought I would have expressed were my name to have replaced "I." Thus, narrow meaning, as articulated by CRS, can be used to explicate a notion of thought *state* distinct from thought *object* that will serve the purpose for which Perry suggested this distinction.[81]

Similar points apply to the examples using names and natural kind terms mentioned in the desideratum on this subject. "Cicero struts" and "Tully struts" have different conceptual roles; so despite the fact that they have identical wide meanings, we can see why believing these different sentences could have different effects on other mental states and behavior.[82]

Let us now turn again to the determination of the function from context to reference and truth-value. I argued in the section on meaning and reference/truth that conceptual role does determine this function. Take "I," for example. If someone says "I am in danger," one can infer that the speaker has said, of himself, that he is in danger. In general, it is part of the conceptual role of "I" that it refers to the producer of the token of "I" (except in contexts such as quotation). However, there are other aspects of conceptual role that are relevant to, say, explanation of behavior, but not to determination of the function from context to reference and truth value. For example, one can infer from "I entirely fill such and such a spatiotemporal volume" to "You do not occupy this volume." But this inference does not seem relevant to the determination of the aforementioned function. Similar points apply to other types of terms. One can infer from "water" to "colorless" (or, at least to "colorless if pure"); but this has little or nothing to do with determination of reference. I would still be referring to the same liquid even if I were under the impression that in its pure state it has a bluish tinge to it. Indeed, it may be that the aspect of conceptual role that determines the function from context to reference is the same for all natural kind terms. My highly tentative conclusion is that the aspect of conceptual role that determines the function from context to reference and truth-value is a small part of the conceptual roles relevant to the explanation of behavior and psychological state.

In conclusion: in this paper, I have not attempted to elaborate CRS, or supply any analyses of language from its perspective. Rather, I have tried to provide reason for suppressing the "put up or shut up" reflex that dogs talk of conceptual roles in the absence of identity conditions for them. My hope is that this theory will get more attention and that more detailed versions of it will allow us to evaluate its prospects better.[83]

Notes

"Advertisement for a Semantics for Psychology" originally appeared in *Midwest Studies in Philosophy*, X (1986). Copyright © 1986 by the Regents of the University of Minnesota. Reprinted by permission of Midwest Studies in Philosophy Inc. and the author.

1 Good sketches of the ideas of the representational theory of mind are to be found in Fodor (1981a) and Lycan (1981). A more detailed treatment is provided in Pylyshyn (1984).

2 See Block (1983) for a discussion of this distinction and for references to the literature on this topic.

3 I hope my "inherited/autonomous" terminology won't make these questions seem trivial.

4 It is commitment to a priori truth (by which I mean truths for which there is no epistemic possibility of refutation) that really causes trouble for friends of analyticity – not our inability to come up with identity conditions for meaning. After all, no one has ever come up with satisfactory identity conditions for people or ships.

5 Perry (1977, 1979); Kaplan (unpublished).

6 A natural variant on the notion of narrow individuation that I described would require in addition that the same properties be attributed in the same way.

7 Note that the claim that narrow meaning is in the head, in this sense, is not incompatible with the idea that what it is for a word to have a certain narrow meaning is for it to express a concept, where concepts are taken to be abstract objects not locatable in space and time; in this respect, "in the head" is not an apt phrase.

8 Of course, one could define a referential notion of meaning that included narrow meaning and therefore better deserved to be called "wide." This would also result in a more intuitive treatment of vacuous reference. Since the main use I'll be making of the notion of wide meaning is to highlight narrow meaning. I'll stick with the simple definition I've introduced.

9 See Loar (1982), p. 279; White (1982); and Fodor (1986a).

10 Cf. Field (1977).

11 This is a controversial reading of the lesson of Kripke's puzzle. I don't have the space here to describe either the puzzle or the conceptual role semantics solution.

12 White (1982) attempts to *define* a narrow meaning notion using such counterfactuals. But this seems misguided, since there is something shared by the twins *in virtue of which* the counterfactuals are true, and that seems a better candidate for narrow meaning.

13 See McGinn (1982), esp. pp. 211–16, for arguments from the nature of representation to narrow content and meaning.

14   Ignore the problem that, since we are made up largely of water, my twin and I can't be duplicates – fixes for this have been proposed by Putnam and Burge.

15   Burge (1979).

16   Actually, my position is that such a multidimensional gradient is needed for full-blooded narrow meaning, but not for the *part* of narrow meaning responsible for mapping contexts onto referents and truth conditions.

17   See Horwich (1982b). Here is the paradox of the preface: I write a book all of whose sentences I believe; nonetheless, I am sure that, being human, I have asserted at least one falsehood. Contradiction. Solution: I have a high degree of belief in each sentence in the book, but that is compatible with a high degree of belief in the falsity of their conjunction.

18   Variance is mean squared deviation from the mean.

19   Burge (1979). Burge constructs cases in which a man has a slight misunderstanding about how a word is used (e.g., he thinks you can have arthritis in the thigh). He then argues, persuasively, that a doppelgänger of this man in a language community in which "arthritis" is standardly used to include rheumatoid inflammations of bones such as the thigh should not be regarded as meaning by "arthritis" what we and our man mean by the word.

20   Loewer and Lepore (1986) seem to object in this way to two-factor conceptual role semantics.

21   See Harman (1974, 1975, and 1982) and Sellars (1963, 1969, and 1974); see also Putnam (1979).

22   Field (1977, 1978).

23   See Churchland (1979), Loar (1981, 1982), Lycan (1981), McGinn (1982), and Schiffer (1981). Loar and Schiffer advocated conceptual role semantics only as a subsidiary semantic theory for the language of thought, if there happens to be one. The semantic theory they advocated for external language is a functionalized Gricean theory.

24   Woods (1977, 1978, and 1981).

25   Johnson-Laird (1977) and Miller and Johnson-Laird (1976).

26   Though in a paper given at the MIT Sloan Conference, 1984, Field suggests a view in which meaning and content are abandoned altogether. Field's 1977 and 1978 papers are quite skeptical about intersubjective comparisons of conceptual role – because of the collateral information problem. For that reason, he placed great weight on the referential component; recent skepticism about the referential component has led to skepticism about meaning and content altogether.

27   That is, the narrow aspect or determinant of meaning.

28   McGinn (1982) states the theory as assigning states of affairs to sentences. This leads Loewer and Lepore (1986) to suppose that a two-factor theory must be more liberal than Davidsonian truth theory in allowing, in the external factor: "Water is wet" is true ↔ H_2O is wet. But a two-factor theorist *can* adopt Davidsonian truth theory for the external factor, even though demanding that the sentence on the right-hand side of the biconditional be a *translation* of the quoted sentence on the left-hand side is a stronger demand than necessary for the two-factor theorist.

29   For purposes of this discussion, I shall be ignoring pictorial internal representations.

30   Brain-writing, as everyone knows, is spelled in capital letters.

31. See Kahneman, Slovic, and Tversky (1982) and references therein for detailed studies of such fallacies.
32 Harman (1970) contrasts code-breaking views of language understanding with incorporation views. On the latter, understanding English is translation into a different language; whereas, on the former, English is part of the language of thought (actually, a system of syntactic structures with English vocabulary items is part of the language of thought), so no translation is involved.
33 Harman (1982), p. 14.
34 See Loar (1982), pp. 278–80, for a different slant on what is wrong with Harman's view. Loar takes the line that devices such as Harman's "normal context" and conceptual role in the minds of experts are ad hoc.
35 Johnson-Laird's reply (1978) to Fodor pretty much abandons this verificationist tendency in favor of a generalized conceptual role much like the idea I've been alluding to here.
36 Fodor (1978); reprinted Fodor (1981a), p. 211.
37 Dretske (1983), p. 88.
38 This is well argued by Stich (1983). (Although, as I think Sterelny 1985, shows, Stich deploys the wrong notion of "potential" in characterizing his functional roles.) Oddly, Stich considers mental representations, functionally individuated, without ever considering whether there is a distinction to be made between the aspect of functional role relevant to semantics and the aspect that might be called syntactic. (Indeed, these are in effect identified on p. 200.) This is a distinction we make with respect to English orthography. If someone writes the letter "a" in an idiosyncratic way, we can identify it *functionally*, by the way it appears in words – e.g., it appears by itself, it appears in "*b*n*n**," in place of the asterisks, etc. At the same time, we can distinguish functionally between two uses of the same syntactic type, "bank."
39 Fodor (1986a).
40 See Hills (1981), pp. 18–19, for a discussion of the two ways of talking about internal symbolism, and Harman (1973) for an application of the representational state version.
41 See Horwich (1982b) for a discussion of this issue in another context.
42 Lycan (unpublished) argues that God could tell us which worlds were the ones in which a sentence is true without telling us what the sentence means. I think he is right, but only for the reason mentioned in the text. God could indicate the possible worlds in a way that allows us to represent which ones they are without representing what they have in common in virtue of which they are the ones in which the sentence is true. See Lycan's paper for a discussion of indexicals and for references to the literature on this topic.
43 See also Loar (1982), p. 277.
44 This is Putnam's claim in an influential series of articles beginning with "The Analytic and the Synthetic" (1962); the few decompositional definitions he allows are those that, like "bachelor" = never-married adult male; involve a single "criterion." The idea is that the term "bachelor" responds to only one "concern," and so there is no possibility that different concerns will "pull apart," creating a situation in which we will have to choose arbitrarily how the word is to apply.

Putnam has also formulated a version of the argument given below against Fodor's innateness thesis.

45   Of course, it is not a particularly *new* story. Indeed, it is just what you would expect if you believed aspects of Quine and Kuhn, or if you accepted Lewis's "functional definition" story in "How to Define Theoretical Terms" (Lewis, 1970). See Kuhn (1983) for semantic views quite close to those of conceptual role semantics.

46   I have heard it said that a conceptual role account of meaningfulness is much more plausible than a conceptual role account of particular meanings. This view is reminiscent of the cognitive theory of emotions that says that what makes a state an emotional state is a certain type of physiological arousal, but what makes such a state joy as opposed to anger is a difference in cognitive "overlay." The application of this idea to semantics cannot be evaluated in the absence of a suggestion as to what it is that accounts for the differences among meanings. Just one comment: in the case of experiential mental states, this type of view is less plausible than the reverse: that some sort of physiological state makes a state experiential, whereas functional *differences* are responsible for the difference between pain and the sensation of red.

47   These theories can often explain semantic defects in complex entities on the basis of the semantic properties of primitives. For example, Katzian semantics can explain why "red idea" is semantically defective on the basis of the semantic values of "red" and "idea." But Katzian semantics can give no answer to the question of what makes a primitive meaningful element meaningful. The Katzian accommodates the difference between "red" and "glub" by putting "red" but not "glub" in his dictionary. But it is not part of the theory to give an account of *why*.

48   This article is a jointly written pseudointerview in which the quoted material is put in Barwise's mouth (p. 51), but Perry continues the line of thought.

49   See Stalnaker (1984) for an attempt to solve this within the possible-worlds framework.

50   I derive this objection by analogy to a point made with regard to truth in Soames (1984), p. 426.

51   This may be Soames's view in the article mentioned in note 50, and I also see a tendency towards this view in Katz (1982), though Katz and Soames probably have different notions of necessity in mind.

52   Though, in the case of at least one version of the Gricean approach, not naturalistic.

53   See the statement of the theory in Schiffer (1982).

54   I used to think that the Fodor-Putnam multiple realizability arguments against physiological reductionism settled the matter. Their point, in essence, was that physiological reductionism was a chauvinist thesis in that, construed as a theory of the mind *simpliciter*, it would exclude intelligent machines or Martians. I now think that the best one is likely to get in the way of a theory of the mind will be a theory of the *human* mind. Such a theory will inevitably be chauvinist. The representational theory of mind that I am adopting here is a theory in that chauvinist tradition. What makes physiological reductionism look so bad is not simply that it is chauvinist – i.e., not just that there are merely *possible* creatures that share our intentional states without sharing our physiology – but rather that we do

have promising theories of the human mind and that they are computational-representational (which is not to say that they are committed to the claim that the brain is a digital computer). If the scientific "essence" of intentional states is computational-representational, then it is not physiological – for the old multiple realizability reasons. So multiple realizability is the nub of the matter, but only because one chauvinist theory of the mind is multiply realizable in terms of another.

55 This comes through loud and clear in Searle (1980).

56 Though in a draft of an article circulated in 1984, Schiffer rejects his earlier approach.

57 See Posner (1978) and Fodor (1982).

58 Sternberg (1969).

59 I can't possibly go into the details here. Dretske's view is couched in terms of the interesting notion of the *most specific information* that a tokening of a representation carries about a state of affairs.

60 Barwise (1984), p. 8.

61 The theory is sketched in Fodor (1983a, 1984) and expounded in detail in Fodor (1990c; see Loar, 1983 for further comments on this paper), which Fodor is now saving for a book he is preparing of the same title. The reason I devote so much space to a largely unpublished account is that the problems with Fodor's account, together with Fodor's refutation of the Dretske-Stampe view, gives us an excellent picture of the type of problem faced by indicator semantics.

62 I am indebted to Paul Horwich here.

63 See, for example, the articles in the relevant section of Sober (1984a).

64 There are disagreements about the *extent* of forces orthogonal to optimality. Lewontin and Gould, for example, are controversial in their insistence that the extent of such orthogonal forces is very great. (See their article in Sober, 1984a.) But this disagreement in the field should not obscure the important agreement mentioned in the text.

65 This issue can be discussed in terms quite distant from evolutionary biology. One example considered by Fodor is that, when it comes to beliefs about poisons, false negatives are much more damaging than false positives. False positives ("This is a poison," said of something that is harmless) can cost you a meal, but false negatives can cost you your life. There are mechanisms in rats and even people that could perhaps be interpreted as inclining one to overattribute noxiousness to foods. Fodor insists that, in such cases, one should *always* interpret the organisms as paying heed to low probabilities of very bad things rather than falsely ascribing high probabilities to the had things. He sees this as a product of a principle of charity. The trouble with this reply is that this is not an a priori issue. If the mental sentence theory of belief is right, there is a difference between acting on a belief that p and acting on an estimate that, though p is unlikely, it would be terrible if true. Independent evidence could be marshalled in favor of one or another alternative. Further, even if Fodor's a priori assumption is right about our cognitive mechanisms, it is contingently right. If we come to understand how our cognitive mechanisms work, perhaps we could build cognitive mechanisms that work otherwise. It would be a strange semantic theory that depends on such a

highly contingent and perhaps quite alterable fact about the cognitive mechanisms that we happen to have. Such a semantic theory would not apply to robots who think, act, and talk almost exactly as we do, but, say, are built to overattribute poisonous qualities to foods on the basis of slim evidence. Will Fodor say we are barred by the logic of the concepts involved from building such a robot?

Another problem with Fodor's a prioristic method of handling these cases is that he is forced to adopt, ad hoc, *other* methods of handling other cases in which supposedly cognitive mechanisms don't aim at truth. In considering the possibility that our cognitive mechanisms are built to *repress* certain unpleasant truths, Fodor stipulates that such mechanisms are not cognitive. He is stuck with simply stipulating which mechanisms are cognitive and which are not.

66 There is a parallel problem in causal theories of reference that *seems* more tractable, but perhaps only because it is more familiar.

67 Quoted in Mandler (1983). On this issue, as on many others, one finds glimmers of quite different views in Piaget. There are other passages where he seems to have some appreciation of the Berkeleyan point I make below. See also the discussion in Fodor (1975).

68 This is not the only argument for the third code. There are powerful empirical reasons for postulating a third code. See Potter, Valian, and Faulconer (1977) for both the good and the bad reasons for believing in a third code. Brison (unpublished) contains an excellent rebuttal of arguments for a third code that make this (and other) mistakes. See also Kolers and Brison (1984).

69 Recall that I am ignoring the mind, concentrating on the brain.

70 The issue of psychologism naturally comes up with respect to this issue, but I have already answered it a number of times.

71 Unless they include in their causal chains the causal roles inside the head, in which case they include CRS itself.

72 Field (1977), p. 390.

73 This example is similar to ones described in Block (1978, 1981b).

74 See the replies in the issue of *Behavioral and Brain Sciences* in which Searle's article appeared and the interchange between Searle and Dennett in *New York Review of Books* (Searle, 1983b; Dennett, 1983a).

75 See Block (1980, 1981b).

76 At the appropriate level of abstraction, of course. In this case, as in others I have mentioned, identity of conceptual role is compatible with a variety of causal differences.

77 The only reply I've seen that contains a glimmer of the CRS reply is Haugeland's in the BBS issue just mentioned (Haugeland, 1980).

78 Burge (1986) objects that this use of "behavior" begs the question in favor of individualistic accounts, behavioral ascriptions often being non-individualistic. I agree that ordinary behavior descriptions are non-individualistic. I would argue along the lines suggested in Desideratum 8 that an important line of work in cognitive psychology *is* individualistic.

79 To make sure it is hungry – an explanation avoided by most of those who condition rats.

80 Actually, I think there is less of a problem here than meets the eye. Letters of the

alphabet are individuated functionally – that is why we recognize shapes that we have never seen before as A's. But what allows us to do this is some degree of stability in the shapes of other letters. It is hard to see how there could fail to be some analogous story about how the brain works – if representationalism is true.

81   This point is similar to the one made by Lycan (1981), (See also Dennett, 1982b.) However, Lycan somehow sees this point as an argument for the internal sentence story (the conceptual role semantics comes in almost incidentally). I talk about thoughts rather than beliefs because the representationalist story is more plausible for occurrent mental states. As many commentators have pointed out, one can ascribe a belief if it follows in a simple way from what a person has explicitly thought, even if the belief ascribed has never actually occurred to the person. See Fodor (1987).

82   On Kripke's puzzle: since "Londres" and "London" have different conceptual roles, it is a mistake to accept Kripke's translation principle. In particular, from the fact that Pierre croit que Londres est jolie, we should not conclude that Pierre believes London is pretty – if the content of his belief is given by "London is pretty." Lycan (1981) and McGinn (1982) have interesting discussions of the conceptual role semantics reponse to Kripke's puzzle, but neither pinpoint the translation principle as the culprit.

83   I am grateful to the John Simon Guggenheim Memorial Foundation and the Center for the Study of Language and Information for support while writing this paper. I would like to thank Michael Bratman, Martin Davies, Hartry Field, Jerry Fodor, Gilbert Harman, Paul Horwich, David Israel, Phil Johnson-Laird, Jerry Katz, Brian Loar, Bill Lycan, and Georges Rey for their helpful comments on earlier drafts.

5 Why Meaning (Probably) Isn't Conceptual Role

Jerry Fodor and Ernest Lepore

Introduction

It's an achievement of the last couple of decades that people who work in linguistic semantics and people who work in the philosophy of language have arrived at a friendly, *de facto* agreement as to their respective job descriptions. The terms of this agreement are that the semanticists do the work and the philosophers do the worrying. The semanticists try to construct actual theories of meaning (or truth theories, or model theories, or whatever) for one or another kind of expression in one or another natural language; for example, they try to figure out how the temperature could be rising compatibly with the substitutivity of identicals. The philosophers, by contrast, keep an eye on the large, foundational issues, such as: what's the relation between sense and denotation; what's the relation between thought and language; whether translation is determinate; and whether life is like a fountain. Every now and then the philosophers and the semanticists are supposed to get together and compare notes on their respective progress. Or lack thereof.

Accordingly, this paper is about not semantics but the philosophy of language. Some of us have been poking around in the basement of meaning theory, and we seem to have discovered a large, nasty crack; as far as we can tell, one of the foundation stones is coming unstuck. We thought we'd better tell you about it before things get worse.

We'll proceed as follows: first we'll try to say where in the foundations the problem is located; then we'll try to say what the problem is; and then we'll make a suggestion or two about what to do about the problem. The first part of the discussion will be very broad; the second part will be rather more specific; the third part will be practically non-existent.

Here goes.

1 Where the Problem Is

A traditional foundational problem in the theory of meaning is: *where do semantic properties come from?* The presupposition of this question is that the fact that a word (or a sentence, or whatever) means what it does can't be a brute fact. It can't be a brute fact, for example, that "dog" means *dog* and not *proton* and that "proton" means *proton* and not *dog*. Rather, "dog" must have some *non*-semantic property in virtue of which it means *dog* and not *proton*; and "proton" must have some (different) non-semantic property in virtue of which it means *proton* and not *dog*. To put it in the standard philosophical jargon, semantic properties must *supervene on* non-semantic properties. There may be some properties that things *just* have; that they have for no reason at all. But if there are, they are the kinds of properties that basic physics talks about (like mass, charge, and charm). They certainly don't include the kinds of properties that semanticists talk about (like meaning *dog* or being a synonym of "bachelor").

We remark in passing that none of this is to be construed as an attempt to legislate physicalism. For present purposes we're content that semantic properties should be, for example, irreducibly intentional, or irreducibly epistemological, or irreducibly teleological. But we take it to be not on the cards that they are irreducibly semantic. In short, we don't care whether semantic properties supervene on something that is *physical* just as long as they supervene on something other than themselves.

So the question arises: what *do* the semantic properties of symbols supervene on? Over the years, philosophers of language have been enthusiastic for two quite different (perhaps, indeed, incompatible) kinds of answers to this question. There's what we will call the "Old Testament" story, according to which the meaning of an expression supervenes on *the expression's relation to things in the world*; and there's what we will call the "New Testament" story, according to which the meaning of an expression supervenes on the expression's *role in a language*. The disagreement between these two sorts of story is venerable, and we don't propose to go into the details here. Just a paragraph or two by way of assembling reminders.

Old Testament semantics derives most directly from the British Empiricists and has, among its modern representatives, behaviorist psychologists like Watson and Skinner and a handful of philosophers in the "naturalized semantics" movement (including Dretske, Millikan, Barwise and Perry in certain of their moods, and one or more of the Fodors). The basic idea is that "dog" means *dog* because of some (non-semantic) relation that holds between the symbol and the animal. If you are a British Empiricist (or, at least, if you're Hume), you say that this relation comes down to some variant on resemblance; "dog" means *dog* rather than *proton* because "dog" is associated to a certain mental image that means *dog* rather than *proton*. And the mental image means *dog* rather than *proton* because it resembles dogs quite a lot but resembles protons hardly at all. If you are a behaviorist psychologist, you say that the symbol-world relation that semantic properties supervene on is *causal* (typically associative); "dog" means *dog* rather than *proton* because, in consequence of the speaker's history of conditioning (or something) dogs cause utterances of "dog" and protons don't. Recent developments of Old Testament semantics propose still other variations on this theme, including, for example, appeals to nomological and/or informational relations between symbols and the world.

Now, this Old Testament story about meaning has come under a lot of criticism, both in philosophy and in linguistics. Perhaps the basic objection is one that derives from Frege: meaning *can't* be a symbol-world relation, according to this objection, because *identity* of symbol-world relations is compatible with *difference* of meaning. Thus, it's plausible that the expressions "The Morning Star" and "The Evening Star" are both attached to the same non-linguistic thing (*viz.* to Venus); but it's also plausible that they don't *mean* the same thing. If they did, you couldn't deny that the Morning Star is the Evening Star without self contradiction or assert that it is without tautology. Both of which, in fact, you can.

So, then, according to this argument, the meaning of an expression doesn't supervene on the way that it's attached to the world. So what *does* it supervene on?

The New Testament story is an elaboration of the following idea: the expressions "The Morning Star" and "The Evening Star" mean different things, despite their both being attached to Venus, because they have different *roles in the (English) language*. "Only in the context of a sentence does a word have a meaning" says Frege, and Wittgenstein adds that "to understand a sentence is to understand a language." The core idea is that it's the way they are connected *to one another* that determines what the expressions in a language mean. Very often (in fact, in all the semantic theories that we will discuss) this notion of "role in the language" is given an epistemological twist: to master a linguistic expression is to be disposed to draw some core set of *inferences* that fix its semantic relation to other expressions in the language. To master the expression "dog" is, *inter alia*, to be prepared to infer from "Rover is a dog" to "Rover is an animal." To master the expression "The Morning Star" is, *inter alia*, to be prepared to infer from "is the Morning Star" to "rises in the Morning." And so forth.

We want to emphasize that, at this stage, we're using notions like *infer* and *disposed to infer* as blank checks. For the moment we'll let any disposition to have one belief cause another count as a disposition to infer the second from the first. So deductive inference, and inductive inferences, and plausible inferences, and prudential inferences, and mere associations, and Heaven knows what all else, are included *pro tem*. A lot of this paper will be about problems that arise when a New Testament semanticist tries to say exactly which inferences are constitutive of the meanings of the terms that enter into them.

The New Testament picture in philosophy is quite close to one that's familiar from structuralist linguistics, according to which the meaning of an expression is its role in a "system of differences." To know what "dog" means is to know that it excludes "cat" and cohabits with "animal." To know what "bachelor" means is to know that it excludes "spinster" and cohabits with "unmarried." Notice that it follows from this view that, if English didn't contain words that mean what "cat" and "animal" do, *it couldn't contain a word that means what "dog" does*. This is a kind of conclusion that structuralists in semantics have, with varying degrees of enthusiasm, quite generally been prepared to embrace.

Although, as far as we can tell, one or other version of the New Testament view is held practically as gospel not only in linguistics and philosophy, but throughout the Cognitive Sciences, it is nevertheless possessed of well-known problems. For example, New Testament semantics appears to be intractably holistic. This is because, once you start identifying the content of a belief with its inferential role in a system of beliefs (*mutatis mutandis*, the meaning of an expression with its inferential role in a language), it's hard to avoid proceeding to identify the content of a belief with its *whole* inferential role in the system of beliefs. And, having gone that far, it's hard to avoid the conclusion that, if belief systems differ at all with respect to the propositions they endorse, then they differ completely with respect to the propositions they endorse. (*Mutatis mutandis*, if languages differ at all in respect of the propositions they can express, then they differ entirely in respect of the propositions they can express.[1]) This is a well-greased, and well travelled, slippery slope; having arrived at the bottom, one finds oneself accepting such *prima facie* outlandish doctrines as that no two people ever share a belief; that there is no such relation as translation; that no two people ever mean the same thing by what they say; that no two time slices of *the same* person ever mean the same thing by what they say; that no one can ever change his mind; that no statements, or beliefs, can ever be contradicted (to say nothing of refuted); and so forth. It's a moot question how to get the goodness out of inferential role semantics without paying this extravagant price. Indeed, it's moot whether it is possible to do so.

Serious though these worries are, however, they are all, as it were, *external* to semantics as such; they impugn its consequences for epistemology and ontology rather than its actual coherence. And a convinced New Testament semanticist might be prepared to bite the bullet. If the doctrine that meaning supervenes on intralinguistic relations has relativistic, idealistic or even solipsistic consequences, then perhaps we had better learn to live with relativism, idealism or even solipsism. There are many, especially on the West Coast, who clearly long to do so.

Well, so much for the background; now here's the problem. It looks to us as though there are serious *linguistic* problems for the functional role approach to meaning. We want to argue that, quite aside from ontology and epistemology, it looks like New Testament semantics can't be squared with a pair of linguistic hypotheses that practically everybody thinks there are very good reasons to endorse; and which, *de facto*, most New Testament semanticists actually *do* endorse. These are, first, that natural languages are compositional, and, second, that the analytic/synthetic (a/s) distinction is unprincipled. (This means not that the distinction is *vague* – what empirical distinction isn't? – but that there aren't any expressions that are true or false solely in virtue of what they mean.) The foundational problem to which we wish to call your attention is that these two principles together with New Testament semantics form an inconsistent triad. At least one of the three will have to go.

The next section of this paper sketches our argument for this claim; the third asks what on earth to do about it.

2   Compositionality, Analyticity and Inferential Role Semantics

There is, we believe, an internal connection between analyticity and compositionality that hasn't previously been remarked upon and that has dire implications for the New Testament identification of meanings with inferential roles. We commence our exploration of this territory with a few remarks about compositionality.

A language is *compositional* iff (idioms aside) the meaning of its syntactically complex expressions is a function of their syntactic structures together with the meanings of their syntactic constituents. For present purposes, a language is compositional iff the meaning of its sentences is a function of their syntactic structural descriptions together with the meanings of their lexical constituents. We take the doctrine that natural languages are compositional to be, as one says in Britain, non-negotiable.

No doubt connectionist psychologists (and a handful of philosophers) have occasionally been moved to dispense with compositionality. But that just indicates the desperateness of their plight. For, compositionality is at the heart of some of the most striking properties that natural languages exhibit. The most obvious of these are *productivity* (roughly, the fact that every natural language can express an open-ended set of propositions) and *systematicity* (roughly, the fact that any natural language that can express the proposition P will also be able to express many propositions that are semantically close to P. If, for example, a language can express the proposition that aRb, then it can express the proposition that bRa; if it can express the proposition that $P \rightarrow Q$, then it can express the proposition that $Q \rightarrow P$; and so forth.)

We digress to remark (since the issue often comes up) that pairs like "John calculated the answer" and *"the answer calculated John" are *not* exceptions to the systematicity of English. Systematicity requires that, generally, if a language can express the proposition P and the proposition P is semantically close to the proposition Q, then the language can also express Q. If, however, there *is no* such proposition as Q, it is no objection to its systematicity that a language can't express it. We are inclined to think that there is no such proposition as that the answer calculated John, hence that the present examples do not constitute an objection to the systematicity of English. We do not, however, wish to dogmatize. If there *is* such a proposition as that the answer calculated John, then English *can* express it; indeed the form of words "the answer calculated John" does so. English is thus systematic on either assumption.

Connected to both productivity and systematicity is a further, apparently perfectly universal, feature of natural languages. The structure of sentences is, in the following sense, *isomorphic* to the structure of the propositions they express: *if a sentence S expresses the proposition that P, then syntactic constituents of S express the constituents of P.* If for example, a sentence expresses the proposition that P and Q, then there will be one syntactic constituent of the sentence that expresses the proposition that P and another syntactic constituent that expresses the proposition that Q. If a sentence expresses the proposition that John loves Mary, then there will be a syntactic constituent of the sentence that refers to John, another syntactic constituent of the sentence that refers to Mary, and another syntactic constituent of the sentence that expresses a relation such that, necessarily, that relation holds between x and y iff x loves y. Notice that, though all of this is patent, none of it is truistic. Idioms and other "holophrastic" constructions are all exceptions, albeit the sorts of exceptions that prove the rule.[2]

Our point is that these three generalizations about natural languages – productivity, systematicity and isomorphism – are connected and explained on the assumption of compositionality; they are all consequences of the principle that the meaning of a sentence is composed from the meanings of its parts. And they appear to be completely baffling otherwise. So, we intend to insist on compositionality in what follows.

Now we get to the crack in the foundation. It turns out that compositionality is an *embarrassment* for the kind of New Testament semantics that identifies the meaning of an expression with its inferential role. In particular, it invites the following kind of *prima facie* argument:

- meanings are compositional
- but inferential roles are *not* compositional
- so meanings can't be inferential roles.

The second step is, of course, the one that's doing the work. But it seems pretty obviously sound. Consider the meaning of the phrase "brown cow"; it depends on the meanings of "brown" and "cow" together with its syntax, just as compositionality requires. To a first approximation, "brown" means – if you like, it connotes the property – BROWN, "cow" means COW, and the semantic interpretation of the syntactic structure $(ADJECTIVE + NOUN)_N$ is property conjunction. (We are aware that there are problems about decoy ducks and the like; but the assumption that language is compositional is the assumption that such problems can be solved.) But now, *prima facie*, the inferential role of "brown cow" depends not only on the inferential role of "brown" and the inferential role of "cow," *but also on what you happen to believe about brown cows.* So, unlike meaning, inferential role is, in the general case, *not* compositional.

Suppose, for example, you happen to think that brown cows are dangerous; then it's part of the inferential role of "brown cow" in your dialect that it does (or can) figure in inferences like *"brown cow → dangerous."* But, first blush anyhow, this fact about the inferential role of "brown cow" doesn't seem to derive from corresponding facts about the inferential roles of its constituents. You can see this by contrasting the present case with, for example, inferences like *"brown cow → brown animal"* or *"brown cow → not-green cow."* "Brown animal" follows from "brown cow" because "cow" entails "animal"; "not-green cow" follows from "brown cow" because "brown" entails "not-green." But it doesn't look like either "brown" or "cow" entails "dangerous," so, to this extent, it doesn't look like the inference from "brown cow" to "dangerous" is compositional.

In short, it appears that some, but not all, of the inferential potential of "brown cow" (some of its role in one's language or belief system) is determined by the respective inferential potentials of "brown" and "cow," the rest being determined by one's "real world" beliefs about brown cows. This should not seem surprising or contentious; it's just a way of saying that "brown cows are dangerous" (unlike "brown cows are animals" and "brown cows are not-green" and "brown cows are brown") is clearly synthetic. That is "brown cows are dangerous" is *contingently* true, true in virtue of the facts about brown cows, not in virtue of the facts about meanings (assuming that it's true at all).

But, to repeat, if meanings are compositional and inferential roles aren't, then if follows that meanings can't be inferential roles.

As far as we can tell, this line of argument is quite robust; in particular, it doesn't depend on detailed assumptions about how an inferential role semantics construes the notion of inferential role. There is, for example, an influential paper by Hartry Field in which inferential role is analyzed in terms of subjective probabilities; in effect, the inferential role of your thought that P is identified with the subjective probability that you (would) assign to P contingent on each of the other thoughts that you (can) entertain (Field, 1977). So, for example, the inferential role of your thought that it's raining is determined in part by the subjective probability that you (would) assign to that thought on the assumption that the streets are wet; and in part by the subjective probability that you (would) assign to it on the assumption that the sun is out; and in part by the subjective probability that you (would) assign to it on the assumption that elephants have wings . . . and so forth. Like other species of New Testament semantics, this treatment generalizes, in fairly obvious ways, from a theory according to which inferential roles are assigned to thoughts to one in which they are assigned to linguistic expressions, or to both.

Our point is that the construal of inferential roles in terms of subjective probabilities, whatever other virtues it may have, does nothing to help with the compositionality problem. This is because *subjective probabilities are not them-selves compositional.* For example, the subjective probability one assigns to the thought that *brown cows are dangerous* is *not* a function of the subjective probability one assigns to the thought that *cows are dangerous*, together with the subjective probability that one assigns to the thought that *brown things are dangerous.* If this seems not obvious, consider a world (or rather a belief world, since the probabilities at issue are supposed to be subjective) where there are very many things that are cows, almost none of which is dangerous, and very many things that are brown, almost none of which is dangerous, and a very small number of brown cows, almost all of which are very, very fierce. On these assumptions, the probability that something that is brown is dangerous is small, and the probability that something that is a cow is dangerous is small, but the probability that a brown cow is dangerous is as big as you please.

We intend the argument so far as one horn of a dilemma, and we anticipate the following reply:

> OK, so if the compositionality of meaning is assumed, meanings can't be iden-tified with inferential roles as such. But this doesn't *really* embarrass New Testament semantics because meanings can still be identified with roles in *analytic* inferences. Thus, on the one hand, the inference "brown cow → brown animal" is compositional (it's inherited from the inference "cow → animal") and, on the other hand, precisely because it is compositional, "brown cow → brown animal" is analytic. Compositional inferences will always be analytic and analytic infer-ences will always be compositional; the compositionality of an inference and its analyticity *are the same thing.*
>
> Look at it this way: if "brown cow → brown animal" is compositional, then it's warranted by the inferential roles of the expressions "brown" and "cow." That's what it is for an inference to be compositional. But, according to New Testament semantics, the inferential roles of "brown" and "cow" *are their meanings.* So, then, that "brown cow → brown animal" is warranted follows from the *meanings* of "brown" and "cow." But for an inference to be analytic *just is* for it to be warranted by the meanings of its constituent expressions. So the com-positionality of "brown cow → brown animal" – or, *mutatis mutandis,* of any other inference – *entails* its analyticity. The same argument also works the other way around. For an inference to be analytic is for it to be warranted by the meanings of its constituents. But, according to New Testament semantics, meanings are inferential roles. So, for an inference to be analytic is for it to be warranted by the inferential roles of its constituents. But for the warrant of an inference to be determined by the inferential roles of its constituents is for the inference to be compositional. So compositionality entails analyticity and vice versa. So, then, meaning is compositional and inferential role isn't and role in analytic inference is. What all that shows is just that we need a revised version of New Testament semantics; one which identifies meaning with role in analytic inference.

The first thing to say about this new suggestion is that the threat of circ-ularity is now very close to the surface. It is proposed that we reconcile New Testament semantics with the compositionality of meaning by identifying the meaning of an expression with its role in analytic inferences. But the difference between analytic inferences and inferences *tout court* is just that the validity of the former is guaranteed *by the meanings* of their constituent expressions. So analyticity and meaning (and compositionality) scrape out a living by doing one another's wash, and Quine gets to say "I told you so."

Notice also that the naturalizability of inferential role semantics is jeopardized by the present proposal. A lot of the attraction of identifying meaning with inferential role lies in the thought that the inferential role of an expression might in turn be identified with *causal* role, thereby conceivably providing the basis for a naturalistic solution to Brentano's problem. That causal relations reconstruct inferential relations is a foundational assumption of computational theories of mental processes, so perhaps there is hope here of a unification of semantics with psychology. But, barring proposals for a causal theory of analyticity, this tactic is unavailable to the philosopher who identifies meaning with the role of an expression in *analytic* inference.[3] The idea that mental processes are computational may provide the basis for a naturalistic account of inference, but it offers no insight at all into the nature of analyticity. Nor, as far as we can see, does anything else.

We can now say pretty exactly what our problem is: you can't identify meanings with inferential roles *tout court*, since, unlike meanings, inferential roles *tout court* aren't compositional. You *can* identify meanings with roles in *analytic* inferences, however, because analytic inferences *are* compositional. But, of course, the cost of identifying meanings with roles in analytic inferences is buying into the analytic/synthetic distinction. So the cost of New Testament semantics is buying into the analytic/synthetic distinction. But, these days, practically everybody thinks that the analytic/synthetic distinction is unprincipled. Indeed, it's widely thought that the discovery that the analytic/synthetic distinction is unprincipled is one of the two most important achievements of modern philosophy of language; the other being precisely the theory that meaning supervenes on inferential role. If, then, we continue to assume that compositionality is non-negotiable, it follows that one of these foundational principles of the philosophy of language is going to have to go. Which one? And with what are we to replace it?

3 What Now?

This is where we ought to tell you how to go about mending the cracked foundations; and we promise you that we would if we could. Since we can't, however, we'll restrict ourselves to a few more or less jaundiced remarks on what we take the visible options to be and on what we think that adopting one or other of them is likely to cost.

The first possibility one might consider is to try resuscitating the analytic/synthetic distinction. There is, we think, a certain face plausibility to this suggestion. We've been seeing that compositionality and analyticity come to much the same thing so long as you accept the New Testament view that meaning supervenes on inferential role. But, in fact, it's plausible that compositionality entails analyticity *whether or not* you accept New Testament semantics. So, for example, it's hard to see how anybody could claim that the meaning of "brown cow" is *compositional* while denying that the inference from "brown cow" to "brown" is *analytically valid*. If it is undeniable that the meaning of "brown cow" is constructed from the meanings of "brown" and "cow," it seems equally undeniable, and for the same reasons, that the inference from "brown cow" to "brown" is guaranteed by the linguistic principles that effect this construction. But an inference that is guaranteed by linguistic principles *just is* an analytic inference. In short, the very structural relations among the constituents of a sentence that ground its compositionality would appear to engender the analyticity of some of the inferences in which its constituents are involved.

So, to repeat, it appears that compositionality underwrites certain analyticities all by itself, without further appeal to the principle that meaning supervenes on inferential roles. A New Testament semanticist might thus reasonably argue that, if compositionality is non-negotiable, so too is analyticity; hence that the rejection of Quine's anti-analyticity arguments is independently motivated. (It's worth mentioning in this respect that Quine says little or nothing about examples like "brown cow → brown," where the analyticity of an inference depends on the *structure* of its premises rather than their lexical contents.) But if the revival of the analytic/synthetic distinction can be defended, it looks as though everything is all right. We're seen that you can't have New Testament semantics and compositionality *and the rejection of a/s*, but you certainly can have the first two if you drop the third.

We emphasize, however, that the kind of a/s distinction that compositionality underwrites holds only between expressions and their *syntactic constituents*. It thus serves to distinguish, say, "brown cow → brown" from "brown cow → dangerous." But it does *not* underwrite a distinction between, say, "brown cow → animal" and "brown cow → dangerous." That is, it doesn't underwrite an analytic/synthetic distinction among inferences that turn on the lexical inventory of the premises as opposed to their linguistic structure. It is, however, precisely these lexically governed inferences that make trouble for New Testament semantics.

If the meaning of "brown cow" derives from the meanings of "brown" and "cow" (as it must if the meaning of "brown cow" is compositional) and if the meaning of "cow" is its inferential role (as it must be if New Testament semantics is right), then it must somehow be arranged that "brown cow" inherits the inference "animal" *but not the inference "dangerous"* from the meanings of its constituents. But that requires that we exclude from the semantic representation of "cow" such information as, for example, "cow →

kind of x such that the brown x-s are dangerous" (and analogously, we must exclude from the semantic representation of "brown" such information as "brown → x such that the cow x-s are dangerous"). But to say that we must treat these inferences as excluded from the semantic representations of "cow" and "brown" is just to say that they are *not* constitutive of the meanings of "cow" and "brown." But to say *that* is to presuppose an analytic/synthetic distinction that applies to lexically governed inferences. And it is precisely an analytic/synthetic distinction for lexically governed inferences that the familiar Quinean polemics are widely supposed to jeopardize.

We've been putting a lot of weight on the difference between analyticities that are engendered by the compositional structure of an expression and those that are generated by the meanings of items in its vocabulary. This distinction is, of course, undermined if you assume that there is a level of representation at which lexical items are semantically decomposed: to posit such a level is, in effect, to hold that lexical meaning is itself compositional. So if there is lexical decomposition, then we can identify the meaning of an expression with its role in those inferences that are determined by its compositional structure *including the compositional structure of its lexical items*. The effect is to assimilate inferences like "brown cow → animal" to inferences like "brown cow → brown" since, at the level of semantic representation, both involve relations between expressions and their constituents. And both are distinguished from "brown cow → dangerous" since, presumably, "dangerous" isn't a constituent of the representations of "brown cow" at *any* linguistic level.

But, of course, to resolve the present worries by taking lexical decomposition for granted simply begs the question against Quine. If lexical meanings were compositional, then lexical items would be definable; and it's part of Quine's story about there being no principled a/s distinction that there is no principled notion of definition. If Quine's arguments show anything, they show that there is no way to reconstruct the intuition that "brown cow → animal" is definitional and "brown cow → dangerous" isn't.

We conclude that, although there may be reasons for resuscitating the analytic/synthetic distinction, the non-negotiability of compositionality isn't one of them. Compositionality licenses a distinction between "brown cow → brown" and "brown cow → dangerous" but not between "brown cow → dangerous" and "brown cow → animal." So the original problem stands: if compositionality isn't negotiable, then either there is an analytic/synthetic distinction for lexically governed inferences (contra Quine), or inferential roles aren't what meaning supervenes on (contra New Testament semantics).

Our second point is that the present situation is rife with ironies. We remarked above that, once you say that the meaning of an expression supervenes on its inferential role, it's hard to stop short of saying that the meaning of an expression supervenes on its *whole* inferential role. That is, it's hard to stop short of relativizing the meaning of an expression to the whole language that contains it, with the consequence that expressions in different languages are semantically incommensurable. There is a sort of linguistic idealist who delights in these holistic implications of New Testament semantics; you see more than a trace of this sensibility among the "cognitive linguistics" crowd, among connectionists, and, of course, among philosophers like Rorty, Putnam, Kuhn and Derrida. It now appears, however, that inferential role semantics *doesn't have* any holistic implications after all, so relativism loses however the argument turns out.

Here, roughly, is how the argument from inferential role semantics to semantic holism was supposed to go:

> *Premise 1, New Testament Semantics*: The meaning of an expression is at least partially constituted by the expression's inferential relations.
>
> *Premise 2, No A/S Distinction*: There is no principled distinction between those of its inferential relations that constitute the meaning of an expression, and those that don't.
>
> *Conclusion, Semantic Holism*: The meaning of an expression is constituted by *all* of its inferential relations, hence by all of its role in a language.

There are, we think, lots of reasons to disapprove of this way of defending semantic holism; not least that it depends, apparently ineliminably, upon a form of slippery slope argument, and these are notorious for leading from true premises to false conclusions. (That is, it depends on arguing from "there's no principled difference between the Fs that are Gs and the Fs that aren't" to "either none of the Fs are Gs or all of them are.") For present purposes, however, we're prepared to ignore all that. The point we want to emphasize is that the argument can't be better than its second premise; that is, the argument from inferential role semantics to semantic holism explicitly *depends on* denying a/s.

So, the situation is this: if the analytic/synthetic distinction is principled, then the second premise is false and the argument for semantic holism is unsound. But if the analytic/synthetic distinction is *un*principled, then the first premise is false. This is because, as we've been seeing, respecting compositionality requires that the meaning of an expression be identified with its role in *analytic* inferences; and compositionality isn't negotiable. But the argument that there is no analytic/synthetic distinction is the argument that there *aren't any* analytic inferences. We assume the law of excluded middle – either there is an analytic/synthetic distinction or there isn't. Either way, the argument from inferential role semantics to semantic holism has to be unsound. We suppose that this demonstration should darken the skies of West Coast semantic holists. So be it; they need the rain.

The foundational problem, to recapitulate, is that you can't do all of the following: endorse inferential role semantics *AND* endorse compositionality *AND* abandon the a/s distinction. If compositionality is non-negotiable, that leaves you with only two options: endorse the a/s distinction or reject the idea that meaning supervenes on inferential role. We can't tell you which of these it would be best to do, but we do want to insist that wriggling isn't likely to get you off the hook. In particular, lots of cognitive scientists have hoped to reconcile themselves to the Quinean arguments by opting for a graded, or a contextualized, or otherwise denatured notion of analyticity. The idea is that, although Quine may have shown that the notion of *identity* of meaning is in trouble, it's still open that a notion of *similarity* of meaning might be evolved. It's supposed that grading the analytic/synthetic distinction would allow us to have *both* compositionality *and* the supervenience of meaning on inferential role. New Testament semantics would thus be vindicated, albeit in a sort of soft-edged version.

Nobody has shown that this can't be done; but nor does anybody have the slightest idea of how to do it. It seems to us that the arguments against a principled notion of identity of meaning work just as well against a principled notion of similarity of meaning, but we won't try to make that case here.[4] Suffice it for present purposes to remark that the connections between analyticity and compositionality that we've been examining make the search for a graded notion of analyticity look unpromising. Compositionality is, after all, a principle that governs relations *among meanings* (it governs the relation between the meaning of a complex expression and the meanings of its constituents). So, if your semantic theory reconstructs meaning in terms of analytic inference, and if you have only a graded notion of analyticity, *then you will have to live with a graded notion of compositionality as well.* But what would a graded notion of compositionality be like? And, in particular, how would such a notion do what compositionality is required to do: *viz.* account for systematicity, isomorphism and productivity?

Wouldn't a graded notion of compositionality entail, at best, that a finite acquaintance with a language is adequate to *sort of understand* expressions not previously encountered? Or that, if a language is capable of expressing the proposition that aRb, then it is *sort of* capable of expressing the proposition that bRa? Or that if the sentence S expresses the proposition P, then the constituents of S *sort of* express the constituents of P? But is there any sense to be made of such claims as, for example, that

> ("John loves Mary" sort of expresses the proposition that John loves Mary) only if "John" sort of refers to "John?"

These are muddy waters and we do not recommend that you wade in them.

Here's where we've gotten to: compositionality is non-negotiable; inferential roles are compositional only if the analytic/synthetic distinction is tenable for inferences that are governed by the lexical inventory. So, if Quine was right about a/s, the only remaining alternative is to give up on the New Testament idea that the meaning of lexical items is constituted by their inferential roles. Barring some proposal for an entirely new kind of semantics, this requires going back of the Old Testament view that what makes "dog" mean *dog* is some sort of symbol-world connection; perhaps some sort of causal or informational or nomological connection between tokens of the expression type and tokens of the animal type. There are, as remarked above, various accounts of this currently on offer and, who knows, maybe one of them can be made to work.

The spinoffs for epistemology would be of some interest since the plausible candidates for the semantically relevant symbol to world relations all look to be *atomistic*. If, for example, "dog" means *dog* because dogs cause "*dog*"s, then it looks like your language could have a word that means what "dog" means in English even if your language didn't have any other words that mean what English words do. *Prima facie*, in fact, it looks as though your language could have a word that means what "dog" means in English even if it doesn't have any other words *at all*. All sorts of holistic arguments against the possibility of translation (and, more generally, against the commensurability of languages and ideologies) would then appear to be likely to collapse. More dark skies on the West Coast.

We aren't, to repeat the point one last time, actually urging you to follow this course. On the contrary, a lot of linguists will have good reason for not wanting to do so. For example, if Old Testament semantics is essentially right, what becomes of such linguistic studies as "lexical semantics"? You can't study the semantic relations among lexical items unless there *are* semantic relations among lexical items; and it's the burden of Old Testament semantics that there aren't. Old Testament semantics has it that semantic relations hold between lexical items *and the world* and *only* between lexical items and the world.[5] Old Testament semantics has, therefore, no truck with semantic fields, lexical decompositions, conceptual networks and the like. If, indeed, what you mean by "the semantic level of linguistic description" is the level of description at which sentences that differ only in synonymous expressions are identically represented, the natural way to read the Old Testament is as denying that there *is* a semantic level of linguistic description. So generative semantics goes, and interpretive semantics *also* goes, and the highest level of linguistic description is, as it might be, syntax or logical form: *viz.* a level where the surface inventory of nonlogico-syntactic vocabulary is preserved. The God of the Old Testament is an austere God.

As previously remarked, our present purpose isn't to sell you any such chilly theology; just to point out that there seems to be this crack in the foundations of the structure in which semanticists and philosophers of language have recently been cohabiting. And to urge that somebody do something about it not later than sometime before the roof falls in.

Notes

"Why Meaning (Probably) Isn't Conceptual Role" originally appeared in *Mind and Language*, 6, 4 (1991) and is reprinted here by permission of Blackwell Publishers and the authors.

1　The issues we'll be concerned with arise in precisely parallel ways for theories of the meanings of linguistic expressions and theories of the contents of thoughts. In the rest of what follows, we will not bother to draw this distinction unless something turns on it.

2　Our statement of the isomorphism principle is intentionally left pretty vague; deep issues arise when more precision is attempted. Suppose, for example, that you hold that (in a null discourse) the sentence "it's raining" expresses the proposition that it's raining in the context of utterance. Then either you must say that "it's raining" has more constituents than appear on its surface or that the isomorphism principle can be violated by pragmatically carried information. For present purposes, we propose not to broach these sorts of issues.

3　There are causal theories of meaning around; see, for example, Skinner (1957), Dretske (1981) and Fodor (1990b) among many others. And each of them implies a corresponding notion of analyticity. But all these theories are externalist and atomist and thus offer no comfort either to New Testament semantics or to holism. They don't legitimate a construal of meaning in terms of *analytic* inference because they reject New Testament semantics; they don't reconstruct meaning in terms of inference at all.

4　See Chapters 1 and 7 of Fodor and Lepore (1992).

5　More precisely, the Old Testament view holds that, if there are semantic relations among lexical items, they are derived not from relations between their roles in the language but from relations between their connections to the world; *ceteris paribus*, two expressions connected to the world in the same way will be synonyms. But it is, of course, precisely the inferential relations among lexical items, and *not* their symbol-world relations, that the semantic level of lexical description has always been supposed to represent.

6 Misrepresentation

Fred Dretske

Epistemology is concerned with knowledge: how do we manage to get things right? There is a deeper question: how do we manage to get things wrong? How is it possible for physical systems to *misrepresent* the state of their surroundings?

The problem is not how, for example, a diagram, d, can misrepresent the world, w. For if we have another system, r, already possessed of representational powers, d can be used as an expressive extension of r, thereby participating in r's representational successes and failures. When this occurs, d can come to mean that w is F when, in fact, w is not F, but d's meaning derives, ultimately, from r. A chart depicting unemployment patterns over the past ten years can misrepresent this condition, but the chart's capacity for misrepresentation is derived from its role as an expressive instrument for agents, speakers of the language, who already have this power.

No, the problem is, rather, one of a system's powers of representation in so far as these powers do not derive from the representational efforts of another source. Unless we have some clue to how this is possible, we do not have a clue how naturally evolving biological systems could have acquired the capacity for belief. For belief is, or so I shall assume, a *non-derived* representational capacity the exercise of which *can* yield a misrepresentation.

The capacity for misrepresentation is a part, perhaps only a small part, of the general problem of meaning or intentionality. Once we have meaning, we can, in our descriptions and explanations of human, animal, and perhaps even machine behaviour, lavish it on the systems we describe. Once we have intentionality, we can (to use Dennett's language) adopt the intentional stance.[1] But what (besides intentionality) gives us (and not, say, machines) the power to adopt this stance? Our ability to adopt this stance is an *expression*, not an analysis, of intentionality. The borrowed meaning of systems towards which we adopt appropriate attitudes tells us no more about the original capacity for misrepresentation than does a misplaced pin on a military map. What we are after, so to speak, is *nature*'s way of making a mistake, the place where the misrepresentational buck stops. Only when we understand this shall we understand how grey matter can misrepresent the weather for tomorrow's picnic.

1   Natural Signs

Naturally occurring signs mean something, and they do so without any assistance from us.[2] Water does not flow uphill; hence, a northerly flowing river means there is a downward gradient in that direction. Shadows to the east mean that the sun is in the west. A sudden force on the passengers in one direction means on acceleration of the train in the opposite direction. The power of these events or conditions to mean what they do is independent of the way we interpret them – or, indeed, of whether we interpret or recognize them at all. The dentist may *use* the X-ray to diagnose the condition of your upper right molar, but the dark shadows mean extensive decay has occurred whether or not he, or anyone else, appreciates this fact. Expanding metal indicates a rising temperature (and in this sense means that the temperature is rising) whether or not anyone, upon observing the former, comes to believe the latter. It meant that *before* intelligent organisms, capable of exploiting this fact (by building thermometers), inhabited the earth. If we are looking for the ultimate source of meaning, and with it an understanding of a system's power of misrepresentation, here, surely, is a promising place to begin.

Natural signs are indicators, more or less reliable indicators, and what they mean is what they indicate to be so. The power of a natural sign to mean something – for example, that Tommy has measles – is underwritten by certain objective constraints, certain lawful relations, between the sign (or the sign's having a certain property) and the condition that constitutes its meaning (Tommy's having measles). In most cases this relation is causal or lawful, one capable of supporting a counterfactual assertion to the effect that, if the one condition had not obtained (if Tommy did not have measles), neither would the other (he would not have those red spots all over his face). Sometimes there are merely regularities, non-lawful but none the less pervasive, that help secure the connection between sign and significance. It is partly the fact, presumably not itself lawful, that animals (for example, squirrels or woodpeckers) do not regularly ring doorbells while foraging for food that makes the ringing bell *mean* that someone (i.e., some *person*) is at the door. If squirrels changed their habits (because, say, doorbells were made out of nuts), then a ringing doorbell would no longer mean what it now does. But as things *now* stand, we can (usually) say that the bell would not be ringing unless someone was at the door, that the bell indicates someone's presence at the door, and that, therefore, that is what it means. But this subjunctively expressed dependency between the ringing bell and someone's presence at the door is a reflection of a regularity which, though not conventional, is not fully lawful either. None the less, the doorbell retains its natural meaning as long as this regularity persists.

Beyond this I have nothing very systematic to say about what constitutes the natural meaning of an event or a condition.[3] I shall proceed with what I hope is a reasonably familiar notion, appealing (when necessary) to concrete examples. The project is to see how far one can go in understanding misrepresentation, the power of a condition (state, event, situation) r to mean (say, indicate) *falsely* that w is F (thereby misrepresenting w), in terms of a natural sign's meaning that w is F. Only when (or if) this project succeeds, or shows reasonable prospects of succeeding, will it, or might it, be necessary to look more carefully at what got smuggled in at the beginning.

Though natural meaning is a promising point of departure, it is hard to see how to get under way. Natural signs, though they mean something, though they can (in this sense) represent w (by indicating or meaning that w is F), are powerless to *misrepresent* anything. Either they do their job right or they don't do it at all. The spots on Tammy's face certainly can mean that he has measles, but they mean this *only* when he has measles. If he doesn't have measles, then the spots don't mean this. Perhaps all they mean is that Tommy has been eating too many sweets.

Grice expresses this point by saying that an occurrence (a tokening of some natural sign) means (in what he calls the natural sense of "meaning" – hereafter meaning$_n$) that P only if P.[4] He contrasts this sense of meaning with nonnatural meaning where a sign can mean that P even though P is false. If we reserve the word "meaning" (minus subscripts) for that species of meaning in which something can mean that w is F when w isn't F, the kind of meaning in which misrepresentation is possible, then meaning$_n$ seems a poorly qualified candidate for understanding meaning.

In speaking of signs and their natural meaning I should always be understood as referring to *particular* events, states or conditions: *this* track, *those* clouds, and *that* smoke. A sign type (for example, smoke) may be said to mean, in some natural sense, that there is fire even when every token of that type fails to mean$_n$ this (because, occasionally, there is no fire). But this type-associated meaning, whatever its proper analysis, does *not* help us understand misrepresentation unless the individual tokens of that type *have* the type-associated meaning, unless particular puffs of smoke mean$_n$ that there is fire when there is no fire. This, though, is not the case. A petrol gauge's registration of "empty" (this *type* of event) can signify an empty tank, but when the tank is not empty, no particular registration of "empty" by the gauge's pointer means$_n$ that the tank is empty. Hence, no particular registration of the gauge misrepresents the amount of gas in the tank (by meaning$_n$ that it is empty when it is not).

The inability of (particular) natural signs to misrepresent anything is sometimes obscured by the way we exploit them in manufactured devices. Interested as we may be in whether, and if so when, w becomes F, we concoct a device d whose various states are designed to function as natural signs of w's condition. Since this is how we use the device, we tend to say of some particular registration that d's being G (assuming this is the natural sign of w's being F) means that w is F even when, through malfunction or misuse, the system is failing to perform satisfactorily and w is not F. But this, clearly, is not what the particular pointer position means$_n$. This is what it is *supposed* to mean$_n$, what it was *designed* to mean$_n$, what (perhaps) tokens of type *normally* mean$_n$, but not what it *does* mean$_n$.

When there is a short circuit, the ring of the doorbell (regardless of what it was designed to indicate, regardless of what it normally indicates) does not indicate that the bellpush is being pressed. It still means$_n$ (indicates) that there is electric current flowing in the doorbell circuit (one of the things it always means$_n$), but the latter no longer means$_n$ that the bellpush is being pressed. What the flow of current *now* means$_n$ – and this is surely how we would judge it if we could *see* the bellpush, *see that* it was *not* being pressed – is that the system is malfunctioning or that there is a short circuit somewhere in the wiring. The *statement*, "There is someone at the door," can mean that there is someone at the door even when no one is there, but the ringing doorbell cannot mean this when no one is there. Not, at least, if we are talking about meaning$_n$. If the bellpush is not being pressed, then we must look for something else for the ringing bell to mean$_n$. Often, we withdraw to some more proximal meaning$_n$, some condition or state of affairs in the normal chain of causal antecedents that *does* obtain (for example, the flow of current or the *cause* of the flow of current – for example, a short circuit) and designate it as the meaning$_n$ of the ringing bell.

2   Functional Meaning

Granted, one may say, the doorbell's ringing cannot mean$_n$ that someone is at the door when no one is there; still, in some related sense of meaning, it means this whether or not anyone is there. If this is not natural meaning (meaning$_n$), it is a close cousin.

Whether it is a cousin or not, there certainly is a kind of meaning that attaches to systems, or components of systems, for which there are identifiable *functions*. Consider, once again, the fuel gauge. It has a function: to pass along information about the amount of petrol in the tank. When things are working properly, the position of the needle is a natural sign of the contents of the tank. Its pointing to the left means$_n$ that the tank is empty. Its pointing to the right means$_n$ that the tank is full. And so on for the intermediate positions. But things sometimes go wrong: connections work loose, the battery goes dead, wires break. The gauge begins to register "empty" when the tank is still full. When this happens there is a tendency to say that the gauge misrepresents the contents of the tank. It *says* the tank is empty when it is not. It *means* (not, of course means$_n$, but still means in *some* sense) that the tank is empty.

When d's being G is, normally, a natural sign of w's being F, when this is what it normally means$_n$, then there is a sense in which it means this whether or not *w* is *F* *if it is the function of d to indicate the condition of w*. Let us call this kind of meaning *meaning*$_f$ – the subscript indicating that this is a functionally derived meaning.

> (M_f) *d*'s being *G* means$_f$ that *w* is *F* = *d*'s function is to indicate the condition of *w*, and the way it performs this function is, in part, by indicating that *w* is F by its (*d*'s) being *G*

The position of the needle on the broken fuel gauge means$_f$ that the tank is empty because it is the gauge's function to indicate the amount of remaining fuel, and the way it performs this function is, in part, by indicating an empty tank when the gauge registers "empty".[5] And, for the same reason and in the same sense, the ringing doorbell says (i.e., means$_f$) that someone is at the door even when no one is there.

Whether or not M_f represents any progress in our attempt to naturalize meaning (and thus understand a system's non-derivative power to misrepresent) depends on whether the functions in question can themselves be understood in some natural way. If these functions are (what I shall call) *assigned* functions, then meaning$_f$ is tainted with the purposes, intentions, and beliefs of those who assign the function from which meaning$_f$ derives its misrepresentational power.[6] We shall not have tracked meaning, in so far as this involves the power of misrepresentation, to its original source. We shall merely have worked our way back, somewhat indirectly, to *our own* mysterious capacity for representation.

To understand what I mean by an *assigned* function, and the way *we* (our intentions, purposes and beliefs) are implicated in a system's having such a function, consider the following case. A sensitive spring-operated scale, calibrated in fractions of a gram, is designed and used to determine the weight of very small objects. Unknown to both designers and users, the instrument is a sensitive indicator of altitude. By registering a reduced weight for things as altitude increases (note: a thing's weight is a function of its height above sea level), the instrument *could* be used as a crude altimeter if the user attached a standard weight and noted the instrument's variable registration as altitude changed. Suppose, now, that under normal use in the laboratory the instrument malfunctions and registers 0.98 g for an object weighing 1 g. Is it misrepresenting the *weight* of the object? Is it misrepresenting the *altitude* of the object? What does the reading of 0.98 g mean? If we are talking about meaning$_n$, it clearly does not mean$_n$ that the object weighs 0.98 g. Nor does it mean$_n$ that the laboratory is 40,000 ft. above sea level. If we ask about meaning$_f$, though, it seems reasonable to say that the instrument's pointer says or indicates (i.e., means$_f$) that the object weighs 0.98 g. It is the function of this instrument to tell us what objects weigh, and it is telling us (incorrectly, as it turns out) that this object weighs 0.98 g.

But is the altitude being misrepresented? No. It should be noticed that the instrument cannot be misrepresenting *both* the altitude and the weight since a representation (or misrepresentation) of one presupposes a *fixity* (hence, non-representation) of the other.[7] Although the instrument *could* be used as an altimeter, it *is not* used that way. That is not its function. Its function is to register weight. That is the function we assign to it, the reason it was built and the explanation why it was built the way it was. Had our purposes been otherwise, it might have meant$_f$ something else. But they were not and it does not.

We sometimes change an instrument's assigned function. When we calibrate it, for example, we do not use it to measure what it is normally used to measure. Instead, we apply it to known quantities in order to use its indication as a (natural) sign of possible malfunction or inaccuracy in the instrument itself. In this case, a reading of 0.98 g (for a weight *known* to be 1 g) indicates that the spring has changed its characteristics, the pointer is bent, or some other component is out of adjustment. We get a new functional meaning because our altered background knowledge (normally a result of different intentions and purposes) changes what the pointer's behaviour means$_n$. With *assigned* functions, the meanings$_f$ change as *our* purposes change.[8]

We sometimes use animals in the same way that we use instruments. Dogs have an acute sense of smell. Exploiting this fact, customs officers use dogs to detect concealed marijuana. When the dog wags it tail, barks, or does whatever it is trained to do when it smells marijuana, the dog's behaviour serves as a natural sign – a sign that the luggage contains marijuana. But this does not mean that the dog's behavior (or the neural condition that triggers this behavior) can misrepresent the contents of the luggage. The dog's behavior may make the customs officer believe (falsely) that there is marijuana in the suitcase, but the dog's behavior means$_f$ this only in a derived way. If the dog is particularly good at its job, barking only when there is marijuana present, we can say that its bark indicates (i.e., means$_n$) that there is marijuana present. Furthermore, it means$_n$ this whether or not anyone interprets it as meaning$_n$ this, whether or not we *use* this natural sign for our own investigative purposes. But when there is no marijuana present, when the dog barks at an innocent box of herbs, the bark does *not* mean$_n$ that there is marijuana present. Nor does it mean$_f$ this in any sense that is independent of *our* interpretative activities. We can, of course, say what the bark means to *us* (that there is marijuana in the suitcase), but this way of talking merely reveals our own involvement in the meaning assigned to the dog's behavior. *We* assign this meaning because this is the information we are *interested* in obtaining, the information we *expect* to get by using the dog in this way, the information the dog was trained to deliver. But if we set aside our interests and purposes, then, *when there is no marijuana present*, there is *no* sense in which the dog's bark means that there is marijuana in the suitcase. The only kind of misrepresentation occurring here is of the derived kind we are familiar with in maps, instruments, and language.

Therefore, if M_f is to serve as a naturalized account of representation, where this is understood to include the power of *mis*representation, then the functions in question must be *natural* functions, functions a thing has which are independent of *our* interpretative intentions and purposes. What we are looking for are functions involving a system of natural signs that give these signs a content, and therefore a meaning (i.e., a meaning$_f$) that is not parasitic on the way *we* exploit them in our information-gathering activities, on the way we choose to interpret them.[9]

We need, then, some characterization of a system's natural functions. More particularly, since we are concerned with the function a system of natural signs might have, we are looking for what a sign is *supposed* to mean$_n$ where the "supposed to" is cashed out in terms of the function of that sign (or sign system) in the organism's *own* cognitive economy. We want to know how *the dog* represents the contents of the luggage – what (if anything) the smell of the box means$_f$ *to it*.

3 Needs

The obvious place to look for natural functions is in biological systems having a variety of organs, mechanisms, and processes that were developed (flourished, preserved) *because* they played a vital information-gathering role in the species' adaptation to its surroundings. An information-gathering function, essential in most cases to the satisfaction of a biological need, can only be successfully realized in a system capable of occupying states that serve as natural signs of external (and sometimes *other* internal) conditions. If that cluster of photoreceptors we call the retina is to perform its function (whatever, exactly, we take this function to be), the various states of these receptors must mean$_n$ something about the character and distribution of one's optical surroundings. Just what the various states of these receptors mean$_f$ will (in accordance with M_f) be determined by two things: (1) what it is the function of this receptor system to indicate, and (2) the meaning$_n$ of the various states that enable the system to perform this function.

To illustrate the way M_f is supposed to work it is convenient to consider simple organisms with obvious biological needs – some thing or condition without which they could not survive. I say this is convenient because this approach to the problem of misrepresentation has its most compelling application to cognitive mechanisms subserving some basic biological need. And the consideration of *primitive* systems gives us the added advantage of avoiding that kind of circularity in the analysis that would be incurred by appealing to those kinds of "needs" (for example, my need for a word processor) that are derived from desires (for example, my desire to produce faster, cleaner copy). We cannot bring desires in at this stage of the analysis since they already possess the kind of representational content that we are trying to understand.

Some marine bacteria have internal magnets (called magnetosomes) that function like compass needles, aligning themselves (and, as a result, the bacteria) parallel to the earth's magnetic field.[10] Since these magnetic lines incline downwards (towards geomagnetic north) in the northern hemisphere (upwards in the southern hemisphere), bacteria in the northern hemisphere, oriented by their internal magnetosomes, propel themselves towards geomagnetic north. The survival value of magnetotaxis (as this sensory mechanism is called) is not obvious, but it is reasonable to suppose that it functions so as to enable the bacteria to avoid surface water. Since these organisms are capable of living only in the absence of oxygen, movement towards diamagnetic north will take the bacteria away from oxygen-rich surface water and towards the comparatively oxygen-free sediment at the bottom. Southern-hemispheric bacteria have their magnetosomes reversed, allowing them to swim towards geomagnetic south with the same beneficial results. Transplant a southern bacterium in the North Atlantic and it will destroy itself – swimming upwards (towards magnetic south) into the toxic, oxygen-rich surface water.

If a bar magnet oriented in the opposite direction to the earth's magnetic field is held near these bacteria, they can be lured into a deadly environment. Although I shall return to the point in a moment (in order to question this line of reasoning), this appears to be a plausible instance of misrepresentation. Since, in the bacteria's normal habitat, the internal orientation of their magnetosomes means$_n$ that there is relatively little oxygen in *that* direction, and since the organism needs precisely this piece of information in order to survive, it seems reasonable to say that it is the function of this sensory mechanism to serve the satisfaction of this need, to deliver this piece of information, to indicate that oxygen-free water is in *that* direction. If this is what it is *supposed* to mean$_n$, this is what it means$_f$. Hence, in the presence of the bar magnet and in accordance with M_f, the organism's sensory state misrepresents the location of oxygen-free water.

This is not to say, of course, that bacteria have *beliefs*, beliefs to the effect that there is little or no oxygen in *that* direction. The capacity for misrepresentation is only *one* dimension of intentionality, only *one* of the properties that a representational system must have to qualify as a belief system. To qualify as a belief, a representational content must also exhibit (among other things) the familiar opacity characteristic of the propositional attitudes, and, unless embellished in some way, meaning$_f$ does not (yet) exhibit *this* level of intentionality. Our project, though, is more modest. We are looking for a naturalized form of misrepresentation and, if we do not yet have an account of false *belief*, we do, it seems have a naturalized account of false *content*.

Apart from some terminological flourishes and a somewhat different way of structuring the problem, nothing I have said so far is particularly original. I have merely been retracing steps, some very significant steps, already taken by others, I am thinking especially of Stampe's seminal analysis of linguistic representation in which the (possibly false) content of a representation is identified with what would cause the representation to have the properties it has under conditions of well-functioning;[11] Enc's development of functional ideas to provide an account of the intentionality of cognitive states;[12] Fodor's application of teleological notions in supplying a semantics for his "language of thought";[13] and Millikan's powerful analysis of meaning in terms of the variety of proper functions a reproducible event (such as a sound or a gesture) might have.[14] I myself have tried to exploit (vaguely) functional ideas in my analysis of belief by defining a structure's semantic content in terms of the information it was developed to carry (hence, acquired the function of carrying).[15]

4 The Indeterminacy of Function

Though this approach to the problem of meaning – and, hence, misrepresentation – has been explored in some depth, there remain obstacles to regarding it as even a promising sketch, let alone a finished portrait, of nature's way of making a mistake.

There is, first, the question of how to understand a system's ability to misrepresent something for which it has no biological need. If O does not need (or need to avoid) F, it cannot (on the present account) be the *natural* function of any of O's cognitive systems to alert it to the presence (absence, location, approach, identity) of F. And, without this, there is no possibility of *mis*representing something *as* F. Some internal state could still mean$_n$ that an F was present (in the way the state of Rover's detector system means$_n$ that the luggage contains marijuana), but this internal state cannot mean$_f$ this. What we have so far is a way of understanding how an organism might misrepresent the presence of food, an obstacle, a predator, or a mate (something there is a biological need to secure or avoid),[16] but no way of understanding how *we* can misrepresent things as, say, can-openers, tennis-rackets, tulips, or the jack of diamonds. Even if we suppose our nervous systems sophisticated enough to indicate (under normal conditions) the presence of such things, it surely cannot be the *natural* function of these neural states to signal the presence – much less, specific kinds – of kitchen utensils, sporting equipment, flowers, and playing cards.

I think this is a formidable, but *not* an insuperable, difficulty. For it seems clear that a cognitive system might develop so as to service, and hence have the natural function of servicing, some biological need without its representational (*and* misrepresentational) efforts being confined to these needs. In order to identify its natural predator, an organism might develop detectors of color, shape, and movement of considerable discriminative power. Equipped, then, with this capacity for differentiating various colors, shapes, and movements, the organism acquires, as a fringe benefit so to speak, the ability to identify (and, hence, misidentify) things for which it has no biological need. The creature may have no need for green leaves, but its need for pink blossoms has led to the development of a cognitive system whose various states are capable, because of their need-related meaning$_f$, to mean$_f$ that there are green leaves present. Perhaps, though having no need for such things, it has developed a taste for them and hence a way of representing them with elements that already have a meaning$_f$.

There is, however, a more serious objection to this approach to the problem of misrepresentation. Consider, once again, the bacteria. It was said that it was the function of their magnetotactic system to indicate the whereabouts of oxygen-free environments. But why describe the function of this system in this way? Why not say that it is the function of this system to indicate the direction of geomagnetic north? Perhaps, to be even more modest, we should assign to this sensor the function of indicating the whereabouts (direction) of magnetic (not necessarily *geo*magnetic) north. This primitive sensory mechanism is, after all, functioning perfectly well when, under the bar magnet's influence, it leads its possessor into a toxic environment. *Something* is going wrong in this case, of course, but I see no reason to place the blame on the sensory mechanism, no reason to say it is not performing *its* function. One may as well complain that a fuel gauge is not performing its function when the petrol tank is filled with water (and the driver is consequently misled about the amount of *petrol* he has left). Under such abnormal circumstances, the instrument is performing its duties in a perfectly satisfactory way – i.e., indicating the amount of liquid in the tank. What has gone wrong is something for which the instrument itself is not responsible: namely, a breakdown in the normal correlations (between the quantity of liquid in the tank and the quantity of petrol in the tank) that make the gauge serviceable as a *fuel* gauge, that allow it (when conditions are normal) to mean$_n$ that there is petrol in the tank. Similarly, there is nothing wrong with one's perceptual system when one consults a slow-running clock and is, as a result, misled about the time of day. It is the function of one's eyes to tell one what *the clock says*; it is the function of *the clock* to say what the time is. Getting things right about what you need to know is often a *shared* responsibility. You have to get G right and G has to get F right. Hence, even if it is F that you need, or need to know about, the function of the perceptual system may be only to inform you of G.

If we think about the bacterium's sensory system in this way, then *its* function is to align the organism with the prevailing magnetic field. It is, so to speak, the job of magnetic north to be the direction of oxygen-free water. By transplanting a northern bacterium in the southern hemisphere we can make things go awry, but *not* because a hemispheric transplant undergoes *sensory* disorientation. No, the magnetotactic system functions as it is supposed to function, as it was (presumably) evolved to function. The most that might be claimed is that there is some *cognitive* slip (the bacterium mistakenly "infers" from its sensory condition that *that* is the direction of oxygen-free water). This sort of reply, however, begs the question by presupposing that the creature *already* has the conceptual or representational capacity to represent something *as* the direction of oxygen-free water. Our question is *whether* the organism has this capacity and, if so, where it comes from.[17]

Northern bacteria, it is true, have no need to live in northerly climes *qua* northerly climes. So to describe the function of the bacterium's detectors in terms of the role they play in identifying geomagnetic north is not to describe them in ways that reveal *how* this function is related to the satisfaction of its needs. But we do not have to describe the function of a mechanism in terms of its possessor's ultimate biological needs.[18] It is the function of the heart to circulate the blood. Just *why* the blood needs to be circulated may be a mystery.

So the sticky question is: *given* that a system needs F, and *given* that mechanism M enables the organism to detect, identify or recognize F, *how* does the mechanism carry out this function? Does it do so by representing *nearby Fs as nearby Fs* or does it, perhaps, represent them merely *as nearby Gs*, trusting to nature (the correlation between F and G) for the satisfaction of its needs? To describe a cognitive mechanism as an F-detector (and, therefore, as a mechanism that plays a vital role in the satisfaction of an organism's needs) is not *yet* to tell the functional story by means of which this mechanism does its job. All we know when we know that O needs F and that m enables O to detect F is that M *either* means$_f$ that F is present *or* it means$_f$ that G is present where G is, in O's natural surroundings, a natural sign of F's presence (where G means$_n$ F).[19] If I need vitamin C, my perceptual-cognitive system should not automatically be credited with the capacity for recognizing objects *as* containing vitamin C (as meaning$_f$ that they contain vitamin C) just because it supplies me with the information required to satisfy this need. Representing things as oranges and lemons will do quite nicely.

The problem we face is the problem of accounting for the misrepresentational capacities of a system *without* doing so by artificially *inflating* the natural functions of such a system. We need some *principled* way of saying what the natural function of a mechanism is, what its various states not only *mean$_n$* but what they *mean$_f$*. It sounds a bit far-fetched (to my ear at least) to describe the bacteria's sensory mechanism as indicating, and having the function of indicating, the whereabouts of oxygen. For this makes it sound as though it is not performing its function under deceptive conditions (for example, in the presence of a bar magnet). This is, after all, a *magneto*tactic, not a *chemo*tactic, sensor. But if we choose to describe the function of this sensor in this more modest way, we no longer have an example of a system with misrepresentational powers. A northern bacterium (transplanted in the southern hemisphere) will not be misrepresenting anything when, under the guidance of its magnetotactic sensor, it moves upwards (towards geomagnetic north) into the lethal surface water.

The alignment of its magnetosomes will mean$_n$ what it has always meant$_n$, what it is its function to mean$_n$, what it is supposed to mean$_n$: namely, that *that* is the direction of magnetic north. The disaster can be blamed on the abnormal surroundings. Nor can we salvage some residual misrepresentational capacity by supposing that the bacterium, under the influence of a bar magnet, at least misrepresents the direction of geomagnetic north. For, once again, the same problem emerges: why suppose it is the function of this mechanism to indicate the direction of *geo*magnetic north rather than, simply, the direction of the surrounding magnetic field? If we describe the function only in the latter way, it becomes impossible to fool the organism, impossible to make it misrepresent anything. For its internal states only mean$_f$ that the magnetic field is pointing in *that* direction and (like a compass) this is always accurate.

5   Functional Determination

For the purpose of clarifying issues, I have confined the discussion to simple organisms with primitive representational capacities. It is not surprising, then, to find no clear and unambiguous capacity for misrepresentation at this level. For this power – and, presumably, the dependent capacity for belief – requires a certain threshold of complexity in the information-processing capabilities of a system. Somewhere between the single cell and man we cross that threshold. It is the purpose of this final section to describe the character of this threshold, to describe the *kind* of complexity responsible for the misrepresentational capabilities of higher organisms.

Suppose an organism (unlike our bacterium) has *two* ways of detecting the presence of some toxic substance F. This may be because the organism is equipped with two sense modalities, each (in their different way) sensitive to F (or some modally specific natural sign of F), or because a single sense modality exploits different external signs (or symptoms) of F. As an example of the latter, consider the way we might identify oak trees visually by either one of two ways: by the distinctive leaf pattern (in the summer) or by the characteristic texture and pattern of the bark (in winter). We have, then, two internal states or conditions, I_1 and I_2, each produced by a different chain of antecedent events that are natural signs of the presence of F. Each means$_n$ that F is present. Suppose, furthermore, that, having a need to escape from the toxic F, these internal states are harnessed to a third state, call it R, which triggers or releases a pattern of avoidance behavior. Figure 6.1 assembles the relevant facts. R, of course, is also a natural sign of F. Under normal circumstances, R does not occur unless F is present. f_1 and f_2 are properties typical of normal Fs. s_1 and s_2 are proximal stimuli.

If, now, we present the system with some ersatz F (analogous to the bar magnet with the bacteria), something exhibiting *some* of the properties of the

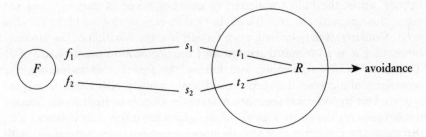

Figure 6.1

real f (say f_1), we trigger a chain of events (s_1, I_1, R and avoidance) that normally occurs, and is really only appropriate, in the presence of F. If we look at the internal state R and ask what it means$_f$ under these deceptive conditions, we find ourselves unable to say (as we could in the case for the bacteria) that it means$_f$ anything short of (i.e., more proximal than) F itself. Even though s_1 (by means of I_1) is triggering the occurrence of R, R does not mean$_n$ (hence, cannot mean$_f$) that s_1 (or f_1) is occurring. R is analogous to a light bulb connected to switches wired in parallel *either* of whose closure will turn the light on. When the bulb lights up, it does not mean$_n$ that switch no. 1 is closed even when it is this switch's closure that causes the light to go on. It does not mean$_n$ this, because there is no regular correlation between the bulb lighting up and switch no. 1 being close (50 per cent of the time it is switch no. 2).

If we think of the detection system described above as having the function of enabling the organism to detect F, then the multiplicity of ways of detecting F has the consequence that certain internal states (for example, R) can indicate (hence mean$_f$) that F is present without indicating anything about the intermediate conditions (i.e., f_1 or s_1) that "tell" it that F is present. Our problem with the bacteria was to find a way of having the orientation of its magnetosomes mean$_f$ that oxygen-free water was in a certain direction without *arbitrarily* dismissing the possibility of its meaning$_f$ that the magnetic field was aligned in that direction. We can now see that, with the multiple resources described in figure 6.1, this possibility can be *non*-arbitrarily dismissed. R *cannot* mean$_f$ that f_1 or s_1 is occurring because it *does* not, even under optimal conditions, mean$_n$ this. We can therefore claim to have found a non-derivative case of misrepresentation (i.e., R's meaning$_f$ that F is present when it is not) which cannot be dismissed by redescribing what R means$_f$ so as to eliminate that appearance of misrepresentation. The threatened inflation of possible meanings$_f$, arising from the variety of ways a system's natural function might be described, has been blocked.

Still, it will be said, we *need not* accept this as a case of genuine misrepresentation *if* we are prepared to recognize that R has a *disjunctive* meaning$_n$. The lighting up of the bulb (connected to switches wired in parallel) does not mean$_n$ that any particular switch is on, but it does indicate that *one* of the switches is on. Similarly, it may be said, even though it is the function of the mechanism having R as its terminal state to alert the organism to the presence of F, it does so by R's indicating, and having the function of indicating, the occurrence of a certain disjunctive condition – namely, that either f_1 or f_2 (or s_1 or s_2). Our hypothetical organism mistakenly withdraws from F, *not* because it misrepresents the ersatz F as F, but because what it correctly indicates (i.e., that the ersatz F is either f_1 or f_2) is no longer correlated in the normal way with something's being F.

No matter how versatile a detection system we might design, no matter how many routes of informational access we might give an organism, the possibility will always exist of describing its function (and therefore the meaning$_f$ of its various states) as the detection of some highly disjunctive property of the proximal input. At least, this will always be possible *if* we have a determinate set of disjuncts to which we can retreat.

Suppose, however, that we have a system capable of some form of associative learning. Suppose, in other words, that through repeated exposures to *cs* (a conditioned stimulus) in the presence of F, a change takes place. R (and, hence, avoidance behavior) can now be triggered by the occurrence of *cs* alone. Furthermore, it becomes clear that there is virtually no limit to the kind of stimulus that can acquire this "displaced" effectiveness in triggering R and subsequent avoidance behavior. Almost any *s* can become a *cs*, thereby assuming "control" over R, by functioning (in the "experience" of the organism) as a sign of F.

We now have a cognitive mechanism that not only transforms a variety of different sensory inputs (the s_i) into *one* output-determining state (R), but is capable of modifying the character of this many – one mapping over time. If we restrict ourselves to the sensory inputs (the s_i of figure 6.1), R means$_n$ one thing at t_1 (for example, that either s_1 or s_2), something else at t_2 (for example, that either s_1 or s_2 or, through learning, cs_3), and something still different at a later time. Just *what* R means$_n$ will depend on the individual's learning history – on *what* s_1 became cs_1 *for it*. There is no *time-invariant* meaning$_n$ for R; hence, nothing that, through time, could be its function to indicate. In terms of the s_i that produce R, R can have no time-invariant meaning$_f$.

Of course, throughout this process, R continues to indicate the presence of F. It does so because, by hypothesis, any new s_i to which R becomes conditioned is a natural sign of F. Learning is a process in which stimuli that indicate the presence of F are, in their turn, indicated by some relevant internal state of the organism (R in this case). Therefore, if we are to think of these cognitive mechanisms as having a time-invariant function at all (something that is implied by their continued – indeed, as a result of learning, more efficient – servicing of the associated need), then we *must* think of their function, not as indicating the nature of the proximal (even distal) conditions that trigger positive responses (the s_1 and f_1), but as indicating the condition (F) for which these diverse stimuli are signs. The mechanism just described has, then, as its natural function, the indication of the presence of F. Hence, the occurrence of R means$_f$ that F is present. It does not mean$_f$ that s_1 or s_2 or . . . s_x obtains, even though, at any given stage of development, it will mean$_n$ this for some definite value of x.

A system at this level of complexity, having not only multiple channels of access to what it needs to know about, but the resources for expanding its information-gathering resources, possesses, I submit, a genuine power of misrepresentation. When there is a breakdown in the normal chain of natural signs, when, say, cs_7 occurs (a learned sign of F) under circumstances in which it does not mean$_n$ that F is present (in the way that the broken clock does not mean$_n$ that it is 3.30 a.m.), R still means$_f$ (though not, of course, means$_n$) that F is present. It means$_f$ this because that is what it is *supposed* to mean$_n$, what it is its natural function to mean$_n$, and there is available to other condition it can mean$_f$.[20]

Notes

1 Dennett (1978c).
2 This needs some qualification, but it will do for the moment. What a natural sign means often does depend on us, on what we *know* about relevant alternative possibilities or on how we *use* an associated device. But if we don't know anything, or if the sign occurs in the operation of a device having no normal use, the sign still means something – just not, specifically, what we say it means under epistemically (or functionally) richer conditions. I return to this point in n. 8 below.
3 I give a fuller account of it in Dretske (1981), chs 1 and 2.
4 Grice (1957).
5 I hope it is clear, that I am not here concerned with the word "empty" (or the letter "E") that might appear on the gauge. This symbol means empty whatever the gauge is doing, but this is purely conventional. I am concerned with what the pointer's position means$_n$ *whatever* we choose to print on the face of the instrument.
6 Wright (1973) calls these "conscious" functions.
7 A doorbell, for example, cannot mean$_n$ *both* that there is someone at the door *and* that there is a short circuit.
8 It isn't the change of purpose *alone* that changes what something means$_n$ (hence, means$_f$). It is the fact that this change in use is accompanied by altered background knowledge, and meaning$_n$ changes as background knowledge changes. If, for example, A depends on both B and C, a changing A can mean$_n$ that C is changing *if* we know that B is constant. If we know that C is constant, it can mean$_n$ that B

is changing. If we know nothing, it only means that either B or C is changing. Natural meaning is relative in this sense, but derelativizing it (by ignoring what we know and how we use a device) does not eliminate natural meaning. It merely makes *less determinate* what things mean$_n$. For a fuller discussion of this point, see ch. 3 in Dretske (1981).

9 I think much of our talk about the representational capacities of computers is of this assigned, hence derived, kind. It tells us nothing about the intrinsic power of a machine to represent or misrepresent anything. Hence, nothing about the cognitive character of its internal states. Cummins (1983), I think, gets it exactly right by distinguishing *cognition (a version of *assigned* meaning) from genuine cognition.

10 My source for this example is Blakemore and Frankel (1981).

11 Stampe (1977).

12 Enc (1982). Enc identified the content of a functional state with the (construction of the) properties of the event to which the system has the function of responding.

13 Fodor (1990c).

14 Millikan (1984).

15 Dretske (1981), part 3.

16 Something for which there is, in Dennett's (earlier) language, an "appropriate efferent continuation"; see Denett (1969).

17 Fodor (in a circulated draft of "Why paramecia don't have mental representations"; see Fodor, 1986b) distinguishes organisms for which a representational theory of mind is not appropriate (paramecia, for example) and ones for which it is (us, for example) in terms of the latter's ability to respond to non-nomic stimulus properties (properties that are not transducer-detectable). We, but not paramecia, are capable of representing something as, say, a crumpled shirt, and *being a crumpled shirt* is not a projectible property. In this article. Fodor is not concerned with the question of *where* we get this extraordinary representational power from (he suggests it requires inferential capacities). He is concerned only with offering it as a way of distinguishing us from a variety of other perceptual and quasi-cognitive systems.

I agree with Fodor about the importance and relevance of this distinction, but my present concern is to understand *how* a system could acquire the power to represent something in this way. The power to represent something *as* a crumpled shirt (where this implies the correlative ability to misrepresent it as such) is certainly not innate.

18 Enc (1982), p. 168, says that a photoreceptor in the fruit-fly has the function of enabling the fly to reach humid spots (in virtue of the correlation between dark spots and humid spots). I have no objection to describing things in this way. But the question remains: *how* does it perform this function. We can answer this question without supposing that there is any mechanism of the fly whose function it is to indicate the degree of humidity. The sensory mechanism can perform this function if there is merely something to indicate the luminosity – i.e., a photoreceptor. *That* will enable the fly to reach humid spots. Likewise, the bacteria's magnetotactic sense *enables* (and, let us say, has the *function* of enabling) the bacteria to avoid oxygen-rich water. But the way it does it (it may be argued) is by having a sensor that indicates, and has the function of indicating, the direction of the magnetic field.

19 In Fodor's way of putting the point (see Fodor, 1987), this is merely a way of saying that his identification of the semantics of M (some mental representation) with entry conditions (relative to a set of normalcy conditions) still leaves some slack. We can say that the entry condition is the absence (presence) of oxygen *or* a specific orientation of the magnetic field Appeal to the sectional history of this mechanism won't decide *which* is the right specification of entry conditions – hence, won't tell us whether the bacteria are capable of *mis*representing anything. Fodor, I think, realizes this residual indeterminacy and makes the suggestive remark (n. 9) that this problem is an analog of the problems of specifying the perceptual object for theories of perception.

20 I am grateful to Berent Enc, Dennis Stampe, and Jerry Fodor for their helpful criticisms, both constructive and destructive, of earlier drafts of this essay.

7   Excerpt from: From Information to Intentionality

Barry Loewer

Dretske's New Account of Misrepresentation

In a recent paper he [Fred Dretske] suggests a different account of misrepresentation.[1] In this paper he doesn't attempt a reduction of belief content but is content to show how a state can be said to misrepresent without presupposing any intentional or semantic notions. The more recent suggestion is that what a brain state (or other internal state of an organism) represents is determined by the information which it is *designed* to carry. Dretske brings in teleological considerations in order to help specify representational content. He defines the "functional meaning" of a structure r's being in a state G as follows:

> r's function is to indicate the condition of w and the way it performs this function is, in part, by indicating that w is F by its (r's) being G. (this volume, p. 161)

The idea is that $G(r)$ functionally means that w is F if when r is functioning properly $G(r)$ carries the information that w is F. Misrepresentation can occur when r is not functioning properly.

According to the account in Dretske (1981), the content of $G(r)$ is determined by the correlations which obtain during the learning period. On the new account it is the correlations that obtain when r is functioning properly that determine the content of $G(r)$. This seems to be an improvement since, as I argued previously (Loewer, 1987), the distinction between the period during which a concept is learned and when it is used is question begging. But, as Dretske recognizes, his new account requires that there be a non-intentional characterization of r's information carrying function. One might worry that we see a structure as having the function to carry certain information not because this is an objective feature of the structure but because of the use that we make of the structure. For example, if the column of mercury registers 70 degrees when it is 80 degrees because the mercury is stuck we will say that the thermometer misrepresents. But certainly this depends on the fact that we use the thermometer to measure temperature. What counts as proper functioning is relative to our purposes. Dretske concludes that the ability of the thermometer to misrepresent (and so to represent) is dependent on human beliefs and purposes. It is not "original representation."

Dretske observes that the natural place to look for original representation is in organisms which contain structures that appear to have evolved, because they play a vital information gathering role in the species' adaptation to its environment. He considers the example of certain anaerobic bacteria which contain internal magnets called "magnetosomes." The magnetosomes of those bacteria that live in the northern hemisphere point to magnetic north and cause the bacteria to swim away from the surface. The survival value of the structure appears to be that it helps the bacteria avoid oxygen-rich, hence toxic, surface water. Dretske considers the claim that the function of the magnetosome is to carry information about the direction of oxygen-rich water. Supporting this is the fact that the bacteria need to avoid oxygen-rich water to survive and it is plausible that they would not have evolved to contain magnetosomes unless these function to detect the direction of oxygen-rich water. If the south pole of a bar magnet is placed near one of these bacteria and it moves upward (toward local magnetic north and in the direction of oxygen-rich water) it is *misrepresenting* the direction of oxygen-rich water. At first, this looks like a case of natural misrepresentation. But Dretske realizes that the information that a structure normally carries and the needs which are satisfied by the information do not uniquely determine the structure's information carrying function (if it has any). In the case under discussion, another account is that the function of the magnetosome is to carry information about the direction of local magnetic north. It so happens that in its usual environment the direction of local magnetic north is correlated with the direction of oxygen-rich water. If this is the magnetosome's function then a bacterium allegedly fooled by the bar magnet really does not misrepresent the direction of oxygen-rich water since it is not the function of the magnetosome to carry information about the direction of oxygen-rich water but about the direction of local magnetic north. It is carrying out this function perfectly. As Dretske says, we "need some principled way of saying what the natural function of a mechanism is."

Dretske next considers a (hypothetical) organism, O, which contains a structure r such that $G(r)$ carries the information that x is F but which is unlike the bacteria in that there are two ways in which O can detect Fs. For example, consider an animal capable of detecting the presence of a lion either by sight or sound. Figure 7.1 illustrates the situation.

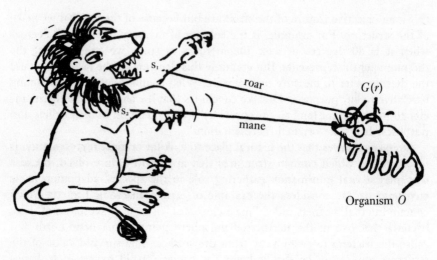

Figure 7.1

F is the property of being a lion, s_1 and s_2 are respectively the proximal stimuli, appearing to have a large mane and a roaring sound; and r is a cognitive structure. When r is functioning properly it is caused to be in state G either by s_1 or by s_2. When conditions are normal only lions appear to have large manes and only lions roar. So if r is G then there must be a lion present. When circumstances are not normal, misrepresentation may occur (e.g., someone dresses up in a lion suit and roars, causing O mistakenly to believe that a lion is present). In the case of the bacterium there is not genuine misrepresentation since the magnetosome represents the direction of local magnetic north, not the direction of oxygen-rich water. Consider the analogous objection that in the present case, when O is confronted with someone dressed in his lion suit, $G(r)$ doesn't misrepresent that a lion is present but correctly represents the occurrence of one of the proximal stimuli, e.g., a roaring sound. Dretske at first suggests that this objection is unfounded. He points out that $G(r)$ does not represent the occurrence of a roaring sound since it does not carry this information even under normal conditions. That is, when r is functioning normally, it is possible for it to be G even though no roaring sound occurs. Similarly, r's being G doesn't represent any other proximal stimuli that normally occasions it. So it appears that Dretske has discovered a principled way of eliminating the proximal conditions as what is represented and so rescues his account of misrepresentation.

However, there is an obvious objection, analogous to the objection we made against the identification of belief content with semantic content, which Dretske himself raises against this proposal. It is that $G(r)$, instead of representing that a lion is present, represents the disjunctive proposition that either s_1 or s_2 has occurred. If this were so then we no longer would have a genuine case of misrepresentation since $G(r)$ *correctly* represents that s, s_2 has occurred. As long as this alternative cannot be dismissed, we do not have an unequivocal case of misrepresentation.

Dretske's response to this is to consider an organism capable of associative learning. Suppose that originally $G(r)$ can be caused either by s_1 or by s_2, as previously. But the organism is capable of "learning" to associate a new proximal stimulus, s_3, with $G(r)$. Dretske further supposes that

> . . . it becomes clear that there is virtually no limit to the kind of stimulus that can acquire this "displaced" effectiveness in triggering r and subsequent avoidance behavior.

He concludes that in this kind of situation it cannot be said that r's being G represents any of the disjunctions $s_1 \vee s_2 \vee \ldots$, since there is no end to the disjunctions which can come to be associated with r's being G. So, none of the disjunctions can be what $G(r)$ represents.

We have been assuming that, although various s_i can come to trigger $G(r)$, those which do are all correlated, *under normal conditions*, with the presence of a lion. Dretske doesn't tell us exactly what constitutes normal conditions but presumably he would count the presence of holographic images of lions or tape-recorded roars as not normal. He claims that $G(r)$ represents the presence of a lion since this is all that is in common among the s_i that come to be correlated with $G(r)$. In "abnormal" circumstances, a stimulus s_k can occur and cause r to be G even though no lion is present. According to Dretske, this is a genuine case of misrepresentation. One cannot now object that $G(r)$ actually represents some disjunction of proximal stimuli $s_1 \vee s_2 \vee \ldots$ since even in normal circumstances it doesn't carry the information that $s_1 \vee s_2 \vee \ldots$.

Has Dretske actually constructed a naturalistic account of misrepresentation? He has told us that $G(r)$ represents for O that x is F if it is the function of $G(r)$ to carry information that x is F. He doesn't provide a positive characterization of "the function of $G(r)$ is to carry the information that p." But he does give us a way of discovering what information it is *not* the function of $G(r)$ to carry. In our example, it was not the function of $G(r)$ to carry the information that s_1 or s_2 occurred, since O could learn to associate other stimuli with $G(r)$. To help evaluate his proposal let's examine the following positive account of representation which is based on his discussion:

> (DD) $G(r)$ represents that x is F iff the most specific information common to every D-possible token of $G(r)$ which occurs when conditions are normal is that x is F and O needs the information that x is F.[2]

It is clear that, in determining what $G(r)$ represents, we must consider not only those tokens of G which occur during O's life, since these will be associated with a finite, perhaps small, set of stimuli, and we would not have eliminated the claim that stimuli $G(r)$ represents the disjunctive proposition that one of these stimuli occurred. Dretske's suggestion for eliminating this alternative is that we consider certain counterfactual tokens of r's being G. These are the D-possible tokens of $G(r)$. These counterfactual tokens are caused by various stimuli other than those which cause actually occurring tokens. By including these tokens in the determination of the informational function of $G(r)$ one might hope that the representational content of $G(r)$ will not include information about proximal stimuli which cause r to be G.

This new account of representation appears to be an improvement over the one found in Dretske (1981). By considering the D-possible tokens of r's being G, the new account seems to avoid our objection to semantic content. We cannot object to the new account that $G(r)$ carries the information that a certain disjunction of stimuli or neural states occurred (making this part of its semantic content), since there may be D-possible tokens which are not caused by any of these stimuli or neural states. The new account does not appeal to the dubious distinction between the period during which a concept is learned and the period when it is used. Instead, misrepresentation is accounted for by the failure of the structure to function normally or by conditions being abnormal. Since my two major objections (in 1987) to the old account concerned problems with the learning period and semantic content, it will be interesting to see if the new account avoids similar objections.

If (DD) is to be a successful naturalistic account of representation, then it must be possible to characterize O's informational needs, normal conditions and functioning, and D-possible tokens of $G(r)$, in non-intentional terms. I have some worries about the first two of these, but the main difficulty is in characterizing the D-possible tokens of $G(r)$. As we observed, we do not want to restrict the D-possible tokens to those which are caused by whatever stimuli O actually learns to associate with r's being G, since then the representational content of $G(r)$ would include that one of these stimuli occurred. So we include possible tokens of $G(r)$ which are caused by other stimuli. But, given the plasticity of neural structures, it is certainly possible for r's being G to be caused by stimuli which are not themselves normally associated with x's being F. That is, there are counterfactual situations in which something other than x's being F causes a stimuli which causes r to be G. If we count such tokens as D-possible then (DD) will not attribute to $G(r)$ the content that x is F. The problem is to distinguish those tokens which, while associated with various stimuli, still represent that x is F from those that represent some other concept, and to do this in a way that does not presuppose semantic or intentional notions. We cannot, for example, say that the D-possible tokens of $G(r)$ are the ones which represent that x is F (or are caused by x's being F) since this obviously appeals to what $G(r)$ represents. Dretske offers no hint as to how to characterize the set of D-possible tokens without employing semantic notions and I see no way in which it can be done. In any case, until he tells us precisely which tokens of $G(r)$ can be considered in determining what $G(r)$ represents, he has not produced an account of misrepresentation.[3]

Notes

"From Information to Intentionality" originally appeared in *Synthese*, 70 (1987), pp. 287–317. Copyright 1987 by D. Reidel Publishing Company. Reprinted by permission of Kluwer Academic Publishers and the author.

1 See Dretske (1986). Dretske doesn't make any reference to his account of mis-representation in Dretske (1981) in this paper.
2 Dretske does not give *DD* as an account of representation but it is implicit in his account of misrepresentation. It is impossible to evaluate an account of misrepresentation without an account of representation.
3 I would like to thank Davis Baird, Paul Boghossian, Mike Costa, Gary Gates, Ernest Lepore, Brian McLaughlin and Dion Scot-Kakures for helpful discussions of information-theoretic semantics.

8 A Theory of Content, II: The Theory

Jerry Fodor

". . . the appeal to teleologically Normal conditions doesn't provide for a univocal notion of intentional content . . . it's just not true that Normally caused intentional states ipso facto mean whatever causes them. So we need a non-teleological solution of the disjunction problem. So be it." So the first part of this discussion (Fodor, 1990b, chapter 3) concluded. But that did rather beg the question against the guy who holds that *there isn't going to be a solution of the disjunction problem* because there are no intentional states, and hence no matters of fact about the disjunctiveness, or otherwise, of their intentional contents. What you need, to put the matter brutally, is one thing; what you are likely to get is quite another. What on earth would a naturalistic and non-teleological theory of content be like?

The rest of this paper explores and extends an approach to the disjunction problem that I first sketched in *Psychosemantics* (1987) and in "Information and Representation" (1990a). This solution is broadly within the tradition of informational approaches to content[1] but it does not equate what a symbol means with the information that its tokens carry; and it does not try to solve the disjunction problem by distinguishing type one situations (those in which whatever causes a symbol to be tokened is ipso facto in its extension from type two situations (those in which symbols are allowed to be caused by things that they don't apply to.)[2] In the second respect, at least, it differs from all the other treatments of the disjunction problem that I've seen in the literature.

I must acknowledge at the outset the existence of what seems to be quite an impressive consensus – among the maybe six or eight people who care about these matters – that my way of doing the disjunction problem won't work. But Granny says I'm not to be disconsolate; Rome wasn't deconstructed in a day, she says. Accordingly, I now propose to run through more or less all of the objections to my treatment of the disjunction problem that I've heard of, and a few that I've dreamed up. Partly this is to show you that I am not disconsolate; partly it is to try to convince you that my story actually copes pretty well with the putative counterexamples; and partly it's to provide an opportunity to refine and deepen the theory.

Asymmetric Dependence (and Teleology for Almost the Last Time)

Errors raise the disjunction problem, but the disjunction problem isn't really, deep down, a problem about error. What the disjunction problem is really about deep down is the difference between *meaning* and *information*. Let's start with this.

Information is tied to etiology in a way that meaning isn't. If the tokens of a symbol have two kinds of etiologies, it follows that there are two kinds of information that tokens of that symbol carry. (If some "cow" tokens are caused by cows and some "cow" tokens aren't then it follows that some "cow" tokens carry information about cows and some "cow" tokens don't). By contrast, *the meaning of a symbol is one of the things that all of its tokens have in common, however they may happen to be caused. All* "cow" tokens mean *cow*; if they didn't, they wouldn't be "cow" tokens.

So, information follows etiology and meaning doesn't, and that's why you get a disjunction problem if you identify the meaning of a symbol with the information that its tokens carry. Error is merely illustrative; it comes into the disjunction problem only because it's so plausible that the false tokens of a symbol have a different kind of causal history (and hence carry different information) than the true ones. But (as can be seen in Fodor, 1990b, chapter 3) there are other sorts of examples of etiological heterogeneity (including representation in thought) and they produce disjunction problems too.

To put the same point another way, solving the disjunction problem requires not a theory of *error* but a theory of *meaning*; if a theory of meaning is any good, the conditions for disjunctive meaning should fall out as a special case (see the discussion in Fodor, 1990a). If one is sympathetic to the Skinner-Dretske tradition, the trick in constructing such a theory is to explain how the meaning of a symbol can be insensitive to the heterogeneity of the (actual and possible) causes of its tokens even though, on the one hand, meaning is supposed somehow to reduce to information and, on the other hand, information varies with etiology.

You can now see what's *really* wrong with teleological theories of content. The heart of a teleological theory is the idea that "in Normal circumstances" the tokens of a symbol can have only *one kind* of cause – viz. the kind of cause that fixes meaning. (Normally, only cows cause "cows," so the teleological story goes.) But surely this underestimates what one might call the *robustness* of meaning: in actual fact, "cow" tokens get caused in *all sorts* of ways, and they all mean *cow* for all of that. Solving the disjunction problem and making clear how a symbol's meaning could be so insensitive to variability in the causes of its tokenings are really two ways of describing the same undertaking. If there's going to be a causal theory of content, there has to be some way of picking out *semantically relevant* causal relations from all the other kinds of causal relations that the tokens of a symbol can enter into. And we'd better not do this by implicitly denying robustness – e.g., by idealizing to contexts of etiological homogeneity.

Well, then, how *are* we to do it? Here's a first approximation to the proposal that I favor: cows cause "cow" tokens, and (let's suppose) cats cause "cow" tokens. But "cow" means *cow* and not *cat* or *cow or cat* because *there being cat-caused "cow" tokens depends on there being cow-caused "cow" tokens, but not the other way around.* "Cow" means *cow* because, as I shall henceforth put it, non-cow-caused "cow" tokens are *asymmetrically dependent upon* cow-caused "cow" tokens. "Cow" means *cow* because *but that "cow" tokens carry information about cows, they wouldn't carry information about anything.*

Notice that this sort of story has the desirable property of not assuming that there are such things as type one situations; in particular, it doesn't assume that there are circumstances – nomologically possible and naturalistically and otherwise non-question-beggingly specifiable – in which it's semantically necessary that only cows cause "cows." Nor does it assume that there are non-question-beggingly specifiable circumstances in which it's semantically necessary that *all* cows would cause "cows."[3] All that's required for "cow" to mean *cow*, according to the present account, is that some "cow" tokens should be caused by (more precisely, that they should carry information about) cows, and that non-cow-caused "cow" tokens should depend asymmetrically on these.

Teleological theories say that what's special about false tokens is that they can't happen when circumstances are Normal; if it's supposed that things actually are Normal some of the time (as, indeed, it must be if the theory is historical/Darwinian) it follows that some of the time what's said (or thought) can't but be true. By contrast, the theory I'm selling says that false tokens can happen whenever they like; only if *they* happen, so too must tokenings of other kinds: no non-cow-caused "cow"s without cow-caused "cow"s; false tokens are metaphysically dependent on true ones.[4] Since the satisfaction of the asymmetric dependence condition is compatible with any amount of heterogeneity in the causal history of "cow" tokens, this way of solving the disjunction problem is compatible with meaning being arbitrarily robust.[5]

This story also has the desirable property of being naturalistic (in the sense discussed in Fodor, 1990b, chapter 3). It's atomistic ("cow"s could be asymmetrically dependent on cows in a world in which no other asymmetric dependencies obtain) and it's physicalistic (you can say what asymmetric dependence is without resort to intentional or semantic idiom).[6] But despite its having these desirable properties, the proposal I've just sketched is *only* a first approximation. As it stands there's lots to be said against it. Before we commence to look at the problems, however, I have three prefatory remarks I want to make: a shortish one about a doctrine that you might call "pansemanticism," a longish one about ontology, and then a very short one about who has the burden of argument.

Pansemanticism

Here's a clash of intuitions for you.
On the one hand:

> . . . symbols and mental states both have representational *content*. And nothing else does that belongs to the causal order: not rocks, or worms or trees or spiral nebulae. . . . the main joint business of the philosophy of language and the philosophy of mind is the problem of representation. . . . How can anything manage to be *about* anything; and why is it that only thoughts and symbols succeed? (Fodor, 1987, p. xi)

And on the other hand:

> Clouds *mean* rain. Spots of a certain kind *mean* measles. . . . In all such cases there is a lawlike or nomological regularity connecting one type of situation with another. Instances of these regularities are cases in which one situation means something or carries information about another: and, of course, in such cases there need be neither minds nor symbols used by minds. (Israel, 1987, p. 3; emphasis his)

In fact, the idea that meaning is just *everywhere* is a natural conclusion to draw from informational analyses of content. If, after all, meaning reduces (more or less)[7] to reliable causal covariance, then, since there is patently a lot of reliable causal covariance around, it looks to follow that there must be a lot of meaning around too. And the intuition that "means" is univocal – and means *carries information about* – in "'smoke' means *smoke*" and "smoke means fire" is close to the heart of information-based semantics.

But this can't be right. If it were, then (since "carries information about" is transitive) it would follow that "smoke" means *fire*; which it doesn't. On the asymmetric dependence account, by contrast, this sort of case comes out all right. "Smoke' tokens carry information about fire (when they're caused by smoke that's caused by fire). But they don't *mean* fire because their dependence on fire is asymmetrically dependent on their dependence on smoke. Break the *fire* → *smoke* connection, and the *smoke* → "*smoke*" connection remains intact; our using "smoke" in situations where there's fire doesn't depend on smoke's carrying information about fire. But break the *smoke* → "*smoke*" connection and the *fire* → "*smoke*" connection goes too; our using "smoke" in situations where there's fire does depend on "smoke"'s carrying information about smoke.

There is, in short, a lot less meaning around than there is information. That's because all you need for information is reliable causal covariance, whereas for meaning you need (at least) asymmetric dependence too. Information is ubiquitous but not robust; meaning is robust but not ubiquitous. So much for pansemanticism.

Ontology

As I remarked in (1990b), chapter 3, I assume that if the generalization that Xs cause Ys is counterfactual supporting, then there is a "covering" law that relates the property of being X to the property of being a cause of Ys: counterfactual supporting causal generalizations are (either identical to or) backed by causal laws, and laws are relations among properties. So, what the story about asymmetric dependence comes down to is that "cow" means *cow* if (*i*) there is a nomic relation between the property of being a cow and the property of being a cause of "cow" tokens; and (*ii*) if there are nomic relations between other properties and the property of being a cause of "cow" tokens, then the latter nomic relations depend asymmetrically upon the former.

Ontologically speaking, I'm inclined to believe that it's bedrock that the world contains properties and their nomic relations; i.e., that truths about nomic relations among properties are deeper than – and hence are not to be analyzed in terms of – counterfactual truths about individuals. In any event, *epistemologically* speaking, I'm quite certain that it's possible to know that there is a nomic relation among properties but not have much idea which counter-factuals are true in virtue of the fact that the relation holds. It is therefore, *methodologically* speaking, probably a bad idea to require of philosophical analyses that are articulated in terms of nomic relations among properties that they be, as one says in the trade, "cashed" by analyses that are articulated in terms of counterfactual relations among individuals.

This methodological point is one about which I feel strongly. So much so that I am prepared to succumb to a digression. Here come several paragraphs about how a philosopher can get into trouble by taking it for granted that truths about laws need to be analyzed by, or into, counterfactual truths.

The context is Kripke's critical discussion (1982) of dispositional accounts of rule following. According to such accounts, meaning *plus* by "+" is analyzed in terms of a disposition to "respond with the sum of [the] two numbers" when asked things like "What's m + n?" Kripke says this sort of analysis won't do because we have no such dispositions: our computational powers are finite; we make mistakes; and so forth. To which he imagines his interlocutor replying that: ". . . the trouble arises solely from too crude a notion of disposition: *ceteris paribus* notions of dispositions, not crude and literal notions, are the ones standardly used in philosophy and in science." So what's imagined is, in effect, a dispositional story about rule following that is backed by an appeal to the performance/competence distinction.

But, according to Kripke, that won't do either. For

... how should we flesh out the *ceteris paribus* clause? Perhaps [by invoking counterfactuals] as something like: If my brain had been stuffed with sufficient extra matter to grasp large enough numbers, and if it were given enough capacity to perform such a large addition ... [etc.] ... , then given an addition problem involving two large numbers *m* and *n*, I would respond with their sum. ... But how can we have any confidence of this? How in the world can I tell what would happen if my brain were stuffed with extra brain matter. ... Surely such speculation should be left to science fiction writers and futurologists. We have no idea what the results of such experiments would be. They might lead me to go insane. ... [and so forth]

Apparently Kripke assumes that we can't have reason to accept that a generalization defined for idealized conditions is lawful unless we can specify the counterfactuals which would be true if the idealized conditions were to obtain. It is, however, hard to see why one should take this methodology seriously. For example: God only knows what would happen if molecules and containers actually met the conditions specified by the ideal gas laws (molecules are perfectly elastic; containers are infinitely impermeable; etc.); for all *I* know, if any of these things were true, the world would come to an end. After all, the satisfaction of these conditions is, presumably, *physically impossible* and who knows what would happen in physically impossible worlds?

But it's not required, in order that the ideal gas laws should be in scientific good repute, that we know anything like all of what would happen if there really were ideal gasses. All that's required is that we know (e.g.) that, if there were ideal gasses, then, ceteris paribus, their volume would vary inversely with the pressure upon them. And *that* counterfactual *the theory itself tells us is true.*[8]

Similarly, if there are psychological laws that idealize to unbounded working memory, it is not required in order for *them* to be in scientific good repute that we know all of what would happen if working memory really were unbounded. All we need to know is that, if we did have unbounded memory, then, ceteris paribus, we would be able to compute the value of $m + n$ for arbitrary m and n.[9] And that counterfactual the theory itself tells us is true.

Similarly again, we can know that there are asymmetric dependences among nomic relations between properties without knowing much about which counterfactuals these asymmetric dependences make true. All we need to know is that, if the nomic relation between $P1$ and $P2$ is asymmetrically dependent on the nomic relation between $P3$ and $P4$, then, ceteris paribus, breaking the relation between $P3$ and $P4$ would break the relation between $P1$ and $P2$. And that counterfactual the theory itself tells us is true. As per above.

Having gotten all that off my chest, I shall join the crowd and talk counterfactuals from time to time, faut de mieux. And, since it's widely supposed that talk about counterfactuals itself translates into talk about possibilia, I shall sometimes equate "there is a nomic dependence between the property of being a *Y* an the property of being a cause of *X*s" with "*Y*s cause *X*s in all (nearby? see below) nomologically possible worlds". But I am not happy about any of this; it seems to me to be just the sort of reductive move that is always blowing up in philosophers' faces. I suspect, in particular, that some of the troubles we're about to survey stem not from there being anything wrong with the proposal that content rests on asymmetrical dependences among nomological relations, but rather from there being everything wrong with the assumption that claims about nomological relations need counterfactual/possible-world translations.[10]

Who Has the Burden of Argument

The theory of meaning that I'm going to propose is elaborated largely in terms of subjunctive conditionals. It has this in common with all informational theories of meaning; it's in the nature of such theories to claim that a symbol means such-and-such because *if there were* instances of such-and-such they *would cause* tokenings of the symbol. So it may occur to you, in the course of these proceedings, to object as follows: "Why should I believe that the counter-factuals that are being invoked are true? Why should I believe that if there actually were such-and-suches they actually would cause symbol tokenings in the ways that your theory requires?"

The answer is: don't forget, this stuff is supposed to be philosophy. In particular, it's an attempt to solve Brentano's problem by showing that there are naturalistically specifiable, and atomistic, sufficient conditions for a physical state to have an intentional content. In *that* context, I get to *stipulate* the counterfactuals. It's enough if I can make good the claim that "*X*" *would mean* such and such if so and so *were to be* the case. It's not also incumbent upon me to argue that, since "*X*" *does* mean such and such, so and so *is* the case. That is, solving Brentano's problem requires giving sufficient conditions for inten-tionality, not *necessary* and sufficient conditions. So, if you want to argue with the metaphysical conclusions of this paper, you've got to construct a world where my counterfactuals are all in place but where "*X*" doesn't mean what I say it does. Fair enough; let's see one.

OK, now to business.

To begin with, not an objection, but something more like a vague discom-fort: *even if you can get the theory to cope with the examples, I don't see why the theory should be true; I don't see why asymmetric dependence should, as it were, make the difference between information and content.*

Let's start by forgetting about the naturalization problem (we'll return to it in a couple of paragraphs). I want to make it seem plausible that asymmetric dependence might have deep roots in the analysis of semantical phenomena when the phenomena are viewed commonsensically, outside the context of metaphysical issues about reduction. And let's, for the moment, talk about linguistic rather than mental representation in order to keep the facts as much as possible out in the open. So, then:

We have, I suppose, a variety of practices with respect to the linguistic expressions we use. And I suppose it's plausible that these practices aren't all on a level; some of them presuppose others in the sense that some work only because others are in place. For a banal example, there's the business of having people paged. How it works is: someone calls out "John" and, if everything goes right, John comes. Why John? I mean, why is it *John* that you get when you call out "John"? Well, because the practice is that the guy who is to come is the guy whose name is the vocable that is called. This much, surely, is untendentious.

Notice that you have to invoke the practice of naming to specify the practice of paging. So the practice of paging is parasitic on the practice of naming; you couldn't have the former but that you have the latter. But not, I suppose, vice versa? Couldn't you have the practices that are constitutive of naming (so that, for example, the convention is that "John" is pink is true if it's the person whose name is "John" that is pink) even if there were no practice of paging people by calling out their names? I take it to be plausible that you could, so I take it to be plausible that paging is *asymmetrically* dependent on naming.

Oh, no doubt, I could have an arrangement with my dog according to which my dog comes when I whistle; and this though the sound that I make when I whistle for my dog isn't, of course, my dog's name. But here learning the language game really *is* just training. The whistling works because there's a *pre*arrangement between me and my dog; I've taught the dog what to do when I make that noise. By contrast, I can page John by calling his name without this sort of prearrangement. When a convention of naming is in place, there's room for a practice of paging that is perfectly abstract: anyone who has a name can be paged just by calling his name.

So, the *productivity* of the paging arrangement depends on there being a convention of naming. Similarly, mutatis mutandis, for the productivity of the practice in virtue of which I bring you a slab when you say "bring me a slab." That it's one of *those* things that you get when you say this has essentially to do with those being the kinds of things that are *called* "slabs" (with its being the case, for example, that those are the kinds of things that have to be pink if "slabs are pink" is true.) But not, surely, vice versa; surely the practices in virtue of our pursuit of which "is a slab" means *is a slab* could be in place even if there were no convention of bringing slabs when they're called for. So then it's plausible that the cluster of practices that center around bringing things when they're called for is asymmetrically dependent on the cluster of practices that fix the extensions of our predicates.

These kinds of considerations show one of the ways that asymmetric dependence gets a foothold in semantic analysis: some of our linguistic practices presuppose some of our others, and it's plausible that practices of *applying* terms (names to their bearers, predicates to things in their extensions) are at the bottom of the pile.[11] But what, precisely, has all this got to do with robustness and with the relation between information and content? The idea is that, although tokens of "slab" that request slabs carry no information about slabs (if anything, they carry information about wants; viz. the information that a slab is wanted), still, *some* tokens of "slab" presumably carry information about slabs (in particular, the tokens that are used to predicate slabhood of slabs do); and, but for there being tokens of "slab" that carry information about slabs, I couldn't get a slab by using "slab" to call for one. My "slab" requests are thus, in a certain sense, *causally dependent on slabs even though there are no slabs in their causal histories.* But they're not, of course, causally dependent on slabs in the way that (according to informational semantics) my "slab" predications are. So then there are *two* semantically relevant ways that "slab" tokens can be causally dependent on slabs consonant with their meaning *slab*: by being "slab" tokens that are caused by slabs, and by being "slab" tokens that are asymmetrically dependent upon "slab" tokens that are caused by slabs. Equivalently: by being "slab" tokens that carry information about slabs, and by being "slab" tokens that asymmetrically depend upon "slab" tokens that carry information about slabs.

So far so good; we can see how asymmetric dependences among our linguistic practices might explain how a token of "slab" could mean *slab* even when, as in the case of slab request, it's a want rather than a slab that causes the tokening; and how a token of "John" could mean *John* even though, if it's used to page John, it's caused not by John but by his absence. Which is to say that we can see something of the connection between asymmetric dependence and robustness.

But, of course, as it stands none of this is of any use to a reductionist. For, in these examples, we've been construing robustness by appeal to asymmetric dependences among *linguistic practices.* And linguistic *practices* depend on linguistic *policies*; the asymmetric dependence of my pagings on my namings comes down to my undertaking that, ceteris paribus, I will call out "John" only when the man I want to come is the one whom I undertake that I will use "John" to name; and so forth. Since, however, being in pursuit of a policy is being in an intentional state, how could asymmetric dependence among linguistic practices help with the naturalization problem?

The first point is that words can't have their meanings *just* because their users undertake to pursue some or other linguistic policies; or, indeed, just because of any purely *mental* phenomenon, anything that happens purely "in your head." Your undertaking to call John "John" doesn't, all by itself, make "John" a name of John. How could it? For "John" to be John's name, there must be some sort of *real relation* between the name and its bearer; and intentions don't, per se, establish real relations. This is because, of course, intentions are (merely) intentional; you can intend that there be a certain relation between

"John" and John and yet there may be no such relation. *A fortiori*, you can intend that there be a certain *semantical* relation between "John" and John – that the one should name the other, for example – and yet there may be no such relation. Mere undertakings connect nothing with nothing; "intentional relation" is an oxymoron. For there to be a relation between "John" and John, something has to happen *in the world*. That's part of what makes the idea of a *causal* construal of semantic relations so attractive. (And it's also, I think, what's right about Wittgenstein's "private language" argument. Though, as I read the text, he has it muddled up with irrelevant epistemology. For "John" to mean *John*, something has to happen in the world. It doesn't follow that for "John" to mean John someone has to be in a position to *tell* that that thing has happened.)

Linguistic policies don't make semantic relations; but maybe they make *causal* relations, and maybe causal relations make semantic relations. This, anyhow, is a hope by which informational semantics lives. I pursue a policy according to which I use "is a slab" to predicate slabhood, and a policy according to which I use "bring a slab" to request slabs, and a policy according to which the second of these practices is asymmetrically dependent on the first. My pursuing these policies is my being in a certain complex mental state, and my being in that mental state has causal consequences: in particular it has the consequence that there is a certain pattern of causal relations between slabs and my tokenings of "is a slab"; and that there is a certain (very different) pattern of causal relations between slabs and my tokenings of "bring a slab"; and that the second pattern of causal relations is asymmetrically dependent on the first.

Now maybe we can kick away the ladder. Perhaps the policies per se aren't what matters for semantics; maybe all that matters is the patterns of causal dependencies that the pursuit of the policies give rise to. That one kind of causal relation between "slab"s and slabs should depend asymmetrically upon another kind of causal relation between "slab"s and slabs might be enough to explain the robustness of "slab" tokenings, *however* the relations are sustained. (Cf. a doctrine of Skinner's cited with approval in Fodor, 1990b, chapter 3: semantics depends on a "functional relation" – a relation of nomic dependence – between symbols and their denotata. How this relation is mediated – e.g., that it is neurologically mediated, or for that matter, psychologically mediated – isn't part of the *semantical* story.)

The point is, if the asymmetric dependence story about robustness can be told just in terms of symbol–world causal relations, then we can tell it *even in a context where the project is naturalization*. No doubt, it's the linguistic policies of speakers that give rise to the asymmetric causal dependences in terms of which the conditions for robustness are defined; but the conditions for robustness *quantify over* the mediating mechanisms, and so can be stated without referring to the policies; hence their compatibility with naturalism.

At a minimum, nobody who is independently committed to the reduction of semantic relations to causal ones should boggle at this way of accommodating the facts about robustness. Informational theories, for example, define "information" in just this sort of way: i.e., they appeal to reliable covariances while quantifying over the causal mechanisms by which these covariances are sustained. By doing so, they explain why information (indeed, why the very *same* information) can be transmitted over so many different kinds of channels.

Well, similarly, if it's the causal patterns themselves that count, rather than the mechanisms whose operations give rise to them, then perhaps our *mental* representations can be robust just in virtue of asymmetric dependences among the causal patterns that our concepts enter into.[12] That is, perhaps there could be mechanisms which sustain asymmetric dependences among the relations between mental representations and the world, even though, patently, we have no policies with respect to the tokenings of our mental representations. If that were so, then the conditions for the robustness of linguistic expressions and the conditions for the robustness of mental representations might be *identical* even though, of course, the mechanisms in virtue of whose operations the two sorts of symbols satisfy the conditions for robustness would be very, very different. Some races are won by sailboats and some are won by steamboats, and the mechanisms whose operation eventuates in winning the two sorts of races are very, very different. But the conditions for winning quantify over the mechanisms and are the same for both sorts of races; however you are driven, all you have to do to win is come in first (on corrected time, to be sure).

So much for some of the intuitions that are running the show. Now let's see to the counterexamples.

1 *First objection*:   What about "unicorn"? It seems implausible that non-unicorn-caused "unicorn" tokens should depend on unicorn-caused "unicorn" tokens since, as you may have noticed, there are many of the former but none of the latter.

First reply: That's one of the reasons why I want to do the thing in terms of nomic relations among properties rather than causal relations among individuals. I take it that there can be nomic relations among properties that aren't instantiated; so it can be true that the property of being a unicorn is nomologically linked with the property of being a cause of "unicorn"'s *even if there aren't any unicorns*. Maybe this cashes out into something like *"there wouldn't be non-unicorn-caused "unicorn" tokens but that unicorns would cause "unicorn" tokens if there were any unicorns*. And maybe *that* cashes out into something like: *there are non-unicorn-caused "unicorn" tokens in worlds that are close to us only if there are unicorn-caused "unicorn" tokens in worlds that are close to them*. But this is very approximate. For example, I suppose that "unicorn" is a (noninstantiated) kind term. It will become clear later, when we worry about doppelgängers of things that are in the extensions of kind terms, that this entails that, ceteris paribus, no world in which only non-unicorns cause "unicorns" can be as close to ours as some world in which only unicorns do. And anyhow, for reasons previously set out, I am not an enthusiast for such translations.

Two subsidiary points should be noticed. First, this way of compensating for the lack of unicorns won't work if the lack of unicorns is *necessary* (e.g., nomologically or metaphysically necessary). For, in that case, it's not a law that if there were unicorns they would cause "unicorn" tokens; laws aren't made true by vacuous satisfactions of their antecedents. Similar lines of argument suggest what appears to be quite a strong consequence of the asymmetric dependence story: *no* primitive symbol can express a property that is necessarily uninstantiated. (There can't, for example, be a primitive symbol that expresses the property of being a round square).

One would think that a theory that makes so strong a claim should be pretty easy to test. Not so, however, in present case. For one thing, the notion of primitiveness that's at issue here isn't entirely clear. You could, presumably, have a *syntactically* primitive symbol[13] that means *is a round square* so long as it is "introduced by" a definition. Whatever, precisely, *that* may mean. In short, although the claim that all necessarily uninstantiated properties may be expressed by complex symbols looks to rule out a lot of possibilities, I, for one, can't think of any way to decide whether it's true. Suggestions are gratefully solicited.

2 *Second objection*: Why doesn't "horse" mean *small horse*, seeing that, after all, if horses cause "horses" it follows that small horses cause "horses".

Second reply: That's another reason why I want to do the thing in terms of nomic relations among properties rather than causal relations among individuals. Being struck by lightning caused the death of the cow. The bolt that killed the cow was the fourth that Tuesday, so being struck by the fourth bolt on that Tuesday caused the death of the cow; "cause" is transparent to that sort of substitution. But though it's true (given the assumptions) that being struck by the fourth bolt on Tuesday killed the cow, the law that "covered" that causal transaction applies to cows and lightning bolts qua cow and lightning bolt (or, perhaps, qua organisms and electrical discharges?); it was because it was a lightning bolt – and not because it was the fourth such bolt that Tuesday – that its hitting the cow caused the cow to die.

Well, similarly in the semantic case. Small horses cause "horse"s if horses do; but nothing follows as to the identity of the properties involved in the law that covers these causal transactions (except that small horses must be in the extension of the one and token "horse"s in the extension of the other). As it turns out, routine application of the method of differences suggests that it must be the property of *being a horse* and not the property of *being a small horse* that is connected with the property of *being a cause of "horse" tokens* since many things that have the first property have the third despite their lack of the second: large horses and medium horses simply spring to mind. (Similar considerations explain why "horse" means *horse* rather than, as it might be, *animal*; consider this a take-home assignment.)

3 *Third objection* (suggested independently by Steven Wagner, Tim Maudlin, and Scott Weinstein, in reverse chronological order):

Aha! But how about this: Consider, on the one hand, Old Paint (hereinafter OP) and, on the other hand, all the horses except Old Paint (hereinafter HEOPs). It's plausible that OP wouldn't cause "horse"s except that HEOPs do; and it's also plausible that HEOPs would cause "horse"s even if OP didn't. So OP's causing "horse"s is asymmetrically dependent on HEOPs causing "horse"s; so "horse" means *all the horses except Old Paint*.

Third reply:　This is a third reason why I want to do it in terms of nomic relations among properties rather than causal relations among individuals. In what follows, I will often have claims to make about what happens when you break the connection between Xs and "X"s. In thinking about these claims *it is essential* to bear in mind that "break the connection between Xs and 'X's" is always shorthand for "break the connection between the property in virtue of which Xs cause 'X's and the property of being a cause of 'X's". In the present case, *by stipulation* the property in virtue of which OP causes "horse"s is the property of *being a horse*. But if you break the connection between *that* property and the property of being a cause of "horse"s, then the connection between HEOPs and "horse"s fails too (since, of course, HEOPs are causes of "horse"s not in virtue of being HEOPs, but in virtue of being horses).

So OP's causing "horse"s is not, after all, asymmetrically dependent on HEOPs causing "horse"s, and the counterexample fails.

Next worry:　Does asymmetric dependence really solve the disjunction problem?

Asymmetric dependence finds *a* difference between, on the one hand, false tokens, representation in thought, and the like and, on the other hand, symbol tokens that are caused by things that they apply to. But is it the *right* difference? Does it, for example, explain why it's only in the case of the latter sort of tokenings that etiology determines meaning? I now propose to look rather closely at some worries about how the asymmetric dependence story copes with the disjunction problem.

4 *Baker's objection*:　Here is a passage from a critical discussion of asymmetric dependence in a recent paper by Lynne Rudder Baker (1989).

> Let us consider this account in light of a particular case. Suppose that, although there are many ordinary cats around, a certain person, *S*, learns a particular Mentalese symbol solely from artifacts (say, Putnam's robot-cats) that impinge on sensory surfaces in exactly the same way as cats. Now (for the first time) *S*

sees a real cat. . . . How should Fodor interpret the cat-caused token?. . . . There seem to be three possibilities . . .

none of which, Baker thinks, is tolerable. These are:

(a) the token means *cat* and is thus true of the cat. But this can't be right because ". . . if there is any asymmetric dependence, it goes the other way. *S*'s present disposition to apply 'cat' to a real cat depends upon her corresponding current disposition to apply it to robot-cats."

(b) the token means *robot-cat* and is thus false of the cat. But this can't be right since it ignores relevant counterfactuals. Specifically, it ignores the fact that – although only robots did cause *S*'s "cats" – cats *would* have caused them if *S* had happened to encounter any. ". . . the [counterfactual supporting] correlation is between tokens of a certain type and (cats or robot-cats). It is simply an accident that the actual causes of *S*'s early representations were all robot cats . . ."

This is a form of argument I accept; see the discussion of Dretske's "learning period" account of the disjunction problem in Fodor (1990b), chapter 3.

(c) the token means *robot-cat or cat* and is thus true of the cat. But this can't be right because it ". . . just rekindles the disjunction problem. . . . [Moreover, on this account] both the cat-caused and the robot-caused tokens are veridical after all – even when *S*, on subsequently discovering the difference between cats and robot-cats, exclaims, 'I mistook that robot for a cat!' [Option C] seems to preclude saying that *S* made an error. We would have to say that her mistake was to think that she had made a mistake, and try . . . to find some way to make sense of her 'second-order' mistake."

So none of the three options is any good. So there must be something wrong with the way the asymmetric dependence story treats the disjunction problem. What to do then, what to do?

For reasons that will become clear when we discuss the *echt* Twin Earth problem (the one about H_2O and XYZ), Baker's case is in certain important respects underdescribed. However, given just the information that she provides and the choices that she offers, I opt for (c); that first "cat"[14] token means *cat or robot* and is thus true of the cat that it's applied to.[15] I am pleased to be able to tell you that at least one other philosopher shares this intuition. Fred Dretske somewhere considers the following variant of a Twin Earth example: there are both H_2O and XYZ on Twin Earth, but, just fortuitously, some speaker of the local dialect learns "water" only from ostensions of samples of H_2O. Dretske's intuition (and mine) is that this speaker's tokens of "water" mean H_2O *or* XYZ; in this case, though not in the standard Twin cases, the fact that the speaker would have called XYZ samples "water" counts for determining the extension that term has in his mouth. Since Baker's cat/robot case seems to be much the same sort of example, I take it that Drestke would share my view that "cat" means *cat or robot-cat* in the circumstances that Baker imagines.[16]

How good are the objections Baker raises against this analysis? Baker says that to opt for (c) "rekindles the disjunction problem," but I don't see that that is so: it is OK for *some* predicates to be disjunctive as long as not all of them are. One can perfectly consistently hold, on the one hand, that "cat" means *robot or cat* when it's *accidental* that you learned it just from robot-cats, while denying, on the other hand, that it would mean *cat or robot* if you had learned it in a world where all you *could* have learned it from were robot-cats (e.g., because there aren't any cats around). Similarly, Dretske can consistently hold that "water" is true of H_2O or XYZ in the case he describes while agreeing that it is true of H_2O and false of XYZ in the case that Putnam describes.

But what of *S*'s sense, on subsequently discovering the difference between robots and cats, that she used to be mistaken when she applied "cats" to robots? If her "cat" tokens meant *cat or robot*, then they were true of *both* the cats and the robots that she applied them to. Is she, then, mistaken to suppose that she used to be mistaken? There is, I think, an easy answer and an interesting answer.

Easy answer: S used not to distinguish between cats and robots; her indiscriminate application of the same term to both was a symptom of her failure to distinguish between them. Not distinguishing between cats and robots was a serious mistake (by *S*'s current lights; and, of course, by ours).

Interesting answer: This depends on formulating the disjunction problem a little more carefully than one usually needs to. A typical instance of the disjunction problem is: "Why does the extension of 'cat' not contain both cats and rats, assuming that both cats and rats cause 'cat's?" This isn't quite the same as: "Why doesn't 'cat' *mean cat or rat* given that both cats and rats cause 'cats'?" The difference makes a difference in Baker's case.

Suppose that option (c) is right. Then, if *S* used to use "cat" in the way that Baker imagines, cats and robots were both in its extension. But this doesn't, of course, imply that *S* used "cat" to express the disjunctive concept CAT OR ROBOT (i.e., to mean *cat or robot*). Quite the contrary, S *couldn't* have used "cat" to express that concept because, by assumption, she didn't *have* that concept. Nobody can have the concept CAT OR ROBOT unless he has the constituent concepts CAT and ROBOT; which by assumption, *S* didn't.

So, then, what concept *did S* use "cat" to express according to option (c)? There just isn't any way to say; English provides only a disjunctive formula (viz. the expression "cat or robot") to pick out the extension {cats U robots}, and this disjunctive formula expresses a disjunctive concept (viz. the concept CAT OR ROBOT), hence not the concept that *S* had in mind. (Rather similar arguments show that English won't let you say what "water" means in the mouth of my Twin Earth twin; and, mutatis mutandis, that English$_2$ won't let my twin say what "water" means in my mouth.)

Now we can see what mistake *S* used to make when she applied "cat" to robots. No doubt what she said when she did so was something true. But she said it because she took it that the robots that she called "cats" had a certain non-disjunctive property which they shared with everything else in the set {cats U robots}. By her present lights, by contrast, *there is no such property*. By her present lights, the only property that cats and robots share qua cats and robots is the disjunctive property of BEING A CAT OR A ROBOT. So, by her present lights, when she used to say "cat" of robots (or of cats for that matter), she was saying something true, but she was saying it *for the wrong reason*. Hence her present (well-founded) intuition that there was some sort of mistake underlying her usage.

Given all this, I take it that Baker's case doesn't refute the asymmetric dependence account of content.

5 *Indeterminacy*:   As can be seen in Fodor (1990b), chapter 3, teleological solutions to the disjunction problem have the following nasty habit: teleology goes soft just when you need it most; you get indeterminacies of function in just the cases where you would like to appeal to function to resolve indeterminacies of content.

In the notorious frog and bug case, for example, one would think that a good theory of content should decide – and should give some reasons for deciding – whether the intentional objects of the frog's snaps are flies or little-black-things (in effect, whether the content of the frog's mental state is "there's a fly" or "there's a fly-or-bee-bee").[17] But, on inspection, the teleological story about content fails to do so. To recapitulate the argument I gave in (1990b), chapter 3: you can say why snapping is a good thing for frogs to do given their situation, which-ever way you describe what they snap *at*. All that's required for frog snaps to be functional is that they normally succeed in getting the flies into the frogs; and, so long as the little black dots in the frog's Normal environment *are* flies, the snaps do this equally well on either account of their intentional objects. The mathematics of survival come out precisely the same either way. (This is the sort of thing that makes philosophers feel – incorrectly but understandably – that, deep down, *content makes no difference*. First Darwinism, then nihilism when Darwinism fails; a career familiar enough from nineteenth-century moral theory.)

The asymmetric dependence story, by contrast, decides the case. The frog's snaps at flies are asymmetrically dependent on its snaps at little black dots. So it is black dots, not flies, that frogs snap at. (De dicto, of course; de re it's true both that frogs snap at little black dots *and* that they snap at flies since Normally flies are the only little black dots that frogs come across.)

Three subsidiary objections now need to be considered. To wit:

(i) "What makes you so sure that the counterfactuals are the way that you're assuming? Who says that the fly snaps are asymmetrically dependent on the black-dot snaps and not vice versa?"

Strictly speaking, this is a sort of question I do not feel obliged to answer; it suffices, for the present metaphysical purposes, that there are naturalistically specifiable conditions, not known to be false, such that *if* they obtain there is a matter of fact about what the frog is snapping at. (See above, the discussion of who has the burden of argument.) However, just this once:

The crucial observation is that frogs continue to snap at (and ingest) bee-bees even when they have plenty of evidence that the bee-bees that they're snapping at aren't flies. That is: frogs continue to snap at dots in worlds where there are dots but no flies; but they don't snap at flies in worlds where there are flies but no dots.[18] (In fact, frogs won't even snap at *dead* flies; it's *moving* black dots they care about.) I take it that this strongly suggests that either there is no nomic relation between the property of being-a-fly and the property of being-a-cause-of-frog-snaps, or that, if there is such a relation, it depends asymmetrically upon the nomic relation between the property of being-a-black-dot and the property of being-a-cause-of-fly-snaps.

So far as I can tell, there's nothing special here; just a routine employment of the method of differences.

(ii) "Doesn't asymmetric dependence capitulate to the argument from illusion? If the intentional object of the frog's fly-snaps is little black dots when (de re) the frog snaps at flies, then maybe the intentional object of my fly-swats is little black dots when (de re) I swat at flies. If the fact that frogs sometimes snap at little black dots that aren't flies means that they haven't got a FLY-concept, doesn't the fact that I sometimes swat at little black dots that aren't flies mean that I haven't got a FLY-concept either?"

The relevant consideration isn't, however, *just* that frogs sometimes go for bee-bees; it's that they are prepared to go on going for bee-bees *forever*. Sometimes I swat at mere fly-appearances; but usually I only swat if there's a fly. Sometimes Macbeth starts at mere dagger appearances; but most of the time he startles only if there's a dagger. What Macbeth and I have in common – and what distinguishes our case from the frog's – is that, *though he and I both make mistakes, we are both in a position to recover.*[19] By contrast, frogs *have no way at all* of telling flies from bee-bees. If you think of frog snaps at black dots as *mistaken* when the black dots are bee-bees, then such mistakes are *nomologically necessary* for the frog; and this not just in the weakish sense that it's a law that black dots elicit snaps if flies do in *this* world, but also in the stronger sense that black dots elicit snaps if flies do in *all* relevant worlds where the frog's psychological constitution is the same as here.

There is no world compatible with the perceptual mechanisms of frogs in which they can avoid mistaking black dots for flies. Whereas even if, freakishly, I mistake all the dagger appearances I actually come across for daggers; and even if, still more freakishly, I never do recover from any of these mistakes, still, that would be an *accident* since it is nomologically consonant with the way that I'm constructed that I should distinguish daggers from dagger appearances some of the time. But it is *not* nomologically consonant with the way that frogs are constructed that they should ever distinguish black dots from flies.

So Macbeth and I have dagger detectors and not dagger-or-dagger-appearance detectors but frogs have black-dot detectors and not fly detectors.

Here, then, is an interesting consequence of the present story about content: an organism can't have a kind of symbol which it *necessarily* misapplies, i.e., which it misapplies in every world compatible with its psychology. Suppose that Xs look a lot like Ys; suppose they look enough like Ys that S-tokens are quite often applied to them. Still, if S means Y and not X, then (according to the theory) there *must* be worlds, consonant with the organism's psychology in *this* world, in which S-tokens are applied to Ys but withheld from Xs. (And, of course, the asymmetric dependence condition requires that, ceteris paribus, some such worlds are nearer to ours then any worlds in which S-tokens are applied to Xs but withheld from Ys; see sections 8 and 10 below.) The bottom line is that it's impossible for frogs to have FLY concepts but not impossible for *us* to have FLY concepts. This is because it's consonant with our psychology, but not with theirs, to sometimes distinguish flies from bee-bees.

This consequence constrains robustness. There are, after all, some mistakes that can't be made; viz. mistakes from which it is nomologically impossible to recover, consonant with the character of one's psychology. To this extent, the asymmetric dependence story is an attenuated sort of verificationism. I think that perhaps it captures what't *true* about verificationism; but, of course, I would think that.[20]

(iii) "How do you avoid saying that frogs are really snapping at their retinas?"

The point about black dots was that (we're assuming) in the frog's ecology, "is a black dot" is a description Normally true of flies. So our problem was to choose – from among the descriptions that flies Normally satisfy when frogs snap at them – the descriptions that frogs snap at them under. There may, however, be Xs other than flies, and Fs other than being a black dot, such that flies getting snapped at by frogs is asymmetrically dependent on Xs being F. If there are such, the question would arise: Why aren't Xs that are Fs the intentional objects of fly snaps?

For example: it's presumably a law that no fly gets snapped at except as some proximal projection of the fly produces some state of excitation of the retina of the frog; a retinal excitation that is, in turn, causally implicated in producing the snap. Moreover, it's plausible that such states of retinal excitation would be sufficient for causing frog snaps even if they (the excitations) weren't produced by proximal projections of flies. If all this is true, then the frog's fly-elicited fly snaps are asymmetrically dependent on these states of retinal excitation. So why aren't the excitation states the intentional objects of the frog's snaps?

I don't know what the story is with frogs, but in the general case there is no reason at all to suppose that the causal dependence of perceptual states on distal objects is asymmetrically dependent on the causal dependence of *specific arrays of proximal stimuli* on the distal objects; e.g., that there are specifiable sorts of proximal traces that a cow has to leave on pain of the cow → COW connection failing. On the contrary, in the usual case there are a heterogeneity of proximal arrays that will eventuate in cow perception, and there's a good reason for this: since – due to the laws of optics, inter alia – cows are mapped one-many onto their proximal projections, the mechanisms of perception – constancy, bias, sharpening, and the like – must map the proximal projections many-one onto tokenings of COW. Given the vast number of ways that cows may impinge upon sensory mechanisms, a perceptual system which made COW tokenings intimately dependent upon specific proximal projections wouldn't work as a cow-spotter.

It might still be said, however, that the dependence of cow thoughts on distal cows is asymmetrically dependent on their dependence on *disjunctions* of proximal cow projections; distal cows wouldn't evoke COW tokens but that they project proximal whiffs or glimpses or snaps or crackles or . . . well, or what? Since, after all, cow spotting can be mediated by theory to any extent you like, the barest whiff or glimpse of cow can do the job for an observer who is suitably attuned. Less, indeed, than a whiff or glimpse; a mere ripple in cow-infested waters may suffice to turn the trick. On the present view, cow thoughts do *not*, of course, owe their intentional content to the belief systems in which they are embedded; what determines their content is simply their asymmetric causal dependence on cows. But it is quite compatible with this that belief systems should *mediate* these semantically salient causal dependencies. They can form links in the causal chain that runs from cows to COW tokens, just as instruments of observation form links in the causal chain that runs from galaxies to GALAXY tokens.[21] To the extent that this is so, just about *any* proximal display might mediate the relation between cows and cow-thoughts for some cow-thinker or other on some or other cow-spotting occasion.

So barring appeals to *open* disjunctions, it seems likely that there is just no way to specify an array of proximal stimulations upon which the dependence of cow-thoughts upon cows is asymmetrically dependent. And here's where I quit.[22] I mean, it does seem to me that the price of intentional univocality is holding that primitive intentional states can't express open disjunctions. The idea might be that, on the one hand, content depends on *nomic* relations among properties and, on the other, nothing falls under a law by satisfying an *open* disjunction (open disjunctions aren't projectible). Like the prohibition against primitive symbols that express impossible properties, this strikes me as a very strong consequence of the present semantical theory, but not an embarrassment because not obviously false.[23]

6 *What about the logical vocabulary?* I don't know what about the logical vocabulary. Since I think that Kripke's objection fails (see above), I'm inclined to think that maybe there is *no* objection to the idea that "+," "and," "all" and the like have the meanings they do because they play a certain causal role in the mental lives of their users. This would, of course, be to accept a distinction in kind between the logical and the non-logical vocabularies. (The semantics for the former would be a kind of "use" theory, whereas the semantics for the latter would depend on nomic, specifically mind-world, relations.) Gilbert Harman somewhere suggests that to be a logical word *just is* to be the sort of word of which a use-theory of meaning is true. That proposal strikes me as plausible.

You may wonder how anybody who claims to be implacably opposed to inferential role semantics can have the gall to identify the meaning of a logical word with its use. Answer: the trouble with use theories is that they invite holism by well-known paths of argument (see Fodor, 1990b, chapter 3, and, more extensively, 1987, chapter 3). But these holistic arguments depend on the acknowledged impossibility of *defining* most terms (specifically, on the impossibility of distinguishing defining from merely nomic biconditionals). It is therefore unclear that they apply to the logical vocabulary since terms in the logical vocabulary generally *are* definable: anything counts as meaning *plus* that expresses a function from the numbers m,n to $m + n$; anything counts as meaning *and* that expresses a function from propositions to truth values and assigns *true* to P,Q iff it assigns *true* to $P \ \& \ Q$.

Correspondingly, it is arguably a sufficient condition for a speaker's meaning *plus* by "+" that, ceteris paribus, he takes "$m + n$" to designate the sum of m and n; a sufficient condition for a speaker's meaning *and* by "and" that, ceteris paribus, he takes "P and Q" to be true iff he takes "P" to be true and "Q" to be true; and so forth. (Relations like "taking to express," "taking to be true" – which, on this construal, hold between symbol users and symbols they use – would have to receive a causal/dispositional reconstruction if circularity is to be avoided. But there are familiar proposals for wedding functionalist construals of these relations to functional role theories of content: thus, a speaker means *and* by "and" iff, ceteris paribus, he has "P and Q" in his belief box iff he has

"*P*" in his belief box and he has "*Q*" in his belief box. In the case of logical vocabulary, I know of no principled reason why some such proposal shouldn't be endorsed.)

7 *What about predicates that express abstractions (like "virtuous")?*   All predicates express properties, and all properties are abstract. The semantics of the word "virtuous," for example, is determined by the nomic relation between the property of being a cause of tokens of that word and the property of being virtuous. It isn't interestingly different from the semantics of "horse."

8 *Block's problem:*   The following characteristically insightful objection was pointed out to me by Ned Block in the following conversation; I suppose I'm grateful to him.

> Look, your theory comes down to: "cow" means *cow* and not *cat* because, though there are nomologically possible worlds in which cows cause "cow"s but cats don't, there are no nomologically possible worlds in which cats cause "cow"s but cows don't. But such face plausibility as this idea may have depends on equivocating between two readings of "cow". In fact, there's a dilemma: if you mean by "cow" something like *the phonological / orthographic sequence* ⌜c^o^w⌝, then there's just no reason at all to believe the claim you're making. For example, there is surely a possible world in which cows don't cause ⌜c^o^w⌝s but trees do, viz. *the world in which* ⌜c^o^w⌝ *means tree*. So, if when you write "cow" what you mean is ⌜c^o^w⌝, then it clearly can't be nomologically necessary in order for "cow" to mean *cow* that nothing causes "cow"s in worlds where cows don't.
>
> Notice that it does no good to protest that the asymmetric dependence condition is supposed to be sufficient but not necessary for content. There is *no* orthographic/phonetic sequence "*X*" which mightn't mean *tree* in some nomologically possible world or other, whatever "*X*" happens to mean here. Given the conventionality of meaning, there couldn't be. It follows that there is no orthographic/phonetic sequence "*X*" the nomologically possibility of tokenings of which is dependent on "*X*"s being caused by *X*s. So there is no such sequence that satisfies your sufficient condition for meaning *X*. A sufficient condition for content that *nothing* satisfies needn't much concern Brentano. Or us.
>
> It wouldn't, of course, be a way out of this to amend the proposal to read "⌜c^o^w⌝ means *cow* only if, in every world in which you break the cow → ⌜c^o^w⌝ connection, *either* nothing causes ⌜c^o^w⌝s, *or* ⌜c^o^w⌝ doesn't mean *cow*." For, though that would indeed exclude the unwanted cases, it would do so by appealing to a semantical condition and would therefore be circular. Well, for the same sort of reason it's also no good arguing that, in the world imagined, tokens of ⌜c^o^w⌝ don't count as tokens of the (viz. *our*) word "cow"; i.e., to read "cow" in "cows's are asymmetrically dependent on cows" as naming the *word* "cow" rather than the orthographic/phonological sequence ⌜c^o^w⌝. For, that would be to appeal implicitly to a semantical construal of the conditions for type identifying words. Barring circularity, the orthographic/phonological construal of "same word" is accessible to a naturalistic semantics, but the semantical construal of "same word" is not.

So, to put it in a nutshell, if you read "cow" orthographically/phonologically the claim that "cow" means *cow* because "cow"s are asymmetrically dependent on cows is false; and if you read "cow" morphemically the claim that "cow" means *cow* because "cow"s are asymmetrically dependent on cows is circular. Either way, it's a claim that seems to be in trouble.

This is a pretty nifty line of argument. Just the same, I think the problem it raises is actually only technical.

Block is, of course, perfectly right that for the purposes of a naturalistic semantics the only non-question-begging reading of "cow" is ⌜cˆoˆw⌝. Henceforth be it so read. However, the asymmetric dependence proposal is that, *all else being equal*, breaking cow → "cow" breaks X → "cow" for all X.[24] Correspondingly – to put the point intuitively – what's wrong with Block's argument is that all else *isn't* equal in the worlds that he imagines. To get those worlds, you need to suppose *not only* that cow → "cow" is broken, *but also and independently* that tree → "cow" is in force. It's this independent supposition that violates the "all else equal" clause.

Here's a way to make the same point in terms of possibilia. If you put in "all else equal," then what the theory requires is *not* that cows cause "cow"s in *every* nomologically possible world where Xs cause cows. Rather, what's required is just that there be worlds where cows cause "cows" and non-cows don't; and that they be nearer to our world than any world in which some non-cows cause "cows" and no cows do. Notice that, on this formulation of the asymmetric dependence condition, the nomological possibility of Block's world where ⌜cˆoˆw⌝ means *tree* is compatible with "cow" meaning (and hence being asymmetrically dependent upon) cows in our world. At least, it is on the intuitively plausible assumption that worlds that are just like ours except that it's the case that cows don't cause "cow"s are ipso facto nearer to us than worlds that are just like ours except that it's both the case that cows don't cause "cows" *and* that trees do.

Let's do this one more time: to get the nearest semantically relevant world to here, you break cow → "cow." All the X → "cow" relations that nomically depend on cow → "cow" will, of course, go too, since to say that X → "cow" is nomically dependent on cow → "cow" is to say that [not (X → "cow") unless (cow → "cow")] is nomologically necessary. What the present theory claims is that, in the world that's just like ours except that cow → "cow" and everything nomologically dependent on it are gone, X → "cow" is false for all X (where, to repeat, "cow" is read as ⌜cˆoˆw⌝). Well, if this is what you mean by "the nearest possible world in which cow → 'cow' is gone," then clearly, Block's world doesn't qualify. To get to Block's world, you have to both break cow → "cow" and to stipulate tree → "cow." So the nomological possibility of Block's world is compatible with "cow" meaning *cow* according to the present version of the asymmetric dependence criterion. So everything would seem to be OK.

Corollary: suppose that, in *this* world, there happens to be a language L in which "cow" (viz. $\ulcorner c\hat{\ }o\hat{\ }w\urcorner$) means *tree*. Presumably *our* (English-speakering) use of "cow" for cows is causally independent of L's use of "cow" for trees. So, then, the nearest world to ours in which cow $\rightarrow$ "cow" goes (taking with it everything that's nomically dependent on it) still has tree $\rightarrow$ "cow" intact; and the nearest world to ours in which tree $\rightarrow$ "cow" goes (taking with it everything that's nomically dependent on it) still has cow $\rightarrow$ "cow" intact. But by assumption (specifically, by the assumption that only L and English use $\ulcorner c\hat{\ }o\hat{\ }w\urcorner$), in the nearest world in which *both* cow $\rightarrow$ "cow" *and* tree $\rightarrow$ "cow" goes for every X. So, for every X, either $X \rightarrow$ "cow" depends on cow $\rightarrow$ "cow" or $X \rightarrow$ "cow" depends on tree $\rightarrow$ "cow", neither of which depends upon the other. So, if there is a language in which "cow" means *cow* and a language in which "cow" means tree, then there are two different ways in which tokens of "cow" satisfy the asymmetric dependence condition. So "cow" (viz. $\ulcorner c\hat{\ }o\hat{\ }w\urcorner$) is ambiguous. This is, I take it, the intuitively correct solution.

Next objection?

9 *Why doesn't "WATER" mean the same as "H_2O"?* After all, it's plausible that they express the same property; in which case, it presumably follows that neither concept is asymmetrically dependent on the other.

Actually, I'm inclined to think that "WATER" *does* mean the same as "H_2O." What doesn't follow – and isn't true – is that having the concept WATER is the same mental state as having the concept H_2O (i.e., it's not the case that concepts are individuated by their contents. For a discussion of this sort of distinction, see Fodor, 1990b, chapter 6). Would you, therefore, kindly rephrase your objection?

OK. Why, given that they express the same property, is having the concept WATER not the same mental state as having the concept H_2O?

Reply:　Because you can't have the concept H_2O without having the concept HYDROGEN and you can have the concept WATER without having the concept HYDROGEN; as, indeed, is evident from the fact that the (Mentalese) expression "H_2O" has internal lexico-syntactic structure.

10 *Do the twin cases*:　Tell me why "water" doesn't mean XYZ. And don't tell me that "water" does mean XYZ; XYZ isn't even in its extension.

I suppose the worry is that an English speaker exposed to XYZ would call it "water," and the truth of this counterfactual suggests that there's a nomic dependence between the property of being a cause of "water" tokens and the disjunctive property of being H_2O or XYZ. Since, according to the present proposal, content arises from such nomic dependencies, the problem is to explain why H_2O is, but XYZ is not, in the extension of "water." (Less precisely, it's to explain why "water" doesn't mean something disjunctive.)

The thing to keep your eye on is this: it's built into the way that one tells the Twin Earth story that it's about kind-terms (mutatis mutandis, kind-concepts). In particular, it's part of the story about "water" being a kind-term that English speakers intended it to apply to all and only stuff of the same (natural) kind as paradigmatic local samples (and similarly for "water2" as it's used by speakers of English2.) A fortiori, it's part of "water" and "water2" being kind-terms that speakers intend *not* to apply them to anything that is distinguishably *not* of the same kind as their local samples. (There are, of course, sorts of expressions with perfectly kosher semantics whose uses are not controlled by these sorts of intentions, that are therefore not used to pick out natural kinds, and whose extensions are therefore disjunctive in the sense that things of more than one natural kind belong to them. The expression "stuff sort of like water" is, I suppose, one such.)

My point is that the intention to use "water" only of stuff of the same kind as the local samples has the effect of making its applications to XYZ asymmetrically dependent on its applications to H_2O ceteris paribus. Given that people are disposed to treat "water" as a kind-term (and, of course, given that the local samples are all in fact H_2O) it follows that – all else equal – they would apply it to XYZ only when they would apply it to H_2O; specifically, they would apply it to XYZ only when they *mistake* XYZ for H_2O; only when (and only because) they can't tell XYZ and H_2O apart. Whereas, given a world in which they *can* tell XYZ and H_2O apart (and in which their intentions with respect to "water" are the same as they are in *this* world), they will continue to apply "water" to H_2O and refrain from applying it to XYZ.

Notice that worlds in which speakers intend to use "water" as a kind-term and XYZ is distinguishable from H_2O are "nearby" relative to worlds in which speakers do not intend to use "water" as a kind-term and XYZ is distinguishable from H_2O. So the possibilities play out like this:

- In nearby worlds where XYZ *can't* be distinguished from H_2O, if you break the H_2O/"water" connection you lose the XYZ/"water" connection and vice versa.
- In nearby worlds where XYZ *can* be distinguished from H_2O, if you break the H_2O/"water" connection you lose the XYZ/"water" connection, but *not* vice versa.

So, ceteris paribus, there are nearby worlds where you get the H_2O/"water" connection without the XYZ/"water" connection, but no nearby worlds where you get the XYZ/"water" connection without the H_2O/"water" connection. I.e., it's nomologically possible for the XYZ/water connection to fail without the H_2O/water connection failing, but not vice versa. So applications of "water" to XYZ are asymmetrically dependent on applications of "water" to H_2O. So "water" means H_2O and not XYZ in the conditions that the Twin Earth story imagines, just as the standard intuitions require.[25]

So much for H_2O and XYZ. It may be useful, by way of summary, to bring together what I've said about the unicorn worry, the Baker worry and the

H_2O/XYZ worry, since all three involve cases where a semantic theory is required to make intuitively correct determinations of the extension of a term with respect to merely possible entities.

To begin with, you can now see why I said that the Baker example (about cats and robot-cats) was underdescribed. In the *echt* Twin cases, it's always assumed that the speaker intends the word in question to be a natural kind-term, and the speaker's having this intention has the effect of making the semantically relevant asymmetric dependencies true of his use of the word. In Baker's case, by contrast, we know that the speaker eventually comes to apply "cat" to cats and not to robots, but we *don't* know whether this is in virtue of a previous standing disposition to use "cat" as a kind-term. Baker doesn't say, so I've assumed that the speaker had no such standing disposition. So Baker's "cat" means *cat or robot* because, on the one hand, *S* would (indeed, does) use "cat" for either; and, on the other, there's nothing in Baker's description of the case that suggests a mechanism (such as an intention to use "cat" as a kind-term) that would make the use for the robots asymmetrically dependent upon the use for the cats (or vice versa).

"Unicorn" means unicorn because you can have lawful relations among uninstantiated properties (and people would apply "unicorn" to unicorns if there were any). By contrast, "water" means water (and not XYZ) because, although people would use "water" of XYZ if there were any (XYZ is supposed to be indistinguishable from H_2O), nevertheless they have a settled policy of using "water" as a kind-term (of using it only for substances actually of the same kind as water), and their adherence to this policy makes their use of "water" for XYZ asymmetrically dependent on their use of "water" for H_2O: there's a break in the XYZ/"water" connection *without* a break in the H_2O/ "water" connection in nearby worlds where H_2O is distinguishable from XYZ. (If, however, you don't like this story about why "water" doesn't mean XYZ, I'll tell you a different one presently.)

11 *Absolutely last objection*:   But *how could* asymmetric dependence be sufficient for content? Surely you can have cases where one nomic relation is asymmetrically dependent on another but where there is no *semantical* relation at issue?

Well, maybe, but I've only been able to think of two candidates: asymmetric dependences that arise from causal chains and asymmetric dependences that involve nomic relations at different levels of analysis. And what's striking about both these cases is that the asymmetric dependences they generate aren't the right kind to produce robustness. Since mere stipulation can ensure that only asymmetric dependencies that do produce robustness count for semantic purposes, neither of these kinds of cases poses a real threat to my story. Let's have a look at this.

Interlevel relations: Suppose you have a case where a microlevel law $(B \rightarrow C)$ provides the mechanism for a macrolevel law $(A \rightarrow D)$ (in the way that, for example, Bernoulli's law provides the mechanism for laws about airfoils). Then it might be that the $A \to D$ law is asymmetrically dependent on the $B \to C$ law. You might get this if, for example, $B \to C$ is necessary but not sufficient to sustain $A \to D$; in that case, breaking the $B \to C$ connection would break the $A \to D$ connection in all nomologically possible worlds, but there might be nomologically possible worlds in which the $A \to D$ connection goes even though the $B \to C$ connection is intact. Since it is, to put it mildly, not obvious that C has to mean B in such cases, it seems that asymmetric dependence isn't sufficient for content after all.

Reply: The point of appeals to asymmetric dependence in theories of content is to show how tokens of the same type could have heterogeneous causes compatible with their all meaning the same thing; i.e., it's to show how robustness is possible. Correspondingly, if a sufficient condition for content is going to be fashioned in terms of asymmetric dependence, it must advert to the dependence of one causal law *about "X" tokens* upon another causal law *about "X" tokens*. But the sort of asymmetric dependences that interlevel cases generate don't meet this condition. What we have in these cases is a law that governs the tokening of one thing (*D*s in the example) that's dependent on a law that governs the tokening of some other thing (*C*s in the example). This sort of asymmetric dependence doesn't produce robustness, so it's not semantically relevant.

Causal chains: We discussed these in a slightly different context when we asked why the frog's retinal irradiations are not the intentional objects of its fly-snaps: the causal link between distal stimuli and mental representations is mediated by (and thus depends asymmetrically upon) causal links between proximal stimuli and mental representations. In that example, we were given a state whose intentional object was assumed to be one of its causes, and the question was *which* one. The present issue is slightly different: since causal chains give rise to a species of asymmetrical dependence, and since every event belongs to some causal chain or other, how are we to avoid concluding that everything means something? Pansemanticism gone mad.

Short form: Suppose *A*s (qua *A*s) cause *B*s (qua *B*s), and *B*s (qua *B*s) cause *C*s (qua *C*s), and assume that *A*s are sufficient but not necessary for the *B*s. Then the law $A \to C$ is asymmetrically dependent on the law $B \to C$. Why doesn't it follow that *C*s mean *B*?

Answer: Because, although the causal chain makes the $A \to C$ connection asymmetrically depend on the $B \to C$ connection, the dependence of *C*s on *B*s that it engenders is not ipso facto robust, and content requires not just causal dependence but robustness too. The dependence of *C*s on *B*s *is robust only if there are non-B-caused Cs*. But the causal chain $A \to B \to C$ engenders an asymmetric dependence in which *all the A-caused Cs are also B-caused*. So the aymmetric dependence of $A \to C$ on $B \to C$ doesn't satisfy the conditions on robustness; so it's not semantically relevant.

But suppose we have both $A \to B \to C$ and $D \to B \to C$.

(i) C still doesn't mean B because every C is B-caused and robustness fails.

(ii) C doesn't mean A because Cs being caused by non-As doesn't depend on Cs being caused by As, (i.e., you don't get $X \to C$ relations that are asymmetrically dependent on $A \to C$ relations). An analogous argument shows that C doesn't mean D either.

(iii) C doesn't mean (A or D) because X-caused Cs that are asymmetrically dependent on A- or D-caused Cs are ipso facto asymmetrically dependent on B-caused Cs. Intuitively, what's wanted is that "X" means X only if Xs are the *only* sorts of things on which Xs are robustly dependent. Take-home problem: Formulate the asymmetric dependence condition to make this the case.

All that this technical fooling around shows is that, if we stipulate that asymmetric dependence engenders content only if it produces robustness, then perhaps we can avoid Crazy Pansemanticism: the doctrine that everything means something. But, of course, some causal chains – viz. the ones that do meet conditions for information and robustness – *will*, ipso facto, meet the present conditions for content. So, the really interesting question is whether meeting the conditions for information and robustness really *is* meeting the conditions for content. We'll return to this at the end.

So much for all the objections I've been able to think of.

Unverificationist Interlude

We arrive at a major watershed. If we accept the theory as it has been developed so far, we're committed to a form of verificationism. For, according to the theory, it's a semantical truth (it follows from the nature of semantical relations as such) that:

P: You cannot have a symbol (/concept) which expresses property X unless it is nomologically possible for you to distinguish X-instantiations from instantiations of any other property.

Or, to put it slightly differently:

P′: If "X" expresses at least X, and if there is a Y which it is not nomologically possible for you to distinguish from X, then "X" expresses Y as well as X (e.g., it expresses the disjunctive property X *or* Y).[26]

Now, I don't know of any perfectly clear counterexamples to P (Paul Boghossian has struggled manfully to produce one, but I'm not convinced that he's succeeded).[27] But, on the other hand, I don't see why P or P′ have to be true. *Why* should having a word that means X but not Y depend on being able, even in principle, to tell Xs and Ys apart? After all (by assumption) being X is a different state of affairs from being Y even if (by assumption) the worlds in which differences between Xs and Ys show up are too far away for us to get to. But if the difference between being X and being Y is real, then so too, surely, is the difference between being X and being $(X$ or $Y)$. And if the difference between being X and being $(X$ or $Y)$ is real, why shouldn't we be able to talk (/think) in ways that respect that difference?

I don't know how convincing you will find that line of thought; I'm not at all sure, for that matter, how convincing *I* find it. Put it, at a minimum, that the successes of verificationist philosophizing have not, over the years, been exactly staggering. Perhaps it would be well, if only as an exercise, to see what we would have to change about the story we've been telling if we want it not to entail P or P′.

I think the answer is pretty clear. The story up to now has had two parts: there's an "information" condition (roughly, "X" expresses X only if Xs qua Xs cause "X"s); and there's an "asymmetric dependence" condition which is supposed to take care of the "robustness" cases; the cases where "X"s are caused by things *other* than Xs.[28] It is the first of these – the information condition – that entrains the verificationism. Correspondingly, the cost of getting rid of the verificationism is a semantical theory that is, in a sense that should presently become clear, not purely informational. I propose to lay out the relevant geography, leaving it to you to decide whether or not being a verificationist is worth it at the price.

You may recall that in Fodor (1990b), chapter 3, when we discussed the Skinner-to-Dretske tradition in semantics, I suggested that the following claim is close to its heart: what your words (/thoughts) mean is dependent entirely on your *dispositions* to token them (on what I called the "subjunctive history" of their tokenings), *the actual history* of their tokenings being semantically irrelevant.

The discussion up till now has stuck with Skinner and Dretske in assuming that this doctrine is correct – that semantic relations are, as I shall now say, purely informational[29] – and it's pretty clear how the verificationism follows. Consider the Twin cases. Perhaps the first thing one is inclined to point to as relevant to distinguishing the WATER concept from the WATER2 concept is that the former, but not the latter, is formed in an environment of H_2O. But (purely) informational theories don't acknowledge this appeal. Such theories distinguish between concepts only if their tokenings are controlled by different laws. Hence only if different counterfactuals are true of their tokenings. Hence only if there are (possible) circumstances in which one concept would be caused to be tokened and the other concept would not. So if you want to have the WATER concept distinct from the WATER2 concept, and you want to play by the rules of a purely informational semantics, you have to assume a world where WATER is under the control of H_2O but *not* under the control of XYZ,[30] i.e., a world where H_2O and XYZ are distinguished (a fortiori, a world in which H_2O and XYZ are distinguishable). That is how you get from informational semantics to verificationism.

Correspondingly, the way you avoid the verificationism is: you relax the demand that semantic relations be construed solely by reference to subjunctive conditionals; you let the actual histories of tokenings count too. What follows is a sketch of a mixed theory of this sort. I propose three conditions on the relation between (a symbol) "X" and (a property) X, such that, when they are simultaneously satisfied, "X" expresses X. Or so I claim. I'll then comment, briefly, on the sorts of considerations that motivate each of these conditions. And then I'll say something about what sorts of facts are hard for this kind of theory to accommodate. And then I'll do a little tidying up and a little moralizing. And then – you'll be glad to hear – I propose to stop.

I claim that "X" means X if:

(1)   "Xs cause 'X's" is a law.
(2)   Some "X"s are actually caused by Xs.
(3)   For all Y not $= X$, if Ys qua Ys actually cause "X"s, then Ys *causing* "X"s is asymmetrically dependent on Xs *causing* "X"s.

Comments:

Condition 1: "$X \rightarrow$ 'X'" is a law.

- This just follows Dretske. It ensures that "X"s *at least* carry information about Xs (but not, N.B., that they carry information *only* about Xs).
- It also explains why "horse" means HORSE and not SMALL HORSE (even though small horses cause "horses" if horses do. The idea is that when small horses cause "horses" the covering law is *horse* → "*horse*" and not *small horse* → "horse" (see above).
- Notice, however, that condition 1 doesn't rule out "horse" means HORSE OR (COW ON A DARK NIGHT) since the connection between the property of being a "horse" token and the property of being an instance of *cow on a dark night* (unlike the connection between the property of being a "horse" token and the property of being an instance of *small horse*) presumably *is* nomic on the operative assumption that cows on dark nights qua cows on dark nights are sometimes mistaken for horses. That is, the information requirement doesn't, in and of itself, solve the disjunction problem. By now this should come as not news.

Condition 2: Some "X"s are actually caused by Xs

- This invokes the actual history of "*X*" tokens as constitutive of the meaning of "*X*" and thereby violates the assumptions of pure informational theories.
- It rules out " 'horse' means Twin-horse," " 'water' means XYZ," and the like.
- It also allows the intuition that the first non-robot-caused "cat" (in Baker's example) was *false*, in case that's the intuition that you feel inclined to have. (It doesn't *require* this intuition, however. If you don't have it, you're free to argue that, for semantical purposes, a causal history that includes only *X*s counts as including *X*s and *Y*s when the exclusion of the *Y*s was accidental; in which case, the intuition should be that the first cat-occasioned "cat" means CAT OR ROBOT and is therefore true.)

Condition 3: Asymmetric dependence

- This is the heart of the solution of the disjunction problem for the mixed theory as it was for the pure one: it rules out "horse" means HORSE OR COW ON A DARK NIGHT, given (a) the assumption that some cows on dark nights actually do cause "horses," and (b) the usual assumption about counterfactuals (viz. that cows on dark nights wouldn't cause "horses" but that horses do).
- Notice that we can't rely on condition 2 to do this job. It's one thing to assume that the actual history of "*X*" must contain *X*s so that "horse" can't mean TWIN HORSE. It's quite another thing to suppose that it must contain *only* *X*s (so that, if some cows on dark nights have caused "horses" then "horse" means HORSE OR COW ON A DARK NIGHT). Having condition 2 in the theory allows actual histories of tokening to be constitutive of the semantic properties of symbols; condition 3 allows symbols to be robust with respect to their actual histories of tokening as well as with respect to their counterfactual histories. That is, it allows tokens of a symbol actually to be caused by things that are not its extension.
- Condition 3 is also required to rule out " 'horse' means HORSE PICTURE," to account for the dependence of the metaphorical uses of "horse" upon its literal uses, and the like. Remember that not all non-horse-occasioned "horse"s are ipso facto false.

General comment: The mixed theory is itself just a *soupçon* verificationist, but only in a way that might surely be considered untendentious. We used to have to say that "*X*"s meaning *X* requires the nomological possibility of distinguishing *X* from any property that would cause "*X*"s *if it were instantiated*. (Hence we had to say that "water" means something disjunctive unless there is a nomologically possible world in which H_2O is distinguished from XYZ, etc.) Now all we require is that it be nomologically possible to distinguish *X* from any property that is *actually* instantiated in the causal history of "*X*"s. (Any property that *doesn't* actually cause "*X*"s ipso facto fails to meet condition 2; that's why "water" doesn't mean XYZ according to the present account.) The theory is residually verificationist only in assuming that if cows-on-dark-nights actually do cause "horses," either "horse" means something disjunctive or it is nomologically possible to distinguish horses from cows-on-a-dark-night. (I.e., the residual verificationism is required so that tokens of "horse" that are caused by cows on dark nights can fall under condition 3.)

I think, in fact, that this much verificationism is probably built into causal theories of content per se. Thus, you get actual causal histories to bear on the semantics of kind-concepts by taking terms like "water" to mean something like *whatever bears the same-kind relation to the local samples*. This will make XYZ be not in the extension of "water" *on the assumption that there's no XYZ in the local samples*. If, by contrast, water tokens actually *are* caused indifferently by H_2O and XYZ, you can't appeal to actual histories to exclude XYZ from the extension of "water." And if they *would be* caused by H_2O and XYZ indifferently in any nomologically accessible world (if, that is to say, it's not nomologically possible to tell them apart) then you can't appeal to subjunctive causal conditionals to exclude XYZ from the extension of "water." So there seems to be *nothing left* to keep XYZ out of the extension of "water" consonant with assuming that what "water" means must have *something* to do with the causation of its tokens. My advice is, if this be verificationism, swallow it.

Notice, by the way, that it's still true, on the mixed view, that frogs snap at black dots rather than flies. For: some frog snaps are caused by black dots (black dots satisfy condition 2); and there is no world compatible with the frog's psychology in which frogs snap at flies but not at black dots (flies fail to satisfy condition 3). Conversely, it's daggers – rather than dagger appearances – that Macbeth's DAGGER concept expresses because, although daggers and dagger appearances both cause DAGGER tokens in this world, still there are possible worlds in which Macbeth can tell them apart. Even if you don't want a *lot* of verificationism, you probably want a *little* verificationism to deal with semantical versions of the argument from illusion.

Here's what's happened: where we used to have a *causal law* account of semantic properties, we now have an account that invokes both causal laws and actual causal histories. The resultant story is only minimally verificationist, which is arguably a good thing. But, of course, there is the usual nothing free for lunch. Pure informational theories aren't gratuitous; there are things they do better than mixed theories can. In particular, they're very good at unicorns.

Pure informational theories can treat "unicorn"s just the same way they treat "table"s and "chair"s. Since, according to such theories, all that semantic relations require is the right nomic connections among properties, and since you can have nomic connections among *uninstantiated* properties, all that's required for "unicorn"s to mean *unicorns* is a nomologically possible world in which the former are elicited by the latter, together with the satisfaction of the usual asymmetric dependence constraints. Uninstantiation is not, according to pure informational theories, a semantically *interesting* property of properties.

Mixed informational theories, by contrast, take quite a serious view of uninstantiation; in particular, "unicorn" can't mean UNICORN in virtue of satisfying conditions 1 to 3 since it fails egregiously to satisfy 2. The upshot is that, whereas pure theories can treat UNICORN as a *primitive* concept, mixed theories have to treat it as, in effect, an abbreviated description. Mixed theories have to say, in effect, that concepts that express uninstantiated properties are ipso facto constructions out of concepts that express instantiated properties; there is, no doubt, something quaintly Russellean in this. Perhaps, however, it's not a tragedy. Even pure theories have to say that "square circle" can't be primitive since, of course, there isn't a nomologically possible world in which "square circles" are caused by instantiations of *square circle*hood. So, if the mixed theory that embraces 1 to 3 can't be *necessary* for content, neither can the corresponding pure theory that omits condition 2.

Pure and mixed theories both have to acknowledge primitive/derived as a distinction of kind. Still, pure theories can tolerate a rather closer connection between being *semantically* primitive and being *syntactically* simple than mixed theories can. I used to think (see "The Current Status of the Innateness Controversy" in Fodor, 1981a) that "primitive concept" just about meant "lexical concept" (viz. concept expressed by a syntactically simple predicate of, as it might be, English). I'm now inclined to think it just about means "lexical and instantiated concept." Extensionally, this probably makes vanishingly close to no difference because *uninstantiated lexical properties are very, very rare.* So rare that one might risk the speculation that their rarity isn't an accident. Maybe the *instantiated lexical concepts* constitute a semantical natural kind.

Summary: How God Knows What You're Thinking

"Even God couldn't tell, just by looking in your head, the intentional content of your neural states."[31] That's a way of summarizing the "externalist" view of content. It's also a way of rejecting "functional role" semantics since, according to functional role theories, when you know the facts about the intramental causal relations of a mental state, you know the facts on which its content supervenes.

Robustness ups the ante. If, as I've been supposing, the etiology of the tokens of an intentional state can be practically arbitrarily heterogeneous consonant with all the tokens having the same content, then it presumably follows that even God couldn't tell what the content of a mental state is just by looking at its *actual* causal relations. And this may seem unsatisfactory, because really *causal* – as opposed to informational – theories would have it that the actual causal relations of a mental state token are what *determines* its content. At the heart of such theories is the intuition that it must be something like *being caused by a cat* that makes a certain thought a *cat*-thought. The tug of war between this sort of intuition and the facts about robustness has been a main theme in our discussion; indeed, the "mixed" story about content is an attempt to give both the causal and the nomic theories their due.

What's in your head doesn't determine content and actual causal relations don't determine content, but: if God has a look at both the actual causal relations of your mental state *and* the surrounding space of counterfactual causal relations, *then* He can tell the content of your state. The content of a state supervenes on its actual causal relations together with certain counterfactuals. Or so I claim.

If this is true then (barring some caveats we'll look at presently) it solves Brentano's problem about the possibility of providing a naturalistic account of content. So if it's true, it's important. Just by way of making the claim graphic, I propose to run through an example that show, how, assuming the theory, Omniscience might consult the actual causal relations of a mental state, together with relevant counterfactuals, to resolve a simple case of the disjunction problem. This may do as a summary of the body of doctrine that I've been developing.

For simplicity, I assume that what God sees when He looks in your head is a lot of light bulbs, each with a letter on it. (High-tech heads have LCDs.) A mental-state type is specified by saying which bulbs are on in your head when you are in the state. A token of a mental-state type is a region of space time in which the corresponding array of bulbs is lit. This is, I imagine, as close to neurological plausibility as it is ever necessary to come for serious philosophical purposes.

What God sees when he looks at the relations between what's in your head and what's in the world is that there are many cases in which the bulbs turn on and off in lawful correlation with features of, say, the local distal environment. He can tell that these relations *are* lawful because he can tell that they are counterfactual supporting. And He can tell that they are counterfactual supporting because, by assumption, He can see not just actual causal relations but the space of counterfactuals that surround them.

Let's suppose that here is how it looks to Him in a particular case; say, in *your* particular case. There is a light bulb marked c that regularly goes on when there are cats around; and there is light bulb marked s that regularly goes on when there are shoes around. We can assume that the right story is that c's being on means *cat* (i.e., it constitutes your entertaining as a token of the concept CAT) and s's being on means *shoe*.

But God can't assume this; at least, not yet. The reason He can't is that He's got problems about robustness. It turns out that, though some of the c tokenings in your head are caused by cats, it's also true that some of your c tokenings are caused by shoes. Moreover, like the cat $\rightarrow c$ causal pattern, the shoe $\rightarrow c$ causal pattern supports counterfactuals; there are circumstances in which shoes cause *c*s *reliably*. (I assume that the statistics don't matter; that is, it doesn't matter to the intentional content of *c*-states what the relative frequency of shoe-caused *c*s to cat-caused *c*s turns out to be. God doesn't play dice with intentional ascriptions.)

Also, God has trouble with Twin-cats. Twin-cats are robots, hence neither cats nor shoes. But they would turn on the *c* bulb in virtue of the similarity between Twin-cats and real cats, and they would turn on the *s*-bulb in virtue of the similarity between Twin-cats and real shoes. Since God can see counterfactuals, He is able to see that all of this is true.

Because God has these troubles with robustness and Twins, He has a disjunction problem. The way it's *supposed* to come out is that the *c*s Twin-cats would cause, like the *c*s that shoes do or would cause, are semantically just like the *c*s that cats do cause, viz. they all mean *cat*. Cases where shoes cause *c*s are cases where shoes are *mistaken* for cats; cases where Twin-cats cause *c*s are cases where Twins would be mistaken for cats if there were any.

God, cannot, however, take the way it's supposed to turn out for granted. Charity requires the He consider an alternative hypothesis, viz. that *c* is ambiguous, with some *c* tokens meaning *shoe* and some meaning *Twin-cat*.[32] Here's how God resolves the dilemma. He asks Himself, "What was the actual causal pattern like?" and "What would the causal patterns have been like in a world that's relevantly like the real one except that, in the counterfactual world, *c*s aren't caused by cats?"

The answer to the first question rules out the Twins; there are no Twin-cats in the actual causal history of *c* tokenings, so *c* tokenings don't mean Twin-cats.[33] The answer to the second question is supposed to rule out the shoes. There are two relevant possibilities here:

One is that you would have gotten the shoe-caused *c* tokens even if the cat → *c* connection hadn't been in place. But then, these shoe-caused *c* tokens can't mean *cat*. For: no symbol means *cat* unless it carries information about cats. But no symbol carries information about cats unless its tokenings are somehow nomically dependent upon cats. But, on the present assumptions, shoe-caused *c*-tokenings *aren't* nomically dependent on cats; you'd get them even in worlds where the cat → *c* connection is broken. The point is that, if shoes causing *c*s isn't *somehow* nomically dependent on cats causing *c*s, then God can only take shoe-caused *c*s to mean *cat* if He is prepared to give up the basic principle of information-based semantics, viz. that the content of a symbol is *somehow* dependent on the lawful causal relations that its tokens enter into. I assume that God is not about to give this up.

The other relevant possibility is that shoes wouldn't cause *c*s if cats didn't cause *c*s. If this counterfactual is true, then God can square the assumption that *c* means *cat* with — on the one hand — there being *c*s that aren't caused by cats (robustness) and — on the other hand — the foundational intuition that a symbol means *cat* in virtue of some sort of reliable causal connection that its tokens bear to cats. If even shoe-caused *c*s are causally dependent, on cats – in the sense that if cats didn't cause *c*s then shoes wouldn't either – then it's OK for God to read a *c*-token as meaning *cat* even when it's caused by a shoe.

So God can tell the intentional content of your neural state by looking at its actual causal relations and at relevant counterfactuals; in effect, He can apply the method of differences, just like any other rational agent. So there's a fact of the matter about what the intentional content of your neural state *is*. So God doesn't have to worry about Brentano's problem. And neither do we.

Or so it seems.

Conclusion: Have We Solved Brentano's Problem?

Suppose that everything in this paper is true. Then what we have is an explication of a semantical relation (viz. the semantical relation between a syntactically primitive predicate and the property it expresses) couched in a vocabulary that involves only naturalistic (specifically causal) expressions and expressions that denote intensional with-an-*s* objects (specifically expressions that denote laws and properties). It comes out of this treatment that symbols can be both robust and informative, consonant with the basic symbol-making relation being nomic dependence. Since, moreover, the account is entirely atomistic, it follows that the connection between intentionality and holism isn't *intrinsic*, ever so many fashionable philosophers recently to the contrary notwithstanding.

So, does this solve Brentano's problem? Or, to put it another way, *does information plus robustness equal content?* Are information and robustness all you need for intentionality?

I don't know the answer to this question. The standard objection to the identification of content with information is the disjunction problem. Correspondingly, I've tacitly assumed throughout this paper that if you can get a theory of content that squares the intuition that "*X*" means *X* only if "*X*" tokens carry information about *X*-instantiation with the intuition that "*X*" means *X* only if you can have *X*-tokens that aren't caused by *X*s, then you've done all that a solution to Brentano's problem is required to do. Maybe, however, there are reasons for wanting more than information and robustness for content. What might these reasons be?

Well, there are people who think that you have to throw in some consciousness, for example. However, to insist on an internal connection between content and consciousness in the face of a successful research program, from Freud to Chomsky, that depends on denying that there is one, seems to me vaguely Luddite.[34] I don't, therefore, propose to take this idea seriously; but I do agree that if I'm wrong, and it is a serious idea, then the problem of intentionality is probably hopeless because the problem of consciousness is probably hopeless.

Another possibility is that you have to throw in some normativity. I am sort of in sympathy with this. Robustness captures the point that some ways of using symbols are ontologically parasitic on others. But we surely want more; we want it to turn out that some ways of using symbols are *wrong*.[35] Where, in the picture of representation that we've been constructing, does the idea get a foothold that there are *mis*representations, and that they are things to be avoided?

One might consider trying to derive the normative relations from the ontological ones, but, at second thought, this seems not plausible. There's no obvious reason why the fact that one way of using a symbol is asymmetrically dependent on another implies that we should prefer the second way of using it to the first. It seems, not just here but also in the general case, that ontological priority is normatively neutral, Plato to the contrary notwithstanding. What to do?

The reader who has followed the argument the whole weary way to here may now be feeling a twinge of nostalgia for the teleological account of content deprecated in Fodor (1990b), chapter 3. As I remarked at the time, talk of function brings (a kind of, anyhow) normative talk in its train; wherever you have functions, you have the logical space for misfunctions and malfunctions too. It's therefore arguable that teleological theories go some way toward reconciling the demands of naturalism with the normativity of intentional ascription, with semantic evaluations being really evaluative. Too bad teleological theories are so rotten at resolving intentional indeterminacy.

It's not, however, out of the question that we might have it both ways. The arguments in Fodor (1990b), chapter 3 seem to me to show pretty conclusively that you cannot derive the intentional content of a mental state from its biological function (not, at least, if your account of its biological function is grounded in its selectional history). But it might be well advised to try going the other way round: given an independent, non-teleological, naturalistic account of content (like, for example, the one that we've been working on), you might try construing the function of a mental state by reference to what it represents. For example, the function of the belief that P is to represent the world as being such that P on (certain) occasions when it's the case that P. Talking this way does nothing to offend naturalistic scruples given that the notion of representation is independently defined.

It is, moreover, an argument for this order of analysis that the account of the function of intentional states that it provides is plausibly *true*. I assume that (anyhow, higher) organisms are species of decision theoretic machines; plus or minus a bit, they act in ways that will maximize their utilities if (and, except by luck, only if) their beliefs are true. What is therefore required of a belief in order that it should perform its function in such a machine is that it should *be* true. So, to that extent, false beliefs ipso facto fail to perform their functions. It might turn out, on this sort of view, that there are no normative implications of representation per se. Representation is just a certain kind of causal relation – it's just information plus asymmetric dependence – and as such it's neither a good thing nor a bad. Evaluation gets a grip when representational states have functions that are defined by reference to their contents (when a state that represents the world as such and such has the function of representing the world as such and such). In these cases, misrepresentations are failures of function and are, as such, to be deplored.

This is, however, all very complicated; there's a lot more to be done if this sort of story is to be made convincing. For example, if Freud was right some false beliefs perform *a* function by screening unbearable truths. Do they thereby perform *their* function? If so, it looks like false beliefs can be functional, so semantic evaluation and functional evaluation come apart. This throws doubt on the current project, which proposes, in effect, that misrepresentation is a bad thing *because* it's a species of malfunction. I don't know how seriously one should take such examples, and I don't propose to explore the issue any further here. Perhaps we could leave it at this: *if* you're moved by the idea of a teleological account of the normativity of intentional ascription, that option is still open even if you think (as I think you ought to) that teleological accounts of *content* are hopeless.

Well, then, suppose we can finesse the normativity issue in something like the way I've just discussed. Would it *then* be reasonable to claim to have solved Brentano's problem? Here's a thought intended to placate philosophers who hold it a matter of principle that no philosophical problem should ever be solved: even if it's true that intentionality equals information plus robustness, it wouldn't have to follow that information plus robustness is sufficient for *mentality*. Sufficient conditions for being in a state with intentional content needn't also be sufficient conditions for having a belief or a desire or, indeed, for being in any other *psychological* condition.

It's arguable, for example, that beliefs aren't just states that have content; they're states that have content *and* whose causal relations obey the axioms of some reasonable decision theory; and the axioms of some reasonable theory of inference, etc. No argument I've heard of shows that you can't satisfy the intentionality condition for being a belief without satisfying these others. (Functional-role theories of content might well entail this since they generally connect content with "minimal rationality"; so much the worse for them.) If content is just information plus robustness, a good theory of content might license the literal ascription of (underived) intentionality to thermometers, thermostats, and the like; that is, it might turn out on a good theory of content that some of the states of such devices are semantically evaluable. I don't think that should count as a reductio, though (in my view) the ascription of beliefs and desires to thermometers or thermostats certainly would.

In short, it might turn out that the intentional is a big superset of the psychological, and that might be acceptable so long as it isn't a *crazy* superset of the psychological (so long as it doesn't include everything, for example). It's good to remember this when you're working over your intuitions, looking for counterexamples to putative solution of Brentano's problem; one does not refute a theory that entails that state *S* has content such-and-such just by showing that *S* is not a propositional attitude. It's also good to remember that the intentional might be a big superset of the psychological if you're inclined to weep over the possibility of Brentano's problem being solved. Solving Brentano's problem might, after all, leave most of the philosophy of mind still in the old familiar mess; so no technological unemployment need result.

Last word: Suppose we had naturalistically sufficient conditions for content. It wouldn't, of course, follow that any of our neural states, or any or our public symbols, have the content that they do because they satisfy the conditions on offer. Indeed, it wouldn't follow from the mere existence of sufficient conditions for content that anything in the universe has actually got any. "*P* implies *Q*" is neutral about *Q*. God can accept the consequents of any true hypotheticals whose antecedents He doesn't know to be false; but we can't.

On the other hand, if there are naturalistic sufficient conditions for content, and if we don't know these conditions not to be satisfied, then we would at least be in a position to claim, for example, that "cat" *could* mean *cat* for all we know to the contrary. This would be a satisfactory situation for the philosophy of mind (or the philosophy of language, or whatever this stuff is) to have finally arrived at. For, the prima facie plausibility that "cat" *does* mean *cat* is, after all, pretty substantial. I don't know about you guys, but when friends in other lines of work ask me what philosophers are into these days, and I tell them that these days philosophers are into claiming that really, deep down – in a first-class conceptual system, you know? – *it's not true* that "cat" means *cat* . . . they laugh at me. I do find that embarrassing.[36]

Notes

"A Theory of Content, II: The Theory" originally appeared as chapter 4 of Jerry Fodor's book *A Theory of Content and Other Essays* (1990), and is reprinted here by permission of MIT Press and the author.

1 A variant of the theory that I'll discuss near the end departs significantly from the letter of informational semantics, though perhaps less significantly from its spirit.
2 For the type one/type two distinction, see Fodor (1990b), chapter 3.
3 Compare *Psychosemantics* (1987), in which I took it for granted – wrongly, as I now think – that an information-based semantics would have to specify such circumstances. As far as I can tell, I assumed this because I thought that any informational theory of content would have to amount to a more or less hedged version of "all

and only cows cause 'cow's". This, too, was a failure to take semantic robustness sufficiently seriously. It's no more plausible that there are non-question-beggingly specifiable situations in which it's semantically necessary that all cows cause "cows" than that there are such situations in which, necessarily, only cows do. How *could* there be circumstances in which the content of a thought guarantees that someone will think it?

4   As are all other "non-labeling" uses of a symbol. See Fodor (1990a).

5   Well, *almost* arbitrarily robust; see below.

6   Though not, of course, without resort to intensional (with-an-"s") idiom. The asymmetric dependence story is up to its ears in Realism about properties, relations, laws, and other abstracta. Whether this sort of Realism prejudices a semantic theory's claim to be physicalistic – and whether, if it does, it *matters* whether a semantic theory is physicalistic – are questions of some interest; but not ones that I propose to take on here. Suffice it that *naturalism*, as I understand the term, needn't imply *materialism* if the latter is understood as denying independent ontological status to abstract entities.

7   The caveat is because informational semanticists rarely straight out identify "meaning that . . ." with "carrying the information that . . ." (though Israel seems to be right on the edge of doing so in the passage cited in the text). Dretske (1987), for example, adds constraints intended to ensure that the information carried should be *perfectly* reliable, and that it should be "digitally" encoded (this is Dretske's way of ensuring that "dog" means *dog* rather than *animal*.) Also, the Stanford theorists generally allow that information can be generated by reliable relations other than causal ones (e.g., entailment relations). These considerations don't, however, affect the point in the text.

8   As Georges Rey remarks, "The viability of a ceteris paribus clause depends not upon the actual specification or realizability of the idealization, but rather upon whether the apparent exceptions to the law to which it is attached can be explained as due to independently specifiable interference. It is a check written on the banks of independent theories, which is only as good as those theories and *their* independent evidence can make it. So the question . . . is not whether the ceteris paribus clause can be replaced, but rather: Can all the errors be explained as independent interference?" (Rey, unpublished) It's worth spelling out an implication of Rey's point: To know what, in general, the consequence of satisfying a ceteris paribus condition would be, we would have to know what would happen if none of the sources of "independent interference" were operative. And to know *that*, we'd have to know, at a minimum, what the sources of independent interference *are*; we'd have to know which other laws can interact with the ceteris paribus law under examination. But, of course, it's never possible to know (much) of this under the conditions actually operative in scientific theory construction; what interactions between L and other laws are possible depends not just on how L turns out, but also on *how the rest of science turns out*.

9   This counterfactual is, of course, by no means vacuous. It claims, in effect, that our capacities to add are bounded *only* by the limitations of our working memory; in particular, they aren't bounded *by what we know about how to add numbers*. Such claims are, to put it mildly, often non-obvious. For example, as of this date nobody knows whether it's true that, but for memory constraints, a normal English

speaker could parse every sentence of his language. ("Garden path" sentences appear to offer counterexamples.) As it turns out, the resolution of some rather deep issues in linguistics depend on this question.

10   For example, Steven Wagner's "Theories of Mental Representation" (unpublished) criticizes one version of the view I'll be proposing by remarking that it "has the *wildly* implausible consequence that there are worlds, remotely like ours in which cows could not be mistaken for horses." In fact, what I hold is only that if "cow" means *cow* and not *horse* then it must be nomologically possible to tell any cow from a horse; which doesn't sound all *that* wild after all. (Actually, there's a version of my story that requires still less; see the discussion of verificationism below.) You get the consequence that Wagner denounces only if you conjoin my story about semantics to the story about modals that says that, if P is nomologically possible, then there is a world in which it's the case that P. So much the worse for that story about modals.

11   To be sure, this can't be the *only* way that asymmetric dependence gets its foothold. For example: if, as I'm claiming, the use of linguistic symbols to effect mislabelings, false predications, and the like is asymmetrically dependent on their being applied correctly, that asymmetry can't arise from linguistic practices in anything like the way that the asymmetric dependence of pagings on namings does; there's a *convention* for paging, but not for mislabeling. And, of course, we have no linguistic practices (no conventions) at all with respect to our mental representations. Patience, dear Reader; all in good time.

12   I'll use "concept" ambiguously; sometimes it refers to a mental representation (thus following psychological usage) and sometimes to the intension of a mental representation (thus following philosophical usage). The context will often make clear which reading is at issue. When I wish to name a concept, I'll use the corresponding English word in caps; hence, "COW" for the concept cow.

13   Roughly, a symbol is syntactically primitive iff it has no semantically evaluable proper parts.

14   Baker raises her problem for tokens of Mentalese, but nothing turns on this, and English is easier to spell.

15   There may be readers who demand a semantics that makes the first "cat" token come out false (i.e., who demand that it mean *robot-cat*). I beg a temporary suspension of their disbelief. We'll see further on how the theory could be revised to accommodate them.

16   I think these sorts of cases throw some interesting side light on the standard Twin Earth examples. It's usual in the literature to take the moral of the Twin cases to be the significance of context in determining content: "water" means H_2O because there isn't any XYZ on earth. But Dretske's case opens the possibility of super-Twins: creatures who not only have type-identical neural structures, but also share a context (in some reasonable sense), but whose intentional states nevertheless differ in content: the extension of A's term "water" includes XYZ and the extension of B's term "water" does not because it's fortuitous for A but not for B that he has encountered no samples of XYZ.

Apparently, then, the content of your term may differ from the content of mine if there's something that prevents tokens of your term from being caused by instantiations of a property whose instantiations could (i.e., really could, not just nomologically possibly could) cause tokenings of mine. This might be true even of two creatures who live in the same world if, as it happens, they live in different parts of the wood. If the nearest XYZ to me is so far away that I can't possibly get there in a lifetime, then, I suppose, "water" means something non-disjunctive in my mouth. Whereas, if the nearest XYZ to you is so close that it's just an accident that you haven't come across any, then, I suppose, "water" does mean something disjunctive in yours.

Does any of this matter? If so, to what?

17   The hyphens are because nobody could think that the frog has the disjunctive concept FLY OR BEE BEE (just as nobody could think that *S* has disjunctive concept CAT OR ROBOT CAT in the Baker case discussed above). The issue, rather, is whether the frog has the concept FLY or the concept of a certain visible property which, de facto, flies and bee bees both exhibit.

18   It's crucial that this claim be read *synchronically* since, presumably, frogs wouldn't develop a disposition to snap at black dots in worlds where the black dots have *never* been flies. The semantically relevant sort of asymmetric dependence is a relation among an organism's *current* dispositions. Take real-world frogs and put them in possible worlds where the black dots are bee-bees and they'll snap away, happy as the day is long. But real-world frogs in possible worlds where the flies aren't black dots are ipso facto snapless.

19   Cf: "Is this a dagger which I see before me . . ./Come, let me clutch thee./I have thee not, and yet I see thee still./ Art thou no, fatal vision, sensible/ To feeling as to sight? or art thou but/ A dagger of the mind, a false creation,/ Proceeding from the heat-oppressed brain?" Macbeth's morals were, no doubt, reprehensible, but his epistemology was spot on.

20   I've thus far made a point of not distinguishing two theses: (a) if *X* and *Y* are distinct concepts, then there must be a world in which *x*s but not *y*s cause "*X*"s; (b) if *X* and *Y* are distinct concepts *and xs and ys both cause "X"s in* this *world* then there must be a world in which *x*s but not *y*s cause "*X*"s. The (b) story is markedly less verificationist than the (a) story and some philosophers may prefer it on that ground. We'll come to this presently; but suffice it for now that both stories say the same things about what frogs snap at and about what Macbeth means by "dagger."

21   For further discussion of the analogy between the function of theories and of instruments of observation in mediating the symbol/world relations upon which content depends, see Fodor (1990b), chapter 3 (especially fn 4); also Fodor (1987), chapter 4.

22   The case is a little different when states of the central nervous system (as opposed, e.g., to retinal states) are proposed as the intentional objects of the thoughts that cows causally occasion. I suppose it might turn out that there are specifiable, *non*-disjunctive states of the brain upon whose tokening the connection of cow-occasioned thoughts to cows asymmetrically depend. Such a discovery would not, however, require us to say that the intentional object of one's cow thoughts are brain states. Rather, we could simply take the brain-state tokens to be tokens of the Mentalese term for cow.

23   I say that one *might* rule out proximal referents for mental representations by appeal to the principle that open disjunctions aren't projectible. But one could

also take the high ground and rule them out by stipulation: just as primitive symbols aren't allowed to express necessarily uninstantiated properties, so too they aren't allowed to express proximal properties. If this seems arbitrary, remember that we're looking for (naturalistically) *sufficient* conditions for representation.

24 And not vice versa. But where the asymmetry of the dependence is not germane to the point at issue I'll leave this clause out to simplify the exposition.

25 I take it that, but for the talk about intentions and policies, the same sort of line applies to kind-concepts. What makes something a kind-concept, according to his view, is what it tracks in worlds where instances of the kind to which it applies are distinguishable from instances of the kinds to which it doesn't.

26 "E.g." rather than "i.e." because, for present purposes, we're not attending to the distinction between disjunctive predicates and ambiguous ones.

27 Boghossian isn't the only critic who has objected to the verificationist implications of the sort of treatment I've been proposing. Cf. Cummins (1989b) and Wagner (unpublished).

28 For those keeping score: the information and asymmetric dependence conditions are clauses in a (putatively) sufficient condition for "X" expressing X; i.e., they are severally necessary and jointly sufficient conditions for the satisfaction of a sufficient condition.

29 Dretske is himself not faithful to purely informational semantics; his proposal for dealing with the disjunction problem requires that facts about the history of acquisition of a concept are relevant to determining its extension (see Fodor, 1990b, chapter 3). There's nothing unreasonable about this – there's no a priori argument that pure informational theories are better than impure ones. But, as we've seen, Dretske's way of adding a dash of causal history to his purely informational story doesn't get him where he wants to go.

30 A world where there is H_2O but not XYZ (or vice versa) doesn't count, because although only H_2O controls the *actual* WATER tokenings in worlds where there is only H_2O, XYZ controls *counterfactual* WATER tokenings in those worlds assuming that the connection between XYZ and WATER tokens is nomic. Remember unicorns: there can be laws about uninstantiated properties.

31 By contrast, He could tell just by looking in your head which of your mental states are in the ranges and domains of which of your mental processes. At least, He could if He's a methodological solipsist, which I'm sure He is.

32 I don't have a story about the difference between ambiguity and disjunctiveness that I feel like telling here so the "disjunction" problem is really the "disjunction or ambiguity" problem, as per note 26.

33 Strictly speaking, of course, the claim is only that if c-tokenings do mean Twins, then it must be in virtue of the satisfaction of some semantic condition other than the one we've been discussing. We've seen, as we've gone along, several reasons why our condition, though it is arguably sufficient for content, can't possibly be necessary.

34 Searle argues that consciousness must come in because nothing else suggests itself as distinguishing "derived" intentionality from the real thing. However, if the present story is right, this isn't so. Roughly, X's intentionality is real if it depends on X's satisfying conditions 1 to 3; X's intentionality is derived if it derives from Y's satisfying conditions 1 to 3, where $Y \neq X$.

35 Compare: "The crux of Kripke's reading of Wittgenstein may be put like this. It is of the essence of meaning an expression in a certain way, that meaning it that way determines how the expression would have to be used if it is to be used correctly. . . . Any proposed candidate for being the property in virtue of which an expression has meaning must be such as to ground the 'normativity' of meaning. . . ." (Boghossian, 1989, pp. 83–4.)

I say that I am *sort of* sympathetic. The trouble is that requiring that normativity be grounded suggests there is more to demand of a naturalized semantics than that it provide a reduction of such notions as, say, *extension*. But what could this "more" amount to? To apply a term to a thing in its extension *is* to apply the term correctly; once you've said what it is that makes the tables the extension of "table"s, there is surely no *further* question about why it's *correct* to apply a "table" to a table. It thus seems that if you have a reductive theory of the semantic relations, there is no job of grounding normativity left to do.

In short, I'm not clear how – or whether – "open question" arguments can get a grip in the present case. I am darkly suspicious that the Kripkensteinian worry about the normative force of meaning is either a non-issue or just the reduction issue over again; anyhow, that it's not a *new* issue. In the text, however, I've suppressed these qualms.

36 I want to express a special indebtedness to Paul Boghossian for very helpful conversations on these topics and for having caught a bad mistake in an earlier draft of this paper. Literally dozens of other people have made suggestions I've found illuminating. They include all, but not only, the following (and I hereby apologize to anyone I have left out): Louise Antony, Lynne Baker, Ned Block, Dan Dennett, Michael Devitt, Joe Levine, Barry Loewer, Tim Maudlin, Brian McLaughlin, Georges Rey, Steve Wagner, and many graduate students at Rutgers and CUNY.

9   Fodorian Semantics

Fred Adams and Ken Aizawa

Janet believes that Bush lost the election. How is this possible? How do states of Janet come to be about or mean something about Bush, elections, or losing? How do thoughts, purely natural, physical states of persons, get to be about the world and acquire their semantic contents? Call the project of answering these questions the "naturalization project." The "naturalized" part of the project is to explain how something with meaning can arise out of purely natural causes and physical objects without depending upon things that already have meaning. It is, if you will, the project of explaining how there can be underived intentionality – unmeant meaners. The "semantic" part is the attempt to get beyond the level of information or indication to the level of meaning, to the level where misrepresentation and falsehood are possible. Smoke may be a natural sign or indicator of fire, but smoke can hardly be falsely tokened and it does not mean anything in the required sense. The English word "smoke" in a thought about smoke or in a sentence, in contrast, semantically means smoke; it can be falsely tokened. Only a semantic representation seems to be capable of misrepresentation (Dretske, 1981, 1986).

Jerry Fodor (Fodor, 1987, 1990a, 1990b) has constructed a naturalized semantics capable of being applied to thoughts. He claims to have discovered a set of naturalistic conditions that are sufficient, if met, to enable a purely natural, physical state to have semantic meaning (content). Fodor does not claim that his conditions are necessary for meaning. Some things may have meaning independently of his conditions. He does claim that his account has advantages over competitors of solving the "disjunction problem" (Fodor, 1990a) and of being able to account for the mental phenomenon of "robust tokening" (Fodor, 1990a, 1990b). Solving the disjunction problem requires showing why not every cause that tokens a symbol "X" is part of "X"'s meaning. If a horse on a dark night tokens "cow" and a cow in the daylight tokens "cow," how does "cow" unequivocally mean cow, rather than equivocally mean cow or horse on a dark night? Accounting for the phenomenon of robust tokening requires that not every non-X-caused tokening of "X" should constitute a false tokening of "X." For example, if a mule causes Janet to think of it as a horse, the mule causes "horse" to be falsely tokened in Janet. However, if a mule causes Janet to think of horses, not because she thinks the mule is a horse, but just because the mule reminds her of a horse she once rode, then the mule has caused a robust (but not false) tokening of "horse" in Janet. Furthermore, Fodor claims that his theory avoids semantic promiscuity. Semantic promiscuity is the nasty practice of attributing meaning to items that have none.

We shall call Fodor's semantic theory the "Asymmetric Causal Dependency Theory." Fodor maintains that among a set of sufficient conditions for a syntactic item "X" to mean X is the condition that the power of any Y (not identical to X) to cause "X"s must depend upon the power of Xs to cause "X"s, but not *vice versa*. In this paper, we review the role that asymmetrical causal dependency plays in Fodor's theory of meaning. It is the key to his whole approach to naturalizing meaning. We present reasons for rejecting Fodor's theory of meaning and his approach. First, the theory assigns meaning to some "X"s that have none. In other words, Fodor's theory is semantically promiscuous. Second, depending on how one interprets Fodor's asymmetrical causal dependency condition, the theory is either vacuous, attributes the wrong content to "X"s, or fails to solve a well-worn version of the disjunction problem. Third, we strongly doubt that Fodor's conditions explain robust tokening. In the penultimate section, we argue that the entire Fodorian asymmetric causal dependency approach to meaning is not merely wrong in the details, but is fundamentally misguided.

1   The Asymmetric Causal Dependency Theory

In "A Theory of Content, II" (see this volume, chapter 8) Fodor claims that "X" means X if:

(1)   "Xs cause 'X's" is a law.
(2)   Some "X"s are actually caused by Xs.
(3)   For all Y not = X, if Ys qua Ys actually cause "X"s, then Ys *causing* "X"s is asymmetrically dependent on X's causing "X"s (see p. 208).
(4)   There are some non-X-caused "X"s (cf. pp. 181, 205).

Here we have a set of sufficient conditions for meaning, each of which is, by metatheoretic assumption, a necessary part of the sufficient conditions. For the most part, the conditions of the theory are clear, but a few points of elaboration are in order.

Condition (1) is Fodor's "information" condition. "This just follows Dretske. It ensures that "X's *at least* carry information about Xs (but not, N.B., that they carry information *only* about Xs" (see p. 208). When stated in full dress, the condition asserts that there is a law connecting the property of being an X with the property of being a syntactic item "X." Fodor is clearly not endorsing an anomic causal theory that would allow an individual object X to cause "X" tokens without specifying the nomically relevant properties of Xs and "X"s. A second important feature of condition (1), and of all four conditions for that matter, is that "X" is a purely syntactic item. It must be identified or individuated exclusively on the basis of its syntactic properties, for to allow semantic properties into the specification of "X" would defeat one of the implicit assumptions of the entire naturalization project. It would undermine the attempt to provide a purely naturalistic analysis of the meaning relation.

Condition (2) is Fodor's flirtation, however brief,[1] with a causal-historical condition on meaning. Condition (2) is clearly both historical and causal. The motivation for (2), however fleeting, seems to be to handle Twin-Earth examples. "This invokes the actual history of 'X' tokens as constitutive of the meaning of 'X' and thereby violates the assumptions of pure informational theories. . . . It rules out ' "horse" means Twin-horse,' ' "water" means XYZ,' and the like" (see p. 209).[2] Fodor shares the common intuition that "water" tokens in the brains of Earthlings mean H_2O, so he must tailor his theory to accommodate this. He believes that, on Earth, it is a law that "H_2O causes 'water' in humans" and it is a law that "XYZ causes 'water' in humans." Adding the second condition, that there must be instances in which Xs causes "X"s, is supposed to make it the case that "water" means H_2O, rather than XYZ, because only the H_2O-"water" law is instantiated.

Condition (3), the asymmetric causal dependency condition, is the heart of Fodor's theory. This condition is designed to help circumvent the disjunction problem, avoid semantic promiscuity, and make possible robust tokening.

> This is the heart of the solution of the disjunction problem . . . it rules out "horse" means HORSE OR COW ON A DARK NIGHT, given (a) the assumption that some cows on dark nights actually do cause "horse"s, and (b) the usual assumption about counterfactuals (viz. that cows on dark nights wouldn't cause "horse"s but that horses do). . . . Condition 3 is also required to rule out " 'horse' means HORSE PICTURE". . . . Remember that not all non-horse-occasioned "horse"s are *ipso facto* false. (see p. 209)

Also, in face of the threat of semantic promiscuity, Fodor adds "There is . . . a lot less meaning around than there is information . . . all you need for information is reliable causal covariance, whereas for meaning you need (at least) asymmetric dependence too" (see pp. 183–4).

The interpretation of condition (3) is a point of contention. For the present, we shall state one interpretation (Adams and Aizawa, 1992) and come back to another (Warfield, forthcoming; Adams and Aizawa, forthcoming) later in the paper. We might take (3) to mean that all the Y-"X" connections found in the actual world depend asymmetrically on the X-"X" connection found in the actual world. That is, if the X-"X" connection found in the actual world is broken, then all of the Y-"X" connections that exist in our world will be broken as well, but even if all the Y-"X" connections of the actual world are broken, the X-"X" connection will remain intact. Fodor takes this condition to be essential to the proper assignment of content to terms. Here is why. We may suppose that it is a law that, under certain conditions of good light with no occluding objects and so forth, a sample of H_2O will cause "water" tokens to occur in Janet's brain. Thus, condition (1) is satisfied. Also, let it be the case that, on at least one occasion, a sample of H_2O has made a "water" token appear in Janet's head, so that condition (2) is satisfied. In addition to the conditions under which H_2O causes "water" to occur in Janet's head, there are conditions, such as poor light or great distance, under which a glass of gin or a glass of water would cause "water" to appear in Janet's head. Further, the question "What would you like to drink?" and the imperative "Name the principal chemical in the human body" would cause a "water" to appear in Janet's head. The problem, then, is that, given conditions (1) and (2) alone, we seem forced to say that Janet's concept "water" does not mean H_2O, but the long disjunction H_2O or gin-in-the-dark-or-at-a-distance or "What would you like to drink?" or "Name the principal chemical in the human body." Condition (3) is designed to save the theory from this problem, since, Fodor suggests, the only reason a glass of gin in the dark or at a distance, or the question "What would you like to drink?" or the imperative "Name the principal chemical in the human body" can cause "water" to occur in Janet's head is because H_2O causes this. If H_2O were not connected to "water," then gin in the dark or at a distance, the question, and the imperative would not be connected to "water." Moreover, the dependency is supposed to be asymmetrical, since the power H_2O has does not depend on the power of gin, the question, or the imperative. In other words, breaking the H_2O-"water" law thereby breaks the gin-in-the-dark-or-at-a-distance-"water", "What would you like to drink?"-"water", and "Name the principal chemical in the human body"-"water" laws, but breaking the gin-in-the-dark-or-at-a-distance-"water", "What would you like to drink?"-"water", and "Name the principal chemical in the human body"-"water" laws does not thereby break the H_2O-"water" law.

We might also emphasize that the dependency Fodor has in mind must be *synchronic*, that is, gin in the dark or at a distance would not now cause "water"s unless H_2O in good light would now cause "water"s. The only reason gin now causes "water"s is that it is mistaken for H_2O. Fodor does not mean that had the H_2O-"water" connection not existed prior to, say, the gin-in-the-dark-or-at-a-distance-"water" connection, then the gin-in-the-dark-or-at-a-distance-"water" connection would not exist. Nor is it that the H_2O-"water" law must have been instantiated before the gin-in-the-dark-or-at-a-distance-"water" law was, or could have been, instantiated. It is that breaking the H_2O-"water" connection now would thereby break the gin-in-the-dark-or-at-a-distance-"water" connection now (Fodor, 1987, p. 109).

2 Pigeons and Semantic Promiscuity

Our first objection to Fodorian semantics will focus upon his attempt to avoid the charge of semantic promiscuity. His theory may avoid pansemanticism – the view that literally everything has a meaning. The really dreadful thing about pansemanticism, however, is not only that it attributes so much meaning, but that it attributes meaning where it does not belong. We shall show that Fodorian semantics is semantically promiscuous in just this latter respect.

Fodor writes, "So, if you want to argue with the metaphysical conclusions of this paper, you've got to construct a world where my counterfactuals are all in place but where 'X' doesn't mean what I say it does. Fair enough; let's see one" (see p. 186). Okay, here goes; a case where "X" satisfies Fodor's conditions but doesn't mean anything. Let pigeons = Xs and pigeon droppings = "X"s. In the world we envision, pigeons produce droppings, an unpleasant chemical mixture. In other words, the world we imagine is like ours in having the instantiated law "pigeons cause droppings." In the imagined world, it is also an instantiated law that demented scientists cause droppings, blobs of an unpleasant mixture qualitatively indistinguishable in every way from the stuff pigeons drop. In order to satisfy the asymmetric causal dependency condition, in our imagined world, the scientists have the power to produce droppings only because pigeons have the power to produce droppings. Here we must strongly emphasize that the dependency we envision is *synchronic*, not diachronic. It is not just that our scientists could not have figured out how to synthesize pigeon droppings without pigeons having first produced the droppings; it is that scientists simply could not now make the droppings if pigeons could not now make the droppings. Further, in this world, only pigeons and scientists can make the droppings. Thus, in this world, all the laws connecting non-pigeons to pigeon droppings depend synchronically and asymmetrically on the law connecting pigeons to pigeon droppings.

In this situation, all four conditions of Fodor's theory are satisfied: it is an instantiated law of this world that pigeons cause such droppings (conditions (1) and (2)); for all non-pigeons, the non-pigeon to droppings laws are asymmetrically and synchronically dependent on the pigeon to droppings law (condition (3)); and there are instances of non-pigeons producing such droppings (condition (4)). Thus, by Fodor's analysis, in the world we have described, pigeon droppings mean (not just indicate) pigeons. We take it to be wildly implausible (not to mention false) that pigeon droppings have a semantic value and a sign of failure that Fodor's theory does not block this result.

A not uncommon reaction to this example is a puzzled look followed by a question about how the ability of the scientists to create droppings depends on the ability of the pigeons to create droppings. One may easily imagine that the scientists would not have developed their ability had not the pigeons developed their ability first. This diachronic dependency might hold, but the puzzle is over how the power of the scientists depends synchronically upon the power of the pigeons. How could it be that, if the pigeons couldn't do their thing, the scientists couldn't do theirs?

First, if we play by Fodor's rules, we are not obliged to explain why the scientists-"droppings" law depends on the pigeons-"droppings" law. Fodor does not take it upon himself to explain why one law (cows on dark nights cause "horse"s) synchronically and asymmetrically depends upon another (horses in good light cause "horse"s). Instead, he delights in pointing out that he gets to stipulate how the dependencies go, since he is dealing with sufficient conditions.

Second, we actually welcome this question about dependencies and we return to it in a later section. For now, however, we offer an explanation of the synchronic asymmetric dependence in the world we imagine. Our scientists are demented. Were it not a law in their world that pigeons produce pigeon droppings, they would *immediately* know this and be so overwhelmed by the complexity of the synthetic process needed to produce synthetic pigeon droppings that they would simply be unable to perform it. They would so lack confidence in the feasibility of such a synthesis that they could not bring themselves even to try to carry out the process. We take it that, in our imagined world, Fodor's conditions are too weak; for they assign semantic properties to things that lack meaning (such as pigeon droppings). Thus, Fodorian semantics is semantically promiscuous.

One may respond that, while pigeon droppings may not *non-naturally* mean pigeons, they may still *naturally* mean pigeons. True, but this won't satisfy the "semantics" part of a program to naturalize semantics, and it is clearly not the kind of meaning for which Fodor intended his conditions to be sufficient. It won't provide a semantics for thoughts because such tokens could not be false, while thoughts can be false. If Fodor wished to have only a theory of natural meaning, he might well have stopped at conditions (1) and (2). He did not because natural meaning is not his quarry.[3]

3   Pathologies and Vacuity

Fodor makes it abundantly clear that his conditions are to be treated as sufficient, but not necessary, for "X" to mean X. In fact, he has told us emphatically in personal communication that his conditions are not to be taken as necessary for anything. The simplest examples showing that his conditions are not necessary for meaning come from Fodor himself. Since there are no unicorns, unicorns have not caused "unicorn"s. Thus, condition (2) is not satisfied and "unicorn" cannot mean unicorn in virtue of satisfying Fodor's Asymmetric Causal Dependency Theory (see p. 210f). Fodor also indicates that logical vocabulary may not mean what it does in virtue of his theory,

I'm inclined to think that maybe there is *no* objection to the idea that "+," "and," "all" and the like have the meanings they do because they play a certain causal role in the mental lives of their users. This would, of course, be to accept a distinction in kind between the logical and the non-logical vocabularies. (The semantics for the former would be a kind of "use" theory, whereas the semantics for the latter would depend on nomic, specifically mind-world, relations.) (see p. 199)

While Fodor mentions these cases, he does not mention another class of terms that he also believes would not be governed by the Asymmetric Causal Dependency Theory, names (personal communication). One reason for this (perhaps) is that Fodor's theory is nomological, rather than causal, and individuals cannot occur in laws. "Rhonda causes 'Rhonda's'" cannot be a law because Rhonda is the wrong sort of thing to occur in a covering law. Fodor suspects that a historical, anomic causal theory is more promising in the case of individual names.

Aside from showing that Fodor's sufficiency conditions are not genuine sufficiency conditions because they do not block semantic promiscuity, it is also possible to attack them by showing that they are uninteresting, since nothing in fact satisfies them. In an earlier paper (Adams and Aizawa, 1992), we suggested that Fodor's conditions are in fact vacuous on the ground that condition (3) is too strong. That is, even if it were not for the problem of the pigeons and semantic promiscuity, Fodorian semantics may not apply to any cognitive agents. This bad result might obtain for at least two reasons. First, it could turn out that, for any syntactic "X" of the sort Fodor has in mind, there is always some Y-"X" law of the actual world that does not depend *asymmetrically* on the X-"X" law. Second, it may be that, for any syntactic "X" of the sort Fodor has in mind, there is an actual Y-"X" connection that depends *symmetrically* on the X-"X" connection. We shall call the first the "pathologies problem" and the second the "Twin-Earth" problem.

Let a *pathological cause* of "X" be any Y not = X such that the Y-"X" law does not depend on the X-"X" law. The use of the term "pathological" may not be entirely happy, insofar as not every instance of what we call a pathological cause will in fact be a disease. Nonetheless, the term connotes a dysfunction of the sort crucial to our objection. The problem for Fodor's theory is that there are pathological causes of mental tokens. Consider how the existence of pathological causes will typically prevent, say, "water" from meaning H_2O in virtue of Fodor's conditions. Let there be instantiations of a nomic connection between H_2O and "water" tokens in Janet's brain, so that conditions (1) and (2) are satisfied. Also let there have been occasions on which thoughts about drinking have caused "water"s in Janet's brain, so that the robustness condition (4) is satisfied. Let it further be the case that thoughts about drinking cause "water"s in Janet only because H_2O causes "water"s in Janet. Even when these conditions are satisfied, there are plenty of properties that nomically cause "water"s in Janet, but not because H_2O nomically causes "water"s in her. A severe blow to the head, a hallucinogenic drug, a brain tumor, a high fever, or a current passed through a series of well-placed microelectrodes in the brain could cause "water"s in Janet. The power of these Ys need not depend synchronically on the power H_2O now has to cause syntactic "water"s in Janet. It may well be that there is a diachronic dependence of, say, the microelectrode-"water" law on the H_2O-"water" law, but this is of course beside the point. Diachronic dependencies are not the issue for Fodor. To avoid the pathology problem, he must claim that laws, such as the microelectrode-"water" law, depend synchronically on the H_2O-"water" law. Thus, insofar as the existence of pathological causes is the rule and not the exception, Fodor's theory appears to be vacuous.

When we claim that the laws connecting such Ys as hallucinogens and brain tumors to "X"s are not asymmetrically dependent on the X-"X" laws, we are aware that we are making an empirical claim. Even though we are not scientists, we can give good reasons for our empirical conjectures. First, our examples tolerate a wide range of empirical developments. We need to make no commitment concerning exactly what property it is of brain tumors that is causally responsible for their producing "X"s. It might be that brain tumors qua producers of electrical activity PDQ cause "X"s. It might be that brain tumors qua disruptors of metabolic activity LMNO cause "X"s. All we need for present purposes is that the power the relevant property has to produce "X"s in the brain does not depend on the power of Xs to produce "X"s. Similarly, for our other putative pathological causes.

Second, and more importantly, our pathological causes involve the contingent, lower-level properties of the instantiation of psychological processes interfering in higher-level psychological processes. As is well known, Fodor believes that the laws relevant to semantics are not basic laws of physics, but are laws of the special sciences. These laws are not strict, but *ceteris paribus* laws. In asserting a special science law, such as,

(*) If a person wants a beer and believes that she can get one by going to the refrigerator, then *ceteris paribus* she will go to the refrigerator,

part of the force of the "ceteris paribus" is to recognize that lower-level properties can interfere with the higher-level laws. The *ceteris paribus* clause recognizes such events as having a massive stroke or having the molecules in one's body fly apart in an extremely improbable quantum mechanical coincidence. In other words, the *ceteris paribus* clause admits the existence of laws such as, "If the molecules in a person's body fly apart, then *ceteris paribus* the person will not go to the refrigerator" or "If a person has a massive stroke, then *ceteris paribus* the person will not go to the refrigerator." In these laws, we assume that the power more basic properties have to cause less basic events does not depend on the power of relatively higher properties to bring about these same less basic events. Stated in terms of our examples, we suppose that the power brain tumors have over a person's going or not going to the refrigerator does not depend synchronically on the power her beliefs and desires have on her going or not going. We suppose that the power certain quantum mechanical possibilities have over a person's visiting the refrigerator does not depend synchronically on the power her beliefs and desires have on her visiting. Our empirical beliefs about the independent causal powers of our Ys are, thus, not secured merely by empirical intuitions cultivated for the present task of challenging Fodor's theory of meaning, but by empirical intuitions concerning the interactions among strict laws and *ceteris paribus* laws.

By touching upon *ceteris paribus* laws, we obtain an added benefit. We can clarify the scope of our argument based on pathologies. In earlier publications we spoke of pathologies only in connection with humans and other higher organisms. One might, therefore, think that the pathologies problem only affects representations in higher organisms. From the foregoing, however, it is clear that pathological causes, in our novel sense of the term, are to be expected wherever *ceteris paribus* laws are in force; that is, in all the special sciences. This is especially damaging for Fodor, since he takes it that the theory of meaning is clearly a part of the special science of psychology. When all of physics is said and done, "meaning" and "reference" will not be among the basic terms. The existence of pathologies rules out Fodor's theory of meaning just where he thinks it must be, in the special sciences.

It might be thought that Fodor could respond to the pathologies problem by claiming that we have not taken seriously enough his claim to be offering merely sufficient conditions for "X"s meaning X. He never claimed, one might say, that anything means what it does in virtue of his conditions. Instead, his sole ambition was to show that there can be purely naturalistic conditions for something "X" to mean X. The question whether the conditions are ever in fact satisfied is another matter. So, technically, this vacuity "problem" we have brought forth does not contradict anything Fodor claims.

This response to our charge of vacuity hardly fits the spirit of Fodor's enterprise. If Fodor genuinely aspires only to a set of conditions for meeting Brentano's problem – conditions that would provide purely naturalistic conditions for "X" meaning X – it is not clear why he needs the Asymmetric Causal Dependency Theory. After all, as we saw, he already believes that "maybe there is *no* objection to the idea that '+,' 'and,' 'all' and the like have the meanings they do because they play a certain causal role in the mental lives of their users." What is the point of solving Brentano's problem in a new way, if functional role semantics already solves the problem? Further, if Fodor genuinely aspires only to a set of conditions for meeting Brentano's problem, it is not clear why he cares if his theory assigns the intuitively *correct* meaning to "X" rather than merely *some* meaning to "X". When facing the objection that his theory would lead "horse" to mean small horse, rather than horse, Fodor does not discard the question as irrelevant, since his conditions still assign content to "horse," hence solve Brentano's problem (cf. p. 191f). Instead, he explains why his conditions lead to "horse" meaning horse, rather than small horse. The reason is that the property of being a "horse" is nomologically connected to the property of being a horse, not the property of being a small horse. Finally, the response would disappoint many expectations about what Fodor has championed for years. It is a considerable disappointment to learn that this theory of mental representation is not a theory that figures in the explanation of human or animal behavior. It is not a theory of the primitive mental representations that figure into the actual compositional semantics of Fodor's hypothetical human language of thought. The theory would not show that meaning as we find it in the actual world is atomistic, rather than holistic. The theory would be largely disconnected from the remainder of Fodor's (and others') conceptions of mental representation. Fodor may win a battle with this move, but he certainly loses the war.

4   Twin-Earth and Vacuity

In his second published installment of the Asymmetric Causal Dependency Theory, Fodor believed that his theory could handle Twin-Earth cases (see pp. 202–3). He assumed that handling such cases is relevant to semantics. Nevertheless, as mentioned above, variations on the basic Twin-Earth theme are highly problematic for the theory. Consider, first, what we might call the *Standard* case. Recall, first of all, that "H_2O causes 'water' tokens in beings like Janet" and "XYZ causes 'water' tokens in begins like Janet" are both laws. Both laws are in place, if one is, because XYZ and H_2O are indistinguishable to Janet and the science of her day. Further, it appears that the H_2O-"water" law is instantiated, even though the XYZ-"water" law is not. We might also say that " 'What is the so-called universal solvent?' causes 'water' in beings like Janet" is an instantiated law allowing the satisfaction of condition (4).

A problem arises for conditon (3). In order to satisfy condition (3), breaking the H_2O-"water" connection must break the XYZ-"water" connection. The problem is that it is also the case that, if one breaks the XYZ-"water" connection, one will break the H_2O-"water" connection. That is, there is a *symmetric* dependence of the XYZ-"water" connection on the H_2O-"water" connection. Fodor's theory requires both (a) and (b) to be true:

(a) Breaking the H_2O-"water" connection thereby breaks the XYZ-"water" connection, and
(b) Breaking the XYZ-"water" connection does not thereby break the H_2O-"water" connection.

In fact, however, on both Earth and Twin-Earth, (a) is true, but (b) is false. Indeed, Fodor agrees with us that the XYZ-"water" and the H_2O-"water" laws are symmetrically dependent (see p. 203). We conclude, therefore, that Twin-Earth examples show that no term for a thing that has a twin[4] means what it does in virtue of satisfying Fodor's conditions. This provides reason to believe that Fodor's conditions are vacuous, hence uninteresting.

5 Fodor's Asymmetry Condition Revisited

A popular response to our objections, both the pathology problem and the Twin-Earth Problem, is to claim that there is a better interpretation of Fodor's third condition.[5] To this point, we have taken condition (3) to mean that all the Y-"X" connections found in the actual world depend asymmetrically on the X-"X" connection. Others propose that (3) be understood in a weaker sense; that only the Y-"X" connections *that are instantiated* in the actual world must depend asymmetrically on the X-"X" connection. We might introduce this as condition (3'):

> (3') For all Y not = X, if there are instances in which Ys qua Ys cause "X"s, then the law "Ys cause 'X's" found in the actual world is asymmetrically dependent on the law "Xs cause 'X's".

According to the previous interpretation of the asymmetric dependency condition (condition (3) above), breaking the X-"X" law will break all the Y-"X" laws, but breaking all the Y-"X" laws will leave the X-"X" law unchanged. According to the new interpretation (condition (3')), it may or may not be the case that *all* the Y-"X" connections depend asymmetrically on the X-"X" connection. Condition (3') is silent on that point. Instead, (3') requires only that all the Y-"X" laws of the actual world that are instantiated depend asymmetrically on the X-"X" law. There may be uninstantiated Y-"X" laws and they may depend on the X-"X" connection for their ability to cause "X"s or they may not. The uninstantiated connections are irrelevant to the meaning of "X."

Consider two points. First, according to condition (3'), the asymmetric dependencies the new interpretation postulates are still dependencies among laws; one set of laws still depends asymmetrically on another single law. Second, condition (3') does not require that instantiations of the Y-"X" laws create dependencies of the Y-"X" laws on the X-"X" law. A given Y-"X" law depends or does not depend on the X-"X" law regardless of whether the Y-"X" law has instantiations or not. Condition (3') changes only the causes of "X" that are to be counted among those asymmetrically dependent on the power of Xs.

The move from (3) to (3') may appear to save Fodor's theory from our vacuity arguments, since condition (3') appears to be satisfied in circumstances where (3) was not satisfied (Warfield, forthcoming). Consider the Standard Twin-Earth case. On condition (3'), the XYZ-"water" connection (which still depends symmetrically on the H_2O-"water" connection) need not be among those that are asymmetrically dependent on the H_2O-"water" connection, since it is uninstantiated. It may also be suggested that (3′) saves Fodor from the problem of pathologies. One can claim that laws such as "brain tumors cause 'water's,'" "hallucinogens cause 'water's,'" "blows to the head cause 'water's,'" "microelectrodes cause 'water's,'" and so forth, govern the psychological processes of some actual person Janet and even admit that these laws are not dependent on the H_2O-"water" law, yet maintain that, since these laws are uninstantiated, the fact that they do not depend on the H_2O-"water" law renders them irrelevant to the meaning of "water." One might suppose that, for most people, neither a brain tumor, nor a hallucinogen, nor a blow to the head, nor any other injury or illness has caused a token of "water," so that, for most people, "water" can mean H_2O in virtue of Fodor's conditions.

Here we wish to observe that condition (3′) appeals again to the actual causal history of "X" and that this does not seem to be the sort of move Fodor himself is now willing to make. We know this, as before, from personal communication, but it can also be seen in his latest book. Fodor and Lepore write,

> For it is unclear that a causal theory must identify the truth conditions of a sentence S with the conditions that *actually* cause S to be tokened. It might be just as good – in fact, it might even be better – to identify the truth conditions of S with what *would* cause it to be tokened *were it the case that* . . . (Notice that none of the *actual* causes of the tokens of a type need satisfy the subjunctive condition.) This is, in fact, the way that causal theories proceed when they invoke nomological connections – rather than causal histories as the metaphysical basis of content. What makes "cat" mean *cat*, according to such theories, is *not* that it *is* caused by cats, but only that it's nomologically necessary that it *would* be caused by cats under some or other circumstances that the theory is obliged to specify. (For examples of this sort of theory, see . . . Fodor, "A Theory of Content"; etc.) (Fodor and Lepore, 1992, p. 157; ellipsis and parenthetical comment in original)

Not only does Fodor now appear to be unwilling to add further conditions or refinements that implicate actual causal history, it seems that in this passage he has even forgotten that he had such a condition (condition 2) in "A Theory of Content, II"!

6   Pathologies and Twin-Earth Revisited

Replacing condition (3) with condition (3′) may appear to provide a solid rejoinder to the pathology and Twin-Earth problems; however, appearances are deceiving (cf. Adams and Aizawa, forthcoming). To see this, let us first revisit the pathologies problem. Let Janet be a perfectly normal, fully functional adult whose syntactic tokens of "cat" mean cat. Let Janet's "cat" tokens also satisfy the Fodorian conditions for meaning cat in the obvious way. So, it looks as though Janet's "cat"s means cat in virtue of Fodor's conditions. Suppose, further, that the meaning of Janet's "cat"s is not overdetermined. Since Fodor offers only sufficient conditions for meaning, there may be two or more sets of sufficient conditions for Janet's "cat"s to mean cat. Therefore, let this not be the case. Let no conditions other than (1), (2), (3′) and (4) conspire to be sufficient for Janet's tokens of "cat" to mean cat. Finally, let it be the case that, prior to Tuesday, "cat" has not been pathologically tokened in Janet. On Tuesday she volunteers for a neuropsychology experiment. She goes into the lab and small electrodes are placed on her scalp. By passing a small current through the electrodes, a single pathological "cat" token is produced in Janet. Thus, on Tuesday, a previously uninstantiated electrode-"cat" law, a law that does not depend on the cat-"cat" law, is instantiated. The experiment is then over and Janet returns to lead a normal psychological life in which "cat" apparently serves as Janet's mental representation of cats.

Prior to Tuesday, Janet's "cat"s appear to mean cat via Fodorian semantics with condition (3′) in place of (3). After Tuesday, however, Janet's "cat" tokens could not mean cat by these conditions. Why not? Because condition (3′) fails to be satisfied. The electrode-"cat" law became relevant on Tuesday; it became one of the instantiated Y-"X" laws that must asymmetrically depend on the X-"X" law for "X" to mean X in virtue of Fodor's conditions (for "cat" to mean cat, in Janet). However, after Tuesday (and now, relevantly) electrodes would cause "cat"s in Janet, even if cats did not cause "cat"s in Janet. Recall that the failure of pathological Y-"X" laws, such as the electrode-"cat" law, to depend on X-"X" laws, such as the cat-"cat" law, was conceded on condition (3) (conceded even by Fodor). The move to (3′) did not change this fact; (3′) only tried to make this fact irrelevant on the ground that the electrode-"cat" law is uninstantiated. After Tuesday, however, this law becomes relevant, and condition (3′) is not satisfied because Janet instantiates the electrode-"cat" law. As we explained when we introduced the pathologies examples, "cat" is a purely syntactic item. It does not require cats to produce it. Whatever the electrodes do to Janet to produce a "cat" can be done with or without the existence of cats.

This is bad for Fodorian semantics for at least three reasons. First, Fodorian semantics cannot explain how Janet's "cat" tokens have their actual meaning. It is very clear to us, and many others agree, that in these circumstances Janet's "cat" tokens mean cat before and after Tuesday. One wild tokening cannot change that.[6] Fodorian semantics with condition (3′), however, cannot explain how Janet's "cat"s mean cat after Tuesday. Second, the meaning Fodorian semantics could assign to Janet's "cat" tokens seems doomed to be incorrect. Fodor's theory would allow saying that after Tuesday Janet's "cat"s lose their meaning or have the disjunctive meaning cat-or-electrode (Fodor, 1991, p. 262), but it would not allow saying that Janet's "cat"s still mean cat in virtue of his conditions. In other words, Fodor's conditions must make the wrong assignment of content in this experimental context. Recall that, in the development of his theory in 1990, Fodor was concerned about the correct assignment of content to terms (cf. especially, pp. 191–5). Showing that this version of the theory assigns the wrong content to terms constitutes a serious objection to the theory.

Third, further reflection suggests that Fodor's conditions are still vacuous. The results of the neuropsychological thought-experiment on Janet casts doubt on the assumption that (before or after Tuesday) "cat" could mean cat in virtue of Fodor's conditions. Intuitively, "cat" means cat before and after Tuesday. To explain this, Fodor might say that "cat" means cat prior to Tuesday exclusively in virtue of his conditions, and means cat after Tuesday in virtue of another set of sufficient conditions.[7] This is wildly implausible. It requires that suddenly and instantaneously, with the passage of electrical current through the electrodes, some other set of conditions takes up where the Fodorian conditions left off and gave "cat" the meaning cat. We think not. Instead, we suppose that, contrary to our original assumption, "cat" *never meant* cat in virtue of Fodor's conditions. This neurophysiological thought-experiment with Janet brings this to light. In fact, insofar as the results of this neurophysiological experiment are reproducible with any mental representation, we have reason to believe that no mental token means what it does in virtue of Fodor's conditions. To show that "dog," "cow," "water," etc. in Janet does not mean dog, cow, water, etc., we need not actually produce pathological tokens of "dog," "cow," "water," etc. Instead, we can see from our one case that Fodor's conditions are not sufficient for meaning (hence, are vacuous).

Upon revisiting the pathologies problem we find that condition (3′) is no salvation for Fodorian semantics. At best, it assigns the wrong content to terms when pathological causes strike (even if they only strike once). At worst, if Fodor's theory cannot explain the meaning of Janet's tokens after Tuesday, it is unlikely that the theory adequately explains the meanings of her mental tokens prior to Tuesday. It is, in our estimation, more likely that Fodorian semantics is still vacuous. No "X" means X in virtue of Fodor's conditions.

Next, let us revisit the Twin-Earth case with condition (3′) in hand. We think that, here too, condition (3′) does not rescue Fodorian semantics because it assigns the wrong content to "X"s. Let's assume that we have the following instantiated laws,

> H_2O causes "water"s
> "What is the so-called universal solvent?" causes "water"s
> Gin in a glass at a distance causes "water"s
> "What is the main component of rain?" causes "water"s,

and that all these instantiated laws connecting non-H_2O to "water" are asymmetrically dependent on the H_2O to "water" law. There is, in addition, an uninstantiated XYZ-"water" law that is symmetrically dependent on the H_2O law, but, since it is uninstantiated, according to (3′), it is not relevant to the meaning of "water." We propose to test condition (3′) by modifying the Standard Twin-Earth story. Rather than having XYZ on some distant planet, let XYZ be found scattered about on Earth.[8] Suppose, that is, that there are puddles, lakes, and drinks that contain XYZ all around (i.e., the conditional probability that something is XYZ, given that it caused a "water" token, is not zero), but merely by chance none of this XYZ has ever caused a "water" token in Janet. Call this environment Modified Earth. Let Janet have lived her entire life on this Modified Earth so that by some freakish set of events she never actually encounters XYZ, only H_2O. Let it also be the case that no one, not Janet nor any of the scientists in her community, can distinguish the two liquids. Under these conditions, we take it that Janet has a disjunctive representation of XYZ or H_2O; that is, Janet's "water" tokens mean XYZ or H_2O.

If we adopt the new version of Fodor's conditions we get the wrong content for Janet's "water" tokens in the Modified Twin-Earth case. Instead of assigning disjunctive content to "water," Fodor's conditions dictate that "water" means H_2O. There is an H_2O-"water" law (condition 1). The law is instantiated by Janet (condition 2). Instances of non-H_2O that have caused "water"s, such as gin at a distance or questions about the principal component of rain, have done so only because H_2O causes "water"s (condition 3′ and condition 4). Thus, Fodorian semantics, with condition (3′), assigns the wrong content to Janet's "water"s. It says her "water" tokens mean H_2O when they actually mean H_2O or XYZ, in the XYZ-rich environment.

Fodor may try to accommodate the intuition that Janet's "water" tokens indeed do mean H_2O or XYZ in this XYZ-infested Modified Earth environment by appealing to the existence of a disjunctive H_2O-or-XYZ-"water" law. The H_2O-or-XYZ-"water" law exists, Fodor might claim, if either the H_2O-"water" law or the XYZ-"water" law exists. Further, the disjunctive law is instantiated if either disjunct is, and the H_2O-"water" law disjunct is instantiated. Notice, however, that, if Fodor tried this move, he would go from the frying pan to the fire for two reasons. First, if there were such a disjunctive law, Fodor's theory would assign the wrong content to Janet's "water" tokens in her standard XYZ-free environment of Earth. Second, if there were such a disjunctive law, the required dependencies among the laws would not be there.

The first problem is clear because the disjunctive H_2O-or-XYZ-"water" law would exist and be instantiated in Janet's standard XYZ-free environment of Earth. If the existence of the disjunctive law in Janet's XYZ-rich environment of Modified Earth were sufficient, given Fodor's conditions, to make her "water" tokens mean H_2O or XYZ there, then the existence of that disjunctive law in her XYZ-free Earth environment would be sufficient to make her "water" tokens have disjunctive meaning there as well. In *both* environments, Fodor's conditions would assign disjunctive content to Janet's "water" tokens.

Therefore, Fodorian semantics would be unable to explain why Janet's "water" tokens. univocally mean H_2O in her normal XYZ-free Earth environment. Thus, the theory still would not solve the Standard version of the Twin-Earth problem discussed above.

The second problem is that asymmetric dependencies do not exist among the singular and the disjunctive laws (Adams, in preparation). For example, could Fodor say that, in the XYZ-infested Modified Earth environment, the H_2O-"water" law asymmetrically depends upon the H_2O-or-XYZ-"water" law (thus, "water" means H_2O or XYZ there) and that, in the XYZ-free Earth environment, the H_2O-or-XYZ-"water" law asymmetrically depends upon the H_2O-"water" law (thus, "water" means H_2O there)? In other words, can he say that the dependencies among the laws depend on the environment? This, one may think, would get the meaning of "water" to come out right in the respective environments. Setting aside the fact that this move is entirely *ad hoc*, it does not help because it does not get the dependencies among the disjunctive and non-disjunctive laws to come out right. If "water" were to mean H_2O, in Janet's XYZ-free Earth environment, in virtue of Fodor's conditions, then the H_2O-or-XYZ-"water" law must asymmetrically depend on the H_2O-"water" law. Clauses (a) and (b) must both be true:

(a)   breaking the H_2O-"water" law must break the H_2O-or-XYZ-"water" law,

(b)   but breaking the H_2O-or-XYZ-"water" law must not break the H_2O-"water" law.

Clause (a) is apparently true, but clause (b) is false. Clause (a) is true because breaking the H_2O-"water" law breaks the XYZ-"water" law and, since breaking both the H_2O-"water" law *and* the XYZ-"water" law breaks the H_2O-or-XYZ-"water" law, the H_2O-or-XYZ "water" law is dependent on the H_2O-"water" law. Clause (b) fails to be true because breaking the H_2O-or-XYZ-"water" law will break the H_2O-"water" law, since if neither H_2O nor XYZ has the power to cause "water"s, then, logically, H_2O does not have the power to cause "water"s. So Fodorian semantics would be unable to explain why Janet's "water" tokens univocally mean H_2O in her normal XYZ-free Earth environment.

The dependencies do not work even in Janet's XYZ-rich Modified Earth environment. Thus, Fodor cannot explain why Janet's "water" tokens mean H_2O or XYZ there. There both clauses (c) and (d) must be true:

(c)   breaking the H_2O-or-XYZ-"water" law would break the H_2O-"water" law,

(d)   but breaking the H_2O-"water" law would not break the H_2O-or-XYZ-"water" law.

While (c) is true, (d) is false, for the reasons we have given above.

Therefore, the Twin-Earth assault on condition (3′) goes like this. Either there is a disjunctive H₂O-or-XYZ-"water" law or there is not. If there is a disjunctive law, Fodorian semantics cannot assign non-disjunctive content to Janet's "water" tokens in Janet's XYZ-free Earth environment. If there is no disjunctive law, Fodorian semantics assigns the wrong content to "water" in Janet's XYZ-rich modified Earth environment. Thus, where Fodorian semantics with condition (3) was vacuous, Fodorian semantics with condition (3′) in one way or another makes the wrong assignment of content to terms. For these reasons, Fodorian semantics fares no better when revisiting the Twin-Earth cases with condition (3′) in place of condition (3) than it does when revisiting the pathologies cases. These failures of Fodorian semantics, regardless of whether one interprets the asymmetric dependency condition as (3) or (3′), lead us to believe that the theory is fundamentally misguided. In closing, we will explain further why we think this is so and suggest why Fodor's account probably does not even account for the phenomena of robust tokening – fundamental data around which the theory was constructed.

7   Robustness: Why Asymmetric Causal Dependency Is Fundamentally Misguided

One of the principal virtues that Fodor touts for his theory is that it is supposed to account for the phenomena of "robust tokening": non-X-caused, non-false tokenings of "X"s. Indeed, the asymmetrical dependency clause itself is clearly crafted to this end. Nonetheless, we doubt seriously that it does explain robustness and we shall close by explaining why. In this way, we shall be casting doubt on the very heart of Fodorian semantics.

Suppose that robust tokening, such as a steak causing "cow" to be tokened in Janet, is to be explained by asymmetric causal dependency, as Fodorian semantics maintains. Then, the required causal asymmetries must be explained purely syntactically. Ys must cause "X"s only because Xs cause "X"s and without regard to the fact that "X" means X. In section 2 we noted the puzzlement we face when we suggest in our pigeon example that the scientists-droppings law depends asymmetrically on the pigeon-droppings law. More generally, we now raise the issue of why it might ever be true that all Y-"X" laws depend asymmetrically on the X-"X" law. What is the mechanism by which this asymmetric dependence is maintained? It cannot be simply a brute fact of nature, since, as Fodor agrees, intentional laws are not basic laws. Further, if the Fodorian account is to naturalize meaning, that is, reduce meaning to non-meaningful concepts, the explanation cannot involve anything semantic. So what could the explanation of the synchronic, asymmetric dependency be, if it involves nothing semantic? Nothing reasonable comes to mind. We believe that the most plausible explanation of the putative fact that the syntactic item "What is the principal chemical component of the human body?" in Janet's head causes a syntactic item "water" in Janet, only because H_2O causes the syntactic item "water" in Janet, violates naturalism. It violates naturalism because the explanation involves meaning. We surmise that the best explanation of this putative fact is that "water" in Janet means water, Janet knows that water is the principal component of the human body, and Janet wants to answer the question. If the syntactic item "water" did not mean water, then the question would not have evoked the "water" token. In other words, the asymmetric dependence apparently arises, at least in part, from the facts about the meanings of syntactic items; they do not themselves form the basis of meaning. Indeed, Fodor himself at one point ventures an explanation of at least one asymmetric causal dependency in which the explanation invokes intentional concepts, threatening to violate his semantic naturalism:

> My point is that the intention to use "water" only of stuff of the same kind as the local samples has the effect of making its application to XYZ asymmetrically dependent on its application to H_2O ceteris paribus. (see p. 203)

We believe this passage betrays the misconception of using asymmetric causal dependencies as the metaphysical basis of meaning.

We suggest that the asymmetric dependencies Fodor has in mind arise, at least in part, from the meanings of terms. In asserting this, we do not mean to claim that this is universally the case. It may occasionally happen that a Y-"X" law depends on an X-"X" law because of nothing more than the physical properties of Ys and Xs and the mere syntactic properties of "X"s, but this would be the exception, rather than the rule. In cases of robust non-false tokenings, where Ys cause "X"s (but not through misidentification, e.g., gin at a glance being mistaken for water or horses on dark nights being mistaken for cows), Ys cause "X"s partly because of the *meanings* of "X"s. Asymmetric causal dependencies derived from purely syntactic features of "cow" tokens would be unlikely candidates to explain why steaks cause non-false tokenings of "cow" in Janet. A much better explanation of this phenomenon of robustness, therefore, is that "cow" means cow, "steak" means steak, and Janet associates steaks with cows (Adams, Aizawa, and Fuller, forthcoming; Adams and Aizawa, forthcoming; Adams, in Preparation).

8 Conclusion

In other papers, we have discouraged acceptance of Fodorian semantics (Adams and Aizawa, 1992; Adams and Aizawa, 1993; Adams and Aizawa, forthcoming). The present paper carries on in this spirit. Here we have examined two principal versions of Fodorian Semantics – differing only on whether the asymmetric causal dependency clause is interpreted as condition (3) or (3'). The first version suffers from semantic promiscuity and vacuity due to pathological causes and Twin-Earth examples. The second version, championed as a response to the problems of vacuity, has insurmountable problems of its own. It fails to meet the problem of vacuity posed by pathological causes and Twin-Earth examples. Further, content assignments it permits are incorrect. In the penultimate section, we have given reasons to believe that the asymmetric causal dependency approach is fundamentally ill-conceived. Fodor (among others) has taken heroic steps to revive the Asymmetric Causal Dependency Theory, but the patient died. It is time to look elsewhere for a naturalized semantic theory.[9]

Notes

"Fodorian Semantics" appears here for the first time by kind permission of the authors.

1 We say "brief" because (a) it did not appear in Fodor's original statement of the conditions (Fodor, 1987, chapter 4), and (b) in conversation and in print (Fodor and Lepore, 1992, p. 157) Fodor has denied that his is a causal-historical account and denied that such accounts are correct.

2 We set aside the question of whether it is true that "pure informational" theories are not historical, but compare Dretske (1981, 1988). Many of the examples below will rely on variations on the basic "Twin-Earth" picture. Many people object to the fact that "Twin-Earth" is an unreal place or that some examples involving XYZ require it to do unrealistic things. Here we continue following Fodor's example, since it is standardized in the literature and we think that the Twin-Earth example easily could be replaced *mutatis mutandis* with a more realistic example, say, jadite-nephrite. We leave it to the reader to supply the necessary changes.

3 Yet another response to our pigeons example has been to accept it as decisive, but to claim that Fodor should add an additional condition to his theory, namely, that "X"s must occur in a language of thought (cf. Warfield, forthcoming). Elsewhere, (Adams and Aizawa, forthcoming), we have argued, among other things, that this proposal still does not save Fodorian semantics.

4 Fodor will say that Twin-Earth is irrelevant, since it does not exist (at least he said this to us and in some manuscripts he is circulating). That, however, misses the point that Twin-Earth examples exemplify. Barn facades, fool's gold, jadeite and other examples of things that persons may fail to discriminate from barns, gold, nephrite, and so on, are just as problematic for Fodor. For these are things that do exist. Janet may grow up on a desert island where only gold (no fool's gold) exists. She may be unable to distinguish the two substances. Yet, her "gold" tokens may mean gold because any fool's gold is too remote to be relevant to the meaning of her "gold" tokens. Still, the gold-"gold" and fool's-gold-"gold" laws may be symmetrically dependent (for Janet). Fodor could not explain why Janet's tokens of "gold" mean only gold. Thus, the problem generalizes beyond XYZ.

5 Presented to us independently by Pat Manfredi, Donna Summerfield, Fritz Warfield,

and Takashi Yagisawa, this response will appear in print in a forthcoming paper by Fritz Warfield, "Fodorian Semantics: A Reply to Adams and Aizawa."

6   In support of our claim is a semantic theory that we favor (Dretske, 1988; Adams, Aizawa, and Fuller, forthcoming). On this theory, if "cat" has acquired the function of indicating cats in Janet, it will still have that function after a single tokening by a microelectrode. If having a meaning is at all similar to having a function, and we think it is, a single misfiring does not change meaning or function. If Janet's heart skips a beat, it does not fail to have the function of circulating the blood, and if "cat" is wildly tokened just once, it does not fail to mean cat if it meant cat all along.

7   He cannot say that the meaning of "cat" is overdetermined by two sets of conditions: the asymmetric causal dependency conditions *and* some conditions C* (where C* = some other as yet unspecified sufficient conditions for "cat" to mean cat) and that "cat" continues to mean cat after Tuesday in virtue of the continued satisfaction of conditions C*. He cannot say this, since one of the stipulations in the original example was that the meaning of "cat" was not overdetermined.

8   If you want to know how the water and XYZ keep from getting mixed or blended together, don't blame us, blame Putnam for the strain on the example. We don't intend to try to patch up the examples that Putnam started in 1975. The point of the examples survives the technical difficulties, in any case. If necessary to diminish the strain on your credulity, we would again suggest you make the necessary substitutions of the "jade" means jadite or nephrite example in place of the water/XYZ example.

9   We would like to thank Kent Bach, Ned Block, Fred Dretske, Jerry Fodor, Gary Fuller, Pat Manfredi, Carol Slater, Donna Summerfield, Fritz Warfield, and Takashi Yagisawa for numerous helpful discussions concerning the subjects in this paper. Adams also thanks The Center for the Study of Language and Information at Stanford University for support during the writing of this paper.

10 Biosemantics

Ruth Millikan

Causal or informational theories of the semantic content of mental states which have had an eye on the problem of false representations have characteristically begun with something like this intuition. There are some circumstances under which an inner representation has its represented as a necessary and/or sufficient cause or condition of production. That is how the content of the representation is fixed. False representations are to be explained as tokens that are produced under other circumstances. The challenge, then, is to tell what defines certain circumstances as the content-fixing ones.

I

Note that the answer cannot be just that these circumstances are *statistically* normal conditions. To gather such statistics, one would need to delimit a reference class of occasions, know how to count its members, and specify description categories. It would not do, for example, just to average over conditions-in-the-universe-any-place-any-time. Nor is it given how to carve out relevant description categories for conditions on occasions. Is it "average" in the summer for it to be (precisely) between 80° and 80.5° Fahrenheit with humidity 87 per cent? And are average conditions those which obtain on at least 50 per cent of the occasions, or is it 90 per cent? Depending on how one sets these parameters, radically different conditions are "statistically normal." But the notion of semantic content clearly is not relative, in this manner, to arbitrary parameters. The content-fixing circumstances must be *non-arbitrarily* determined.

A number of recent writers have made an appeal to teleology here, specifically to conditions of normal function or well-functioning of the systems that produce inner representations. Where the represented is R and its representation is "R," under conditions of well-functioning, we might suppose, only Rs can or are likely to produce "Rs." Or perhaps "R" is a representation of R just in case the system was designed to react to Rs by producing "Rs." But this sort of move yields too many representations. Every state of every functional system has normal causes, things that it is a response to in accordance with design. These causes may be proximate or remote, and many are disjunctive. Thus, a proximate normal cause of dilation of the skin capillaries is certain substances in the blood, more remote causes include muscular effort, sunburn, and being in an overheated environment. To each of these causes the vascular system responds by design, yet the response (a red face), though it may be a natural sign of burn or exertion or overheating, certainly is not a representation of that. If not every state of a system represents its normal causes, which are the states that do?

Jerry Fodor[1] has said that, whereas the content of an inner representation is determined by some sort of causal story, its status *as* a representation is determined by the functional organization of the part of the system which uses it. There is such a thing, it seems, as behaving like a representation without behaving like a representation of anything in particular. What the thing is a representation of is then determined by its cause under content-fixing conditions. It would be interesting to have the character of universal I-am-a-representation behavior spelled out for us. Yet, as Fodor well knows, there would still be the problem of demonstrating that there was only one normal cause per representation type.

A number of writers, including Dennis Stampe,[2] Fred Dretske,[3] and Mohan Matthen,[4] have suggested that what is different about effects that are representations is that their function is, precisely, to represent, "indicate," or "detect." For example, Matthen says of (fullfledged) perceptual states that they are "state[s] that [have] the function of *detecting* the presence of things of a certain type . . ." (1988, p. 20). It does not help to be told that inner representations are things that have representing (indicating, detecting) as their function, however, unless we are also told what kind of activity representing (indicating, detecting) is. Matthen does not tell us how to naturalize the notion "detecting." If "detecting" is a function of a representational state, it must be something that the state effects or produces. For example, it cannot be the function of a state to have been produced in response to something. Or does Matthen mean that it is not the representational states themselves, but the part of the system which produces them, which has the function of detecting? It has the function, say, of producing states that correspond to or covary with something in the outside world? But, unfortunately, not every device whose job description includes producing items that vary with the world is a representation producer. The devices in me that produce calluses are supposed to vary their placement according to where the friction is, but calluses are not representations. The pigment arrangers in the skin of a chameleon, the function of which is to vary the chameleon's color with what it sits on, are not representation producers.

Stampe and Dretske do address the question what representing or (Dretske) "detecting" is. Each brings in his own description of what a natural sign or natural representation is, then assimilates *having the function of representing R* to being a natural sign or representer of *R* when the system functions normally. Now, the production of natural signs is undoubtedly an accidental side effect of normal operation of many systems. From my red face you can tell that either I have been exerting myself, or I have been in the heat, or I am burned. But the production of an accidental side effect, no matter how regular, is not one of a system's functions; that goes by definition. More damaging, however, it simply is not true that representations must carry natural information. Consider the signals with which various animals signal danger. Nature knows that it is better to err on the side of caution, and it is likely that many of these signs occur more often in the absence than in the presence of any real danger. Certainly there is nothing incoherent in the idea that this might be so, hence that many of these signals do not carry natural information concerning the dangers they signal.

II

I fully agree, however, that an appeal to teleology, to function, is what is needed to fly a naturalist theory of content. Moreover, what makes a thing into an inner representation is, near enough, that its function is to represent. But, I shall argue, the way to unpack this insight is to focus on representation *consumption*, rather than representation production. It is the devices that *use* representations which determine these to be representations and, at the same time (contra Fodor), determine their content. If it really is the function of an inner representation to indicate its represented, clearly it is not just a natural sign, a sign that you or I looking on might interpret. It must be one that functions as a sign or representation *for the system itself.* What is it then for a system to use a representation *as* a representation?

The conception of function on which I shall rely was defined in my *Language, Thought, and Other Biological Categories*[5] and defended in "In Defense of Proper Functions"[6] under the label "proper function." Proper functions are determined by the histories of the items possessing them; functions that were "selected for" are paradigm cases.[7] The notions "function" and "design" should not be read, however, as referring only to origin. Natural selection does not slack after the emergence of a structure but actively preserves it by acting against the later emergence of less fit structures. And structures can be preserved due to performance of new functions unrelated to the forces that originally shaped them. Such functions are "proper functions," too, and are "performed in accordance with design."

The notion "design" should not be read – and this is very important – as a reference to innateness. A system may have been designed to be altered by its experience, perhaps to learn from its experience in a prescribed manner. Doing what it has learned to do in this manner is then "behaving in accordance with design" or "functioning properly."[8]

My term "normal" should be read normatively, historically, and relative to specific function. In the first instance, "normal" applies to explanations. A "normal explanation" explains the performance of a particular function, telling how it was (typically) historically performed on those (perhaps rare) occasions when it was properly performed. Normal explanations do not tell, say, why it has been common for a function to be performed; they are not statistical explanations. They cover only past times of actual performance, showing how these performances were entailed by natural law, given certain conditions, coupled with the dispositions and structures of the relevant functional devices.[9] In the second instance, "normal" applies to conditions. A "normal condition for performance of a function" is a condition, the presence of which must be mentioned in giving a full normal explanation for performance of that function. Other functions of the same organism or system may have other normal conditions. For example, normal conditions for discriminating colors are not the same as normal conditions for discriminating tastes, and normal conditions for seeing very large objects are not the same as for seeing very small ones. It follows that "normal conditions" must not be read as having anything to do with what is typical or average or even, in many cases, at all common. First, many functions are performed only rarely. For example, very few wild seeds land in conditions normal for their growth and development, and the protective colorings of caterpillars seldom actually succeed in preventing them from being eaten. Indeed, normal conditions might almost better be called "historically optimal" conditions. (If normal conditions for proper functioning, hence survival and proliferation, were a statistical norm, imagine how many rabbits there would be in the world.) Second, many proper functions only need to be performed under rare conditions. Consider, for example, the vomiting reflex, the function of which is to prevent (further) toxification of the body. A normal condition for performance of this function is presence, specifically of poison in the stomach, for (I am guessing) it is only under that condition that this reflex has historically had beneficial effects. But poison in the stomach certainly is not an average condition. (Nor, of course, is it a normal condition for other functions of the digestive system.)[10]

If it is actually one of a system's functions to produce representations, as we have said, these representations must function as representations for the system itself. Let us view the system, then, as divided into two parts or two aspects, one of which produces representations for the other to consume. What we need to look at is the consumer part, at what it is to use a thing *as* a representation. Indeed, a good look at the consumer part of the system ought to be all that is needed to determine not only representational status but representational content. We argue this as follows. First, the part of the system which consumes representations must understand the representations proffered to it.

Suppose, for example, that there were abundant "natural information" (in Dretske's[11] sense) contained in numerous natural signs all present in a certain state of a system. This information could still not serve the system *as* information, unless the signs were understood by the system, and, furthermore, understood as bearers of whatever specific information they, in fact, do bear. (Contrast Fodor's notion that something could function like a representation without functioning like a representation of anything in particular.) So there must be something about the consumer that *constitutes* its taking the signs to indicate, say, *p*, *q*, and *r* rather than *s*, *t*, and *u*. But, if we know what constitutes the consumer's *taking* a sign to indicate *p*, what *q*, what *r*, etc., then, granted that the consumer's takings are in some way systematically derived from the structures of the signs so taken, we can construct a semantics for the consumer's language. Anything the signs may indicate qua natural signs or natural information carriers then drops out as entirely irrelevant; the representation-producing side of the system had better pay undivided attention to the language of its consumer. The sign producer's function will be to produce signs that are true *as the consumer reads the language*.

The problem for the naturalist bent on describing intentionality, then, does not concern representation production at all. Although a representation always is something that is produced by a system whose proper function is to make that representation correspond by rule to the world, what the rule of correspondence is, what gives definition to this function, is determined entirely by the representation's consumers.

For a system to use an inner item as a representation, I propose, is for the following two conditions to be met. First, unless the representation accords, *so* (by a certain rule), with a represented, the consumer's normal use of, or response to, the representation will not be able to fulfill all of the consumer's proper functions in so responding – not, at least, in accordance with a normal explanation. (Of course, it might still fulfill these functions by freak accident, but not in the historically normal way.) Putting this more formally, that the representation and the represented accord with one another, so, is a normal condition for proper functioning of the consumer device as it reacts to the representation.[12] Note that the proposal is not that the content of the representation rests on the function of the representation or of the consumer, on what these do. The idea is not that there is such a thing as behaving like a representation of *X* or as being treated like a representation of *X*. The content hangs only on there being a certain condition that would be *normal* for performance of the consumer's functions – namely, that a certain correspondence relation hold between sign and world – whatever those functions may happen to be. For example, suppose the semantic rules for my belief representations are determined by the fact that belief tokens in me will aid the devices that use them to perform certain of their tasks in accordance with a normal explanation for success only under the condition that the forms or "shapes" of these belief tokens correspond, in accordance with said rules, to conditions in the world. Just what these user tasks are need not be mentioned.[13]

Second, represented conditions are conditions that vary, depending on the *form* of the representation, in accordance with specifiable correspondence rules that give the semantics for the relevant *system* of representation. More precisely, representations always admit of significant transformations (in the mathematical sense), which accord with transformations of their corresponding representeds, thus displaying significant articulation into variant and invariant aspects. If an item considered as compounded of certain variant and invariant aspects can be said to be "composed" of these, then we can also say that every representation is, as such, a member of a representational system having a "compositional semantics." For it is not that the represented condition is itself a normal condition for proper operation of the representation consumer. A certain correspondence between the representation and the world is what is normal. Coordinately, there is no such thing as a representation consumer that can understand only one representation. There are always other representations, composed other ways, saying other things, which it could have understood as well, in accordance with the same principles of operation. A couple of very elementary examples should make this clear.[14]

First, consider beavers, who splash the water smartly with their tails to signal danger. This instinctive behavior has the function of causing other beavers to take cover. The splash means danger, because only when it corresponds to danger does the instinctive response to the splash on the part of the interpreter beavers, the consumers, serve a purpose. If there is no danger present, the interpreter beavers interrupt their activities uselessly. Hence, that the splash corresponds to danger is a normal condition for proper functioning of the interpreter beavers' instinctive reaction to the splash. (It does not follow, of course, that it is a usual condition. Beavers being skittish, most beaver splashes possibly occur in response to things not in fact endangering the beaver.) In the beaver splash semantic system, the time and place of the splash varies with, "corresponds to," the time and place of danger. The representation is articulate: properly speaking, it is not a splash but a splash-at-a-time-and-a-place. Other representations in the same system, splashes at other times and places, indicate other danger locations.

Second, consider honey bees, which perform "dances" to indicate the location of sources of nectar they have discovered. Variations in the tempo of the dance and in the angle of its long axis vary with the distance and direction of the nectar. The interpreter mechanisms in the watching bees – these are the representation consumers – will not perform their full proper functions of aiding the process of nectar collection in accordance with a normal explanation unless the location of nectar corresponds correctly to the dance. So, the dances are representations of the location of nectar. The full representation here is a dance-at-a-time-in-a-place-at-a-tempo-with-an-orientation.

Notice that, on this account, it is not necessary to assume that most representations are true. Many biological devices perform their proper functions not on the average, but just often enough. The protective coloring of the juveniles of many animal species, for example, is an adaptation passed on because *occasionally* it prevents a juvenile from being eaten, though most of the juveniles of these species get eaten anyway. Similarly, it is conceivable that the devices that fix human beliefs fix true ones not on the average, but just often enough. If the true beliefs are functional and the false beliefs are, for the most part, no worse than having an empty mind, then even very fallible belief-fixing devices might be better than no belief-fixing devices at all. These devices might even be, in a sense, "designed to deliver some falsehoods." Perhaps, given the difficulty of designing highly accurate belief-fixing mechanisms, it is actually advantageous to fix too many beliefs, letting some of these be false, rather than fix too few beliefs. Coordinately, perhaps our belief-consuming mechanisms are carefully designed to tolerate a large proportion of false beliefs. It would not follow, of course, that the belief consumers are designed to *use* false beliefs, certainly not that false beliefs can serve all of the functions that true ones can. Indeed, surely if none of the mechanisms that used beliefs ever cared at all how or whether these beliefs corresponded to anything in the world, beliefs would not be functioning as representations, but in some other capacity.

Shifting our focus from producing devices to consuming devices in our search for naturalized semantic content is important. But the shift from the *function* of consumers to *normal conditions* for proper operation is equally important. Matthen, for example, characterizes what he calls a "quasi-perceptual state" as, roughly, one whose job is to cause the system to do what it must do to perform its function, given that it is in certain circumstances, which are what it represents. Matthen is thus looking pretty squarely at the representation consumers, but at what it is the representation's job to get these consumers to do, rather than at normal conditions for their proper operation. As a result, Matthen now retreats. The description he has given of quasi-perceptual states he says, cannot cover "real perception such as that which we humans experience. Quite simply, there is no such thing as *the* proper response, or even a range of functionally appropriate responses, to what perception tells us" (Matthen, 1988, p. 20).[15] On the contrary, representational content rests not on univocity of consumer function but on sameness of normal conditions for those functions. The same percept of the world may be used to guide any of very many and diverse activities, practical or theoretical. What stays the same is that the percept must correspond to environmental configurations in accordance with the same correspondence rules for each of these activities. For example, if the position of the chair in the room does not correspond, so, to my visual representation of its position, that will hinder me equally in my attempts to avoid the chair when passing through the room, to move the chair, to sit in it, to remove the cat from it, to make judgments about it, etc. Similarly, my belief that New York is large may be turned to any of diverse purposes, but those which require it to be a *representation* require also that New York indeed be large if these purposes are to succeed in accordance with a normal explanation for functioning of my cognitive systems.

III

We have just cleanly bypassed the whole genre of causal/informational accounts of mental content. To illustrate this, we consider an example of Dretske's. Dretske tells of a certain species of northern hemisphere bacteria which orient themselves away from toxic oxygen-rich surface water by attending to their magnetosomes, tiny inner magnets, which pull toward the magnetic north pole, hence pull down (Dretske, 1986). (Southern hemisphere bacteria have their magnetosomes reversed.) The function of the magnetosome thus appears to be to effect that the bacterium moves into oxygen-free water. Correlatively, intuition tells us that what the pull of the magnetosome represents is the whereabouts of oxygen-free water. The direction of oxygen-free water is not, however, a factor in *causing* the direction of pull of the magnetosome. And the most reliable natural information that the magnetosome carries is surely not about oxygen-free water but about distal and proximal causes of the pull, about the direction of geomagnetic or, better, just plain magnetic north. One can, after all, easily deflect the magnetosome away from the direction of lesser oxygen merely by holding a bar magnet overhead. Moreover, it is surely a function of the magnetosome to respond to that magnetic field; that is part of its normal mechanism of operation, whereas responding to oxygen density is not. None of this makes any sense on a causal or informational approach.

But on the biosemantic theory it does make sense. What the magnetosome represents is only what its *consumers* require that it correspond to in order to perform *their* tasks. Ignore, then, how the representation (a pull-in-a-direction-at-a-time) is normally produced. Concentrate, instead on how the systems that react to the representation work, on what these systems need in order to do their job. What they need is only that the pull be in the direction of oxygen-free water at the time. For example, they care not at all how it came about that the pull is in that direction; the magnetosome that points toward oxygen-free water quite by accident and not in accordance with any normal explanation will do just as well as one that points that way for the normal reasons. (As Socrates concedes in the *Meno*, true opinion is just as good as knowledge so long as it stays put.) What the magnetosome represents then is univocal; it represents only the direction of oxygen-free water. For that is the only thing that corresponds (by a compositional rule) to it, the absence of which would matter – the absence of which would disrupt the function of those mechanisms which rely on the magnetosome for guidance.

It is worth noting that what is represented by the magnetosome is not proximal but distal; no proximal stimulus is represented at all. Nor, of course, does the bacterium perform an inference from the existence of the proximal stimulus (the magnetic field) to the existence of the represented. These are good results for a theory of content to have, for otherwise one needs to introduce a derivative theory of content for mental representations that do not refer, say, to sensory stimulations, and also a foundationalist account of belief fixation. Note also that, on the present view, representations manufactured in identical ways by different species of animal might have different contents. Thus, a certain kind of small swift image on the toad's retina, manufactured by his eye lens, represents a bug, for that is what it must correspond to if the reflex it (invariably) triggers is to perform its proper functions normally, while exactly the same kind of small swift image on the retina of a male hoverfly, manufactured, let us suppose, by a nearly identical lens, represents a passing female hoverfly, for that is what it must correspond to if the female-chasing reflex it (invariably) triggers is to perform its proper functions normally. Turning the coin over, representations with the same content may be normally manufactured in a diversity of ways, even in the same species. How many different ways do you have, for example, of telling a lemon or your spouse? Nor is it necessary that any of the ways one has of manufacturing a given representation be especially reliable ways in order for the representation to have determinate content. These various results cut the biosemantic approach off from all varieties of verificationism and foundationalism with a clean, sharp knife.

IV

But perhaps it will be thought that belief fixation and consumption are not biologically proper activities, hence that there are no normal explanations, in our defined sense, for proper performances of human beliefs. Unlike bee dances, which are all variations on the same simple theme, beliefs in dinosaurs, in quarks, and in the instability of the dollar are recent, novel, and innumerably diverse, as are their possible uses. How could there be anything *biologically* normal or abnormal about the details of the consumption of such beliefs?

But what an organism does in accordance with evolutionary design can be very novel and surprising, for the more complex of nature's creatures are designed to learn. Unlike evolutionary adaptation, learning is not accomplished by *random* generate-and-test procedures. Even when learning involves trial and error (probably the exception rather than the rule), there are principles in accordance with which responses are selected by the system to try, and there are specific principles of generalization and discrimination, etc., which have been built into the system by natural selection. How these principles normally work, that is, how they work given normal (i.e., historically optimal) environments, to produce changes in the learner's nervous system which will effect the furthering of ends of the system has, of course, an explanation – the normal explanation for proper performance of the learning mechanism and of the states of the nervous system it produces.

Using a worn-out comparison, there is an infinity of functions which a modern computer mainframe is capable of performing, depending upon its input and on the program it is running. Each of these things it can do, so long as it is not damaged or broken, "in accordance with design," and to each of these capacities there corresponds an explanation of how it would be activated or fulfilled normally. The human's mainframe takes, roughly, stimulations of the afferent nerves as input, both to program and to run it.[16] It responds, in part, by developing concepts, by acquiring beliefs and desires in accordance with these concepts, by engaging in practical inference leading ultimately to action. Each of these activities may, of course, involve circumscribed sorts of trial and error learning. When conditions are optimal, all this aids survival and proliferation in accordance with a historically normal explanation – one of high generality, of course. When conditions are not optimal, it may yield, among other things, empty or confused concepts, biologically useless desires, and false beliefs. But, even when the desires are biologically useless (though probably not when the concepts expressed in them are empty or confused), there are still biologically normal ways for them to get fulfilled, the most obvious of which require reliance on true beliefs.[17]

Yet how do we know that our contemporary ways of forming concepts, desires, and beliefs do occur in accordance with evolutionary design? Fodor, for example, is ready with the labels "pop Darwinism" and "naive adaptationism" to abuse anyone who supposes that our cognitive systems were actually selected for their belief and desire using capacities.[18] Clearly, to believe that every structure must have a function would be naive. Nor is it wise uncritically to adopt hypotheses about the functions of structures when these functions are obscure. It does not follow that we should balk at the sort of adaptationist who, having found a highly complex structure that quite evidently is currently and effectively performing a highly complex and obviously indispensable function, then concludes, *ceteris paribus*, that this function has been the most recent historical task stabilizing the structure. To suspect that the brain has not been preserved for thinking with or that the eye has not been preserved for seeing with – to suspect this, moreover, in the absence of any alternative hypotheses about causes of the stability of these structures – would be totally irresponsible. Consider: nearly every human behavior is bound up with intentional action. Are we really to suppose that the degree to which our behaviors help to fulfill intentions, and the degree to which intentions result from logically related desires plus beliefs, is a sheer coincidence – that these patterns are irrelevant to survival and proliferation or, though relevant, have had no stabilizing effect on the gene pool? But the only alternative to biological design, in our sense of "design," is sheer coincidence, freak accident – unless there is a ghost running the machine!

Indeed, it is reasonable to suppose that the brain structures we have recently been using in developing space technology and elementary particle physics have been operating in accordance with the very same general principles as when prehistoric man used them for more primitive ventures. They are no more performing new and different functions or operating in accordance with new and different principles nowadays than are the eyes when what they see is television screens and space shuttles. Compare: the wheel was invented for the purpose of rolling ox carts, and did not come into its own (pulleys, gears, etc.) for several thousand years thereafter, during the industrial revolution. Similarly, it is reasonable that the cognitive structures with which man is endowed were originally nature's solution to some very simple demands made by man's evolutionary niche. But the solution nature stumbled on was elegant, supremely general, and powerful, indeed; I believe it was a solution that cut to the very bone of the ontological structure of the world. That solution involved the introduction of representations, inner and/or outer, having a subject/predicate structure, and subject to a negation transformation. (Why I believe that that particular development was so radical and so powerful has been explained in depth in Millikan, 1984, chapters 14–19. But see also section V (6) below.)

V

One last worry about our sort of position is voiced by Daniel Dennett[19] and discussed at length by Fodor.[20] Is it really plausible that bacteria and paramecia, or even birds and bees, have inner representations in the same sense that we do? Am I really prepared to say that these creatures, too, have mental states, that they think? I am not prepared to say that. On the contrary, the representations that they have must differ from human beliefs in at least six very fundamental ways.[21]

(1) Self-representing elements

The representations that the magnetosome produces have three significant variables, each of which refers to itself. The time of the pull refers to the time of the oxygen-free water, the locale of the pull refers to the locale of the oxygen-free water, and the direction of pull refers to the direction of oxygen-free water. The beaver's splash has two self-referring variables: a splash at a certain time and place indicates that there is danger at that same time and place. (There is nothing necessary about this. It might have meant that there would be danger at the nearest beaver dam in five minutes.) Compare the standard color coding on the outsides of colored markers: each color stands for itself. True, it may be that sophisticated indexical representations such as percepts and indexical beliefs also have their time or place or both as significant self-representing elements, but they also have other significant variables that are not self-representing. The magnetosome does not.

(2)   Storing representations

Any representation the time or place of which is a significant variable obviously cannot be stored away, carried about with the organism for use on future occasions. Most beliefs are representations that can be stored away. Clearly this is an important difference.

(3)   Indicative and imperative representations

The theory I have sketched here of the content of inner representations applies only to indicative representations, representations which are supposed to be determined by the facts, which tell what is the case. It does not apply to imperative representations, representations which are supposed to determine the facts, which tell the interpreter what to do. Neither do causal-informational theories of content apply to the contents of imperative representations. True, some philosophers seem to have assumed that having defined the content of various mental symbols by reference to what causes them to enter the "belief box," then when one finds these same symbols in, say, the "desire box" or the "intention box," one already knows what they mean. But how do we know that the desire box or the intention box use the same representational system as the belief box? To answer that question we would have to know what constitutes a desire box's or an intention box's using one representational system rather than another which, turned around, is the very question at issue. In Millikan (1984) and "Thoughts Without Laws; Cognitive Science With Content,"[22] I developed a parallel theory of the content of imperative representations. Very roughly, one of the proper functions of the consumer system for an imperative representations is to help *produce* a correspondence between the representation and the world. (Of course, this proper function often is not performed.) I also argued that desires and intentions are imperative representations.

Consider, then, the beaver's splash. It tells that there is danger here now. Or why not say, instead, that it tells other nearby beavers what to do now, namely, to seek cover? Consider the magnetosome. It tells which is the direction of oxygen-free water. Or why not say, instead, that it tells the bacterium which way to go? Simple animal signals are invariably both indicative and imperative. Even the dance of the honey bee, which is certainly no simple signal, is both indicative and imperative. It tells the worker bees where the nectar is; equally, it tells them where to go. The step from these primitive representations to human beliefs is an enormous one, for it involves the separation of indicative from imperative functions of the representational system. Representations, that are undifferentiated between indicative and imperative connect states of affairs directly to actions, to specific things to be done in the face of those states of affairs. Human beliefs are not tied directly to actions. Unless combined with appropriate desires, human beliefs are impotent. And human desires are equally impotent unless combined with suitable beliefs.[23]

(4) Inference

As indicative and imperative functions are separated in the central inner representational systems of humans, they need to be reintegrated. Thus, humans engage in practical inference, combining beliefs and desires in novel ways to yield first intentions and then action. Humans also combine beliefs with beliefs to yield new beliefs. Surely nothing remotely like this takes place inside the bacterium.

(5) Acts of identifying

Mediate inferences always turn on something like a middle term, which must have the same representational value in both premises for the inference to go through. Indeed, the representation consumers in us perform many functions that require them to use two or more overlapping representations together, and in such a manner that, unless the representeds corresponding to these indeed have a common element, these functions will not be properly performed. Put informally, the consumer device *takes* these represented elements to be the same, thus identifying their representational values. Suppose, for example, that you intend to speak to Henry about something. In order to carry out this intention you must, when the time comes, be able to recognize Henry in perception as the person to whom you intend to speak. You must identify Henry as represented in perception with Henry as represented in your intention. Activities that involve the coordinated use of representations from different sensory modalities, as in the case of eye-hand coordination, visual-tactile coordination, also require that certain objects, contours, places, or directions, etc., be identified as the same through the two modalities. Now, the foundation upon which modern representational theories of thought are built depends upon a denial that what is thought of is ever placed before a naked mind. Clearly, we can never know what an inner representation represents by a direct comparison of representation to represented. Rather, acts of identifying are our ways of "knowing what our representations represent." The bacterium is quite incapable of knowing, in this sense, what its representations are about. This might be a reason to say that it does not understand its own representations, not really.

(6)   *Negation and propositional content*

The representational system to which the magnetosome pull belongs does not contain negation. Indeed, it does not even contain contrary representations, for the magnetosome cannot pull in two directions at once. Similarly, if two beavers splash at different times or places, or if two bees dance different dances at the same time, it may well be that there is indeed beaver danger two times or in two places and that there is indeed nectar in two different locations.[24] Without contrariety, no conflict, of course, and, more specifically, no contradiction. If the law of non-contradiction plays as significant a role in the development of human concepts and knowledge as has traditionally been supposed, this is a large difference between us and the bacterium indeed.[25] In Millikan (1984) I argued that negation, hence explicit contradiction, is dependent upon subject-predicate, that is, propositional, structure and vice versa. Thus, representations that are simpler also do not have propositional content.

In sum, these six differences between our representations and those of the bacterium, or Fodor's paramecia, ought to be enough amply to secure our superiority, to make us feel comfortably more endowed with mind.

Notes

"Biosemantics" originally appeared in *Journal of Philosophy*, 86, 6 (1989), and is reprinted here by permission of the *Journal of Philosophy* and the author.

1   Fodor (1986a, 1987).
2   Stampe (1977).
3   Dretske (1986).
4   Matthen (1988).
5   Millikan (1984).
6   Millikan (1989).
7   An odd custom exists of identifying this sort of view with Larry Wright, who does not hold it. See Millikan (1989). Natural selection is not the only source of proper functions. See Millikan (1984), chs. 1 and 2.
8   See Millikan (1984, 1990a).
9   This last clarification is offered to aid Fodor ("On There Not Being an Evolutionary Theory of Content," unpublished), who uses my term 'Normal' (here I am not capitalizing it but the idea has not changed) in a multiply confused way, making a parody of my views on representation. In this connection, see also notes 13 and 17.
10   "Normal explanation" and "normal condition for performance of a function," along with "proper function," are defined with considerable detail in Millikan (1984). The reader may wish, in particular, to consult the discussion of normal explanations for performance of "adapted and derived proper functions" in chapter 2, for these functions cover the functions of states of the nervous system which result in part from learning, such as states of human belief and desire.

11   Dretske (1981).
12   Strictly, this normal condition must derive from a "most proximate normal explanation" of the consumer's proper functioning. See Millikan (1984), chapter 6, where a more precise account of what I am here calling "representations" is given under the heading "intentional icons."
13   In this particular case, one task is, surely, contributing, in conformity with certain general principles or rules, to practical inference processes, hence to the fulfillment of current desires. So, if you like, all beliefs have the *same* proper function. Or, since the rules or principles that govern practical inference dictate that a belief's "shape" determines what other inner representations it may properly be combined with to form what products, we could say that each belief has a *different* range of proper functions. Take your pick. Cf. Fodor (1990a, unpublished).
14   These examples are of representations that are not "inner" but out in the open. As in the case of inner representations, however, they are produced and consumed by mechanisms designed to cooperate with one another; each such representation stands intermediate between two parts of a single biological system.
15   Dretske (1986), p. 28 and Papineau (1987), p. 67ff have similar concerns.
16   This is a broad metaphor. I am not advocating computationalism.
17   A word of caution. The normal conditions for a desire's fulfillment are not necessarily fulfillable conditions. In general, normal conditions for fulfillment of a function are not quite the same as conditions which, when you add them and stir, always effect proper function, because they may well be impossible conditions. For example, Fodor (1990a, unpublished) has questioned me about the normal conditions under which his desire that it should rain tomorrow will perform its proper function of *getting* it to rain. Now, the biologically normal way for such a desire to be fulfilled is exactly the same as for any other desire: one has or acquires true beliefs about how to effect the fulfillment of the desire and acts on them. Biologically normal conditions for fulfillment of the desire for rain thus include the condition that one has true beliefs about how to make it rain. Clearly this is an example in which the biological norm fails to accord with the statistical norm: most desires about the weather are fulfilled, if at all, by biological accident. It may even be that the laws of nature, coupled with my situation, prohibit my having any true beliefs about how to make it rain; the needed general condition cannot be realized in the particular case. Similarly, normal conditions for proper function of beliefs in impossible things are, of course, impossible conditions: these beliefs are such that they cannot correspond, in accordance with the rules of Mentalese, to conditions in the world.
18   Fodor (1987, unpublished).
19   Dennett (1978a).
20   Fodor (1986b).
21   Accordingly, in Millikan (1984) I did not call these primitive forms "representations" but "intentional signals" and, for items like bee dances, "intentional icons," reserving the term "representation" for those icons, the representational values of which must be identified if their consumers are to function properly – see section V (5).
22   Millikan (1986).

23   Possibly human intentions are in both indicative and imperative mood, however, functioning simultaneously to represent settled facts about one's future and to direct one's action.
24   On the other hand, the bees cannot go to two places at once.
25   In Millikan (1984) I defend the position that the law of non-contradiction plays a crucial role in allowing us to develop new methods of mapping the world with representations.

11 A Continuum of Semantic Optimism

Peter Godfrey-Smith

I Pessimism

If our aim is to understand the semantic theory of Ruth Millikan, one unlikely way to start is to consider the theory of truth defended by William James. James, after all, is usually thought to have been as soft about truth as any famous philosopher has been; a belief is true for James if it helps you to get by. Millikan, on the other hand, has said that she holds a correspondence theory of truth of "the strongest possible kind," and a positively "flatfooted" version of the truth-conditional approach to semantics (1990a, p. 324). Yet James and Millikan can be seen as occupying two points on one interval of semantic views. Theories along this line agree about a particular link between truth and success. They disagree about the possibility of there being a certain kind of unified *explanation* of the success that is linked to truth. James occupies one pessimistic extreme with respect to this explanatory task. Millikan occupies an intermediate position. David Papineau's view is more optimistic, and a position of extreme optimism has been defended by Jamie Whyte. By moving from point to point on this line it will be possible eventually to gain a clearer conception of Millikan's proposal, and appreciate its links to other views.

James's discussions of truth will support a variety of interpretations. Some might excuse this, as consonant with James's conviction that human concepts are never really adequate to capture reality, and that dressed-up formal "precision" in philosophy only pretends to solve a problem, while sucking the life out of the enterprise. Others – and this is the more common reaction – find in James a constant, fatal vacillation on central issues about truth and its link to experience. Part of the point of the idea of truth appears to lie in the fact that an idea can turn out to be practically useful and yet not be true. Yet usefulness for actual agents in their real-world projects is the only coherent epistemic standard there is, for a pragmatist, so if a pragmatist is to use the concept of truth coherently, he or she must have in mind something along those lines.

Without claiming there is a single view in James, I will separate out one strand of his thought, look at it from an angle James himself would probably never permit, and use it to tie down the pessimistic end of the continuum on which we will find Millikan.

James asserts a necessary connection between the truth of an idea and its usefulness in enabling us to deal with experience:

> *"The true," to put it very briefly, is only the expedient in the way of our thinking, just as "the right" is only the expedient in the way of our behaving.* Expedient in almost any fashion; and expedient in the long run and on the whole of course; for what meets expediently all the experiences in sight won't necessarily meet all further experiences equally satisfactorily. Experience, as we know, has a way of *boiling over*, and making us correct our present formulas. (1907, p. 106)

> Those thoughts are true which guide us to *beneficial interaction* with sensible particulars as they occur, whether they copy these in advance or not. (1909, p. 217)

True beliefs, for James, are those that help the agent to anticipate and productively shape experience; truth helps us to get by. But to the modern reader, this claim apparently has a corollary: the truth-*conditions* of a belief will then be the conditions under which that belief helps us to get by. Presumably, when we act on a belief, we will get by or fail according to how things are in the world. So we could also say: the belief is true if certain conditions in the world obtain, conditions under which actions guided by that belief are success-ful. We seem to have the material here for a *correspondence* theory of truth, after all.[1]

No doubt there are several parts of this chain of reasoning James might find unconvincing, but one is especially useful for us. Experience, James says, has a way of *boiling over*. Our expectations are often thwarted, and our attempts to get by must be imaginatively revised. The reason for this is the fact that our concepts are rarely adequate to capture the world. They are human creations, which at best will give us some useful answers temporarily, but can never tell the whole story.

If we ask *why* this boiling over is inevitable, why the world is that way, we may be asking a question which James would find too transcendental. But there are ways to push the story along further. First, it seems that no matter how primitive our concepts could be, there would always be *some* world in which they were of permanent and stable value. If the world was simple enough, then once we had hit on some ways to behave successfully, this success should stay put. For James the *actual* universe is not like that. It is a capricious, changeable place whose structure is inaccessible to us and which is constantly producing new combinations of things. The world impinges on us via experience, and the world's changeable qualities show up there as a frequent "boiling over."[2]

Consequently, James could resist being propelled into a modern corre-spondence view with the claim that, when some type of belief helps us get by, there *is* no single condition in the world that lies behind and explains this. When an idea fails us, this is an indication that the world has gotten away from us again, but when an idea helps us on successive occasions, this is no guarantee that things have really stayed put. The world is simmering with variety, and when it produces something new sometimes we will fall flat and sometimes we will get by nonetheless. There is just our getting by, or our being forced to back up and revise, and that's the end of it. For James, this is all we need in any case. If we had a choice between having ideas that "copied" the world and ideas which worked well for us, without copying anything, why should we care about copying? (James, 1907, pp. 112–13): "If our symbols *fit* the world, in the sense of determining our expectations rightly, they may be even the better for not copying its terms" (1909, p. 217).[3]

It should be clear in what sense this view shows an explanatory pessimism (I am not claiming that any other aspects of James's thought should be called "pessimistic"). This view is also "pragmatism" in roughly the sense of Rorty (1982). Rorty sees a pragmatist view, with respect to a given domain, as the view that there is no interesting explanation to be had of those phenomena; there are just particular cases, which may be important to us in a variety of specific ways, and about which nothing deep and general can be said. Parts of Stich's attack on truth, which also flies a pragmatist flag, may express a similar view in different terms (Stich, 1990). Whether or not this "realist anti-essentialist" view captures much of the historical James, as it is inspired by James I will call it a "Jamesian" view, and this view establishes for us the pessimistic end of the continuum of semantic optimism.[4]

II Optimism

We will now jump over Millikan, and tie down the other, optimistic end of the line. Whyte (1990) proposes the following theory of the content of beliefs:

(R)   A belief's truth condition is that which guarantees the fulfillment of any desire by the action which that belief and desire would combine to cause. (p. 150)

This is roughly what the previous section attempted to press on James.[5] A true belief is one which helps us pursue our practical projects successfully; the truth-condition is the state of affairs in the world which ensures that actions based on the belief do in fact aid the pursuit of our projects. Whyte understands success as the fulfillment of the agent's desires, and hence he has to give an independent account of the content of desires. This he defers for another occasion, and I will assume for the purposes of discussion that this can be done.

As Whyte recognizes that beliefs can combine with each other and with desires in indefinitely many ways, he faces an immediate problem involving the multiplicity of the actions a belief can affect and of the successful outcomes which can result. In the first instance Whyte defines the truth-condition for a large complex of beliefs as they interact with some specified desire. The truth-condition for the complex of beliefs is the entire set of states of affairs that would guarantee success of the associated action. We are to find the truth-condition of a particular belief B by finding what is in common between all the sets of states of affairs which guarantee the success of actions based on all the complexes of beliefs of which B is a part.

A further problem Whyte confronts stems from the fact that some world-conditions are apparently a necessary part of *every* action's success-condition. He discusses the example of there being terrestrial gravity, which is assumed by nearly every action undertaken on earth. His response is to widen the range of cases which are relevant. In counterfactual situations, an action's success may depend on there *not* being gravity. In my own view, this internal problem is probably solved more easily. An analysis of an agent along Whyte's lines should try to find the state of affairs that is common to *and peculiar* to all the success-conditions associated with actions associated with a particular belief. Universally necessary parts of success-conditions can be factored out of truth-conditions just because they are universal. This, we will find, is Millikan's way of dealing with this problem as it appears in her theory.

In any case, the point of this discussion of Whyte is not to discuss internal details, but to note where it resembles the Jamesian position of the previous section, and where it differs from it. James and Whyte agree that it is a necessary truth that true beliefs lead to successful actions, that they help us to get by. Whyte, unlike James, believes that for any belief there is some particular state of the world which guarantees the success of action based on the belief.

To see the optimism in this view we should focus not on the idea that a state of affairs *guarantees* success, but on the idea that there is *one* state of affairs that guarantees success. Indeed, it should always be possible to specify *some* state of affairs which will guarantee the success of action based on a belief or belief complex; the question is whether this state of affairs can always be taken to be the truth-condition, or part of the truth-condition. Indeed, much of the comic potential of the idea of a "guardian angel" is based on the idea that truth is not required for success in this way. If someone is looking out for you effectively enough, you will get by no matter how badly awry your beliefs are; this is the evil demon for success semantics.[6] This evil demon, like more familiar ones, can be dismissed when the scenario exceeds some boundary for relevant possibility. However, guardian angel scenarios which might be relevant need not be far-fetched. Recall the early behavior of Bond's foe Red Grant, in the movie of *From Russia with Love*. Bond meets with success when he acts on the assumption that there is no knife-wielding thug behind him (B), not because this assumption is true, but because he has, unknown to him, someone looking out for him. Bond is guaranteed to succeed when he believes B if there really is no thug behind him *or* if there is a thug, but Red is watching his back *or* . . . So this objection to Whyte takes the familiar form of a "disjunction problem" (Fodor, 1984).[7]

Various replies can be made to arguments of this kind, but the important point for us is the contrast between this view and the Jamesian view. If one believes that our cognitive apparatus is imperfectly matched to an unpredictable world, then there is no reason to expect for a moment that all actions based on a belief share some one non-disjunctive condition which guarantees the action's success.[8] Compare Dretske (1981), which insisted that meaning and knowledge require the effectively flawless transmission of information through the world from distal conditions to cognitive states. Critics doubted that inner states will often have such cast-iron nomic specificity to one environmental condition (see commentaries to Dretske, 1983). *Some* inner states might be connected to some external states in this simple a way, but it is optimistic to build this requirement into a general semantic theory. Dretske's optimism about the informational specificity of inner states, with respect to the "input" end of the system, is mirrored by Whyte's optimism about the causal specificity of such states with respect to the "output" end.

Perhaps the basic idea of "success semantics" can be applied in a more cautious way, though. David Papineau (1987, 1990) reaches a position of this type. Papineau begins with a formula similar to Whyte's: "the truth-condition of a given belief type is that circumstance whose presence guarantees the success of actions based upon that belief" (1987, p. 56). Papineau's problem with this view stems from the need to tie down "success" independently. The satisfaction of desire seems to be the obvious way, but this is an intentional concept itself. Papineau finds a solution to this problem in an appeal to teleology. Papineau's proposal is as follows:

> The biological function of a given belief type is to be present when a certain condition obtains: that then is the belief's truth-condition. And, correspondingly, the biological function of any given desire type is to give rise to a certain result: that result is then the desire's satisfaction-condition. (1987, p. 64)

This may not look initially like a view along the continuum of theories we are considering. Its being a theory of this type is a consequence of the way Papineau understands biological functions. Papineau adopts a version of an approach to functions due originally to Larry Wright (1973); he sees a thing's function as "some effect of that thing which accounts for it being there" (1987, p. 64). One way a (type of) thing can survive and proliferate as a consequence of its effects is to be favored in a regime of natural selection. The function of a disposition to form a belief of a certain type will then be whatever that belief type has historically done which explains its survival in the cognitive system of the agent. For Papineau, *being present* (and hence producing a particular behavior) *under certain circumstances* is the thing a belief type can do which will explain why it is there. "For it is specifically when trees, and not tree replicas, were present, that belief about trees would have had advantageous behavioral effects" (1987, p. 65).

The question now is: what exactly is the connection, on this theory, between success and some special explanatory state of affairs? How optimistic is this view, in comparison to Whyte's, for instance?

We must distinguish at this point two aspects of the link between a belief and success. There are firstly the questions we are concerned with: *given* that a belief is true, what are the consequences for success, and is there some single state of affairs that guarantees success in these cases? Then there is the separate question of *how often* a belief is true, and hence how often the success due to truth will accrue. Papineau is concerned that his account of representation makes error possible. He raises the following objection to his own view:

> On my story, beliefs get selected because of the good results they produce when they are (as we say) true. And this seems to imply that beliefs must at least usually be true, even if they aren't always so. For surely, if they didn't usually produce good results, they wouldn't be favored by natural selection in the first place. (1987, p. 89)

Papineau's reply to this point is to accept that, on his view, "any given belief type must usually have been true *up till now*" (1987, p. 89). As with all selective explanations, the beneficial effects of the entity in question need only occur in the past; they may have ceased at the present time. If the environment has changed, then what was once useful can now be neutral or detrimental. This has a consequence for the assessment of the link between truth and success which we are concerned with, and here Papineau may make a weaker claim than Whyte. Papineau need not say that a belief must always produce success when it is true, and produce it as a consequence of the same condition in the world. He must only say that this was true in the relevant historical environment of the cognitive system in question. Things may have changed since then.[9]

There is also a sense in which Papineau's theory here makes a stronger claim than Whyte's theory – aside from the obvious fact that Papineau's historical and evolutionary commitments are stronger. Whyte claims that, when a belief is true, it must produce success, but he does not make any claims about how often beliefs are true. Truth might be very rare, as long as there are certain consequences when it does come around. Thus Whyte avoids some well-known problems for indicator semantics, a program which struggles with the consequence that in normal conditions beliefs must be true (Fodor, 1984, 1987; Dretske, 1986, 1988). Papineau, however, claims that not only must beliefs be helpful when true, but in the past they must have *usually* been true. In the 1990 presentation of Papineau's view a similar commitment is found: "beliefs have been selected because they are characteristically co-present with certain conditions" (p. 37). Thus Papineau lands his teleological approach squarely in the middle of the problems which have long beset the indicator program.

This is an incidental problem with Papineau's theory, though. Our primary focus is on what a theory says must occur when a belief is true, not on what a theory says about how often a belief is true. In this respect Papineau's commitments are probably weaker than Whyte's, though they are still very strong from a Jamesian perspective. Millikan's theory, we will find, makes more moderate commitments along both dimensions.

III Millikan's Meaning

Suppose at this point we think there is something to be said about a necessary link between truth and success, but we are inclined towards neither extreme optimism nor extreme pessimism about locating truth-conditions with the aid of this link. On the one hand it seems simplistic to think that, for any type of belief, there is some one distal condition in the world that is "the" condition which guarantees the success of action based on the belief (or some range of conditions small and similar enough to be thought of as "the" truth-condition). On the other hand, the Jamesian position gives up the game very early; might a single state of affairs play *some* kind of special role in explaining the success of action based on a belief? One way to proceed from here would be to start marshalling qualifications and exceptions, to modify a basic formula of Whyte's type. Millikan shows another way ahead.

A simple way to approach Millikan's view is to take issue with some assumptions made about functions by Papineau. Millikan and Papineau share the view that functions are selectively salient historical effects; they are effects or dispositions of past tokens of a type which help explain the existence of present tokens. For example, it is usually supposed that the spectacular neck-expanding display of the frill-necked lizard has the function of startling or deceiving a potentially dangerous intruder, such as a predator.[10] This effect, let us suppose, has led to the survival and proliferation of the display and the structural traits which make it possible. But note that this can seem a compelling explanation without our making the assumption that this maneuver actually helps individual lizards very often. Perhaps the majority of foes are unaffected or even amused by the display. All that is required is that *occasionally* a lizard is helped by the display, and that the general costs of the trait do not outweigh this occasional benefit.[11]

The benefits of such a display can be merely occasional in two respects. It may be that most displays by lizards are not produced in response to any real danger, and it is a hair-trigger response prone to false alarms. It may also be that, when there is a real danger present, even then the display only rarely helps. Both these things could be true without affecting the fact that the explanation for the display is its deterring dangerous intruders.

Using this case, we can now outline a central concept in Millikan's framework, that of a historically normal condition for the performance of a function. Once embedded in a psychological context, this is where Millikan will make the link between truth and success characteristic of the theories we are considering. On Millikan's view the special connection between a certain state of the world and a functionally characterized entity is based in the role that state plays in explanation. In the frill-necked lizard case, there is a certain type of sequence of events which, however rare, explains the selection of the display. The sequence involves the presence of some dangerous intruder, the production of the display, and a startled or frightened reaction in the intruder. There might be ways in which the display could work to produce lizard success which do not involve this sequence of events – the display might lead to the lizard being singled out for special consideration by conservation groups, for instance. The condition *there being a photographer from the Australian Conservation Foundation nearby looking for striking images* is a condition under which producing the display will tend to lead to practical success. It may be even more likely to result in success (for both type and token) than displaying in response to a predator. But though this is a situation in which the display will help the lizard, it is not why the display is there. The explanation for the display's selection makes reference to the special sequence of events involving predators. Given the explanatory importance of this sequence of events, we can say that a certain condition in the world also has explanatory importance. The presence of an intruder (of a certain type) is a world-condition required for the display to fulfill its functions in a historically explanatory way. This explanatory link will replace the "guarantee of success" used by Whyte and the more demanding explanatory link used by Papineau.

At this point we can begin to define another of Millikan's concepts, that of an "intentional icon." Intentional icons come in "indicative" and "imperative" varieties. The paradigm cases of both are sentences, but not all intentional icons need have many pre-theoretic similarities with sentences. English statements, human beliefs, beaver tail splashes (danger signals) and adrenalin flows are all indicative intentional icons. Imperative intentional icons include English commands, human desires, beaver tail splashes and adrenalin flows. The two categories are only exclusive in the case of sophisticated icons. Simpler icons tend to be both indicative and imperative.

An indicative intentional icon "stands midway between two cooperating devices" (Millikan, 1984, p. 96). One is the producer of the icon, the other is the interpreter or consumer. Producer and consumer can be in the same body, or in the different bodies – this is one source of the generality of Millikan's theory. A consumer is something which has functions, and which is supposed to modify its functions according to the icons it consumes. The essential feature of an indicative intentional icon (hereafter simply "icon") is the way it affects the activities of its consumers, and – most importantly – the states of affairs in the world that are required for the icon to assist the well-functioning of its consumers in a historically explanatory way, a way which explains the survival and proliferation of this mode of icon production and consumption. In fact, the truth-condition of an icon is the state of the world such that the icon will assist the proper functioning of its consumers in a historically explanatory way only if that state of affairs obtains.[12]

Indicative icons are belief-like, "how things are" states. Imperative icons are more akin to desires. An imperative icon affects its consumers in such a way that the consumers acquire the function to produce a certain state of affairs in the world. This state of affairs is the icon's compliance condition, its content. In this discussion I will focus almost entirely on indicative icons. I will also present the theory of indicative icons as a theory of representation and meaning, even though in her 1984 treatment Millikan reserves the term "representation" for a richer concept and distinguishes three "aspects" of meaning. My aim is to focus on the most basic ways in which truth-conditions can be assigned using Millikan's framework, and on the relations she needs there to be between truth, explanation, and success.[13]

The truth-condition is supposed to be "the" condition required for the icon to make its historically explanatory contribution to its consumers' activities. But as we saw earlier, there are likely to be many states of the world that must cooperate to bring this about. The organism must not be under a ton of granite, there must be terrestrial gravity, as Whyte said, and so on. But these favorable worldly conditions are required alike by nearly every functional component of the organism, including other icons. Such conditions are to be abstracted away, and the truth-condition is identified as the distinctive state(s) of the world required by that icon in particular. Putting it very metaphorically, it is as if each icon tells its consumers: "act on the assumption that this state of affairs, over and above the ones you always assume, obtains."

Male fireflies signal their sex and species with patterns of light flashes, and females give a special response to accept a male. Consider the situation of a male who signals and receives an apparent response. The answering flash strikes his eyes and produces a certain pattern of neural activity. This state is what we will try to interpret. Now, there is a variety of things that could cause this state. One of the more unusual hazards faced by male fireflies involves certain female fireflies (*Photuris versicolor*) which mimic the response patterns of other species in order to attract males of these other species close enough to be trapped and eaten (Gerhardt, 1983). So there is ambiguity as far as the causes of the neural state are concerned. But this state also has consequences for the rest of the firefly – it induces an approach to the flash. Our interpretation of the state proceeds by asking: what condition in the world must obtain for this state to assist the proper functioning of those parts of the firefly which have their activities modified by this icon, in a historically explanatory way? This condition in the world is *there being a conspecific female nearby*. That is the state's truth-condition.[14]

In this case we assumed the neural state has only one typical effect on its behavior-generating consumers. This singularity of response is not needed by Millikan. Her theory can tolerate indefinite diversity in the causes of a representation, and she can also tolerate indefinite diversity in the effects this representation has on the rest of the system. What must be constant is the world-condition required for the icon to assist the functioning of its consumers in a normal way, whatever these consumers are and however diverse their functions are.

This completes a preliminary sketch of Millikan's view, and one which locates it as a close relative of "success semantics" doctrines. It is distinguished from other theories of this type by its more guarded claims about the relation between a belief and its success-conditions. But Millikan's presentations sometimes draw also on the vocabulary of another, largely discredited, approach to truth and meaning, the "picture" theory. Although Millikan's theory is intended to be a correspondence view, in my presentation above it was at no point necessary to say that the icon "pictures," has a "likeness" to, or "mirrors" the world. On my presentation Millikan's appears to be a correspondence view in the sense that many other naturalistic theories are; a "correspondence" between sign and world is the end-product of the theory, but not something that does any work along the way. The normal conditions for icons aiding consumers' functions line icons up with states of affairs, without anything in these icons being *like* anything in these states of affairs. Yet Millikan does regard her theory as a kind of picture theory, as showing exactly that all signs picture or "map" the world, in a rarified sense (1984, p. 314; 1986, pp. 73–7). To see why this is, we must look more closely at the form of the explanations Millikan uses to assign content, explanations of how icons have assisted their consumers' functioning. This will take us into some of the more intricate machinery of the theory.

In the discussion of the firefly, I said that a type of icon, a neural state, has historically aided the functioning of its consumers when a certain state obtains in the world, and that this explains the survival of this process of production and consumption of inner signs. What has actually been the object of selection here? Each icon appears, has an effect for good or ill, and is then gone. The thing which persists, which is shaped and maintained by the sequence of successes and failures, is the set of general principles, or rules, by which icons are produced and consumed. Insofar as they are relevant to a history of selection, all icons exist within systems alongside other actual and possible icons, and, as various kinds of structuralists have insisted, each icon's identity depends on the identity of others. Icons are related to each other by the existence of "transformations" which take us from one icon to another. The link between sign and world, the "correspondence," in Millikan's system is, in the first instance, a link between a set of systematically related icons and a set of systematically related states of the world.

This can be illustrated simply in the case of the firefly. Although we do not need to see the neural state as built up out of words, Millikan would insist that this state is "articulated." There are aspects of the icon which can be changed, resulting in a new icon. An example is the time and place at which the icon occurs. Similarly, the icon's truth condition is not strictly "female conspecific" but "female conspecific at place x_1 at time t_1." The icon has what philosophers ordinarily call "indexical" components, and, if we change the time and place at which the icon occurs, we get a different icon with a different truth-condition.

In many discussions in naturalistic semantics, cases are used in which inner signs are indexical in some way. Little attention is usually paid to this fact, and it is not usually regarded as itself a significant step towards a compositional approach to semantics. Millikan, on the other hand, regards indexicality as a low-level case of the necessary articulation of icons. It is no different in kind from the articulation seen in natural languages, where the aspects of a sentence that can be transformed include the names of people, verbs, and so on. Apparent indexicality of simple icons makes the point that all icons exist in systems. For Millikan, an icon without a system would be an icon tokened once, at a certain place, without any re-usable aspects at all. This, she holds, is a semiotic impossibility. Its impossibility is seen in the fact that a lone icon of this sort could never figure in or have a history of selection, could never have a historically explanatory condition for aiding the functioning of its consumers.

Millikan's account is a "picture" theory in a similar way to the theory of Wittgenstein's *Tractatus* (1922); the fact that the icon exemplifies a certain one of its range of possible transformations represents that a world affair exemplifies a certain one of its range of possible transformations, and an icon is a picture of its state of affairs only insofar as it is articulated. The familiar problem with such a "pure" correspondence theory of truth is the fact that there are too many ways to map icons onto states of affairs by transforming each. Millikan's theory is designed to tell us which of the mapping rules is historically, explanatorily special. One might even see Millikan's theory as a reconciliation of the approach to correspondence seen in the early Wittgenstein with some of the characteristic concerns of the later (1958). The *Tractatus* claimed that signs can correspond to the facts. But abstract correspondences are legion. Wittgenstein later said that meaning, if it is anything, is use. Millikan's view is that attention to (historical) *function*, rather than (mere) use, will show us that there is a privileged abstract correspondence between signs and the world after all. The privileged rule is the mapping rule which explains the maintenance and proliferation of the signing system.

At this point some naturalists may wonder what is gained theoretically by talking about maps and alluding to Wittgenstein. In the firefly case, suppose we simply said that icons occurring at different times and places are all of a certain general type, and this type has a history of making useful contributions to the activities of its consumers, and that is why it has been selected. Would this accomplish just as much as Millikan's "mapping" account?

In the firefly case, perhaps it would.[15] In order to see the advantages of Millikan's view, we should switch to a slightly more complex example.

Bush crickets are thought to detect the direction of sounds with "pressure-gradient" ears (Hopkins, 1983). A pressure-gradient ear has a membrane open to the world from both sides, unlike human ears, which are open on one side only. The movement of the membrane is determined by both routes of input. If the sound is equidistant from both sides of the membrane, the two inputs cancel out. If there is a difference in distance, caused by the source of the sound being on one side or the other, there will be a net movement of the membrane determined by the location of the source. The crickets have two ears, but they are individually sensitive to direction in this way. If a line is drawn head to tail along a cricket, a sound from a source at angle Q to this line will differ in phase in its arrival at each side of the membrane by a specific amount – if the source is on the right, that side of the membrane will be a certain way into the wave before the left side gets the signal. This difference in phase determines how vigorously the auditory neurons on that side fire.

Suppose the firing rate of these neurons can be taken as an icon of the direction of sound. That is, the firing rate is taken into account, is "consumed" by the rest of the cricket, in a way which will ultimately affect behavior. If a given firing rate is an icon of the direction of a sound, then this firing rate will help its consumers perform their functions in a historically explanatory way only if the sound is in fact coming from a certain direction. But if we do not adopt Millikan's talk about rules and transformations, then we can *only* say this about a given firing rate if this exact firing rate has in fact aided its consumers in this way. If this exact firing rate has not been tokened before, or has never helped before, it cannot be interpreted. Here the details of Millikan's view pay off. Though a given firing rate may have no history, it is of a general type which makes certain transformations applicable to it. It is the product of mechanisms which have been selected to produce signs in a way which cooperates with consumers, so that the consumption of the icon – ultimately, its effect on behavior – is a function of the specific form of the sign. This effect on the consumers will assist them in a historically explanatory way only if the world is a certain way, related mathematically to the form of the icon.

So suppose the new icon is a firing rate of r^* per second. Though tokens of r^* have not been usefully consumed in the history of the cricket, other rates have been. Suppose the consumers have had their activities modified by rates r in a way which has been historically adaptive when the angle of the sound Q with respect to the cricket is $r/3$ degrees. The explanation for the selection of the cricket's mode of producing and consuming signs includes this rule relating firing rates and salient conditions in the world. If all this is so, then the truth condition of icon r^* is the presence of a sound at $r^*/3$ degrees.

Though Millikan has recently stressed the role of icon consumers in order to sharpen the distinction between her view and indicator theories, which are driven primarily by properties of the production of inner representations, in fact there is a symmetry between the roles of producer and consumer in her picture. In the case above, there are two ways we could imagine the explanation being constructed. Firstly, we could assume that the relation between the physical properties of the icon and its producers is simply given, either by history or physiological constraints. The transducers emit various firing rates according to how they are physically stimulated. Then the explanatory focus is on the consumers: how have the consumers been selected to treat icons of the various possible forms? How have they been selected to respond to an incoming icon, when they use it to modify their activities? If some rule relating the state of the world and the icon explains this selective process, then that determines the content of the icon. Alternately, we could hold the way the icons are consumed fixed, and place the explanatory weight upon the mode of icon production, and the same result should emerge. An explanation could also exhibit some of both these forms. In empirically different cases, different mixtures of the explanatory burden could be assigned to producer and consumer.

It is important not to confuse the rule used by the consumers, in having their activities affected by the icon, with the rule relating icons to the world which determines content. As I said earlier, the rule(s) by which an icon is consumed can be complicated or simple, fixed or changing. The cricket, for example, might do a variety of things to different kinds of sounds at Q degrees. That does not matter. What matters is the rule relating icon to world, when the icon has been adaptively consumed.

So has Millikan struck a principled balance between optimistic and pessimistic extremes along the continuum of success-linked views about truth? The overtly mathematical character of the bush cricket example has probably suggested to many readers one way in which a pessimist might try to show a residual and questionable optimism in Millikan's view. In the cricket example, a rule extracted from past events was used to project the semantic characteristics of a new icon. But the analytic philosopher has learned, from Goodman's "new riddle of induction" (Goodman, 1953) and Kripke's treatment of the later Wittgenstein (Kripke, 1982), that claims for a unique projection from a finite sample to a general principle which will cover new cases are vulnerable to powerful skeptical attacks. Goodman asked an epistemological question about why we regard it as rational to project from a large sample of observed green emeralds to the hypothesis that all emeralds are green, rather than the hypothesis that all emeralds are grue, where something is grue if first observed before 2000 AD and green, blue otherwise. Kripke asks a semantic question concerning why we take someone to be following the "standard" rule for addition when everything about the person's actual behavior, dispositions, and inner life is compatible with taking them to be following another rule, which coincides with the addition rule most of the time but diverges in some cases. The problem Millikan faces is an explanatory one. The problem is whether it is possible to project from the finite historical range of cases where an icon assisted the functioning of its consumers to a *single* explanatory rule which applies also to new cases. So, in the case of the cricket, given that rate r* has never been tokened before, why should the rule interpreting icons be "Q = r/3" rather than "Q = r/3 unless r = r*, in which case Q = r/11"?

Millikan has discussed this problem herself (1990a). Her view is that, though the selectively salient episodes which are the basis for projection to a mapping rule can be described in a variety of ways, each of which would determine a different projection, one account has special explanatory status.

> In saying that, I don't have any particular theory of the nature of explanation up my sleeve. But surely, on any reasonable account, a complexity that can simply be dropped from the explanans without affecting the tightness of the relation of explanans to explanandum is not a *functioning* part of the explanation. For example, my coat does not keep me warm in winter because it is fur-lined *and red*, nor because it is fur-lined *in the winter*, but just because it is fur-lined. (1990a, p. 334)

It is not claimed that there is something semantically special in an a priori way about one rule relating icons to the world, but there is something explanatorily special about these rules. Millikan admits that she assumes that the "qualifications and additions" that change an explanation in terms of a standard mapping rule into a non-standard one are objectively additions and qualifications, but she regards this as a commitment to nothing more than "commonsense ontology," which distinguishes natural properties and kinds from artificially synthesized ones (p. 334). In this way what is alleged to be a special problem with meaning is shown to be an instance of a more general problem about realism and explanation.

This is the right general line of reply to the problem, but the particular way Millikan proceeds here is not the best way. Firstly, the coat example makes the task look easier than it is. That a coat is fur-lined and red *implies* that it is fur-lined, as does the fact that it is fur-lined in winter. Here there is straight-forward sense to be made of the idea that one explanation of the coat's effects is simpler than the other. In explanation we should look, ceteris paribus, for the least specific set of properties that will account for the phenomenon. This principle will not help when we compare rival mapping rules where one is a Kripke-Wittgenstein variant of the other, as in the two rules for the interpretation of r* above. Neither is simpler, in the sense of being less specific than the other. So the coat example makes the task look too easy.

Another aspect of Millikan's reply makes the task seem more difficult than it is. She aligns her assumptions about explanation with "commonsense" ontology's commitment to the additional reality or naturalness of certain properties and kinds. But the problem might be solved without making this claim. One might hold that there is no general metaphysical sense to be made of the idea that some properties are more "natural" overall, while still holding that, in a particular causal-explanatory context, some properties have powers that others do not. There is no need to assume a general ontological thesis, even if it is a plausible one; all that is needed is a local thesis about causal explanations. That is the right place to make a stand.

Let us suppose that a stand can be made at this point. That is, when we assign content with Millikan's apparatus, we are able to narrow down possible interpretations of an intentional icon by finding mapping rules which are truly explanatory in the history of the selection of that mode of icon-consumption, and rejecting rules which are not. If this can be done, there will nonetheless remain a principled limit to the precision of these assignments of content. There is a certain degree of specificity we cannot go beyond, with the apparatus laid out so far. This barrier is a relative of one constructed by Jerry Fodor (1987, 1990b).

Fodor argued that the evolutionary approach to semantics is doomed because appeals to mechanisms of selection "won't decide between *reliably equivalent* content ascriptions" (1990b, p. 73). For example, if all F's are also G's, then according to Fodor anything which has been selected for responding to F's has also, ipso facto, been selected for responding to G's. So if it is reliable that, in the frill-necked lizard's historical environment, the predicates "predator" and "predator or Elvis impersonator" are reliably coextensive, we cannot distinguish between these predicates when specifying the class of conditions to which the lizard's display has been selected as a response.[16] Millikan has replied, correctly, that "selection for" is a causal matter (Millikan, 1990b; Sober, 1984b). Fitness differences between traits are among the causes of evolutionary change, and properties of the environment are among the causes of these fitness differences. As a consequence, selective explanation generates exactly as much opacity, in its description of states of the world, as causal explanation in general does (Sterelny, 1990, §6.6). How much is this? It depends on one's general understanding of causation; Humeans will find themselves in a different position from strong realists here. And any indeterminacy rooted in basic facts about causation will show up similarly in a great many naturalistic theories of content.

Though Fodor's argument does not succeed, the foregoing discussion of explanation and its role in Millikan's account should make clear the location of a detoxified Fodor-style limitation on the specificity of content for her view: evolutionary accounts such as Millikan's will be unable to distinguish between *causal-explanatorily equivalent* content attributions.

So as long as it is true that "being a predator" and "being a predator or Elvis impersonator" have different causal-explanatory significance in a particular case, their coextensiveness is not a problem. The real location of indeterminacy for Millikan's view lies in the question of whether to take some icon to map onto the presence of a predator, rather than a dangerous thing in general, or a particular class of predator, and so on. Assessing the importance of this indeterminacy is a large task, as it depends both on issues in the philosophy of science, concerning the nature of causation and the opacity of causal claims, and also on semantic issues about whether the degree of indeterminacy forced on us by our analysis of cause is an acceptable degree.

IV   Looking Back

William James's biographer, R. B. Perry, claims that James "consistently refused to identify meanings with origins" (1954, p. 252). Perry has in mind a different sense of meaning from ours; this is meaning in the broadest sense of "significance." Yet this refusal may resonate with some present readers contemplating the larger intellectual significance of accepting a view like Millikan's. Many contemporary theories of meaning have the consequence that semantic facts have some involvement with the past, often the distant past. Looking backward in order to resolve indeterminacy is a noticeable feature of recent semantic thinking (Dretske, 1986; Papineau, 1987; Matthen, 1988; McGinn, 1989; Sterelny, 1990). I have discussed success-based theories in this paper in a similar spirit: casting backwards into history, with Millikan, is the most promising way to balance optimism and pessimism about explanations of practical success and their relation to truth.

Further, Millikan is aware that all backward-looking views have obvious prima facie problems with novel thoughts, with beliefs and concepts that have no clear relation to any kind of selective history. In addressing this problem, Millikan has developed a detailed account of how entirely novel structures in bodies and minds can have biological functions if they are the products of general programs or learning rules which are *supposed* to produce novel structures in response to experience. This is not just a feature of Millikan's account of meaning; it is built into her general analysis of functions from the outset (1984, chapter 2).[17] A young chick which imprints on Konrad Lorenz, the first moving thing it sees, has acquired a program which has some novel and unhistorical properties. Konrad, after all, has played no role in the selective history of imprinting. But it is also true that the chick has acquired this unusual program in accordance with a general rule which does have a selective history; it has been designed to memorize the appearance of the first moving thing seen, and to follow that thing around. Consequently, we should be able to say that the new program in the chick has the function to encode the appearance *of Konrad Lorenz*, and to make the chick follow *him* around. Millikan's account of functions is explicitly designed to make sense of such cases, and more complex ones as well. It is no part of Millikan's program to deny the reality of novelty and individuality in morphological or conceptual structure.

All the same, and however well Millikan can accommodate novelty within a historical view, a person who is determined to minimize their debts and bonds to the past, and who resolves to maintain a forward-looking view in every aspect of their conception of human cognition and agency, might feel that the determination of content must remain a more present-tense matter. James's own reaction might, counterfactually, have been something like this. So it may be that we will be left with a choice: we can hold fast to an ahistorical view of meaning, in success semantics or indicator semantics or some other, but abandon then the attempt to resolve the semantic indeterminacies which have become familiar over recent decades. Or we can adopt a theory such as Millikan's, and feel firm in our focus on the objects of thought, at the expense of another tie to the past.[18]

Notes

"A Continuum of Semantic Optimism" appears here for the first time by kind permission of the author.

1   I was alerted to this way of looking at pragmatist views of truth by a talk on C. S. Peirce given by Tom Baldwin at Dubrovnik in 1990. Peirce says, for instance, "For truth is neither more nor less than that character of a proposition which consists in this, that belief in the proposition would, with sufficient experience and reflection, lead us to such conduct as would tend to satisfy the desires we should then have" (1903 note to Peirce, 1877, p. 100; see also p. 103). Peirce is a less useful figure in the present context, though, as he does not play the role of "explanatory pessimist" as well as James.

2   "I think the centre of my whole *Anschauung*, since years ago I read Renouvier, has been the belief that something is doing in the universe, and that *novelty* is real." From a letter to James Ward, 1909, quoted in Perry (1954), p. 356.

3   Thayer finds the central shortcoming in James's account of truth to be not a denial of objective controls on what is true, but "the assumption that the conspicuous nature of the controls in question required little or no supplementary explanation" (Thayer, 1981, p. 152). Here I agree with Thayer on the question of whether there are such controls for James, but I am taking James's refusal to supply explanations of these controls to be more a consequence of his metaphysical outlook than an assumption about what explanations are "required."

4   There are passages which may not fit too well with this view as an interpretation of James: "*The true is the name of whatever proves itself to be good in the way of belief, and good, too, for definite, assignable reasons*" (1907, p. 42). Thayer (1981), p. 545, discusses a half-developed idea seen in some of James's presentations, stressing the fact that a true idea must have some property which accounts for its tendency to help us to get by. This is not a central theme in James, though; his stress is more often on the possibility of discarding, when pragmatically appropriate, the usual relation thought of as an explanation of why truth is useful – the relation of copying.

5   This idea is also found in various other writers; I am focusing on Whyte because his version is straightforward and optimistic. Later we will discuss Papineau's teleological theory, but Papineau does discuss, and reject, a simpler success-based view along the lines of (R) – see Papineau (1987), pp. 55–7. For the origins of this idea, Whyte and Papineau cite Ramsey (1927). Ramsey's version, which he calls a "pragmatist view," is behavioristic. It identifies believing that p, for a certain class of simple beliefs, with acting in a way which would be successful if and only if p (1927, p. 144; contrast Ramsey's explicit "if and only if" with Whyte's and Papineau's expressions). Mellor (1988) endorses Ramsey's view, though he may implicitly drop the "only if" in Ramsey. Papineau also cites Putnam (1978), Appiah (1986), and Stalnaker (1986).

6   Similarly, Mr Magoo, discussed in a related connection by Dennett (1982b), succeeds without truth via a comical pre-established harmony.

7   It might also be objected to Whyte's theory that no *distal* state of affairs is such that a certain kind of action is guaranteed to succeed when that state of affairs holds. The only state of affairs that will generate such a guarantee is one which has many more of the proximal details filled in. These details function like the "channel conditions" of Dretske (1981). I am focusing on the other line of objection in order to link Whyte's theory to other problems standardly discussed in the literature on belief content.

8   Stich (1990) attacks the instrumental value of truth with a case in which true beliefs about a flight lead a man to catch a doomed plane. If he'd known even more – that the flight was doomed – he would not have caught the plane, but Stich says "the question at hand is not whether omniscience would foster survival but whether more true beliefs are always better than fewer" (p. 123). But note how strong a view linking truth and success has to be before Stich's case is a problem. Stich's opponent apparently holds that adding any further truths to a set, in any order, must be helpful, and dropping truths, in any order, must be harmful. Success must not just tend to increase with the number of truths believed, but this function must be never decreasing, and never decreasing regardless of the order in which truths are added. Advocates of success semantics do not hold such extreme views. Generally, they make use only of the idealized case in which all relevant beliefs operating in a situation are true. See also Devitt (1991), chapter 6, for a skeptical discussion of whether truth has any special explanatory powers here, which weaker properties do not have.

9   In Papineau's 1987 and 1990 presentations, the reason for moving from a simple success-based formula to an evolutionary view is the need to specify success independently, not the need to weaken the link between truth and success. I am assuming that Papineau would take the opportunity to make the less optimistic claim, given that his evolutionary framework allows him to do this.

    Sterelny (1990), chapter 6, distinguishes between "modest" and "less modest" teleological theories of content. Papineau is one of the most immodest, in virtue of his attempt to combine the evolutionary approach with a simple kind of compositional semantics. Most of Millikan is also immodest. Sterelny's modesty is orthogonal to my optimism.

10 Strictly, this is apparently *a* function, though in this paper I will assume, perhaps counterfactually, that it is the chief, original one. Recent research suggests that the

frill and its display serve several functions. Males also use it in territorial display, and females use it to reject unwelcome males (Shine, 1992). The large number of blood vessels in the frill have suggested to some that it is used in thermoregulation also. I am grateful to Nicholas Godfrey-Smith of the Australian Museum for his assistance with this case.

11 I am not suggesting that this is all that is needed for an adaptationist explanation to be compelling. A variety of genetic assumptions must be made, and so on. This is a point about the cost-benefit *part* of an adaptationist explanation.

12 Technically, the functions of the consumer which must be furthered are what Millikan (1984) calls "adapted" functions, where the adaptor is the icon.

13 There is an official account of why beliefs are intentional icons in Millikan (1984), pp. 144–6. It may seem strange, but I will ignore this account completely. This official discussion of belief uses concepts from the farthest reaches of Millikan's warehouse, and it is not the most convincing part of the book. An account of belief-like representational states as indicative intentional icons can be fashioned more simply and directly. Millikan's own work since 1984 has also tended in this direction.

14 See Pietroski (forthcoming) for an interesting argument that Millikan's explanation-based account does not always deliver such intuitive results.

15 This confused me in an earlier (1988) discussion.

16 Fodor's example with "fly" and "fly or bee-bee" might be potentially misleading. Flies and bee-bees look similar. If Fodor's general claim about the transparency of the context "selected for responding to . . ." is right, though, we must take selective explanation and attributions of function to be blind between states of affairs which even the organism can easily distinguish. I take it this makes Fodor's claim seem counter-intuitively strong.

17 Evolutionary accounts of meaning and cognition sometimes go another way here, and appeal to individual, within-generation mechanisms of "selection" of beliefs or concepts (e.g., Papineau 1987, p. 66). These are held to be *analogous* to the usual between-generation mechanisms of selection. Millikan's view, on the other hand, stresses that these individual learning processes are *products* of selection. It is true that taking the analogy route potentially reduces the dependence of meaning on the distant past. This idea is less likely to work, however, and Millikan's handling of learning is better. Papineau's way relies entirely on a strong *empirical* similarity between all or most mechanisms of learning and the mechanisms of evolution – a very questionable assumption.

18 I would like to thank Ruth Millikan, who has generously spent a great deal of time over several years helping me to understand her work. This acknowledgement should not be taken to suggest that the interpretation of her writings presented in this paper has her endorsement. Thanks also to David Papineau.

12 Interpretational Semantics[1]

Robert Cummins

Summary and Advertisement

A central insight of the seventeenth century was that mental meaning cannot be understood in terms of resemblance. If the semantic relations between mind and world cannot be understood on the hypothesis that the mind is *like* the world, literally sharing properties with the things it represents, how can it be understood? In the hands of Locke and his successors, covariance replaced resemblance. But whatever advantages this had for Locke, mental representation cannot be understood in terms of covariation by those who want to follow the Computational Theory of Cognition (CTC) in supposing that mental representation *explains* how system manage to get into states that covary with the states of the world. And the attempt to understand mental representation in terms of adaptational roles also appears to reverse the explanatory order central to the CTC, and to be inconsistent with the thesis that cognition (and hence representation) supervenes on abstract formal structure that need not be historically specified.

What is next? The demise of similarity, idealized covariance, and adaptationist theories leaves us with only one candidate: functional role. The approach I will sketch in this chapter – "Interpretational Semantics" – turns out to be ontologically equivalent to a kind of functional-role semantics. However, Interpretational Semantics has, to my intellectual palate, a very different flavor than functional-role semantics; it is motivated in a very different way than typical functional-role theories, it directs our attention to quite different issues, and it generates a different dialectic. These virtues, I think, swamp the significance of the underlying ontological equivalence I note in Cummins 1989a, chapter 9.

Interpretational Semantics is really not an alternative to the traditional theories, which are best construed as answers to a different question. Interpretational Semantics is an account of representation in the CTC, whereas most philosophical discussion of mental representation has to do with Intentionality – i.e., with the contents of thoughts – rather than with the contents of the representations of a computational system. The theory I called the

Representational Theory of Intentionality in Cummins 1989a, chapter 2, would forge a tight link between representation and intentionality. But this, as we see in Cummins 1989a, chapter 10, is extremely problematic if we accept the CTC and the Interpretational Semantics that (I claim) inevitably goes with it. The kind of meaning required by the CTC is, I think, not Intentional Content anymore than entropy is history. There is a connection, of course, but at bottom representation in the CTC is very different from intentionality. To keep this point in the foreground, I will eventually introduce the special term *s-representation* (for simulation-based representation) to stand for the kind of representation described below. The thesis of Interpretational Semantics is that s-representation is the kind of representation the CTC requires to ground its explanatory appeals to representation.

It seems clear that if we are going to understand what representation is in the CTC, we should begin by understanding clearly what it does, and how. Representation is an explanatory construct in the CTC. Until we understand its explanatory role in that framework, we have no serious chance of understanding how it should be grounded for that framework. In order to get a clear picture of how the CTC proposes to exploit representation in the explanation of cognition, it is essential that we also gain a clear picture of the role of computation, for the main thesis of the CTC is that cognitive systems cognize by computing representations. The concepts of representation and computation are correlative in CTC and must be understood together.

Explaining Addition

The CTC proposes to explain cognitive capacities by appeal to representation and computation in exactly the way that arithmetical capacities of calculators (such as addition) are standardly explained by appeal to representation and computation. The main explanatory strength of the CTC is that it proposes to explain cognition in terms of antecedently understood notions of representation and computation – notions the CTC takes to be unproblematic in a variety of familiar non-cognitive contexts such as calculating and elementary computer programming. We would do well to begin, then, by reviewing the "received" explanation of addition in adding machines.

To add is to be described by the plus function, $+(\langle m, n\rangle)= s$. Hence, to explain what makes a system an adder is to explain the fact that the system is described by $+$. But $+$ is a function whose arguments and values are numbers; and whatever numbers are, they are not states or processes or events in any physical system. How, then, can a physical system be described by $+$? How can a physical system traffic in numbers and hence add? The answer, of course, is that *numerals* – i.e., representations of numbers – can be states of a physical system, even if the numbers themselves cannot. A physical system adds by trafficking in numerals and hence, indirectly, in the numbers those numerals represent.

The input to a typical adding machine is a sequence of button pressings: $\langle C,$ $M, +, N, =\rangle$, i.e., $\langle clear,\ first\ addend,\ plus,\ second\ addend,\ equals\rangle$. The output is a display state, D, which is a numeral representing the sum of the two addends. We may think of the button-pressing sequences as arguments to a function g that gives display states as values. An adding machine *satisfies* g; that is, the arguments and values of g are literally states of the physical system.[2] Addition, as was remarked above, relates numbers, not physical states of some machine, so a physical system cannot literally satisfy the plus function. What an adding machine does is *instantiate* the plus function. It *instantiates* addition by *satisfying* the function g whose arguments and values represent the arguments and values of the addition function, or, in other words, have those arguments and values as interpretations.

Putting all this together, we have that something is an adding machine because

(1) we can interpret button pressings (or the internal states they cause) as numbers,[3]
(2) we can interpret displays (or the internal states that cause them) as numbers,
(3) the device causally associates sequences of button pressings with displays (i.e., it satisfies a button-pressing-to-display function),

and, given all this,

(4) if a token of the button-pressing events interpreted as n and m were to occur, then a token display event interpreted as $n + m$ would normally occur as a consequence. The device instantiates the addition function by satisfying the function mentioned in step 3, for that function is interpretable as the addition function.

To get a physical device to add, you have to get it to satisfy a function interpretable as addition. And that means you have to design it so that getting it to represent a pair of addends causes it to represent their sum.

The following is a useful picture of this whole conception of adding machines. I call it the Tower Bridge picture because it reminds me of London's Tower Bridge.

$$+: I(\langle C, N, +, M, =\rangle) = \langle n, m\rangle \longrightarrow I\,(D) = n + m$$

$$\uparrow I \qquad\qquad\qquad\qquad \uparrow I$$

$$g: \langle C, N, +, M, =\rangle = \text{(computation)} == D \Longrightarrow$$

The top span pictures the function instantiated: $+$, in our present case. It takes a pair of numbers onto their sum. The bottom span corresponds to the function satisfied (called simply *g*). It takes a quintuple of button pressings onto a display. The vertical arrows correspond to interpretation: $I (\langle C, N, +, M, = \rangle)$ is the interpretation of $(\langle C, N, +, M, = \rangle)$, namely $\langle n, m \rangle$, the pair of numbers represented by N and M. $I(D)$ is the interpretation of the display, which will be the sum of n and m if the thing works right. Under interpretation, the bottom span is revealed as an instantiation of the top span; computation is revealed as addition.

Computation

We have reduced the problem of explaining addition to the problem of explaining why the machine satisfies *g*, the function that instantiates addition. In standard adding machines, the values of *g* are *computed* from the corresponding arguments; adding machines add by computing the appropriate representations.

Of course, functions need not be computed to be satisfied. Set mousetraps satisfy a function from trippings to snappings without computing it, and physical objects of all kinds satisfy mechanical functions without computing them. The planets stay in their orbits without computing them. Missiles, on the other hand, compute their trajectories (sometimes), and, in general, complex systems often satisfy functions by computing them. Humans, in particular, routinely satisfy functions by computing them. This is how recipes and instruction manuals enable you to satisfy functions you don't know how to satisfy directly. The recipe for hollandaise sauce, for example, specifies such things as eggs and double boilers as inputs and hollandaise sauce as output. When you execute such a recipe, you satisfy a function having the recipe inputs as arguments and the hollandaise (the recipe output) as value. Recipes analyze such functions into simple functions you know how to satisfy directly – e.g., add three eggs to the contents of the bowl.[4]

To compute a function *g* is to execute a program that gives *o* as its output on input *i* just in case $g(i) = o$. Computing reduces to program execution, so our problem reduces to explaining what it is to execute a program.

The obvious strategy is to exploit the idea that program execution involves *steps*, and to treat each elementary step as a function that the executing system simply *satisfies*. To execute a program is to satisfy the steps.

But what guarantees that the steps are executed – i.e., satisfied – "in the right order"? Program execution is surely disciplined step satisfaction. Where does the discipline come in? The discipline takes care of itself. Functions satisfied by *d* specify causal connections between events in *d*, so if *d* satisfies *f* and *g* and if the current value of *f* is an argument for *g*, then an execution of the *f* step will produce an execution of the *g* step. Program execution reduces to step satisfaction.[5]

You won't go far wrong if you think of it this way. Imagine the program expressed as a flow chart. Each box in the chart represents a step. To execute a step is to satisfy its characteristic function, i.e., the function specified by the input/output properties of the box. If you think of the arrows between the boxes as causal arrows, the result is a causal network with steps (i.e., functions to be satisfied) at the nodes. A system executes the program if that causal network gives the (or a) causal structure of the system.[6]

The Role of Representation in This Explanation

The arguments and values of the button-pressing-to-display function that play the role of representations – i.e., the button-pressing sequences and the display states themselves – need not be symbols with any use or meaning outside the system that computes them. What matters is only that the system satisfy a function g that instantiates $+$. That is, there must exist an interpretation I such that

$$g(x) = y \qquad \text{iff} \qquad +(I(x)) = I(y).$$

It is, in short, simply the fact that g is isomorphic to $+$ that makes the arguments and values of g representations of numbers for a system that satisfies g. It is sufficient for the arguments and values of g's being representations of addends and sums that there exist an interpretation mapping g onto $+$: the arguments and values of g's being representations of numbers is *constituted* by the fact that g instantiates $+$; representation is just a name for the relation induced by the interpretation mapping between the elements of g and the elements of $+$.

That there is no "further fact"[7] to representation in this case beyond g's instantiating $+$ is obscured by the use of symbols with a meaning that is independent of their use in the system. One is tempted to suppose that the display state that looks like "5" would mean five regardless of whether g actually instantiates $+$. And so it would – *to us*. But its meaning in the system might be something quite different. To see this, we simply have to imagine that the buttons are mislabeled and that the display wires are crossed. In such a case we would have to discover what represented what, and this we would do by establishing mapping, I, between g and $+$ such that

$$g(x) = y \qquad \text{iff} \qquad +(I(x)) = I(y).$$

Indeed, it suffices to notice that it *makes sense* to suppose that the buttons *could* be mislabeled, or that the display wires *could* be scrambled, for this would make no sense if the meanings of input and output states were determined by the conventional meanings of those states considered as symbol tokens. We say that a display is scrambled because the conventional meanings of the display don't match the meanings that they have in the system, and this evidently requires that displays have a meaning in the system that is independent of their conventional meanings.

We are now in a position to see that it is somewhat misleading to speak of the explanatory role of representation in this context. The explanatory burden is carried by the fact of simulation and the correlative concept of interpretation. There is a sense in which an adding machine adds because it represents numbers, but there is a more important sense in which it represents numbers because it adds: we can speak of it as representing numbers only because it stimulates + under some interpretation.

From an explanatory point of view, what interpretation provides is a link between mere state crunching (button-pressing-to-display transitions) and *addition*: under interpretation, the state transitions of the system are revealed as adding. You can get a feel for the explanatory role of interpretation by imagining that the device is an archaeological discovery. Perhaps you know from documents that the thing is an adding machine; however, looking at it, you have no idea, at first, how to give inputs or read outputs. You can "make it go," let's say, by turning a handle, but this is just more or less random manipulation until you find an interpretation that reveals the state transitions of the device as sum calculations and hence establishes the representational status and contents of those states. To know how to use it is to know how to see it as simulating +, and that means knowing how to "make it go" and how to interpret it.

The concept of representation that is operative here can be brought more clearly into focus by considering again Galileo's ingenious use of geometrical figures to represent mechanical magnitudes (figure 12.1). The crucial point is that, given Galileo's interpretation of the lines and volumes, the laws of Euclidean geometry discipline those representations in a way that mirrors the way the laws of mechanics discipline the represented magnitudes: the geometrical discipline mirrors the natural discipline of the domain. That is, geometrical relationships among the symbols have counterparts in the natural relations among mechanical variables[8] in such a way that computational transformations on the symbols track[9] natural transformations of the system. That is what makes it correct to say that the symbols – lines and volumes – *represent* times, velocities, and distances.

Of course, this is what Galileo *intended* them to represent; that is the interpretation he stipulated. But it is one thing to intend to represent something, another to succeed. Galileo's figures *actually do* represent mechanical variables because the computational discipline *actually does* track the natural one. This is the natural discipline we have in mind when we say that the system behaves according to natural law. I call Galileo's interpretation a proper interpretation because under that interpretation the natural system and the geometrical system that represents it march in step: the geometrical system *simulates* the natural one.[10] A proper interpretation is an interpretation that gets it right: the symbols actually represent what the interpretation says they represent.

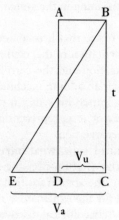

Figure 12.1   Galileo's diagram

Representation, in this context, is simply a convenient way of talking about an aspect of more or less successful simulation.[11] The volumes behave in the geometrical system in a way analogous to the way certain distances behave in the natural system. Hence, the volumes are said to represent those distances; those distances are proper interpretations of those volumes. For instance, the volume of the triangle tracks the distance traveled by the uniformly accelerated body; the volume of the triangle is the *geometrical analogue* of the distance traveled by the accelerated body. This is what makes it correct to say that the volume of the triangle *represents* the distance traveled by the accelerated body, i.e., that the distance traveled by that body is a proper interpretation of that volume. Representation enters into this story in a way exactly analogous to the way it enters into the story about adding machines. In both cases, it is the fact that one function simulates the other under a fixed interpretation that makes it possible to think of the arguments and values of one function as representing the arguments and values of the other. The causal structure of an adding machine – the fact that it executes an appropriate program and hence satisfies the function g – guarantees that the arguments and values of g track the numbers; it guarantees, for example, that "3" is the computational analogue (in the machine) of three in the addition function. This is what makes it possible to think of "3" as a symbol *in the system* for three. Analogously, the formal structure of Euclidian geometry guarantees that the volume of the rectangle in Galileo's figure will track the distance traveled by the unaccelerated body, and this is what makes it possible to think of that volume as representing that distance.[12] The analogy between Galileo's geometrical treatment of mechanics and the computational treatment of addition is brought out by noticing that the Tower Bridge picture applies naturally to the former as well as the latter:

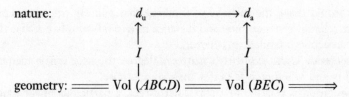

nature: d_u ⟶ d_a

geometry: ══ Vol (*ABCD*) ══ Vol (*BEC*) ═══⟹

Nature maps the distance traveled by the unaccelerated body onto the distance traveled by the accelerated body; geometry maps the volume of the rectangle onto the volume of the triangle.

s-Representation

The concept of representation invoked by the CTC is the same concept that is implicit in the sort of mathematical science that Galileo invented. It is the sense in which

- a graph or equation represents a set of data
- a linear equation represents the relation between time to solution and the absolute value of the multiplier when a product is computed by a successive addition algorithm
- a parabola represents the trajectory of a projectile
- intelligence cannot be represented on a ratio scale (when we say "twice as smart," we misrepresent intelligence) and
- we ask whether social or economic dynamics can be adequately represented by a set of linear equations (knowing that the nonlinear case is computationally intractable).

It will be useful to give this sort of representation a special name. I will call it "s-representation" – "s" for "simulation," because s-representation is simply a consequence of (one might almost say an artifact of) simulation.

Since s-representation is familiar from the context of mathematical modeling, it is useful to list several features of s-representations that are uncontroversial in that context:

- When we are dealing with mathematical models of a natural phenomenon, the criteria of adequate representation are just the criteria of adequate modeling. Typically, we use a battery of statistical techniques to determine how well a mathematical model simulates nature's discipline observed and recorded as "the data." A failure of fit between data and model shows that the model does not adequately s-represent the world (or that aspect of the world that we are trying to s-represent).
- We draw a strong distinction in this context between what we intend to represent, or are trying to represent, and what we succeed in representing.

No one would make the mistake of thinking that a linear equation represents the relation between time and distance in free fall simply because that is what someone intended or believed.

- s-representation is also explicitly a matter of degree; the issue is *how* adequate a model is and whether it is better than competitors.
- s-representation is relative to a particular target: a particular linear model may be a better model of system S than it is of system S', but it would be out of place – a misunderstanding – to ask which system, if either, it "really" represents.
- Failures of s-representation are often not "localizable": When a model is not adequate, it is sometimes possible to pin the blame on a particular culprit (the wrong empirical value for a parameter, say), but, notoriously, it is often not possible to make more than rather vague and global judgments of culpability.
- There is often a pragmatic element to representation in this context: a linear model of a complex social system may be an adequate representation for some purposes and not others, and may be preferable to non-linear models simply because it is mathematically more tractable.

All of these points (and, no doubt, more that I haven't thought of) apply to representation in a computational context. When we write programs – even very simple ones – we often *intend* interpretations that turn out to be Improper. The computational discipline we have designed is inadequate, and the desired tracking fails, at least in part. Discussing a bridge-playing program, I might say, to myself or to a colleague, "This data structure represents the opponent's bridge hand." But if the program is a failure, so is the representation. The upper and lower spans of the Tower Bridge fail to connect properly. Strictly speaking, what I should say in such a case is "I meant this data structure to represent (s-represent) the opponent's hand, but it doesn't seem to work."[13] This commonplace experience of programmers highlights the fact that successful representation in computational systems is not simply a matter between the symbol and its interpretation but depends essentially on the processes that have computational access to (are "defined over") the symbol. A bug in the "logic" of a program can lead to a failure of representation – a failure that may well be correctable without altering the data structures in question at all. It follows from this consideration that misrepresentation in programming, like misrepresentation in mathematical modeling, may be a global affair, with no obvious culprit. It is often difficult to say whether unsatisfactory performance is best improved by altering the data structures (i.e., by finding a better knowledge representation), or by altering the processes that operate on them.[14]

As was pointed out above in connection with addition, the fact that s-representation is simply an offspring of more or less successful simulation is often obscured by the common use of "near English" (or some other natural language) in coding data structures in high-level programming languages. If a data structure for a program intended to play bridge has symbols such as "K-clubs," it is natural to suppose that what we have is a representation of the king of clubs. And so we do; that is what "K-clubs" means *to us* in "near English." But "K-clubs" doesn't succeed in representing the king of clubs *in the system* if the program is a radical failure. We must be careful to distinguish what we intend a data structure to represent in the system we are building from what, if anything, it *does* represent in the system, and to distinguish both of these from what it represents in some independent representational scheme such as our own natural language. There is no "further fact" required for successful s-representation beyond what is required for successful simulation.

In programming, as in mathematical modeling, failure comes in degrees; the tracking may be imperfect but not fail utterly. The computational and natural systems mostly march in step, but with lapses in coordination. We can bring out this point, and the analogy with mathematical modeling, by imagining Galileo's system "automated," i.e., realized as a computational system for solving problems of mechanics. As Galileo set up the system, it isn't quite right. Moreover, given the geometry he was working with, there *is* no way to get it exactly right. The Galilean geometry misrepresents mechanical reality; it does not, and cannot, perfectly simulate the natural order. Galileo had an inadequate "knowledge representation," but one that went a long way nonetheless. Thus, in the world of s-representation, misrepresentation differs from failure to represent only in degree; failed representation becomes misrepresentation when the failure isn't too bad. This is especially true if the failures are identifiable and (more or less) correctable or avoidable.[15] We usually think of the case of Galileo as one of misrepresentation rather than one of failure to represent, because his system is a great deal better than the competition was and because we know how to improve performance; that is, we can specify conditions under which the system's performance is quite good – correct "for all practical purposes" – so there is a sense in which we think of it as "being on the right track."

But isn't it more correct to say that Galileo intended to represent mechanical reality but failed? Misrepresentation is representation, after all, not simple failure to represent.

We could say that Galileo failed to represent mechanical reality rather than that he misrepresented it. "Absolutely speaking" (whatever that means, exactly), it is a failure. Relatively speaking – relative to historical context and available competitors – it was a ground-breaking success. Thus, we could say either that Galileo came closer to representing mechanical reality than the competition, or that he represented mechanical reality better than the competition. If we think of matters in the first way, we will not speak of misrepresentation except as a synonym for intended representation that fails to some extent. If we think of matters in the second way, we will say that Galileo misrepresented mechanical reality, but not as badly as, say, Buridan. The important point is that the imagined objection (in quotation marks above) simply presupposes that representation isn't a matter of degree. The underlying thought is something like this: "Either we have representation or we don't have it, and only if we have it can we speak of misrepresentation."

It is all too easy to think of representation as like identification (the speech act), and of the processes that act on them as like predication. Successful identification (hence reference of one kind) is prior to predication, and hence prior to truth. First there is the issue of what, if anything, you have managed to identify; *then* there is the issue of what to predicate of it, and whether the result is something true. But we cannot suppose analogously that first there is the issue of what (if anything) is represented and then there is the issue of what processes act on the representations. What is s-represented is essentially a matter of the processes, for it is essentially a matter of simulation. And simulation is essentially a matter of degree.

s-representation is relative to a target of simulation. Since (as we will see shortly) proper interpretations are not unique, g may be an imperfect simulation of f but a perfect (or better) simulation of g. Indeed, given any f imperfectly simulated by g, it is (I suppose) always possible to find an f' that g simulates better than f. Thus, it makes no sense to speak of s-representation *simpliciter*; s-representation (and, hence mis-s-representation) must be relativized to the function simulated. Given an interpretation function I, g is a more or less accurate simulation of f. Against this background, we can say that some symbol – one of g's arguments or values – accurately tracks (i.e., represents) or imperfectly tracks (misrepresents) its interpretation under I. But the very same symbol may be said to represent or misrepresent something entirely different given a different interpretation under which g simulates (more or less successfully) a different function, f'. Galileo's symbols are imperfect representations of mechanical variables, but they are perfect representations of plane figures in Euclidian space. Geometry is better geometry than mechanics. Big surprise.

Once we admit these relativizations, we can see why nothing comparable to the "disjunction problem" that arises in connection with covariance theories arises for Interpretational Semantics. We needn't *worry* that we can always trade misrepresentation of x for accurate representation of Something Else; we *can* do that, but it doesn't *matter*. The fact that a system satisfying g thereby perfectly simulates f under I has no tendency to show that the system doesn't also thereby imperfectly simulate f' under I'. And it is the fact of simulation (and its degree of adequacy) that bears the explanatory load in the Tower Bridge strategy. No doubt adding machines simulate functions other than $+$, but that does not compromise the standard explanation of addition in adding machines.

Is this playing fair? Couldn't the covariance theorist pull the same stunt? Here is how it would go: we prefer imperfect correlation with C to perfect correlation with B on the grounds that C, but not B, is an important property of D, where what we are trying to do is explain the system's performance in D (not D', where B looms large).

I have some sympathy with this line of defense, but I suspect that this sort of relativization (or lack of uniqueness, if you like) is just what the covariance theorist was trying to avoid. I leave it to the reader to determine whether covariance is worth saving (for some framework other than the CTC) and, if so, whether this move will help.

But notice that Interpretational Semantics allows for cheap representational contents, and learns to live with them by pointing out that their low price doesn't compromise their explanatory role in the CTC. That defense isn't available to the covariance theorist, because covariance theories cannot explain what representation is in a way that is consistent with the CTC.

Interpretation

There is a deep problem about the notion of interpretation that needs to be canvassed before we go any farther. The simple way to understand an interpretation function is to think of it as any one-to-one mapping. But this is evidently much too liberal. To see why, notice that there is a one-to-one mapping between multiplication and addition. Thus, if $+$ interprets g (our button-pressing-to-display function), then so does $\times$ (by transitivity of one-to-one mappings). It will follow that g instantiates $\times$ as well as $+$; i.e., anything that is an adding machine is automatically a multiplication machine as well. This is surely unacceptable.

Given this simple-minded and liberal understanding of interpretation, the whole business of getting a system to instantiate a given function f becomes *trivial*. It is not trivial in general; designing calculators was a major achievement, and designing calculators that multiply as well as add was a non-trivial achievement as well. So there must be something wrong with understanding interpretation simply as one-to-one mappings.

Let us return to our example. Let A be an adding machine that instantiates $+ \langle x, y \rangle = z$ as $g(\langle C, N, +, M, = \rangle) = d$, a function that maps button-pressing sequences onto display states. Now, since the multiplication function, $\times (\langle x, y \rangle) = z$, is one-to-one mappable to $+$, if we take interpretation to be any one-to-one mapping it will follow that A instantiates $\times$ as g too. But what is the interpretation function? The obvious choice is this:

$$I_+ (\langle C, N, +, M, = \rangle) = I_\times (\langle C, N, +, M, = \rangle),$$

and if $g (\langle C, N, +, M, = \rangle) = d$, then

$$I_\times(d) = \times (I_\times (\langle C, N, +, M, = \rangle)).$$

There are a number of other possibilities, but – and here are the crucial points – *they all involve computing* ×, *and they all involve ignoring the display*. And that's cheating! It is evidently *cheating* to build the function to be instantiated into the interpretation function, because if you do *that* then you will need *another* system (yourself with paper and pencil, typically) to instantiate the function *directly*, i.e., without cheating. In the example, you will need a multiplication machine to compute the values of $I_\times$. And if you have one of those, why bother with A? It is also cheating to interpret the display in a way that ignores the display. If we try to treat $I_\times$ as a function of the display, we will rapidly get a contradiction. When we enter two plus two, the display will read "4". So $I_\times$ ("4") = 4, since that's 2×2. But when we enter one plus three, the display will read "4" again, but we must interpret it as 3, since $1 \times 3 = 3$. $I_\times$ can get around this only by ignoring the display – i.e., by taking the display as a context-sensitive symbol whose interpretation is sensitive *only* to the context.

This particular example can be undercut by requiring that interpretation functions be structure-preserving as well as one-to-one – i.e., by requiring that f and g be isomorphic, which addition and multiplication are not. (In addition, no number plays the role played by zero in multiplication.) But requiring that interpretations establish isomorphism is still much too weak. $x + y$ *is* isomorphic to $2\pi(x + y)$, yet a simple adding machine does not compute $2\pi(x + y)$; it computes $x + y$ and the interpretation has to do the rest (compute $2\pi(z)$).

The obvious moral is that the only really interesting interpretation is what we might call *direct* interpretation. But I must confess that I don't know how to define *directness*. It seems that not building the function to be instantiated into the interpretation function should be a necessary condition, as should not ignoring the arguments and values of the instantiating function. But these are very shaky conditions. First, in any finite device, such as an adding machine, it is possible to get around the first problem – the problem of building the target function into the interpretation – by defining the interpretation function via a (no doubt huge) lookup table. Of course, one would construct such a table by doing the forbidden calculation, but I'm not at all sure how to exploit that fact in formulating a careful definition of what I'm calling *direct* interpretation, because one can obviously *use* such a table without doing the calculations required to build it in the first place. One might counter this move by pointing out, with some justification, that table lookup is a form of computation, and hence that the interpretation does incorporate a computation of the function to be instantiated.

However this may be, some legitimate interpretation surely involves non-trivial calculation, at least for some of us. I am not prepared to disqualify base-3 adding machines just because in order to use them I have to do some translations that, intuitively, are as difficult as adding itself. I suppose someone could get so good at $I_\times$ that it would seem like "reading" the product off A's display rather than like calculating it. Something very much like this surely happens when we learn new notations (e.g., Polish notation in logic) or a new language. More important, one doesn't want the notion of interpretation to be tied in this way to what an interpreter has to do; rather, it should be tied to the complexity (or something) of the proposed interpretation function.[16]

The second problem – ignoring the arguments and values of the instantiating function – can be got around by defining an interpretation that is like I_x but does take the display into account in some trivial way. For example, define I'_x as like I_x except that when the display is "5" the interpretation is that there is no answer. This will force an interpreter to look at the display every time to check that it isn't "5".

Reflections such as these make *direct interpretation* seem like a rather subjective and relativistic affair. Nevertheless, it appears to me to be absolutely central to the notion of function instantiation (and hence computation), so I'm simply going to assume it, leaving to someone else the task of filling this hole or widening it enough to sink the ship. *Something* must account for the fact that instantiating f isn't enough to instantiate every function isomorphic to f.[17] I am inclined to accept a kind of transcendental argument for the solvability of the directness problem: the standard Tower Bridge explanation of addition is *correct*, after all, and it presupposes a non-trivial concept of interpretation; therefore, such a concept of interpretation exists. On the strength of this, when I speak of interpretation I will mean *direct interpretation*, assuming there is such a thing. The intuitive content is, after all, fairly clear: interpretation must be relatively trivial; the system has to do the work, not the interpretation function.

Even on the assumption of direct interpretation, it might seem that if A s-represents anything at all, then A s-represents any content you like. Let g be a button-pressing-to-display function satisfied by S, and let g be interpretable as addition. Let f' be identical to $+$ except that $f'(\langle n, m \rangle) =$ Richard Nixon when $n + m = 5$, and $+(\langle n, \text{Richard Nixon} \rangle) = +(\langle n, 5 \rangle)$. Then g is interpretable as f' – the new interpretation function is just like the old one except that a display of "5" represents Richard Nixon instead of 5. Thus, we seem to have the consequence that representational contents are not just cheap, they are free. But isn't it clear that calculators represent numbers *all the time*, and that they don't represent numbers most of the time and Richard Nixon on occasion?

The trouble with the argument that saddles us with adding machines s-representing Nixon is that, whereas g simulates f', it isn't really the case that "5" is the computational analogue of Richard Nixon. "5" doesn't track Richard Nixon as he is buffeted about by any natural discipline except the discipline enforced on him by f', which is evidently "cooked up." Once again, I am embarrassed by the fact that I have no general account of what makes f' a degenerate target for simulation, but it seems intuitively clear that f' *isn't* a proper object of simulation, and hence that adding machines don't represent Richard Nixon in virtue of simulating f'.

Whatever one thinks about degenerate simulation targets like the one just described, it is clear that any system that simulates *f* is bound to simulate a lot of other functions as well – e.g., the numerical function that relates the Gödel number of a standard expression of an argument of *f* to the Gödel number of a standard expression of *f*'s corresponding value. These won't typically be *familiar* functions, or *interesting* functions, but they will be simulated nonetheless. And this still leaves s-representational content relatively cheap, on the assumption that price varies inversely with supply.[18] We have already seen that the availability of alternative interpretations in no way undermines the explanatory use to which s-representation is put by the CTC. Nevertheless, it is tempting to suppose that some interpretations are improper on grounds external to the facts of simulation – viz. on the grounds that only some simulations matter (i.e., are actually used by a containing system). The idea here is that an s-representation of *f* isn't a representation of *f to the system itself* unless s-representing *f* actually has a function in the system. Both Millikan and Dretske utilize this idea, though in different ways. The basic idea is to choose, from among possible interpretations, the interpretation that tracks the function of the process interpreted, and call *that* the representational content. We might call this the selection-by-function approach to representation – a kind of two-phase approach in which we add a functional requirement to s-representation in order to get "the real thing."

The selection-by-function approach can be made very attractive by the following reflection: whether the inputs and outputs of a program (I include all the data structures a program constructs as among its outputs) should be considered representations at all, or whether (like eggs and hollandaise) they should be construed simply as inputs and outputs, seems to depend on how they are used – i.e., on their *functions*. The inputs and outputs of a recipe *could* be treated as symbols. There is, after all, nothing intrinsic about eggs and hollandaise that unsuits them for a representational career; it is just that no one and no thing actually *does* treat them as representations of something else. And this makes it seem that whether something actually is a representation, as opposed to merely being capable of representing, is a matter of whether it actually gets used as a representation.

The trouble with the selection-by-function approach is that it actually adds nothing new; it enforces no new constraint beyond what is already present in s-representation. What is it, after all, for a computational system to use a simulation of *f*? Well, the values of *f* must be arguments for *h*. Hence, the values of g_f must be arguments for g_h. So what we have here is a super-function *F* having *f* and *h* as components, instantiated as *G*, having g_f and g_h as components. In short, we have a computation of the values of *G*. The problem of how the simulation of *f* is used resolves into the problem of how to interpret the computation of *G* – i.e., into the problem of what the computation of *G* simulates. The selection-by-function approach provides no constraints beyond what is provided by the requirement that an interpretation of *G* must interpret its computation, i.e., its component functions, i.e., the steps of the program execution of which explains satisfaction of *G*. This is not a trivial constraint by any means, but it will not rule out the alternative numerical (and other) interpretations whose existence is guaranteed by model theory.

Perhaps we could understand use non-computationally, as Millikan does. But this appears to be no help either. If *I* and *I'* are alternative interpretations of a system *S* having the same domain and isomorphic ranges, then the physical structure that we specify when we say that *S* has the s-representational content provided by *I* is the same physical structure that we specify when we say that *S* has the content provided by *I'*. For *S*, having *I*-content will be nomologically equivalent to having *I'*-content. Hence, any causal or evolutionary interactions tracked by the fact that *S* has *I*-content will be tracked equally by the fact that *S* has *I'*-content. The problem is that any causal/selective interactions will be sensitive only to the physical structure, and we pick out by reference to the one content the very same physical structure that we pick out by reference to the other. So it looks as if non-computational but non-intentional interactions won't distinguish among alternative interpretations. To put the point intuitively, if somewhat misleadingly: a robot that "thinks" it is simulating a numerical function *N* will do just as well in *E* as one that "thinks" it is simulating natural processes in *E'*, as specified by $f_{E'}$ provided *N* and f_E are isomorphic. Both will be equally good (or bad) at picking up trash, for example. Narrow content can be a lot narrower than one might have thought!

Cognition

The CTC proposes to understand cognitive systems as systems that computationally instantiate cognitive functions. This idea requires a bit of unpacking.

The CTC embraces a thoroughly rationalist conception of cognition. A system is cognitive, according to this conception, in virtue of respecting epistemological constraints appropriate to its task domain (the domain it is said to cognize). That is, its behavior is cogent, or warranted, or rational relative to its inputs and internal states. This is what makes it correct to think of it as cognizing a domain rather than merely responding to an environment. It follows from this conception that we have no reason to think of a system as cognitive except insofar as we can describe what it does – its capacities – in semantic terms, for epistemological constraints are defined only for propositions, or things with propositional contents – things with truth values, in short.[19] We thus arrive at the idea that having a cognitive capacity is instantiating a function that relates propositional contents, i.e., a function that takes propositional contents as arguments and values and relates them as premises to conclusion. A cognitive system, in short, is an *inference engine* – a system that merits an inferential characterization. Thus, to explain cognition is to explain how a system can merit an inferential characterization – i.e., to explain how it can reason. This is the conception I put forward in Cummins (1983). It is explicit also in Haugeland (1978), Dennett (1978a, 1987), and Pollock (1987). It is at least implicit in the work of those (e.g., Fodor) who think of cognitive systems as systems that realize some form of belief-desire psychology; as Dennett points out, belief-desire psychology is essentially a psychology of rationality. Under this conception, the problem of cognition becomes the problem of explaining the fact that the system is described by a *cognitive function*, or, for AI, of building a system that is described by a cognitive function.[20]

It is possible to think of cognitive functions as relating intentional states (e.g., beliefs and desires) to one another, since epistemological constraints make sense when applied to these as well. If we go this route, we are free to think of physical systems as actually satisfying (rather than instantiating) cognitive functions. But this wiggle really makes no difference. Cognitive science generally assumes that cognition is a matter of generating the right representations. One then supposes either that the representations have as interpretations intensions (the proposition that Nixon is a crook, say) that are the arguments and values of cognitive functions – in which case we think of those functions as instantiated – or that the representations figure as constituents of intentional states, the intentional states inheriting their intentional properties (being a belief that Nixon is a crook, say) form the semantic properties of the representations (the proposition that Nixon is a crook). Either way, the representations wind up having the same interpretations, and the system winds up instantiating the same abstract function.

The CTC's proposal is that cognitive systems are computational systems: a cognitive system is described by a cognitive function because it computes representations whose contents are the values of the cognitive function, and computes these from representations of the function's arguments. If we suppose that the objects of computation – the things over which the computations are defined – are *symbols*, some of which are *content-equivalent* to the inferential descriptions that figure in the specification of the target cognitive function, we can explain why the system merits inferential characterization, i.e., why it is cognitive: the system merits inferential characterization because it computes symbols representing conclusions from symbols representing the corresponding premises. To move in a disciplined manner from symbol to symbol – to *compute* symbols – is, *under interpretation*, to move in a disciplined manner from content to content. If we get the discipline right, we get inference and hence cognition.[21]

To say that there are cognitive engines, then, is, on this conception, to say that the behavior of certain things is describable via an interpretation that reveals their activity as epistemologically constrained – as rational. Once the rationality of the activity is revealed, we are led to ask how such activity is possible. The strategy employed by the CTC is designed to answer this question by providing a program (computation) and interpretation such that the system executes the program and, under interpretation, execution of the program is revealed as the very cognizing identified as the explanandum. The basic assumption of the CTC is that, under proper interpretation, symbol crunching is cognition.

Semantics enters into the picture because to understand how a physical device could satisfy a cognitive description we need to forge a conceptual connection between computations and inferences (broadly construed). The CTC explains a cognitive capacity by showing how it is computationally instantiated, and this requires linking the arguments and values of cognitive functions. Interpretations specify the links you need to see in order to see computation as cognition (or as addition, for that matter). Objects of computation seen under interpretation – i.e., individuated *semantically* – are representations. We call an object of computation a representation when it is important to see the computation as an instantiation of something else. That is why the display states of a calculator are properly regarded as representations but the outputs of a recipe (as in hollandaise) are not.

It is useful to put the explanatory role of interpretation into a broader perspective. The goal of science is, in part, to develop concepts (or a vocabulary, if you like) that enable us to solve particular explanatory problems. To a first approximation, what a good conceptual scheme does is force us to characterize the system under study in a way that screens out all the information that is irrelevant to the problem at hand, leaving only what is essential. Think of the conceptual scheme provided by Newtonian mechanics as a kind of filter, like a pair of conceptual glasses that allow you to see only what matters for the solution of mechanical problems. Provided with a pair of Newton glasses, when you look at a pool table, what you see is a lot of arrows on a plane normal to gravity. The point at which an arrow originates represents the center of gravity of a ball. The length and direction of the arrow s-represent the momentum of the ball. And it turns out that, when you see pool tables that way, you can see them simply as conservers of momentum and kinetic energy. Newton glasses, in short, reveal pool as a certain kind of conservation system. Analogously, the proper semantics – i.e., the right interpretation – will allow you to see certain computations as adding and (if the CTC is right) others as cognizing. A proper interpretation of an adding machine takes a physical process and filters out everything but what matters to seeing addition. The CTC is just the thesis that what works for addition will work for cognition.

The Specification Problem

I will conclude this chapter by briefly sketching a potential difficulty with the CTC. My goal here is not serious criticism. My point is that the criticism in question gives us another perspective on the CTC's explanatory strategy and, hence, on its use of the concept of representation.

Crucial to the CTC's conception of cognitive theory is the idea that there are independently specifiable cognitive functions. The idea is that cognitive capacities can be specified as functions on contents in a way that is independent of the way any particular system instantiates or computes those functions. The analogy with calculating is exact and historically important. Multiplication, addition, sine, square root, etc. can be specified independent of any instantiating device. The function so specified is the upper span of the Tower Bridge. We can then ask whether there is a lower span (a computation) and towers (an interpretation) that will support that upper span. If the same strategy is going to work for cognition, we will need comparable independent specifications of cognitive capacities to form the upper span.[22]

It is becoming increasingly clear that the specification problem is the hardest part of the program. The CTC – which is, necessarily, rationalist to the core – is just the idea that cognizing generally is like doing science: *automate* Galileo's geometry and what you have, under the appropriate interpretation, is a system that simulates mechanics. But since this amounts to mapping mechanical propositions onto other mechanical propositions that "follow," it is also cognition. Cognition is just computational simulation of "natural functions" via the instantiation of cognitive functions that give a theory of the natural function in question.

But suppose there is no natural function to simulate. Perhaps remembering faces and finding your way home isn't like doing mechanics – can't be like doing mechanics-because these domains, unlike mechanics, aren't governed by laws special to them. The analogy with science makes this seem rather plausible. After all, science works only where there are natural kinds. A science of temperature *per se* is possible only if, as we say, thermal phenomena form an autonomous domain of inquiry. What this means is that thermodynamics is possible only to the extent that thermal phenomena are governed by laws that describe those phenomena "in their own terms" – i.e., autonomously. In contrast, an autonomous special science of clothing is hardly possible, as Fodor (1984) has emphasized in another connection, because there are no special laws of clothing. Clothing, of course, falls under laws (e.g., the laws of physics, chemistry, and economics), so there is no question that scientific study of clothing is possible. There are also, no doubt, "rules" in the clothing domain: how to dress for different occasions and effects, what needs ironing, what can be washed, and so on. But it is doubtful that these rules could be compiled into an expert system that captures human intelligence in the clothing domain. Perhaps, as Dreyfus and Dreyfus (1985) argue, expert human performance in such domains is, at bottom, not rule-driven but example-driven. But this would mean that we cannot specify the explanandum as a set of cognitive functions that take as arguments and values states of, or propositions about, "the clothing domain." We can have a Rationalist specification of cognition only where we can have a special science. But, while we can perhaps have science anywhere, we surely cannot have a special science for every possible domain of intelligent thought.

It seems to follow that the CTC, like mathematical science, will work only for the cognition of autonomously law-governed domains. The precondition for success is the same in both cases: there must be a well-defined upper span to the Tower Bridge. Special science isn't always possible. If cognition is possible where special science is not – in the cases of clothing and faces of conspecifics, for example – then the CTC's Tower Bridge picture of cognition can't be the whole story.[23]

If, as seems increasingly likely, the specification problem for cognition should prove to be intractable, or to be tractable only in special ways, where will that leave us? I think it will leave us with a kind of biological chauvinism (Block, 1978). Cognition will simply be identified ostensively, and hence extrinsically, as *what humans do when they solve problems, find their way home, etc*. We will be left, in short, with Turing's (1950) conception that a cognitive system is just one that is indistinguishable from humans (or other *known cognizers*) in the relevant respects.

Perhaps the CTC could learn to live with this eventuality, but not very comfortably, I suspect. It is difficult to see what methodology will move you from function satisfaction (program execution) to Turing equivalence if the *target* – the human, or whatever – has no known or knowable characteristic function that might be analyzed ultimately into steps that have known computational instantiations. Synthesis works best if the thing you are trying to synthesize has a known analysis. Otherwise, it is trial and error. That is *nature's* way, of course, but it takes a long time. For now, anyway, the CTC has no way to make progress without functionally specifying the target and trying for an analysis that will eventually lead to computational instantiations.

Notes

"Interpretational Semantics" originally appeared as chapter 8 of Robert Cummins's book *Meaning and Mental Representation* (1989), and is reprinted here by permission of MIT Press and the author.

1 Since this paper was written, in 1988, I have changed my views substantially. The view described here is a version of functional role semantics, and I now believe that no such view is workable, for reasons I set out in "Conceptual role semantics and the explanatory role of content," *Philosophical Studies*, 65 (1992), pp. 103–27, and more completely in *Representations, Targets and Attitudes* (Cambridge, MA: MIT Press [Bradford Books], 1994). I do still hold, however, that the essence of mental representation is an isomorphism between representations and their contents. My fundamental take on the problem is still the same: what makes sophisticated

cognition possible is the fact that the mind can operate on something that has the same structure as the domain it is said to cognize. The mind, in short, must be able to model the world, not just denote things in it. Denotational theories of mental representation are just too philosophical for my taste: They concentrate on understanding the attribution of propositional attitudes rather than on how representational structures enable intelligent behavior.

2   Functions associate values with arguments. To see a device as satisfying a function, therefore, is to see it as having inputs and outputs – starting and ending configurations, perhaps – and to see these as *arguments* and *values*, respectively. This suggests the following:

> d satisfies $g = {}_{df}g(x) = y$ iff, were x to occur in d, then, normally, y would occur in d.

As it stands, this is not adequate. It will fail when f is many-one, i.e., when there is more than one way to get a given output; we need to specify that y is x's output and not, say, z's. Unfortunately, there is no general way to say what it is for y to be x's output for arbitrary d, y, and x. We have to do it case by case. In calculators, the output is typically the first stable display after input, i.e., the first display after input such that no other display occurs until another input occurs. But this definition won't generalize, nor will any other. We must, then, suppose that, for a given device d and function g, we can specify an input-output criterion – a criterion that allows us to say of a given state in d whether it is a value and, if so, which state of d is its input. The first stable output after input criterion lately mentioned is the standard input/output criterion for calculators. Let us write $a_d \Rightarrow v_d$ and mean "Were a to occur in d, then, normally, v would occur in d as a's output." Then

> d satisfies $g = {}_{df}$ there is an input/output criterion d and g such that $a_d \Rightarrow v_d$ iff $g(a) = v$.

3   Of course, adding machines don't have to have buttons or displays. Any set of events or states will do so long as I/O behavior turns out to be addition under interpretation, i.e., so long as it is possible to treat those states or events as representations of addends and their sums.

4   Viewers of "It's the Easter Beagle, Charlie Brown!" will recognize that not everyone knows how to satisfy even this simple function.

To some it sounds odd to say that hollandaise is *computed*, but it is essential to see that a fundamental insight of the theory of computation is that the objects of computation are precisely *arbitrary objects*. With our attention riveted on computational theories of cognition, we tend to think exclusively of the symbolic case – the case in which it is symbols (representations) that are computed. But, notoriously, the symbolic status of the objects of computation is irrelevant to the computation itself; what matters to the computation is just that the objects of computation can be reliably typed. See Haugeland (1981).

5   This definition might seem wrong, given that in a program one often has many calls to the same function; what determines which call is executed first? Well, the program counter keeps track of the flow of control. So, simply think of each function having a hidden argument – MYTURN – which is the state of control (a

physical state of the system, of course) that must obtain for the function to be called.

6   It is easy to think of LISP or OPS5 programs in this way, as well as PASCAL. PROLOG and SMALLTALK are a little trickier because the functional structure is rather more implicit.

When thinking about general-purpose computing systems, you must be careful to distinguish three different ways such systems execute programs: (i) A program may be stored as a data structure for an interpreter. (An interpreter is a program that accesses other programs and executes them.) Here, the program defines a virtual machine which is equivalent to a machine that (ii) simply has that program hardwired in the way that an addition program is hardwired in an adding machine. In the first case, the program defines the functional architecture (Pylyshyn, 1984) of a virtual machine; in the second case, it defines a non-virtual functional architecture. (iii) A program (usually called a rule in this context) may be stored as a data structure and accessed by a program that simply uses the rule to solve some problem or accomplish some task, as when one recalls and uses the rule to solve some problem or accomplish some task, as when one recalls and uses the program for taking square roots.

The functional architecture of a computing system is a program in the sense defined in the text. That is, it is a set of interlocking functions satisfied by the system. Pylyshyn often makes it sound as if the primitive operations of a programming language define a functional architecture, but this cannot be right. The functional architecture of the mind is supposed to be that aspect of the mind's structure that remains fixed across changes in data structures (i.e., in what is represented). This is the program (sense ii) itself, including its control structure, not the primitive operations of a language we might write it in.

7   I take this formulation from Parfit (1984), who argues that there is no "further fact" to personal identity beyond the facts of interpsychological state relations.

8   By mechanical variables, here, I mean real mechanical properties that vary in magnitude. I do NOT mean symbols.

9   The tracking referred to here is not causal, of course. A computational system can simulate a natural one without there being any significant causal relations between a symbol and the property it tracks in the simulated system. This is important because it allows for the fact that a computational system can simulate hypothetical systems and counterfactual systems, as well as abstract systems and systems that are actual and concrete but not in any significant causal interaction with the similator.

10 As I use these terms, instantiation is a special case of simulation, viz. the case in which the interpretations are abstract objects of some kind: numbers, sets, propositions, concepts (construed not as psychological items but as corresponding to predicates in the way propositions correspond to sentences), truth-conditions, and the like. I restrict instantiation to abstract functions (functions with abstracta as arguments and values) because instantiation seems most natural as a relation between something abstract and an instance. Simulation is just like instantiation except that the arguments and values of the function simulated needn't be abstracta.

11 For those who like definition: r s-represents x in $S =_{df}$ there are functions f, g, and I such that S satisfies g, g simulates f under interpretation I, and $I(r) = x$.

12   Here we are talking not about a particular distance (3 meters, say) but about *whatever* distance an unaccelerated body travels for an arbitrarily specified velocity and time. Plug a velocity and a time into the geometry as the base and the height of the rectangle, respectively, and the volume is the distance traveled.

13   A "buggy" bridge program may *have* no Proper Interpretation in the bridge domain, if it is buggy enough. It might, by coincidence, have a Proper Interpretation in some other domain – a domain no one has thought of. In such a case, we have representation without realizing it, but not the representation we intended.

14   Indeed, this is something of a false dichotomy, since a data structure is what it is to some extent because of the processes that operate on it. The difference between a representation of a list and a set, after all, is typically simply a matter of whether it is possible to exploit order. We think of the fundamental data structures in LISP as lists because (car 'list) returns the *first* member of a list rather than some element or other (e.g., the one that *happens* to be first *on this particular occasion*).

15   Correction involves getting it right after all, perhaps by adding a special-case rule. Avoiding the error involves refusing to deal with cases in which failure is likely or inevitable.

16   Actually, I'm not at all sure about this. On the one hand, what makes an adding machine usable for us isn't what makes an adding machine. On the other hand, the question of explaining addition (or building an adding machine) comes up only in the context of some antecedently specified interpretation scheme – a scheme we know to be "workable" (i.e., usable by the systems that will need to use it).

17   In the mathematical cases it cannot be causal connections between symbol and number, because numbers have no causal powers.

18   It is sometimes important that a system can simulate a non-numerical function f while instantiating a numerical function f'. If we know what it is (i.e., if we can give it a standard mathematical expression), the numerical function f' will give us a mathematical handle on the instantiating function g, and hence (indirectly) a handle on f.

19   Actions are said to be rational or irrational, of course, but only because they are themselves Intentional (as well as, sometimes, intentional). Actions, as Aristotle pointed out, are assessable as rational just to the extent that they can be treated as *conclusions* (of practical syllogisms, say) and, hence, as having propositional contents. Mere behaviors – mere motions, Aristotle would have called them – cannot be so assessed. Actions are what Dretske (1981) would call digitized behaviors.

20   Part of the difficulty in reconciling covariance theories with the CTC is that they take the empiricist view that perception is the paradigm of cognition. But perception, as the empiricists conceived it, is not an inferential process, and hence there is no room for a CTC explanation of perception as empiricists conceived it. The CTC, of course, treats perception as an inferential process. This provides the CTC with an explanandum – a target function to simulate – and hence with some space for s-representation to play an explanatory role. But a corollary of this approach is that the distal object to percept relation is mediated by representation, and hence cannot be invoked to define the representation relation.

21   I mean here inference in the sense of Harman (1987), not inference in the sense of deductive proof.

Systems of formal logic contain what are called rules of inference. But such rules don't tell you what to infer; they are only part of a system that determines the validity, not rationality, of an inference already made. They thus have little to do with inference as it is meant here, i.e., with inference construed as the essence of cognition: *generating* a result that is *rational* (rational enough) relative to the situation you are in.

22. The specification of a cognitive function is what Marr (1982) calls (somewhat misleadingly) giving a computational theory.

23 There is another possibility: that cognitive systems don't deal with clothing and faces "in their own terms"; they deal with such matters such as physics and chemistry deal with them. My suspicion is that this is not plausible on empirical grounds; for example, the psychological evidence that faces constitute a "special" domain for people seems quite strong. See, e.g., Gregory (1970).

13 Computation and Mental Representation

Terence Horgan

In this paper, which is largely excerpted from sections 5 and 6 of Horgan (1992), first I summarize the account of mental representation proposed in Cummins (1989a); then I pose several challenges to the account; finally I raise a question about the philosophical rationale for Cummins's project and others like it, and I urge the importance of an alternative philosophical project that has been largely overlooked in recent philosophy of mind.

I

Cummins's book is directed at what he calls The Problem of Representation, which he characterizes this way:

> [T]he Problem of Representation . . . is, at least as I understand it, a paradigmatic problem in the philosophy of science. To a large extent, empirical theories of cognition can and do take a notion of mental content as an explanatory primitive. But this is a kind of explanatory loan (Dennett, 1978a): if it turns out that the notion of mental representation cannot be given a satisfactory explication – if, in particular, no account of the nature of the (mental) representation relation can be given that is consistent with the empirical theory that assumes it – then, at least in this respect, that theory must be regarded as ill founded, and hence as a less than adequate response to the drive for the kind of thorough intellectual understanding that motivates the scientific theory in the first place. (pp. 1–2)

Cummins does not say explicitly what would count, by his lights, as a "satisfactory explication" of mental representation. But presumably he has in mind something like tractable conditions, formulable in non-intentional and non-semantic vocabulary, that are either *necessary and sufficient* for something's being a mental representation with a specific representational content, or anyway are at least *sufficient*. Tractability is my own term; roughly, a specification is tractable if it is relatively compact, relatively non-baroque, non-disjunctive, and cognitively surveyable. The deep methodological assumption underlying

Cummins's whole enterprise is that the notion of mental representation, as employed in empirical theory, will turn out to be illegitimate ("ill founded") *unless* such an account of it can be given. (I will return to this assumption in section III.)

His principal concern is the notion of mental representation employed in computational theories of cognition. Thus he seeks an account, within the context of such theories, of what it is for a state of system to have a representational content, and of what determines the specific content it has. He holds that the idea of mental representation plays somewhat different explanatory roles in ordinary belief/desire intentional psychology, in orthodox computational cognitive science, in connectionist cognitive science, and in neuroscience. So we should not assume, he cautions, that the relevant notion of mental representation for the Computational Theory of Cognition (the CTC) is the same one required by ordinary belief/desire psychology.

Nor should we assume that a mature computational account of cognition would traffic directly in states that play the role of the propositional attitudes of common sense and that involve computational relations to representations whose contents are those of the attitudes themselves. "We need to keep open the possibility that, e.g., belief attribution, though a legitimate case of semantic characterization, is not a semantic characterization of any representation in the believer" (p. 15).

He discusses four kinds of answers that have been proposed to the problem of mental representation, both as this problem was posed in the history of modern philosophy and as it is posed nowadays: answers that appeal respectively to similarity, to covariance, to adaptational role, and to functional role.

After a brief discussion of why it became clear in the seventeenth century that similarity theories, appealing to the alleged resemblance between mental representations and the things they represent, are not tenable, he turns to Locke's version of the theory that the essence of mental representation is covariance between the occurrence of the mental representation and the presence of the thing represented. He argues that Locke's account faces insurmountable problems, and that these same problems also arise for contemporary covariance accounts – notably Fodor's and Dretske's. The most fundamental difficulty is that such theories cannot satisfactorily accommodate the phenomenon of *mis*-representation. He maintains that the standard way of trying to handle misrepresentation – viz. via appeal to covariation in an *idealized* cognitive system – is not tenable. Among other reasons, idealizing away error must inevitably involve envisioning a cognitive system whose design is fundamentally different from that of systems describable by the CTC. "Error," he argues, "is the inevitable price of computational tractability" (p. 54).

Adaptational role accounts of mental representation, such as Millikan's, get dismissed rather quickly as not applicable to the notion of representation assumed by the CTC. For, these accounts are committed to a "historical" notion of representation – a notion under which a state's being a representation with a specific content depends upon its ontogenetic history, in the individual organism and/or the organism's species. But the CTC, Cummins claims, assumes an ahistorical notion of representation.

He then proposes an account of mental representation he calls "interpretational semantics." Although this position is ontologically equivalent to a kind of functional role semantics, he says, it is not really an alternative to traditional theories of mental representation, because it is specifically tailored to the CTC's version of this notion; it is *not* an account of the kind of representation presupposed by commonsense belief/desire psychology.

The account goes as follows. For a physical system that counts as a computational system, such as an adding machine or a digital computer, there will be some function g that is literally *satisfied* by the system: the entities in the domain and range of the function will be entities physically tokened in the machine, and temporal sequences of tokenings of these entities in the machine will accord with the function itself. For instance,

> The input to a typical adding machine is a sequence of button pressings: $\langle C,$ $M, +, N, = \rangle$, i.e., $\langle clear, first\ addend, plus, second\ addend, equals \rangle$. The output is a display state, D, which is a numeral representing the sum of the two addends. We may think of the button-pressing sequences as arguments to a function g that gives display states as values. An adding machine *satisfies* g; that is, the arguments and values of g are literally states of the physical system. (see this volume, p. 280)

The function g is automatically computed by the physical system, by virtue of the system's casual architecture – computation being program execution, and program execution being "disciplined step satisfaction" (see p. 281). Representation enters the scene when there is some further function I, involving entities in its domain and range that are not literally tokened in the physical system itself, that is suitably related to the function g. In the case of a typical adding machine, for instance, this is the *addition* function, whose domain and range traffic in numbers rather than in states literally tokened in the physical device:

> Addition . . . relates numbers, not physical states of some machine, so a physical system cannot literally satisfy the plus function. What an adding machine does is *instantiate* the plus function. It *instantiates* addition by *satisfying* the function g whose arguments and values represent the arguments and values of the addition function, or, in other words, have those arguments and values as interpretations. (see p. 280)

Representation is just the pairwise relation that holds between entities in the domain and range of g and associated entities in the domain and range of I, when g and I are themselves suitably related. For this interpretation relation between g and I to obtain, there must be a structure preserving 1–1 mapping from g to I (i.e., g and I must be isomorphic); and certain further conditions must also be met – more about these presently. When all the conditions are met, the function *g* *simulates* the function *I*. Accordingly, Cummins calls pairing relation between *g* entities and *I* entities, *s-representation* (for "simulation representation").

Three features of Cummins's account deserve special emphasis. First is his way with *mis*-representation:

> [I]n the world of s-representation, misrepresentation differs from failure to represent only in degree; failed representation becomes misrepresentation when the failure isn't too bad . . . [W]e cannot suppose . . . that first there is the issue of what (if anything) is represented and then there is the issue of what processes act on the representations. What is s-represented is essentially a matter of the processes, for it is essentially a matter of simulation. And simulation is essentially a matter of degree. (see pp. 287–8)

Thus, in the end he does not really hold that s-representation requires a full-fledged isomorphism between *g* and *I*; evidently it is enough that there be something like an *approximate* isomorphism (the sort of relation that is easy to understand but hard to "explicate").

Second, he regards s-representation as non-unique: normally a variety of different functions will be simulated, either perfectly or imperfectly, by a given function *g* satisfied by a computational system. Thus, there is no such thing as s-representation *simpliciter*, but only s-representation relative to a specific function, a "target of simulation." For him, this is a virtue:

> We needn't *worry* that we can always trade misrepresentation of *x* for accurate representation of Something Else; we *can* do that, but it doesn't *matter*. . . . No doubt adding machines simulate functions other than +, but that does not compromise the standard explanation of addition in adding machines. (see p. 288)

Third, he never explicitly spells out the additional conditions for s-representation, over and above the requirement that the simulating function *g* should be (approximately) isomorphic to the simulated function *I*. He admits that the isomorphism requirement alone is much too weak. (If structure preservation is all that's required, then any symbol in any physical computational system will represent virtually anything at all – will have virtually any content – relative to *some* function simulated by the system's *g*-function.) And he does describe intuitively, via examples, the sorts of further restrictions he thinks are needed. One is that simulated function should provide a *direct* interpretation of the physical system's symbolic data structures – so that the adding machine computes $x + y$ but not $2\pi(x + y)$. "I must confess that I don't know how to define *directness*" (see p. 290). Another is that the simulated function should not be a "degenerate" target for simulation – as is the function *f* that is identical to the addition function except that the number 5 is everywhere replaced, in the function's domain and range, by Richard Nixon. Intuitively, the trouble is that the numeral "5" in the adding machine "doesn't track Richard Nixon as he is buffeted around by any natural discipline" (see p. 291). "Once again, I am embarrassed by the fact that I have no general account of what makes [this function] a degenerate target for simulation" (see p. 291).

Mental representation, as construed by the CTC, is just a special case of s-representation, claims Cummins.

> [H]aving a cognitive capacity is instantiating a function that relates propositional contents, i.e., a function that takes propositional contents as arguments and values and relates them as premises to conclusion. A cognitive system, in short, is an *inference engine* – a system that merits an inferential characterization ... Under this conception, the problem of cognition becomes the problem of explaining the fact that the system is described by a *cognitive function*, or, for AI, of building a system that is described by a cognitive function. (see pp. 293–4)

Since, on this account, the notion of representation presupposed by the CTC is non-unique, it is not the same as the notion presupposed by commonsense belief/desire psychology. Underlying our ascriptions of beliefs and other propositional attitudes to one another, he recognizes, is the assumption that the contents of these states are (by and large) unique. Hence, he thinks, belief/desire psychology will not, and cannot, emerge as simply a component of a developed computational theory of cognition; the intentionality of beliefs cannot turn out to be just a byproduct of the account of content that is appropriate for the CTC. He makes a few brief and speculative remarks about how commonsense psychology might actually be related to the CTC, but leaves this matter largely open.

II

I turn now from summary to commentary. Let me raise three concerns about Cummins's positive proposal. First is a worry about the explanatory relevance of content, given his (cheerful) admission that s-representational content generally will be non-unique. To the extent that any of various different, mutually incompatible, contents are all correctly assignable to the symbolic data structures that count (under the CTC) as mental representations, there arises the *prima facie* presumption that none of these contents really has any explanatory relevance to the system's performance. If the distinct content assignments to the data structures are all on a par *vis-à-vis* explanation of why the system does what it does, then it appears that they cancel each other out – i.e., none of them has any real explanatory relevance at all. Thus, to the extent that the CTC assumes the explanatory relevance of mental representation (and I agree with Cummins that it does), his account seems inadequate.

Of course the explanatory relevance of content is itself a highly vexed issue in contemporary philosophy of mind. Cummins does have some things to say about it. He lays down some plausible-looking conditions on explanatory relevance; and he argues that s-representational contents, despite their non-uniqueness, satisfy these conditions. But the trouble is that the conditions do not seem *sufficient* for explanatory relevance, because they do not rule out cases of properties that seem intuitively to be mere epiphenomenal correlates of the properties that are genuinely explanatorily relevant to a system's behavior. If the representational content of symbolic data structures is non-unique, and if the various distinct but incompatible contents correctly assignable to data structures are on a par explanatorily, then it is hard not to conclude that these contents are all mere epiphenomenal correlates of those properties of the data structures that do real explanatory work.

My second concern involves Cummins's contention that there is a generic notion of representation that is both (i) non-unique, and (ii) applicable to computational systems at all levels of complexity – from lowly adding machines, to microcomputers and mainframes, to (if the CTC is right) human beings. There is a very different way of viewing representation in this complexity hierarchy, which many of us find more plausible than Cummins's. To wit: symbolic data structures in adding machines are not representations *for the system* at all, but are only representations for the community of people who design and/or use these artifacts. Likewise, *mutatis mutandis*, for the microcomputers and mainframes that currently exist. Although it is a highly vexed question what it would be for data structures to be representations "for a system," presumably the answer has something to do with how those structures would contribute to that system's capacity to successfully navigate a sufficiently complex body through the vicissitudes of embodied existence in the world. (The embodied system would successfully get around in the world, despite all these vicissitudes, because – and only because – of systematically content-appropriate ways that these structures figure in its behavioral control systems.)[1]

Those, like me, who find this alternative perspective more plausible than Cummins's are not likely to find persuasive his argument that the notion of representation presupposed by the CTC is a non-unique one. For, much of the dialectical force of his argument rests on the fact that in general there need not be any unique function that is mirrored by a computational system's inner symbol-manipulating activity. But this fact becomes relevant to the computational theory of *cognition* only if one accepts the contention that data structures in artifacts such as adding machines are representations *for the system itself*. Only then does it begin to seem natural to say that, for computational systems generically, for-the-system representation is mere simulation.

A third concern about Cummins's proposal is the size of the gap between what he seeks – viz. a "satisfactory explication," in non-intentional, non-semantic terms, of mental representation as this notion figures in the CTC, and what he actually delivers. As noted already, he leaves the explication unfinished: he does not cash the notions of *direct interpretation* and *degenerate target of simulation*, to which he resorts in his account; and he admits that he has no idea *how* to cash them. This admission lends credence to the suspicion that a tractable naturalistic "explication" of the concept of mental representation is not to be had – not even for the relatively weak, non-unique notion of s-representation which Cummins claims is the only one presupposed by the CTC. Still less, then, is such an explication likely to be possible for the stronger kind of intentionality that Cummins himself concedes is presupposed by commonsense belief/desire psychology.

III

Why should one even *expect* such an explication to be possible, for either kind of intentionality? Cummins states his reason in the passage I quoted at the beginning. He says in effect that a notion of mental content cannot be an "explanatory primitive" within our overall scientific account of the world, even if it is an explanatory primitive within computational cognitive science *per se*. He evidently reasons this way: if a notion of mental content is not an explanatory primitive in our overall intellectual understanding of things, then it must be susceptible to a tractable naturalistic explication.

Other philosophers have been pursuing similar "explication" projects for similar reasons. A notable case in point is Jerry Fodor, who writes:

> I suppose that sooner or later the physicists will complete the catalogue they've been compiling of the ultimate and irreducible properties of things. When they do, the likes of *spin*, *charm*, and *charge* will perhaps appear upon their list. But *aboutness* surely won't; intentionality simply doesn't go that deep. It's hard to see, in the face of this consideration, how one can be a Realist about intentionality without also being, to some extent or other, a Reductionist. If the semantic and the intentional are real properties of things, it must be in virtue of their identity with (or maybe their supervenience on?) properties that are themselves *neither* intentional *nor* semantic. If aboutness is real, it must really be something else.
>
> And, indeed, the deepest motivation for intentional irrealism derives . . . from a certain ontological intuition: that there is no place for intentional categories in a physicalistc view of the world; that the intentional can't be *naturalized*. (Fodor, 1987, p. 97)

Fodor too supposes that if aboutness is not an explanatorily basic feature of the world – if it is *not* among the "ultimate and irreducible properties of things" – then it must be susceptible to a tractable naturalistic explication. He and others have lately been using the term "naturalization" for the project of *giving* such an explication – that is, giving a tractable specification, in non-intentional and non-semantic terms, of sufficient conditions (or sufficient and necessary conditions) for a state's being an intentional state with a specific content.

So there is an underlying assumption behind philosophical projects such as Cummins's and Fodor's. It might be formulated this way:

> Either (i) there are tractably specifiable non-intentional, non-semantic, sufficient conditions (or sufficient and necessary conditions) for something's being a mental representation with a specific representational content, or (ii) mental content is among the ultimate, fundamental, and unexplainable properties of things.

This assumption is evidently so deeply ingrained that is not clearly noticed *as* an assumption.[2]

I think it is time for philosophers to notice it, to subject it to critical scrutiny, and to rethink the question of how to accommodate intentionality within a broadly naturalistic metaphysical worldview. I will close with a few remarks on this theme.

First, *one* aspect of the non-basic metaphysical status of mental-content properties, in contrast to the likes of such properties as spin, charm, and change, is that intentional properties are probably *supervenient* on physico-chemical properties and relations.

Second, the thesis that semantic and intentional properties supervene on natural properties does not entail the existence of naturalistic sufficient conditions of the sort that Cummins, Fodor, and others seek to provide. For, things might be like this: although the intentional is supervenient upon the non-intentional, in general there is no way *tractably to specify* the non-semantic, non-intentional, conditions that suffice for intentional phenomena. Although a physical supervenience base might always exist for any manifestation of aboutness, in general any adequate non-intentional, non-semantic characterization of the supervenience base might be enormously baroque and complex. Perhaps, for instance, the supervenience base for the intentional content of a token thought (or token utterance, or token inscription) generally involves a good-sized chunk of space-time extending well beyond the cognizer's own body and well beyond the time at which the token thought occurs; perhaps it involves a rather gargantuan number of physico-chemical goings-on within that extended spatio-temporal region; and perhaps there isn't any simple way to describe, in non-intentional and non-semantic vocabulary, all the *relevant* aspects of this hugely complex supervenience base. Perhaps, in addition, the supervenience of the intentional on the non-intentional is largely a holistic matter – with the intentionality of thoughts, utterances, and inscriptions supervening not individually (one token at a time), but rather collectively, as part of the correct global intentional interpretation of a cognizer – or perhaps of the cognizer's whole community or whole species. In short, it might be that the search for tractably specifiable, cognitively surveyable, non-intentional and non-semantic sufficient conditions for intentionality is utterly hopeless – and yet that the intentional supervenes upon the non-intentional nonetheless.

Third, there are a variety of reasons for being skeptical about the very possibility of providing the kinds of tractably specifiable naturalistic conditions for intentionality that Cummins, Fodor, and others seek to provide. For one thing, there is no particular reason to *expect* such conditions, given that supervenience itself does not presuppose them. Moreover, proposals of this kind usually end up susceptible to counterexamples of one sort or another; inductive evidence based on past failures both in this arena, and in other philosophical arenas where attempts at reductive analyses have been pursued, is that there always *will* be counterexamples to such proposals. In addition, it seems fairly likely that human semantic and intentional concepts, like most other human concepts, don't have cleanly delineatable necessary and sufficient conditions at all; the general claim about the structure of human concepts is strongly suggested by work in cognitive science on concepts and categories by Eleanor Rosch and others (Rosch, 1973, 1975, 1978; Rips, 1975; Smith and Medin, 1981). (These kinds of considerations are adumbrated at greater length in Stich, 1992; Tye, 1992; and Stich and Laurence, 1994.)

Fourth, the supervenience of the intentional on the physical does not, by itself, suffice for the naturalistic accommodation of intentionality. Consider again Fodor's observation, in the above-quoted passage, that aboutness will not be in the physicists' eventual catalogue of the ultimate and irreducible properties of things. For anyone who professes to hold what Fodor calls a "physicalistic view of the world," this non-ultimacy of intentionality should not be construed as *merely* a matter of supervenience upon the non-intentional. For, if certain interlevel supervenience facts are themselves *sui generis* and unexplainable, then the supervening properties will thereby qualify for inclusion on the list of ultimate and irreducible properties of things – supervenience notwithstanding. (From a physicalist/naturalist perspective, one reason to reject G. E. Moore's meta-ethical position is his claim that there are certain synthetic necessary truths, of the form "Anything with natural property N is intrinsically valuable," that are utterly unexplainable and thus are metaphysically rock-bottom.) So metaphysical physicalism/naturalism should not merely assert that the intentional supervenes upon the non-intentional; it should also assert that interlevel supervenience facts are (at least in principle) *explainable*, rather than being themselves included among the fundamental, unexplainable facts about the world.[3]

In sum, recent naturalistic programs in the philosophy of mind have been too stringent in one respect, and too lax in another. On one hand, it is excessive to insist on tractably specifiable sufficient conditions for intentionality, as Cummins and Fodor do; but on the other hand, it is not kosher to invoke supervenience relations unless they are subject to naturalistically acceptable modes of explanation. So some rethinking of programs is called for, especially for those who seek a philosophical account that accommodates intentionality within the natural order described by physical science. Philosophers should be asking (i) what kind(s) of explanation of physical/intentional supervenience relations would count as naturalistically kosher, and why; and (ii) whether these supervenence relations are *in fact* susceptible to such explanations (cf. Horgan, 1984, forthcoming; Horgan and Timmons, 1992). It seems entirely possible that things could turn out this way: although (a) there are no *tractably specifiable* non-semantic and non-intentional sufficient conditions for intentionality, nevertheless (b) the supervenience of the intentional on the physical is indeed susceptible, in principle, to naturalistically acceptable modes of explanation.

Notes

"Computation and Mental Representation" appears here for the first time by kind permission of the author.

1   Is it necessary for the system actually to be navigationally tethered to such a body, or for the system's representations of its environment actually to be caused by an environment of the kind represented? I am inclined to say no; the Brentano intentionality of the system's representations could be radically at odds with its actual environment, and with the actual etiology and actual effects of those representations. The system could be, and could have always been, a brain in a vat. Cf. Tienson (forthcoming).

2   The tendency not to notice it is enhanced by terminology. The term "explication," for instance, does double duty: on one hand, it evokes the idea that mental content is somehow explainable via something more basic, rather than being explanatorily *sui generis*; on the other hand, given its history of usage in analytic philosophy, it evokes philosophical projects seeking reductive, tractably specifiable, sufficient and necessary conditions for some term or concept. The term "naturalization," as recently employed in philosophy of mind, does the same kind of double duty. The upshot is a tendency to reason this way: "A physicalistic worldview is surely right, and realism about intentionality is surely right; hence the intentional can be naturalized (explicated); hence the sort of project Cummins, Fodor, and company are pursuing can be successfully carried out."

3   An analogous point holds even if intentionality turns out to be *identical* to some physical relation, rather than being a non-physical relation that supervenes on the physical. Now the key questions are about interlevel linkages between terms and/ or concepts. In virtue of what, one wants to know, does such-and-such physical relation, rather than various other candidate physical relations, count as the relation picked by our *term* "reference," and by the concept that term expresses?

14 True Believers: The Intentional Strategy and Why it Works

Daniel Dennett

Death Speaks

There was a merchant in Baghdad who sent his servant to market to buy provisions and in a little while the servant came back, white and trembling, and said, Master, just now when I was in the market-place I was jostled by a woman in the crowd and when I turned I saw it was Death that jostled me. She looked at me and made a threatening gesture; now, lend me your horse, and I will ride away from this city and avoid my fate. I will go to Samarra and there Death will not find me. The merchant lent him his horse, and the servant mounted it, and he dug his spurs in its flanks and as fast as the horse could gallop he went. Then the merchant went down to the market-place and he saw me standing in the crowd, and he came to me and said, why did you make a threatening gesture to my servant when you saw him this morning? That was not a threatening gesture, I said, it was only a start of surprise. I was astonished to see him in Baghdad, for I had an appointment with him tonight in Samarra.

W. Somerset Maugham

In the social sciences, talk about *belief* is ubiquitous. Since social scientists are typically self-conscious about their methods, there is also a lot of talk about *talk about belief*. And since belief is a genuinely curious and perplexing phenomenon, showing many different faces to the world, there is abundant controversy. Sometimes belief attribution appears to be a dark, risky, and imponderable business – especially when exotic, and more particularly religious or superstitious, beliefs are in the limelight. These are not the only troublesome cases; we also court argument and skepticism when we attribute beliefs to non-human animals, or to infants, or to computers or robots. Or when the beliefs we feel constrained to attribute to an apparently healthy, adult member of our own society are contradictory, or even just wildly false. A biologist colleague of mine was once called on the telephone by a man in a bar who wanted him to settle a bet. The man asked: "Are rabbits birds?" "No," said the biologist. "Damn!" said the man as he hung up. Now could he *really* have believed that rabbits were birds? Could anyone really and truly be attributed that belief? Perhaps, but it would take a bit of a story to bring us to accept it.

In all of these cases belief attribution appears beset with subjectivity, infected with cultural relativism, prone to "indeterminacy of radical translation" – clearly an enterprise demanding special talents: the art of phenomenological analysis, hermeneutics, empathy, *Verstehen*, and all that. On other occasions, normal occasions, when familiar beliefs are the topic, belief attribution looks as easy as speaking prose and as objective and reliable as counting beans in a dish. Particularly when these straightforward cases are before us, it is quite plausible to suppose that in principle (if not yet in practice) it would be possible to confirm these simple, objective belief attributions by *finding something inside the believer's head* – by finding the beliefs themselves, in effect. "Look," someone might say, "You either believe there's milk in the fridge or you don't believe there's milk in the fridge" (you might have no opinion, in the latter case). But if you do believe this, that's a perfectly objective fact about you, and it must come down in the end to your brain's being in some particular physical state. If we knew more about physiological psychology, we could in principle determine the facts about your brain state and thereby determine whether or not you believe there is milk in the fridge, even if you were determined to be silent or disingenuous on the topic. In principle, on this view physiological psychology could trump the results – or non-results – of any "black box" method in the social sciences that divines beliefs (and other mental features) by behavioral, cultural, social, historical, *external* criteria.

These differing reflections congeal into two opposing views on the nature of belief attribution, and hence on the nature of belief. The latter, a variety of *realism*, likens the question of whether a person has a particular belief to the question of whether a person is infected with a particular virus – a perfectly objective internal matter of fact about which an observer can often make educated guesses of great reliability. The former, which we could call *interpretationism* if we absolutely had to give it a name, likens the question of whether a person has a particular belief to the question of whether a person is immoral, or has style, or talent, or would make a good wife. Faced with such questions, we preface our answers with "well, it all depends on what you're interested in," or make some similar acknowledgment of the relativity of the issue. "It's a matter of interpretation," we say. These two opposing views, so baldly stated, do not fairly represent any serious theorists' positions, but they do express views that are typically seen as mutually exclusive and exhaustive; the theorist must be friendly with one and only one of these themes.

I think this is a mistake. My thesis will be that, while belief is a perfectly objective phenomenon (that apparently makes me a realist), it can be discerned only from the point of view of one who adopts a certain *predictive strategy*, and its existence can be confirmed only by an assessment of the success of that strategy (that apparently makes me an interpretationist).

First I will describe the strategy, which I call the intentional strategy or adopting the intentional stance. To a first approximation, the intentional strategy consists of treating the object whose behavior you want to predict as a rational agent with beliefs and desires and other mental stages exhibiting what Brentano and others call *intentionality*. The strategy has often been described before, but I shall try to put this very familiar material in a new light by showing *how* it works and by showing *how well* it works.

Then I will argue that any object – or, as I shall say, any *system* – whose behavior is well predicted by this strategy is in the fullest sense of the word a believer. *What it is* to be a true believer is to be an *intentional system*, a system whose behavior is reliably and voluminously predictable via the intentional strategy. I have argued for this position before (Dennett, 1971, 1976, 1978a), and my arguments have so far garnered few converts and many presumed counterexamples. I shall try again here, harder, and shall also deal with several compelling objections.

The Intentional Strategy and How it Works

There are many strategies, some good, some bad. Here is a strategy, for instance, for predicting the future behavior of a person: determine the date and hour of the person's birth and then feed this modest datum into one or another astrological algorithm for generating predictions of the person's prospects. This strategy is deplorably popular. Its popularity is deplorable only because we have such good reasons for believing that it does not work (*pace* Feyerabend, 1978). When astrological predictions come true this is sheer luck, or the result of such vagueness or ambiguity in the prophecy that almost any eventuality can be construed to confirm it. But suppose the astrological strategy did in fact work well on some people. We could call those people *astrological systems* – systems whose behavior was, as a matter of fact, predictable by the astrological strategy. If there were such people, such astrological systems, we would be more interested than most of us in fact are in *how the astrological strategy works* – that is, we would be interested in the rules, principles, or methods of astrology. We could find out how the strategy works by asking astrologers, reading their books, and observing them in action. But we would also be curious about *why* it worked. We might find that astrologers had no useful opinions about this latter question – they either had no theory of why it worked or their theories were pure hokum. Having a good strategy is one thing; knowing why it works is another.

So far as we know, however, the class of astrological systems is empty, so the astrological strategy is of interest only as a social curiosity. Other strategies have better credentials. Consider the physical strategy, or physical stance; if you want to predict the behavior of a system, determine its physical constitution (perhaps all the way down to the microphysical level) and the physical nature of the impingements upon it, and use your knowledge of the laws of physics to predict the outcome for any input. This is the grand and impractical strategy of Laplace for predicting the entire future of everything in the universe, but it has more modest, local, actually usable versions. The chemist or physicist in the laboratory can use this strategy to predict the behavior of exotic materials, but equally the cook in the kitchen can predict the effect of leaving the pot on the burner too long. The strategy is not always practically available, but that it will always work *in principle* is a dogma of the physical sciences (I ignore the minor complications raised by the subatomic indeterminacies of quantum physics).

Sometimes, in any event, it is more effective to switch from the physical stance to what I call the design stance, where one ignores the actual (possibly messy) details of the physical constitution of an object, and, on the assumption that it has a certain design, predicts that it will behave *as it is designed to behave* under various circumstances. For instance, most users of computers have not the foggiest idea what physical principles are responsible for the computer's highly reliable, and hence predictable, behavior. But if they have a good idea of what the computer is designed to do (a description of its operation at any one of the many possible levels of abstraction), they can predict its behavior with great accuracy and reliability, subject to disconfirmation only in cases of physical malfunction. Less dramatically, almost anyone can predict when an alarm clock will sound on the basis of the most casual inspection of its exterior. One does not know or care to know whether it is spring wound, battery driven, sunlight powered, made of brass wheels and jewel bearings or silicon chips – one just assumes that it is designed so that the alarm will sound when it is set to sound, and it is set to sound where it appears to be set to sound, and the clock will keep on running until that time and beyond, and is designed to run more or less accurately, and so forth. For more accurate and detailed design stance predictions of the alarm clock, one must descend to a less abstract level of description of its design; for instance, to the level at which gears are described, but their material is not specified.

Only the designed behavior of a system is predictable from the design stance, of course. If you want to predict the behavior of an alarm clock when it is pumped full of liquid helium, revert to the physical stance. Not just artifacts but also many biological objects (plants and animals, kidneys and hearts, stamens and pistils) behave in ways that can be predicted from the design stance. They are not just physical systems but designed systems.

Sometimes even the design stance is practically inaccessible, and then there is yet another stance or strategy one can adopt: the intentional stance. Here is how it works: first you decide to treat the object whose behavior is to be predicted as a rational agent; then you figure out what beliefs that agent ought to have, given its place in the world and its purpose. Then you figure out what desires it ought to have, on the same considerations, and finally you predict that this rational agent will act to further its goals in the light of its beliefs. A little practical reasoning from the chosen set of beliefs and desires will in many – but not all – instances yield a decision about what the agent ought to do; that is what you predict the agent *will* do.

The strategy becomes clearer with a little elaboration. Consider first how we go about populating each other's heads with beliefs. A few truisms: sheltered people tend to be ignorant; if you expose someone to something he comes to know all about it. In general, it seems, we come to believe all the truths about the parts of the world around us we are put in a position to learn about. Exposure to *x*, that is, sensory confrontation with *x* over some suitable period of time, is the *normally sufficient* condition for knowing (or having true beliefs) about *x*. As we say, we come to *know all about* the things around us. Such exposure is only *normally* sufficient for knowledge, but this is not the large escape hatch it might appear; our threshold for accepting abnormal ignorance in the face of exposure is quite high. "I didn't know the gun was loaded," said by one who was observed to be present, sighted, and awake during the loading, meets with a variety of utter skepticism that only the most outlandish supporting tale could overwhelm.

Of course we do not come to learn or remember all the truths our sensory histories avail us. In spite of the phrase "know all about," what we come to know, normally, are only all the *relevant* truths our sensory histories avail us. I do not typically come to know the ratio of spectacle-wearing people to trousered people in a room I inhabit, though if this interested me, it would be readily learnable. It is not just that some facts about my environment are below my thresholds of discrimination or beyond the integration and holding power of my memory (such as the height in inches of all the people present), but that many perfectly detectable, graspable, memorable facts are of no interest to me and hence do not come to be believed by me. So one rule for attributing beliefs in the intentional strategy is this: attribute as beliefs all the truths relevant to the system's interests (or desires) that the system's experience to date has made available. This rule leads to attributing somewhat too much – since we all are somewhat forgetful, even of important things. It also fails to capture the false beliefs we are all known to have. But the attribution of false belief, *any* false belief, requires a special genealogy, which will be seen to consist in the main in true beliefs. Two paradigm cases: *S* believes (falsely) that *p*, because *S* believes (truly) that Jones told him that *p*, that Jones is pretty clever, that Jones did not intend to deceive him, . . . etc. Second case: *S* believes (falsely) that there is a snake on the barstool, because *S* believes (truly) that he seems to see a snake on the barstool, is himself sitting in a bar not a yard from the barstool he sees, and so forth. The falsehood has to start somewhere; the seed may be sown in hallucination, illusion, a normal variety of simple misperception, memory deterioration, or deliberate fraud, for instance, but the false beliefs that are reaped grow in a culture medium of true beliefs.

Then there are the arcane and sophisticated beliefs, true and false, that are so often at the focus of attention in discussions of belief attribution. They do not arise directly, goodness knows, from exposure to mundane things and events, but their attribution requires tracing out a lineage of mainly good argument or reasoning from the bulk of beliefs already attributed. An implication of the intentional strategy, then, is that true believers mainly believe truths. If anyone could devise an agreed-upon method of individuating and counting beliefs (which I doubt very much), we would see that all but the smallest portion (say, less than ten percent) of a person's beliefs were attributable under our first rule.[1]

Note that this rule is a derived rule, an elaboration and further specification of the fundamental rule: attribute those beliefs the system *ought to have*. Note also that the rule interacts with the attribution of desires. How do we attribute the desires (preferences, goals, interests) on whose basis we will shape the list of beliefs? We attribute the desires the system *ought to have*. That is the fundamental rule. It dictates, on a first pass, that we attribute the familiar list of highest, or most basic, desires to people: survival, absence of pain, food, comfort, procreation, entertainment. Citing any one of these desires typically terminates the "Why?" game of reason giving. One is not supposed to need an ulterior motive for desiring comfort or pleasure or the prolongation of one's existence. Derived rules of desire attribution interact with belief attributions. Trivially, we have the rule: attribute desires for those things a system believes to be good for it. Somewhat more informatively, attribute desires for those things a system believes to be best means to other ends it desires. The attribution of bizarre and detrimental desires thus requires, like the attribution of false beliefs, special stories.

The interaction between belief and desire becomes trickier when we consider what desires we attribute on the basis of verbal behavior. The capacity to *express* desires in language opens the floodgates of desire attribution. "I want a two-egg mushroom omelette, some French bread and butter, and a half bottle of lightly chilled white Burgundy." How could one begin to attribute a desire for anything so specific in the absence of such verbal declaration? How, indeed, could a creature come to *contract* such a specific desire without the aid of language? Language *enables* us to formulate highly specific desires, but it also *forces* us on occasion to commit ourselves to desires altogether more stringent in their conditions of satisfaction than anything we would otherwise have any reason to endeavor to satisfy. Since in order to get what you want you often have to say what you want, and since you often cannot say what you want without saying something more specific than you antecedently mean, you often end up giving others evidence – the very best of evidence, your unextorted word – that you desire things or states of affairs far more particular than would satisfy you – or better, than would have satisfied you, for once you have declared, being a man of your word, you acquire an interest in satisfying exactly the desire you declared and no other.

"I'd like some baked beans, please."

"Yes sir. How many?"

You might well object to having such a specification of desire demanded of you, but in fact we are all socialized to accede to similar requirements in daily life – to the point of not noticing it, and certainly not feeling oppressed by it. I dwell on this because it has a parallel in the realm of belief, where our linguistic environment is forever forcing us to give – or concede – precise verbal expression to convictions that lack the hard edges verbalization endows them with (see Dennett, 1969, pp. 184–5, and 1978a, chapter 16). By concentrating on the *results* of this social force, while ignoring its distorting effect, one can easily be misled into thinking that it is *obvious* that beliefs and desires are rather like sentences stored in the head. Being language-using creatures, it is inevitable that we should often come to believe that some particular, actually formulated, spelled and punctuated sentence *is true*, and that on other occasions we should come to want such a sentence to *come true*, but these are special cases of belief and desire and as such may not be reliable models for the whole domain.

That is enough, on this occasion, about the principles of belief and desire attribution to be found in the intentional strategy. What about the rationality one attributes to an intentional system? One starts with the ideal of perfect rationality and revises downward as circumstances dictate. That is, one starts with the assumption that people believe all the implications of their beliefs and believe no contradictory pairs of beliefs. This does not create a practical problem of clutter (infinitely many implications, for instance), for one is interested only in ensuring that the system one is predicting is rational enough to get to the particular implications that are relevant to its behavioral predicament of the moment. Instances of irrationality, or of finitely powerful capacities of inference, raise particularly knotty problems of interpretation, which I will set aside on this occasion (see Dennett, 1981a, and Cherniak, 1986).

For I want to turn from the description of the strategy to the question of its use. Do people actually use this strategy? Yes, all the time. There may someday be other strategies for attributing belief and desire and for predicting behavior, but this is the only one we all know now. And when does it work? It works with people almost all the time. Why would it *not* be a good idea to allow individual Oxford colleges to create and grant academic degrees whenever they saw fit? The answer is a long story, but very easy to generate. And there would be widespread agreement about the major points. We have no difficulty thinking of the reasons people would then have for acting in such ways as to give others reasons for acting in such ways as to give others reasons for . . . creating a circumstance we would not want. Our use of the intentional strategy is so habitual and effortless that the role it plays in shaping our expectations about people is easily overlooked. The strategy also works on most other mammals most of the time. For instance, you can use it to design better traps to catch those mammals, by reasoning about what the creature knows or believes about various things, what it prefers, what it wants to avoid. The strategy works on birds, and on fish, and on reptiles, and on insects and spiders, and even on such lowly and unenterprising creatures as clams (once a clam believes there is danger about, it will not relax its grip on its closed shell until it is convinced that the danger has passed). It also works on some artifacts: the chess-playing computer will not take your knight because it knows that there is a line of ensuing play that would lead to losing its rook, and it does not want that to happen. More modestly, the thermostat will turn off the boiler as soon as it comes to believe the room has reached the desired temperature.

The strategy even works for plants. In a locale with late spring storms, you should plant apple varieties that are particularly *cautious* about *concluding* that it is spring – which is when they *want* to blossom, of course. It even works for such inanimate and apparently undesigned phenomena as lightning. An electrician once explained to me how he worked out how to protect my underground water pump from lightning damage: lightning, he said, always wants to find the best way to ground, but sometimes it gets tricked into taking second-best paths. You can protect the pump by making another, better path more *obvious* to the lightning.

True-Believers as Intentional Systems

Now clearly this is a motley assortment of "serious" belief attributions, dubious belief attributions, pedagogically useful metaphors, *façons de parler*, and, perhaps worse, outright frauds. The next task would seem to be distinguishing those intentional systems that *really* have beliefs and desires from those we may find it handy to treat *as if* they had beliefs and desires. But that would be a Sisyphean labor, or else would be terminated by fiat. A better understanding of the phenomenon of belief begins with the observation that even in the worst of these cases, even when we are surest that the strategy works *for the wrong reasons*, it is nevertheless true that it does work, at least a little bit. This is an interesting fact, which distinguishes this class of objects, the class of *intentional systems*, from the class of objects for which the strategy never works. But is this so? Does our definition of an intentional system exclude any objects at all? For instance, it seems the lectern in this lecture room can be construed as an intentional system, fully rational, believing that it is currently located at the center of the civilized world (as some of you may also think), and desiring above all else to remain at that center. What should such a rational agent so equipped with belief and desire do? Stay put, clearly, which is just what the lectern does. I predict the lectern's behavior, accurately, from the intentional stance, so is it an intentional system? If it is, anything at all is.

What should disqualify the lectern? For one thing, the strategy does not recommend itself in this case, for we get no predictive power from it that we did not antecedently have. We already knew what the lectern was going to do – namely nothing – and tailored the beliefs and desires to fit in a quite unprincipled way. In the case of people or animals or computers, however, the situation is different. In these cases often the only strategy that is at all practical is the intentional strategy; it gives us predictive power we can get by no other method. But, it will be urged, this is no difference in nature, but merely a difference that reflects upon our limited capacities as scientists. The Laplacean omniscient physicist could predict the behavior of a computer – or of a live human body, assuming it to be ultimately governed by the laws of physics – without any need for the risky, short-cut methods of either the design or intentional strategies. For people of limited mechanical aptitude, the intentional interpretation of a simple thermostat is a handy and largely innocuous crutch, but the engineers among us can quite fully grasp its internal operation without the aid of this anthropomorphizing. It may be true that the cleverest engineers find it practically impossible to maintain a clear conception of more complex systems, such as a time-sharing computer system or remote-controlled space probe, without lapsing into an intentional stance (and viewing these devices as asking and telling, trying and avoiding, wanting and believing), but this is just a more advanced case of human epistemic frailty. We would not want to classify these artifacts with the true believers – ourselves – on such variable and parochial grounds, would we? Would it not be intolerable to hold that some artifact or creature or person was a believer from the point of view of one observer, but not a believer at all from the point of view of another, cleverer observer? That would be a particularly radical version of interpretationism, and some have thought I espoused it in urging that belief be viewed in terms of the success of the intentional strategy. I must confess that my presentation of the view has sometimes invited that reading, but I now want to discourage it. The decision to adopt the intentional stance is free, but the facts about the success or failure of the stance, were one to adopt it, are perfectly objective.

Once the intentional strategy is in place, it is an extraordinarily powerful tool in prediction – a fact that is largely concealed by our typical concentration on the cases in which it yields dubious or unreliable results. Consider, for instance, predicting moves in a chess game. What makes chess an interesting game, one can see, is the *un*predictability of one's opponent's moves, except in those cases where moves are "forced" – where there is *clearly* one best move – typically the least of the available evils. But this unpredictability is put in context when one recognizes that in the typical chess situation there are very many perfectly legal and hence available moves, but only a few – perhaps half a dozen – with anything to be said for them, and hence only a few high-probability moves according to the intentional strategy. Even when the intentional strategy fails to distinguish a single move with a highest probability, it can dramatically reduce the number of live options.

The same feature is apparent when the intentional strategy is applied to "real world" cases. It is notoriously unable to predict the exact purchase and sell decisions of stock traders, for instance, or the exact sequence of words a politician will utter when making a scheduled speech, but one's confidence can be very high indeed about slightly less specific predictions: that the particular trader *will not buy utilities today*, or that the politician *will side with the unions against his party*, for example. This inability to predict fine-grained descriptions of actions, looked at another way, is a source of strength for the intentional strategy, for it is this neutrality with regard to details of implementation that permits one to exploit the intentional strategy in complex cases, for instance, in *chaining predictions* (see Dennett, 1978a). Suppose the US Secretary of State were to announce he was a paid agent of the KGB. What an unparalleled event! How unpredictable its consequences! Yet in fact we can predict dozens of not terribly interesting but perfectly salient consequences, and consequences of consequences. The President would confer with the rest of the Cabinet, which would support his decision to relieve the Secretary of State of his duties pending the results of various investigations, psychiatric and political, and all this would be reported at a news conference to people who would write stories that would be commented upon in editorials that would be read by people who would write letters to the editors, and so forth. None of that is daring prognostication, but note that it describes an arc of causation in space-time that could not be predicted under *any* description by any imaginable practical extension of physics or biology.

The power of the intentional strategy can be seen even more sharply with the aid of an objection first raised by Robert Nozick some years ago. Suppose, he suggested, some beings of vastly superior intelligence – from Mars, let us say – were to descend upon us, and suppose that we were to them as simple thermostats are to clever engineers. Suppose, that is, that they did not *need* the intentional stance – or even the design stance – to predict our behavior in all its detail. They can be supposed to be Laplacean super-physicists, capable of comprehending the activity on Wall Street, for instance, at the microphysical level. Where we see brokers and buildings and sell orders and bids, they see vast congeries of subatomic particles milling about – and they are such good physicists that they can predict days in advance what ink marks will appear each day on the paper tape labeled "Closing Dow Jones Industrial Average." They can predict the individual behaviors of all the various moving bodies they observe without ever treating any of them as intentional systems. Would we be right then to say that from *their* point of view we really were not believers at all (any more than a simple thermostat is)? If so, then our status as believers is nothing objective, but rather something in the eye of the beholder – provided the beholder shares our intellectual limitations.

Our imagined Martians might be able to predict the future of the human race by Laplacean methods, but if they did not also see us as intentional systems, they would be missing something perfectly objective; the *patterns* in human behavior that are describable from the intentional stance, and only from that stance, and that support generalizations and predictions. Take a particular instance in which the Martians observe a stockbroker deciding to place an order for 500 shares of General Motors. They predict the exact motions of his fingers as he dials the phone and the exact vibrations of his vocal cords as he intones his order. But if the Martians do not see that indefinitely many *different* patterns of finger motions and vocal cord vibrations – even the motions of indefinitely many different individuals – could have been substituted for the actual particulars without perturbing the subsequent operation of the market, then they have failed to see a real pattern in the world they are observing. Just as there are indefinitely many ways of *being a spark plug* – and one has not understood what an internal combustion engine is unless one realizes that a variety of different devices can be screwed into these sockets without affecting the performance of the engine – so there are indefinitely many ways of *ordering 500 shares of General Motors,* and there are societal sockets in which one of these ways will produce just about the same effect as any other. There are also societal pivot points, as it were, where which way people go depends on whether they *believe that p,* or *desire A,* and does not depend on any of the other infinitely many ways they may be alike or different.

Suppose, pursuing our Martian fantasy a little further, that one of the Martians were to engage in a predicting contest with an Earthling. The Earthling and the Martian observe (and observe each other observing) a particular bit of local physical transaction. From the Earthling's point of view, this is what is observed. The telephone rings in Mrs. Gardner's kitchen. She answers, and this is what she says: "Oh, hello dear. You're coming home early? Within the hour? And bringing the boss to dinner? Pick up a bottle of wine on the way home, then, and drive carefully." On the basis of this observation, our Earthling predicts that a large metallic vehicle with rubber tires will come to a stop in the drive within one hour, disgorging two human beings, one of whom will be holding a paper bag containing a bottle containing an alcoholic fluid. The prediction is a bit risky, perhaps, but a good bet on all counts. The Martian makes the same prediction, but has to avail himself of much more information about an extraordinary number of interactions of which, so far as he can tell, the Earthling is entirely ignorant. For instance, the deceleration of the vehicle at intersection *A*, five miles from the house, without which there would have been a collision with another vehicle – whose collision course had been laboriously calculated over some hundreds of meters by the Martian. The Earthling's performance would look like magic! How did the Earthling know that the human being who got out of the car and got the bottle in the shop would get back in? The coming true of the Earthling's prediction, after all the vagaries, intersections, and branches in the paths charted by the Martian, would seem to anyone bereft of the intentional strategy as marvelous and inexplicable as the fatalistic inevitability of the appointment in Samarra. Fatalists – for instance, astrologers – believe that there is a pattern in human affairs that is inexorable, that will impose itself *come what may,* that is, no matter how the victims scheme and second-guess, no matter how they twist and turn in their chains. These fatalists are wrong, but they are *almost* right. There *are* patterns in human affairs that impose themselves, not quite inexorably but with great vigor, absorbing physical perturbations and variations that might as well be considered random; these are the patterns that we characterize in terms of the beliefs, desires, and intentions of rational agents.

No doubt you will have noticed, and been distracted by, a serious flaw in our thought experiment: the Martian is presumed to treat his Earthling opponent as an intelligent being like himself, with whom communication is possible, a being with whom one can make a wager, against whom one can compete. In short, a being with beliefs (such as the belief he expressed in his prediction) and desires (such as the desire to win the prediction contest). So if the Martian sees the pattern in one Earthling, how can he fail to see it in the others? As a bit of narrative, our example could be strengthened by supposing that our Earthling cleverly learned Martian (which is transmitted by X-ray modulation) and disguised himself as a Martian, counting on the species-chauvinism of these otherwise brilliant aliens to permit him to pass as an intentional system while not giving away the secret of his fellow human beings. This addition might get us over a bad twist in the tale, but might obscure the moral to be drawn: namely, *the unavoidability of the intentional stance with regard to oneself and one's fellow intelligent beings.* This unavoidability is itself interest relative; it is perfectly possible to adopt a physical stance, for instance, with regard to an intelligent being, oneself included, but not to the exclusion of maintaining at the same time an intentional stance with regard to oneself at a minimum, and one's fellows *if* one intends, for instance, to learn what they know (a point that has been powerfully made by Stuart Hampshire in a number of writings). We can perhaps suppose our super-intelligent Martians fail to recognize *us* as intentional systems, but we cannot suppose them to lack the requisite concepts.[2] If they observe, theorize, predict, communicate, they view *themselves* as intentional systems.[3] Where there are intelligent beings, the patterns must be there to be described, whether or nor we care to see them.

It is important to recognize the objective reality of the intentional patterns discernible in the activities of intelligent creatures, but also important to recognize the incompleteness and imperfections in the patterns. The objective fact is that the intentional strategy *works as well as it does,* which is not perfectly. No one is perfectly rational, perfectly unforgetful, all-observant, or invulnerable to fatigue, malfunction, or design imperfection. This leads inevitably to circumstances beyond the power of the intentional strategy to describe, in much the same way that physical damage to an artifact, such as a telephone or an automobile, may render it indescribable by the normal design terminology for that artifact. How do you draw the schematic wiring diagram of an audio amplifier that has been partially melted, or how do you characterize the program state of a malfunctioning computer? In cases of even the mildest and most familiar cognitive pathology – where people seem to hold contradictory beliefs or to be deceiving themselves, for instance – the canons of interpretation of the intentional strategy fail to yield clear, stable verdicts about which beliefs and desires to attribute to a person.

Now a *strong* realist position on beliefs and desires would claim that in these cases the person in question really does have some particular beliefs and desires which the intentional strategy, as I have described it, is simply unable to divine. On the milder sort of realism I am advocating, there is no fact of the matter of exactly which beliefs and desires a person has in these degenerate cases, but this is not a surrender to relativism or subjectivism, for *when* and *why* there is no fact of the matter is itself a matter of objective fact. On this view one can even acknowledge the *interest relativity* of belief attributions and grant that, given the different interests of different cultures, for instance, the beliefs and desires one culture would attribute to a member might be quite different from the beliefs and desires another culture would attribute to that very same person. But supposing that were so in a particular case, there would be the further facts about *how well* each of the rival intentional strategies worked for predicting the behavior of that person. We can be sure in advance that no intentional interpretation of an individual will work to perfection, and it may be that two rival schemes are about equally good, and better than any others we can devise. That this is the case is itself something about which there can be a fact of the matter. The objective presence of one pattern (with whatever imperfections) does not rule out the objective presence of another pattern (with whatever imperfections).

The bogey of radically different interpretations with equal warrant from the intentional strategy is theoretically important – one might better say metaphysically important – but practically negligible once one restricts one's attention to the largest and most complex intentional systems we know: human beings.[4]

Until now I have been stressing our kinship to clams and thermostats in order to emphasize a view of the logical status of belief attribution, but the time has come to acknowledge the obvious differences and say what can be made of them. The perverse claim remains: *all there is* to being a true believer is being a system whose behavior is reliably predictable via the intentional strategy, and hence *all there is* to really and truly believing that p (for any proposition p) is being an intentional system for which p occurs as a belief in the best (most predictive) interpretation. But once we turn our attention to the truly interesting and versatile intentional systems, we see that this apparently shallow and instrumentalistic criterion of belief puts a severe constraint on the internal constitution of a genuine believer, and thus yields a robust version of belief after all.

Consider the lowly thermostat, as degenerate a case of an intentional system as could conceivably hold our attention for more than a moment. Going along with the gag, we might agree to grant it the capacity for about half a dozen different beliefs and fewer desires – it can believe the room is too cold or too hot, that the boiler is on or off, and that if it wants the room warmer it should turn on the boiler, and so forth. But surely this is imputing too much to the thermostat; it has no concept of heat or of a boiler, for instance. So suppose we *de-interpret* its beliefs and desires: it can believe the *A* is too *F* or *G*, and if it wants the *A* to be more *F* it should do *K*, and so forth. After all, by attaching the thermostatic control mechanism to different input and output devices, it could be made to regulate the amount of water in a tank, or the speed of a train, for instance. Its attachment to a heat-sensitive transducer and a boiler is too impoverished a link to the world to grant any rich semantics to its belief-like states.

But suppose we then enrich these modes of attachment. Suppose we give it more than one way of learning about the temperature, for instance. We give it an eye of sorts that can distinguish huddled, shivering occupants of the room and an ear so that it can be told how cold it is. We give it some facts about geography so that it can conclude that it is probably in a cold place if it learns that its spatio-temporal location is Winnipeg in December. Of course giving it a visual system that is multipurpose and general – not a mere shivering-object detector – will require vast complications of its inner structure. Suppose we also give our system more behavioral versatility: it chooses the boiler fuel, purchases it from the cheapest and most reliable dealer, checks the weather stripping, and so forth. This adds another dimension of internal complexity; it gives individual belief-like states *more to do*, in effect, by providing more and different occasions for their derivation or deduction from other states, and by providing more and different occasions for them to serve as premises for further reasoning. The cumulative effect of enriching these connections between the device and the world in which it resides is to enrich the semantics of its dummy predicates, *F* and *G* and the rest. The more of this we add, the less amenable our device becomes to serving as the control structure of anything other than a room-temperature maintenance system. A more formal way of saying this is that the class of indistinguishably satisfactory models of the formal system embodied in its internal states gets smaller and smaller as we add such complexities; the more we add, the richer or more demanding or specific the semantics of the system, until eventually we reach systems for which a unique semantic interpretation is practically (but never in principle) dictated (cf. Hayes, 1979). At that point we say this device (or animal or person) has beliefs *about heat* and *about this very room*, and so forth, not only because of the system's actual location in, and operations on, the world, but because we cannot imagine another niche in which it could be placed *where it would work* (see also Dennett, 1982b and 1983b).

Our original simple thermostat had a state we called a belief about a particular boiler, to the effect that it was on or off. Why about *that* boiler? Well, what other boiler would you want to say it was about? The belief is about the boiler because it is *fastened* to the boiler.[5] Given the actual, if mimimal, causal link to the world that happened to be in effect, we could endow a state of the device with *meaning* (of a sort) and *truth conditions*, but it was altogether too easy to substitute a different minimal link and completely change the meaning (in this impoverished sense) of that internal state. But as systems become perceptually richer and behaviorally more versatile, it becomes harder and harder to make substitutions in the actual links of the system to the world without changing the organization of the system itself. If you change its environment, it will *notice*, in effect, and make a change in its internal state in response. There comes to be a two-way constraint of growing specificity between the device and the environment. Fix the device in any one state and it demands a very specific environment in which to operate properly (you can no longer switch it easily from regulating temperature to regulating speed or anything else); but at the same time, if you do not *fix* the state it is in, but just plonk it down in a changed environment, its sensory attachments will be sensitive and discriminative enough to respond appropriately to the change, driving the system into a new state, in which it will operate effectively in the new environment. There is a familiar way of alluding to this tight relationship that can exist between the organization of a system and its environment: you say that the organism continuously *mirrors* the environment, or that there is a *representation* of the environment in – or implicit in – the organization of the system.

It is not that we attribute (or should attribute) beliefs and desires only to things in which we find internal representations, but rather that, when we discover some object for which the intentional strategy works, we endeavor to interpret some of its internal states or processes as internal representations. What makes some internal feature of a thing a representation could only be its role in regulating the behavior of an intentional system.

Now the reason for stressing our kinship with the thermostat should be clear. There is no magic moment in the transition from a simple thermostat to a system that *really* has an internal representation of the world around it. The thermostat has a minimally demanding representation of the world, fancier thermostats have more demanding representations of the world, fancier robots for helping around the house would have still more demanding representations of the world. Finally you reach us. We are so multifariously and intricately connected to the world that almost no substitution is possible – though it is clearly imaginable in a thought experiment. Hilary Putnam imagines the planet Twin Earth, which is just like Earth right down to the scuff marks on the shoes of the Twin Earth replica of your neighbor, but which differs from Earth in some property that is entirely beneath the thresholds of your capacities to discriminate. (What they call water on Twin Earth has a different chemical analysis.) Were *you* to be whisked instantaneously to Twin Earth and exchanged for your Twin Earth replica, you would never be the wiser – just like the simple control system that cannot tell whether it is regulating temperature, speed, or volume of water in a tank. It is easy to devise radically different Twin Earths for something as simple and sensorily deprived as a thermostat, but your internal organization puts a much more stringent demand on substitution. Your Twin Earth and Earth must be virtual replicas or you will change state dramatically on arrival.

So which boiler are *your* beliefs about when you believe the boiler is on? Why, the boiler in your cellar (rather than its twin on Twin Earth, for instance). What other boiler would your beliefs be about? The completion of the semantic interpretation of your beliefs, fixing the referents of your beliefs, requires, as in the case of the thermostat, facts about your actual embedding in the world. The principles, and problems, of interpretation that we discover when we attribute beliefs to people are the *same* principles and problems we discover when we look at the ludicrous, but blessedly simple, problem of attributing beliefs to a thermostat. The differences are of degree, but nevertheless of such great degree that understanding the internal organization of a simple intentional system gives one very little basis for understanding the internal organization of a complex intentional system, such as a human being.

Why Does the Intentional Strategy Work?

When we turn to the question of *why* the intentional strategy works as well as it does, we find that the question is ambiguous, admitting of two very different sorts of answers. If the intentional system is a simple thermostat, one answer is simply this: the intentional strategy works because the thermostat is well designed; it was designed to be a system that could be easily and reliably comprehended and manipulated from this stance. That is true, but not very informative, if what we are after are the actual features of its design that explain its performance. Fortunately, however, in the case of a simple thermostat those features are easily discovered and understood, so the other answer to our *why* question, which is really an answer about *how the machinery works*, is readily available.

If the intentional system in question is a person, there is also an ambiguity in our question. The first answer to the question of why the intentional strategy works is that evolution has designed human beings to be rational, to believe what they ought to believe and want what they ought to want. The fact that we are products of a long and demanding evolutionary process guarantees that using the intentional strategy on us is a safe bet. This answer has the virtues of truth and brevity, and on this occasion the additional virtue of being an answer Herbert Spencer would applaud, but it is also strikingly uninformative. The more difficult version of the question asks, in effect, how the machinery which Nature has provided us works. And we cannot yet give a good answer to that question. We just do not know. We do know how the *strategy* works, and we know the easy answer to the question of why it works, but knowing these does not help us much with the hard answer.

It is not that there is any dearth of doctrine, however. A Skinnerian behaviorist, for instance, would say that the strategy works because its imputations of beliefs and desires are shorthand, in effect, for as yet unimaginably complex descriptions of the effects of prior histories of response and reinforcement. To say that someone wants some ice cream is to say that in the past the ingestion of ice cream has been reinforced in him by the results, creating a propensity under certain background conditions (also too complex to describe) to engage in ice-cream-acquiring behavior. In the absence of detailed knowledge of those historical facts we can nevertheless make shrewd guesses on inductive grounds; these guesses are embodied in our intentional stance claims. Even if all this were true, it would tell us very little about the way such propensities were regulated by the internal machinery.

A currently more popular explanation is that the account of how the strategy works and the account of how the mechanism works will (roughly) *coincide:* for each predictively attributable belief, there will be a functionally salient internal state of the machinery, decomposable into functional parts in just about the same way the sentence expressing the belief is decomposable into parts – that is, words or terms. The inferences we attribute to rational creatures will be mirrored by physical, causal processes in the hardware; the *logical* form of the propositions believed will be copied in the *structural* form of the states in correspondence with them. This is the hypothesis that there is a *language of thought* coded in our brains, and our brains will eventually be understood as symbol manipulating systems in at least rough analogy with computers. Many different versions of this view are currently being explored, in the new research program called cognitive science, and provided one allows great latitude for attenuation of the basic, bold claim, I think some version of it will prove correct.

But I do not believe that this is *obvious*. Those who think that it is obvious, or inevitable, that such a theory will prove true (and there are many who do) are confusing two different empirical claims. The first is that intentional stance description yields an objective, real pattern in the world – the pattern our imaginary Martians missed. This is an empirical claim, but one that is confirmed beyond skepticism. The second is that this real pattern is *produced by* another real pattern roughly isomorphic to it within the brains of intelligent creatures. Doubting the existence of the second real pattern is not doubting the existence of the first. There *are* reasons for believing in the second pattern, but they are not overwhelming. The best simple account I can give of the reasons is as follows.

As we ascend the scale of complexity from simple thermostat, through sophisticated robot, to human being, we discover that our efforts to design systems with the requisite behavior increasingly run foul of the problem of *combinatorial explosion*. Increasing some parameter by, say, ten percent – ten percent more inputs or more degrees of freedom in the behavior to be controlled or more words to be recognized or whatever – tends to increase the internal complexity of the system being designed by orders of magnitude. Things get out of hand very fast and, for instance, can lead to computer programs that will swamp the largest, fastest machines. Now somehow the brain has solved the problem of combinatorial explosion. It is a gigantic network of billions of cells, but still finite, compact, reliable, and swift, and capable of learning new behaviors, vocabularies, theories, almost without limit. Some elegant, *generative*, indefinitely extendable principles of representation must be responsible. We have only one model of such a representation system: a human language. So the argument for a language of thought comes down to this: what else could it be? We have so far been unable to imagine any plausible alternative in any detail. That is a good enough reason, I think, for recommending as a matter of scientific tactics that we pursue the hypothesis in its various forms as far as we can.[6] But we will engage in that exploration more circumspectly, and fruitfully, if we bear in mind that its inevitable rightness is far from assured. One does not well understand even a true empirical hypothesis so long as one is under the misapprehension that it is necessarily true.

Notes

Copyright Oxford University Press 1981. Reprinted from *Scientific Explanation*, ed. A. F. Heath (1981), by permission of Oxford University Press and the author.

1 The idea that most of anyone's beliefs *must* be true seems obvious to some people. Support for the idea can be found in works by Quine, Putnam, Shoemaker, Davidson, and myself. Other people find the idea equally incredible – so probably each side is calling a different phenomenon belief. Once one makes the distinction between belief and opinion (in my technical sense – see "How to Change Your Mind" in Dennett, 1978a, chapter 16), according to which opinions are linguistically infected, relatively sophisticated cognitive states – *roughly* states of betting on the truth of a particular, formulated sentence – one can see the near trivality of the claim that most beliefs are true. A few reflections on peripheral matters should bring it out. Consider Democritus, who had a systematic, all-embracing, but (let us say, for the sake of argument) entirely false physics. He had things *all wrong*, though

his views held together and had a sort of systematic utility. But even if every *claim* that scholarship permits us to attribute to Democritus (either explicit or implicit in his writings) is false, these represent a vanishingly small fraction of his *beliefs*, which include both the vast numbers of humdrum standing beliefs he must have had (about which house he lived in, what to look for in a good pair of sandals, and so forth) and also those occasional beliefs that came and went by the millions as his perceptual experience changed.

But, it may be urged, this isolation of his humdrum beliefs from his science relies on an insupportable distinction between truths of observation and truths of theory; all Democritus' beliefs are theory-laden, and since his theory is false, they are false. The reply is as follows: granted that all observation beliefs are theory laden, why should we choose Democritus' *explicit*, sophisticated theory (couched in his *opinions*) as the theory with which to burden his quotidian observations? Note that the least theoretical compatriot of Democritus also had myriads of theory-laden observation beliefs – and was, in one sense, none the wiser for it. Why should we not suppose Democritus' observations are laden with the same (presumably innocuous) theory? If Democritus forgot his theory, or changed his mind, his observational beliefs would be *largely* untouched. To the extent that his sophisticated theory played a discernible role in his routine behavior and expectations and so forth, it would be quite appropriate to couch his humdrum beliefs in terms of the sophisticated theory, but this will not yield a *mainly false* catalogue of beliefs, since so few of his beliefs will be affected. (The effect of theory on observation is nevertheless often underrated. See Churchland (1979) for dramatic and convincing examples of the tight relationship that can sometimes exist between theory and experience. [The discussion in this note was distilled from a useful conversation with Paul and Patricia Churchland and Michael Stack.])

2   A member of the audience in Oxford pointed out that, if the Martian included the Earthling in his physical stance purview (a possibility I had not explicitly excluded), he would not be surprised by the Earthling's prediction. He would indeed have predicted exactly the pattern of X-ray modulations produced by the Earthling speaking Martian. True, but as the Martian wrote down the results of his calculations, his prediction of the Earthling's prediction would appear, word by Martian word, as on a Ouija board, and what would be baffling to the Martian was how this chunk of mechanism, the Earthling predictor dressed up like a Martian, was able to yield this *true* sentence of Martian when it was so informationally isolated from the events the Martian needed to know of in order to make his own prediction about the arriving automobile.

3   Might there not be intelligent beings who had no use for communicating, predicting, observing . . . ? There might be marvelous, nifty, invulnerable entities lacking these modes of action, but I cannot see what would lead us to call them *intelligent*.

4   John McCarthy's analogy to cryptography nicely makes this point. The larger the corpus of cipher text, the less chance there is of dual, systematically unrelated decipherings. For a very useful discussion of the principles and presuppositions of the intentional stance applied to machines – explicitly including thermostats – see McCarthy (1979).

5   This idea is the ancestor in effect of the species of different ideas lumped together under the rubric of *de re* belief. If one builds from this idea toward its scions, one

can see better the difficulties with them, and how to repair them. (For more on this topic, see Dennett, 1982b.)

6 The fact that all *language of thought* models of mental representation so far proposed fall victim to combinatorial explosion in one way or another should temper one's enthusiasm for engaging in what Fodor aptly calls "the only game in town."

15 Instrumental Intentionality

Lynne Rudder Baker

The suspicion that beliefs, desires, intentions and other attitudes identified by content resist scientific treatment has driven a number of physicalists to conclude that putative intentional phenomena should be dismissed as illusions of prescientific theorizing (Churchland, 1981; Stich, 1983). At least one physicalist, however, has come to a different conclusion. Daniel C. Dennett has proposed an instrumentalism that promises to remove attributions of attitudes from the path of science altogether. If the project can be sustained, it will secure a place, shielded from the claims of advancing science, for intentionality construed instrumentalistically.

Although Dennett's bold attempt to combine physicalism with an instrumentalistic account of attitudes is the most developed theory of its kind, I believe that ultimately it is unsuccessful. And it is unsuccessful not just because it has counterintuitive consequences, but because it lacks internal coherence. There runs throughout Dennett's view, I think, a systematic discrepancy between his official theory and his actual treatment of key concepts. My aim is to bring out inconsistencies in the treatment of the concepts of belief, rationality and design, to expose difficulties concerning the status of what Dennett calls "stances," and to show that removal of these defects would jeopardize either Dennett's realism concerning physical phenomena or his instrumentalism concerning propositional attitudes.

1 Intentional System Theory

Dennett's concept of an intentional system depends upon what Dennett calls "stances." Stances are strategies that one may adopt to predict the behavior of a person or machine. From the physical stance, objects are described and their behavior predicted on the basis of physical constitution. From the design stance, objects are described and their behavior predicted in terms of normal operation or function. Such predictions assume no breakdown or malfunction. From the intentional stance, objects are described and their behavior predicted by attributing rationality to them – that is, "by ascribing to the system *the possession of certain information* and supposing it to be *directed by certain goals*, and then by working out the most reasonable or appropriate action on the basis of these ascriptions and suppositions" (Dennett, 1971, p. 6). In addition to assuming no breakdown or malfunction, predictions from the intentional stance assume that the agent will select an optimal strategy to reach his or her or its goals.

An intentional system is one whose behavior is predictable from the intentional stance, from which attitudes like belief are attributable:

> . . . *all there is* to being a true believer is being a system whose behavior is reliably predictable via the intentional strategy, and hence *all there is* to really and truly believing that *p* (for any proposition *p*) is being an intentional system for which *p* occurs as a belief in the best (most predictive) interpretation. (see this volume, pp. 324–5)

In sum, "being rational is being intentional is being the object of a certain stance" (1976, p. 271). And further:

> The success of the stance is of course a matter settled pragmatically, without reference to whether the object *really* has beliefs, intentions, and so forth; so whether or not any computer can be conscious, or have thoughts or desires, some computers undeniably *are* intentional systems, for they are systems whose behavior can be predicted, and most efficiently predicted, by adopting the intentional stance toward them. (Dennett, 1973, p. 238)

Since "the choice of stance is 'up to us,' a matter of *decision*, not discovery" (1973, p. 239), a system has beliefs and other attitudes attributed from the intentional stance only in virtue of its relation to the (possible) predictive strategies of someone else. On intentional system theory, then, systems have beliefs, and attributions of beliefs may be unproblematically true; but – here is the instrumentalism – what makes such an attribution true is neither that the believer has any particular property, nor that the believer is related to its physical environment in any particular way, but rather the fact that the believer succumbs to a certain strategy or stance. Dennett's instrumentalism is explicit: *x* believes that *p* if and only if the belief that *p* is predictively attributable to *x* (1978a, p. xviii).

An intentional explanation, for all its heuristic value, is never more than an intermediate step on the way to an explanation in terms of design or physical constitution. "Intentional theory is vacuous as psychology because it presupposes and does not explain rationality or intelligence" (1971, p. 15). Although it is a free decision to adopt the intentional stance for convenience, the business of a scientific psychology is to illuminate mentality from the deeper, more explanatory stances: "if one wants to predict and explain the 'actual, empirical' behavior of believers, one must . . . cease talking of belief, and descend to the design stance or physical stance for one's account" (1971, p. 22). In short, the intentional stance, which presupposes neither of the "lower" stances (1973, p. 240), is only a resting place on the way to the "lower," more mechanistic stances, from which genuine explanations are advanced.

It will be useful in what follows to make explicit a distinction implied by Dennett. I shall use the term "feature" with next to no ontological commitment: a system S has a feature F if and only if sentences of the form "S is F" are true. Dennett's program invites contrast between those features that a system has by virtue of (possibly) being the object of a stance, and those features that a system has that are independent of (the possibility of) anyone's taking any stance toward it. For example, although one may correctly predict that a certain glass of water will freeze at 0 degrees Centigrade, the water's having the property of freezing at 0 degrees Centigrade does not depend on anyone's (possible) predictive strategies. On intentional system theory, on the other hand, the feature that someone has of *believing* that water freezes at 0 degrees is determined by the (possible) predictive strategies of others.

So, let us distinguish between features that are *stance-dependent* and features that are *stance-independent* as follows. Suppose that x has a feature F. Then F is a stance-independent feature of x if and only if x's having F is independent of any strategies, attitudes or ascriptions toward x of any y, $y \neq x$; otherwise, F is a stance-dependent feature, or a feature by attribution, of x. Stance-dependent features are those features that a system has only in virtue of its (possibly) being an object of a certain stance.

The distinction between stance-dependent and stance-independent features is motivated by Dennett's ontology. About putative entities like beliefs, experiences and pains, Dennett is an eliminative materialist (1978a, p. xx). At the same time, Dennett is at pains to argue that sentences of the form "S believes that p" have truth value, and not all are false (this volume, chapter 14). As Dennett remarks, "Attributions of belief and desire are not just "convenient fictions'; there are plenty of honest-to-goodness instrumentalist *truths*" (1983b, p. 380). The innocuous construal of "feature" permits the distinction between stance-dependent and stance-independent features to accommodate both aspects of Dennett's view: on the one hand, in line with eliminative materialism, we may deny that beliefs are stance-independent features, but on the other hand, we may understand the truth of sentences of the form "S believes that p" in terms of stance-dependent features of the systems that have them.

The point of distinguishing between stance-dependent and stance-independent features is to contrast Dennett's instrumentalism about the intentional with his realism about the physical. Since he is explicitly committed to what I am calling the "stance-dependence" of features attributed from the intentional stance,[1] Dennett could reject my formulation of the stance-dependent/stance-independent distinction only by rejecting the stance-independence of features attributed from the non-intentional stances. And since to do that would be to abandon realism about physical phenomena, I think that the distinction is unavoidable for Dennett – as long as he remains in any sense a realist.

It is important to see that the distinction between stance-dependent and stance-independent features is, in the first instance, not between the characteristic vocabularies of the stances, but between the kinds of features that make descriptions in those vocabularies true.[2] On Dennett's official view, what makes it the case that x has F, where F is a physical feature, is independent of anyone's strategies (that is, F is stance-independent); but what makes it the case that x has F', where F' is an intentional feature, depends upon someone's (possible) strategies (that is, F' is stance-dependent).

The stance-dependent/stance-independent distinction should not be confused with other distinctions in the literature, such as the intrinsic/extrinsic or intrinsic/relational distinction.[3] Velocity is relative to inertial frame, and hence is not an intrinsic feature. But it is not thereby a stance-dependent feature; the velocity of an object does not depend on anyone's possible predictive strategies any more than its temperature does. (To insist here that velocity depends upon someone's *choice* of frame would be misleading.) Not all relational features are stance-dependent, only those whose possession depends upon someone's strategies.

Further elaboration of exactly what stance-dependence is would require explication of what strategies are and would take us afield. (I have characterized stance-dependence as sharply as Dennett has characterized the intentional stance.) What matters for the arguments that follow is that Dennett is explicitly committed to the idea of stance-dependence (if not to the phrase), and that the stance-dependence/stance-independence distinction is exhaustive and hence can ground the premise common to a series of dilemmas.

2 Belief, Rationality and Design

Dennett puts his intentional system theory to two distinct uses: one broadly ethical and the other proto-scientific. He uses intentional system theory to vindicate our view of ourselves as persons, as moral and rational agents acting on beliefs and desires; and he uses it as a vehicle of discovery, a source of testable hypotheses in psychology and biology. As we shall see, neither of these purposes is well served by instrumentalism.

2.1 Belief and other attitudes

On the official view, believing that p and other attitudes are stance-dependent features of systems. However, when discussing ethical issues, Dennett often implies that the features attributed from the intentional stance are more than mere stance-dependent features.

For example, Dennett says, "a belief is essentially something that has been *endorsed* (by commission or omission) by the agent on the basis of its conformity with the rest of his beliefs" (1973, p. 252). Although endorsement by the agent is eminently plausible as a requirement of belief and is required in many contexts of ethical evaluation, it goes well beyond the view of belief as what is predictively attributable. Since what is predictively attributable to an individual need not coincide with what that individual endorses (think of a chess-playing computer), Dennett is not entitled to this claim.

A natural move for an intentional system theorist to make here is to point out that endorsing is no less intentioal than believing, and that the intentional system approach to belief extends to all intentional concepts worth preserving; so, one may counter, a person endorses something if and only if endorsement of it may be predictively attributed to the person. Although Dennett's own remarks lend little support to this interpretation, the interpretation may have the merit of rendering the account consistent by treating intentional concepts like endorsement in terms of intentional system theory – but at the price of robbing Dennett's claims about agency and decision making of any plausibility. If endorsement were taken as no more than what can be predictively attributed, then whether or not I endorse a claim would not be something that I do (with no conceptual dependence on a would-be ascriber), but something that someone else would find it useful to attribute to me. The difficulties that we find in belief understood in terms of intentional system theory would simply accrue to endorsement.

Moreover, throughout *Elbow Room*, Dennett takes beliefs to provide reasons that cause us to behave one way rather than another (1984, chap. 2). But if beliefs have such causal efficacy, they can hardly be merely stance-dependent features of believers. On the one hand, it is difficult to see how an eliminative materialist can suppose that features whose possession depends upon the (possible) predictive strategies of others can cause anything at all. On the other hand, one who takes beliefs to have causal powers is in no position to be an instrumentalist with regard to belief (unless he is also an instrumentalist with regard to causation).

The difficulty would be removed if Dennett were also an instrumentalist about causation and took causal efficacy to be a stance-dependent feature. Not only do I suspect that Dennett would find this move unpalatable and unhelpful in the context of his discussion of free will, but also it would threaten his realism about physical phenomena, a paradigm of which is causation. To be an instrumentalist about causation would leave one very little about which to be a realist.

Thus, the plausibility of Dennett's *rapprochement* of the physical and the intentional seems to require sleight-of-hand deployment of intentional system theory, deployment that conflicts with the theory's official instrumentalism. The conflict is unresolvable, because consistent instrumentalism is inadequate to bear the weight of the ethical claims.

2.2 Rationality

Officially, rationality is attributed from the intentional stance, and features attributed from the intentional stance are stance-dependent. Yet, much of Dennett's discussion suggests that rationality is as stance-independent as a design feature like vision. For example, he advises that we think in terms of design "*all the way in* – not just for eye-design, but for deliberation-design and belief-design and strategy-concoctor design" (1981b, p. 43). And, since Dennett offers an explicitly design-level model of practical reasoning, he further implies that rationality is a design feature (1978d, p. 295). Finally, Dennett accounts for the success of the intentional stance by appeal to adaptation. In evolved organisms, rationality is produced by mechanisms of natural selection.

So, quite often, Dennett emphasizes his construal of rationality as part of a system's design (1971, pp. 5–6). He sounds as if the intentional stance, with its presupposition of rationality, simply offers a handy, alternative vocabulary to designate those design features that make a system predictable in a certain way. But if the intentional stance just offered a convenient vocabulary for designating certain design features, then attributions of rationality and of design would designate a single set of features, and rationality and design features would both be stance-dependent or both be stance-independent.

Rationality, like belief, cannot be stance-independent without aborting intentional system theory: if ascriptions of rationality simply ascribed features equally (or better) describable from the design or physical stance, they would be true in virtue of the obtaining of some actual (that is, physical) state of affairs. In that case, the grounds for instrumentalism would be thoroughly eroded. So, rationality is *not* a stance-independent feature of systems that have it.

On the other hand, Dennett often seems to hold that design features, at least in evolved organisms, *are* stance-independent: any feature produced by natural selection may be fully specified and understood without adverting to anyone's predictive strategies or attitudes. For example, whether or not a plant undergoes photosynthesis seems independent of anyone's possible predictive strategies. So, it seems that features produced by natural selection are stance-independent and rationality is stance-dependent. But in that case, Dennett cannot consistently explain rationality as the product of natural selection.

One may be tempted to object: a feature is stance-dependent just in case its attribution allows prediction from the intentional stance. Although mechanisms of natural selection are stance-independent, they may produce features that make an organism predictable from the intentional stance. So, the objection may go, there is no contradiction in supposing that stance-independent features may also be stance-dependent features.

The objection is misguided, because it construes stance-dependence in a way that undercuts Dennett's instrumentalism: if stance-dependence were merely a matter of an alternative vocabulary for designating features which a system has independently of anyone's taking a stance, then there would be a physical fact of the matter as to whether or not the system has the feature, specified in a stance-dependent way, and ascriptions of rationality would be true or false in exactly the same way as physical descriptions. In that case, construing the intentional stance as intrumentalistic but the physical stance as realistic would be wholly unmotivated, and, again, the instrumentalism would dissolve.

An objector may go on to claim that, at least, there is a strong similarity between optimality of design (at the design level) and rationality (at the intentional level): they both have survival value. But, I should reply, the appearance of similarity here is vitiated by an equivocation on "has survival value." Assuming (for the moment) realism about the design level and instrumentalism about the intentional level, to say that optimality of design has survival value is to say that the design causally contributes to an organism's survival; but to say that rationality has survival value is only to say that certain attributions have predictive power.

Dennett simply treats rationality inconsistently. Although officially a stance-dependent feature, rationality is often implied by Dennett to be a stance-independent feature, a feature that an organism has per se, without regard to the predictive strategies of others. And this shift over to suggesting that rationality is a stance-independent feature is nowhere more prominent than when Dennett invokes evolution; he almost always speaks of rationality as something that an organism has per se. Indeed, the "creation and improvement of intelligence is one of evolution's most impressive products" (1984, p. 57; compare 1981a). But a feature that an organism has per se is possessed independently of the predictive strategies of others; it is a stance-independent feature.

To sum up the discussion of rationality: on the official theory, rationality cannot be understood as a feature that an organism has per se, apart from predictive strategies. For, officially, "being rational is being intentional is being the object of a certain stance" (1976, p. 271). But when Dennett links rationality to design in the various ways, he treats rationality as a feature that an organism has per se, as opposed to a feature that an organism has in virtue of its (possibly) being the object of a certain stance. One cannot consistently suppose that rationality is acquired by natural selection if one is a realist about the products of natural selection but an instrumentalist about rationality.

2.3   Design

Just as the concept of rationality seems to wobble back and forth between the intentional and design stances, the design stance itself wobbles between stance-independent features attributed from the physical stance and stance-dependent features attributed from the intentional stance. This latter instability, I believe, has obscured the inconsistency in the treatment of rationality.

In keeping with Dennett's scientific realism and the status of theories of natural selection as scientific, I have been supposing that, officially, Dennett takes design features to be stance-independent. Since descriptions from the design stance assume absence of breakdown or malfunction, however, it is time to question that supposition: can the relevant concept of malfunction or breakdown be understood in a stance-independent way?

For artifacts familiar to us, the answer is no. As a simple-minded illustration, suppose that someone presses the brake pedal of an automobile and there is no response. One natural way to describe this episode is as a malfunction of the brakes. However, there is no fact of the matter in terms of stance-independent features as to whether an occurrence should be described as a breakdown or, more neutrally, as a reorganization or change of disposition. The "failure" of the brakes is only clearly a malfunction or breakdown relative to someone's (probably the designer's and/or user's) intentions. But since on intentional system theory, beliefs, desires, and intentions are stance-dependent, to describe an event as a malfunction or breakdown, in the case of artifacts, is to attribute to it a stance-dependent feature.[4]

Dennett has observed that Darwin did not dethrone design as an explanatory concept, but rather showed that design need not be construed anthropomorphically (1975a, p. 73); thus, to say that a feature is part of the design of a system is not to imply that the system was designed by an intelligent being. Nevertheless, the facts remain that malfunctions are relative to design, that artifacts are designed by intelligent beings, and that what design an artifact has is relative to the intentions of the designer. What warrants the description "breakdown" or "malfunction" depends upon such stance-dependent features as intentions. Therefore, at least in cases of artifacts, features attributed from the design stance cannot be understood in a stance-independent way.

Are malfunctions in evolved organisms also stance-dependent features? If malfunctions in evolved organisms are *not* stance-dependent features, then the fact that malfunctions in artifacts are stance-dependent features puts Dennett's goal of a general theory of intelligence that applies equally to organisms and artifacts permanently out of reach. If, on the other hand, malfunctions in evolved organisms *are* stance-dependent features, then there remains nothing in the design stance untainted by the intentional.

Suppose that Dennett takes design features generally to be stance-dependent. This would seem to allow for a unified view of humans and artifacts: functions of a machine are relative to the intentions of the designers (namely, humans), and functions of evolved organisms are relative to the intentions of Mother Nature. But to say that Nature has intentions, officially, is to say no more than that attribution of intentions is predictive. Thus, the cost of taking design features to be stance-dependent seems to be instrumentalism about theories of natural selection.

Dennett thus seems faced with a deep dilemma regarding the design stance.

If design features are stance-independent, then there is no place for malfunc-tion, at least in the case of artifacts (since having brakes, etc., is not stance-independent); but if design features are stance-dependent, then theories of natural selection, as theories explaining design features of evolved organisms, must be construed instrumentalistically. In the first case, the design level tends to collapse into the physical; in the second case, the design level tends to collapse into the intentional. The result is that the design stance is inherently unstable.

The unavoidable inconsistencies in the treatment of belief, rationality and design suggest that instrumental intentionality is an illusion. This suspicion will be further confirmed on consideration of the status of the physical and intentional stances.

3 The Status of the Stances

Suppose that Dennett were to fend off the difficulties of design. Still, the problems would persist. The one that I shall focus on concerns another aspect of the relation between the physical and intentional stances; is the intentional stance dispensable without cognitive loss? Attempts to answer this question lead, I believe, to another dilemma, which has been obscured by the inconsistency of treatment of the intentional stance.

Apart from the difficulties engendered by ambiguity, the attempt to render physical and intentional explanations compatible leads, I believe, to a kind of metaphysical dilemma, one which can be resolved within a physicalist framework (if at all) only at the expense of the vocabulary of the intentional stance that Dennett aims to preserve. On the one hand, if there is something that eludes the physical stance, then Dennett's instrumentalism is imperiled; but on the other hand, if nothing eludes the physical stance, then Dennett's intentionalism cannot play its assigned role.

If Dennett is correct, then any system, human or not, may be described exhaustively and its operations explained wholly in terms of its physical con-stitution. Dennett points out that "if some version of mechanistic physicalism is true (as I believe), we will never *need* absolutely to ascribe any intentions to anything . . ." (1976, p. 273). This seems to imply that the intentional stance is in principle (even if not in practice) dispensable.

On the other hand, Dennett has suggested, to fail to take an intentional stance is, in some cases, to miss certain "objective patterns." Surely, this claim, which would help give the intentional stance the weight it needs to be more than a "sham," leads straight to a dilemma for Dennett; for the existence of *objective* patterns that would be missed by a physical stance would seem to falsify Dennett's instrumentalism concerning the intentional level.

For example, consider Dennett's superior Martians, who can predict all our behavior, every physical movement, from the physical stance. Despite this ability, Dennett says,

> if they did not also see us as intentional systems, they would be *missing something* perfectly objective: the *patterns* in human behavior that are describable from the intentional stance, and only from that stance, and which support generalizations and predictions. (see this volume, p. 322)

If Dennett's view is that, in failing to take the intentional stance, the Martians would miss something objective about us, he would seem to have revised his earlier view that "a particular thing is an intentional system only in relation to the strategies of someone who is trying to explain and predict its behavior" (1971, pp. 3–4). For this example purports to show that our being intentional systems is something perfectly objective apart from the strategies of the ascribers, which, ex hypothesi, are wholly served by the physical stance. What might be missed from the physical stance?

> Take a particular instance in which the Martians observe a stock broker deciding to place an order for 500 shares of General Motors. They predict the exact motions of his fingers as he dials the phone, and the exact vibrations of his vocal cords as he intones his order. But if the Martians do not see that indefinitely many *different* patterns of finger motions and vocal cord vibrations – even the motions of indefinitely many different individuals – could have been substituted for the actual particulars without perturbing the subsequent operation of the market, then they have failed to see a real pattern in the world they are observing. (see this volume, p. 322)

But whether or not the pattern Dennett indicates requires the intentional stance for discerning it depends upon how the expression "perturbing the subsequent operation of the market" is understood. If it is cashed out in physical terms, then he has not shown any "perfectly objective" pattern that is missed by the physical stance. On the other hand, if it cannot be cashed out in physical terms, then the claim would have to be that there are things that elude the physical stance.

Either way, the example illustrates the dilemma suggested earlier: if there is something intentional that eludes the physical stance, then Dennett's instrumentalism about the intentional is endangered; if there is nothing that eludes the physical stance, then the intentional stance seems, in principle, dispensable without cognitive loss, in which case Dennett's intentional stance is "just a sham and a word game" (Haugeland, 1982, p. 616).

4 Ersatz Intentionality

Dennett's instrumentalism concerning intentionality does not deliver the goods. If intentional system theory is genuinely instrumentalistic, if the features that are designated from the intentional stance are stance-dependent features, then the theory cannot play either the ethical or proto-scientific role that Dennett assigns to it: it cannot play the ethical role unless inconsistently applied, and it cannot play the proto-scientific role, because, as mere "interpretation," the intentional stance swings free of the design and physical stances.

On the other hand, if Dennett means the intentional stance to offer a special vocabulary for describing features equally well describable in the vocabulary of the design or physical stance, and he remains a realist about entities posited from these other stances, then it is not even instrumentalistic. To attribute a belief that p would be to attribute a design or physical property (that is, a stance-independent feature) in a special vocabulary. This would be straightforward reduction, to which appeals to hermeneutics would be irrelevant. It also would expose intentional system theory as a "sham and mere word play," in which case the "legitimacy" that intentional system theory holds out for attributions of attitudes is spurious.

These critical points have been submerged, in part because Dennett has not been altogether consistent in his construal of instrumentalism. Throughout *Brainstorms*, he understands attitudes solely in terms of predictive attributability, and it is on this basis that I distinguished between stance-dependent and stance-independent features. Elsewhere, however, in comparing beliefs to centers of gravity, he implies that all he means by his instrumentalism is that beliefs are not to be identified with any particular inner physical state. But, clearly, non-identity with a particular inner state is only a necessary, not a sufficient, condition for an instrumentalistic account of belief; one could be a realist about belief and identify a belief with a complex state of a subject and the environment.

In addition, if the aim is to give an instrumentalistic account of attitudes, the analogy between beliefs and centers of gravity is off the mark. Although we do not identify an object's center of gravity with any inner state or particle, we do not take attributions of centers of gravity to be instrumentalistic, and for good reason: an object's center of gravity is fully determined by the physical properties of the object; it is not a matter of "interpretation." Like the use of exponents in mathematics, employment of the concept of a center of gravity provides a kind of shorthand for genuine properties (stance-independent features) that an object really has. Centers of gravity, unlike beliefs on Dennett's view, are independent of anyone's attitudes, ascriptions or strategies.

The analogy is further vitiated by the fact that the idea of a center of gravity is ensconced in a genuine theory, while the idea of belief is not. As Dennett says, he derives his conclusions about intentional systems from what "seems . . . to be a slapdash, informal sort of thinking that I explicitly deny to be a theory in the strict sense of the term" (1983b, p. 382). Thus, the comparison of the concept of a belief to that of concept of a center of gravity is likely to mislead and to obscure the deep dilemma of Dennett's instrumentalism.[5]

It has been easy to see from the outset that on a consistent intentional system theory, too many things (such as game-playing computers, perhaps even lecterns) have beliefs and have them in the same sense that we do: officially, beliefs are nothing but stance-dependent features whose attribution enables the attributor to predict behavior described in certain ways. Although there is little predictive advantage in attributing beliefs to a lectern (since its behavioral repertoire is so limited), it cannot be deemed an error to do so by intentional system theory. Moreover, to be consistent on intentional system theory, one must regard one's own beliefs as no more than aids for predicting behavior, and even the regarding of them must be cashed out in terms of predictive attributability. Although not emphasized here, the wildness of the consequences of the theory should not be overlooked.

Quite apart from its counterintuitive consequences however, Dennett's instrumentalism is beset, as we have seen, by difficulties. It is plagued by a series of inconsistencies in the treatment of the concepts of belief, rationality and design; and it is caught in a dilemma concerning the epistemic completeness of the physical stance. For these reasons, I think it unlikely that intentional system theory will be made coherent.[6]

Notes

"Instrumental Intentionality" originally appeared in *Philosophy of Science*, 56 (1989), and is reprinted here by permission of *Philosophy of Science*, Princeton University Press and the author.

1 The expression "stance-dependent feature" may be eliminated in favor of the more cumbersome, but more explicitly Dennettian, "feature possessed only in relation to someone's strategies." (Compare a "particular thing is an intentional system only in relation to the strategies of someone who is trying to explain and predict its behavior" (Dennett, 1971, pp. 3–4).) Not only is my formulation of the relevant distinction shorter, but also it makes plain the unity of my objections. All of my arguments point to a single, central flaw in Dennett's conception – namely, an inconsistency in the use of the idea of being a feature possessed only in relation to someone's strategies, or, more briefly, of stance-dependence.

2 Dennett's view may be contrasted with Davidson's here. On Davidson's view, mental events are simply physical events described in a special (mentalistic) vocabulary. If this were Dennett's view, as we shall see in the discussion of rationality below, his instrumentalism would collapse.

3 If the stance-dependence/stance-independence distinction is similar to any other distinction common in the literature, it is to the mind-dependence/mind-independence distinction as used in discussions of temporal becoming. (See Grünbaum, 1968.) Nevertheless, I would not want to push the comparison too far, nor is it relevant to current purposes to push it at all.

4 It may be thought that we can avoid regarding brake failures as dependent on intentions if our theory about cars is an idealization that permits identifying

non-responsive brakes as breakdowns relative to that idealization. However, which idealization is the correct one will be determined in part by the intentions of the designers.

5   If, as Dennett says (1983b, p. 380), there are "physical facts in virtue of which a monkey believes what it believes," and if those facts (whatever they are) fully determine the monkey's beliefs in the way that the comparison to centers of gravity suggests, then there remains little point in calling the position instrumentalistic.

6   I wish to thank Hilary Kornblith, Derk Pereboom, and Daniel Dennett for comments on an earlier version of this article. Since Dennett continues to develop his position, he may no longer hold all the views that I attribute to him here. (See Dennett, 1987). Nevertheless, these views well illustrate the difficulties of working out the details of an instrumentalism about belief.

Part III

Epilogue

16 What Is a Theory of Mental Representation?

Stephen Stich

1 Introduction

Theories of mental content or mental representation are very fashionable these days. And, as with many fashionable products, the market offers a dizzying range of options. There are causal covariation theories, teleological theories, functional role theories, and theories inspired by the causal theory of reference. There are single factor theories, multiple factor theories, narrow theories, wide theories, and a profusion of variations on all of these themes.[1] Indeed, it often seems that it is hard to find a current volume of a major journal in the area that does not have at least one article offering an argument for, or (more typically) against, someone's theory of mental representation. Moreover much of this literature has an unmistakable tone of urgency to it. The quest for an adequate theory of mental representation is not just a popular pursuit; many writers insist it is a vitally important one. Jerry Fodor, who is rarely accused of understating the case, tells us that producing a naturalistic theory of mental content is an essential step in vindicating commonsense intentional psychology. And "if commonsense intentional psychology really were to collapse, that would be, beyond comparison, the greatest intellectual catastrophe in the history of our species" (Fodor, 1987, p. xii). Fred Dretske uses similarly apocalyptic terms. Without a suitably naturalistic theory of mental content, he suggests darkly, we might ultimately have to "relinquish a conception of ourselves as human agents" (1988, p. x).

While there is no shortage of debate about the merits and demerits of various accounts of mental content, there has been remarkably little discussion about what a theory of mental representation is supposed to do: what question (or questions) is a theory of mental representation supposed to answer? And what would count as getting the answer right? These are the questions that will be center stage in the current paper. In trying to answer them, it will prove useful to start by asking another question: why do so many people *want* a theory of mental representation; what makes the project of producing such a theory seem so urgent? This is the question I'll try to answer in section 2.

Though it is unfortunate that questions about what a theory of mental representation is supposed to do have been so often neglected, it is hardly surprising. The sort of methodological self-consciousness that these questions engender has rarely been fashionable in philosophy. As a result, it is all too often the case that philosophers provide elaborate solutions for which there is no clear problem – or, as Fodor has put it, they offer cures for which there is no adequate disease. Thus I would urge, as a basic principle of philosophical method, that we spend a fair amount of time getting clear about the question, before we start worrying about the answer. When we apply this strategy to theorizing about mental representation, some very surprising conclusions begin to emerge.

Here is a preview of the conclusions that I will be defending in the pages to follow.

(1) Once we start thinking about what a theory of mental representation is supposed to do, it becomes clear that there are actually several very different answers that might be offered. There is not one project here but several. These projects divide into two different families, though even within a single family there are important differences to be noted.

(2) With a single (and controversial) exception, the projects that I will sketch cannot readily be pursued by philosophers using the familiar techniques of philosophical analysis that predominate in the literature. Rather, they are intrinsically interdisciplinary projects in which the construction and testing of empirical theories plays a central role. However (again with a few exceptions), the sort of interdisciplinary work that would be necessary to make serious progress on these projects is notably absent in the literature.

(3) This last fact might be taken as an indication that the projects people are actually pursuing are different from the ones that I will describe – that I have simply failed to figure out what those who are searching for a theory of mental representation are up to. But without some details on what those alternative projects might be, I am inclined to draw a darker conclusion: it is my contention that most of the players in this very crowded field have *no* coherent project that could possibly be pursued successfully with the methods they are using.

(4) Even if we put these worries to one side, it is unlikely that any of the projects I will sketch will be of much help in responding to the concerns that have led many to feel it is a matter of some urgency to produce a theory of mental representation.

(5) But I will also argue that those concerns themselves are deeply misguided.

So much for threats and promises. It is time to get to work.

2 Why Would We Want a Theory of Mental Representation?

No doubt there are lots of reasons why people might want a theory of mental representation. But among these many motives, one stands out. Concern about *eliminativism* has been a central theme in the philosophy of mind during the last decade, and producing a theory of mental representation is seen to be a central step in the debate. Though eliminativists have rarely been clear or careful in setting out their thesis, I think the doctrine is best viewed as making a pair of ontological claims, one of which is much stronger, and more unsettling, than the other. The weaker claim is that the representational states of commonsense psychology – states like beliefs and desires – will play no role in a mature theory about the causes of human behavior. If we use the label "cognitive science" as a catch-all for the various scientific disciplines that will play a role in the explanation of human behavior, then what the eliminativist is claiming is that the intentional states posited by commonsense psychology are not part of the ontology of cognitive science. The stronger claim is that these commonsense mental states do not even exist. *There are no such things*, just as there are no such things as phlogiston, or caloric fluid, or witches. Those who endorse both of these claims typically suppose that the first can be marshalled in support of the second, though it is far from clear how the argument is supposed to run.[2] There can be little doubt that many people think a theory of mental representation has a major role to play in the debate over eliminativism. But exactly what this role is supposed to be is less clear. In sections 3 and 4 we will be looking at a pair of views on what a theory of mental representation is. When we've made some progress on the topic, we will return, in section 5, to the question of how a theory of mental representation might be exploited in arguing for or against eliminativism.

There are various arguments for the weaker of the two eliminativist theses – the claim that beliefs and desires won't play a role in a mature cognitive science. One family of arguments focuses on the *structure* of the cognitive processes and mechanisms portrayed by folk psychology. These structures, it is maintained, are incompatible with the structures posited in one or another putatively promising scientific paradigm.[3] A second family of arguments focuses on the *semantic* or *intentional* properties of mental states, as these are construed in commonsense psychology. Some of the arguments in this second family are fairly fussy and technical. They exploit sophisticated notions such as supervenience, individualism, and meaning holism. But, as Fodor has noted, for many people the most worrisome fact about semantic properties is their intuitive ontological oddness.

> [T]he deepest motivation for intentional irrealism derives not from . . . relatively technical worries about individualism and holism . . . but rather from a certain

ontological intuition: that there is no place for intentional categories in a physicalistic view of the world; that the intentional can't be *naturalized*. (1987, p. 97)

This worry goes a long way toward explaining a widely accepted *constraint* on any acceptable theory of mental representation. The theory must be *naturalistic*. It must show how representational properties of mental states can be explained in terms that are compatible with the broader, physicalistic view of nature provided by the natural sciences. Despite its widespread acceptance, I am inclined to think that the naturalism constraint is deeply misguided. I will say a bit about the reasons for my misgivings in section 6.

Even if one accepts the naturalism constraint, however, it is obvious that this constraint can only be part of the story about what it is to get a theory of mental representation right. For on any plausible unpacking of the naturalism constraint, it will be possible to tell lots of naturalistic stories about mental representation, and these stories will differ from one another in lots of ways. We surely don't want to say that all of these accounts are correct. So let us now ask what distinguishes the good ones from the bad ones. What counts as getting a theory *right*?

3   Describing a Commonsense Concept: A First Family of Projects

A prominent feature of our everyday discourse about ourselves and about other people is our practice of identifying mental states by adverting to their content. Examples are everywhere:

> Bush believes that Gorbachev is in Moscow.
> I think it is going to rain this afternoon.
> My wife hopes that I won't be late for dinner.

In these, and in a vast range of other cases, the attribution of content is effortless, unproblematic and unquestionably useful. Moreover, in the typical case, there is widespread intersubjective agreement about these attributions. Plainly, there must be a mental mechanism of some complexity underlying this ubiquitous practice, and it seems plausible to suppose that the mechanism in question includes a store of largely tacit knowledge about the conditions under which it is (and is not) appropriate to characterize a mental state as the belief or the desire *that p*. If we adopt the relatively loose use of the term "concept" that prevails in psychology, this amounts to the assumption that the mechanism underlying our practice embodies a concept of mental representation. And one perfectly plausible goal for a theory of mental content would be to describe that concept. To get the theory right is to give an accurate description of the concept, or the body of tacit knowledge, that underlies our quotidian practice.[4]

The project of describing the conceptual structure underlying judgments about content is at least roughly analogous to a variety of other projects that have been pursued in philosophy and cognitive science. In generative linguistics it is common to assume that a speaker's linguistic judgments and practice are subserved by a substantial body of tacit grammatical knowledge, and that the task of the linguist is to give an explicit account of what the speaker tacitly knows. In cognitive psychology there has been a fair amount of work aimed at making explicit the concepts and knowledge structures underlying various social and practical skills. One of the most fascinating projects along these lines has been the effort to uncover the concepts and principles of "folk physics" – the system of information about the physical world that we exploit as we wander around in it. What makes this research particularly intriguing is the finding that many people exploit a folk physics that is mistaken about the physical world, and not just in detail. The tacit theory that apparently guides these people's physical judgments and their actions is closer to medieval impetus theory than it is to Newtonian physics.[5] Findings like this may make the eliminativist's thesis a bit more plausible. If people can rely on a seriously mistaken physical theory to assist them in moving around in the world, surely it is at least possible that they rely on an equally mistaken psychological theory when they describe, explain and predict people's behavior.

A third endeavor that bears a significant resemblance to the project of describing our commonsense concept of mental representation is the sort of conceptual analysis that has provided intermittent employment for philosophers since the time of Socrates. The rules of the game have changed very little over the last 2500 years. It goes something like this:

s: (Socrates, as it might be): Tell me please, what is X? (where "X" may be replaced by "justice" or "piety" or "knowledge" or "causation" or "freedom" . . .)
c: (Cephalus, perhaps, or Chisholm): I will tell you gladly. To be an instance of X, something must be y and z.
s: But that can't be right. For surely you will grant that a is X, but it is neither y nor z.
c: You are quite right. Let me try again. To be an instance of X something must be either y and z or it must be w.
s: I'm afraid that won't work either, since b is w, but clearly it is not X.

The game comes to an end when S runs out of counterexamples, or C runs out of definitions. And, though no one has kept careful records in this sport, the smart money usually bets on S.

This philosophical game of definition and counterexample makes little sense unless we make a pair of assumptions about the concepts it aims to analyze.

The first of these is that the target concept can be characterized – or defined – by specifying necessary and sufficient conditions. To win a round, S can either produce an example which is an instance of the concept but is not captured by the definition, or he can produce an example which fits the definition but is not an instance of the concept. Moreover, it is generally assumed that the definition will be a Boolean concatenation of properties, or some relatively straightforward variation on that theme. The second assumption is that the players come equipped with enough information about the target concept to enable them to judge whether or not it applies in a wide range of cases, real and hypothetical, that they have never before imagined. To see this second point, consider a pair of well-known examples:

(i)   If someone asks you to keep his weapons, and then asks for them back after he has gone insane, does justice demand that you return them?

(ii) Suppose that Smith has just signed the papers to buy the Ford in the dealership showroom. Though Smith doesn't know it, the dealership does not have clear title to the car. However, moments before and far away, Granny Smith died, and title to her old Ford passes to Smith. So Smith believes he owns a Ford, and his belief is both justified and true. Does Smith *know* he owns a Ford?

It is hard to see how we could expect people to answer questions like these, or why we should take their answers seriously, unless we suppose that they already tacitly know something very much like the set of necessary and sufficient conditions that we are trying to make explicit.

There are two reasons why I have gone on at some length about the traditional philosophical approach to conceptual analysis. The first is that much of the philosophical literature on mental representation seems to fit squarely within the definition and counterexample paradigm. Philosophical theories about the nature of mental representation typically offer what purport to be necessary and sufficient conditions for claims of the form:

Mental state M has the content p.

And objections to these theories typically turn on intuitive counterexamples – cases in which the definition says that M has the content p, but intuition denies it, or vice versa.[6] The second reason is that there is now a fair amount of evidence suggesting that the assumptions underlying this traditional philosophical project may be simply mistaken. And if they are, then the project which dominates the philosophical literature on mental representation will be seriously undermined.

In the psychological literature, perhaps the most widely known challenge to the assumptions underlying traditional philosophical analysis derives from the work of Eleanor Rosch and her co-workers.[7] On the Roschian view, the mental structures that underlie people's judgments when they classify items into categories do not exploit tacitly known necessary and sufficient conditions for category membership, or anything roughly equivalent. Exactly what they do use is an issue that has motivated a great deal of empirical research during the last fifteen years, and continues to be actively explored. Early on Rosch proposed that categorization relies on *prototypes*, which may be thought of as idealized descriptions of the most typical or characteristic members of the category. The prototype for *bird*, for example, might include such features as flying, having feathers, singing, and a variety of others. In determining whether a particular instance falls within the category, subjects assess the *similarity* between the prototype and the instance being categorized. However, the features specified in the prototype are not even close to being necessary or sufficient conditions for membership. So, for example, an animal can lack one or many of the features of the prototypical bird, and still be classified as a bird. Emus are classified as birds though they neither fly nor sing. An alternative to the prototype theory is the hypothesis that categorization is subserved by *exemplars*, which can be thought of as detailed mental descriptions of specific members of the category that are familiar to the person doing the categorizing. On this account, too, people determine whether an item is a member of a category by making a tacit similarity judgment. However, on the exemplar theory, the item being classified is compared to exemplary members of the category.[8]

More recent research has made it clear that, for many concepts, neither the prototype nor the exemplar account will explain all the data comfortably. For some concepts it has been proposed that subjects' judgments rely on something very much like a tacitly known scientific theory. In other cases it has been suggested that there is no enduring concept underlying categorization judgments. Rather, it is argued, subjects construct concepts of various different sorts "on the fly," in response to the situation in which the need to categorize arises.[9]

Although there has been an enormous amount of work on concepts and categorization in recent years, there has been no systematic empirical study of *intentional* categories – categories such as *believing that p*, or *desiring that q*. Thus at present we can only speculate about what such an investigation would reveal. Perhaps the safest bet is that, whatever the mental mechanism underlying intentional categorization may be, it will not utilize "classical" concepts – the sort that can be defined with a set of necessary and sufficient conditions. The argument here is straightforwardly inductive: *no* commonsense concept that has been studied has turned out to be analyzable into a set of necessary and sufficient conditions. Indeed, given currently available evidence, it looks like there are no classical concepts. A second plausible speculation is that the concepts or "knowledge structures" underlying intentional categorization are much more complex than those traditionally offered in philosophical analysis. It's my guess that our "concept" of mental content is going to look more like a theory than like a Platonic definition.

Suppose these speculations are right, what follows? The most obvious consequence is that, in seeking to build a theory of mental representation, the traditional philosophical method of proposing definitions and hunting for intuitive counterexamples will have to be abandoned. That method tries to specify a set of conditions that all and only the cases which intuitively fall under the target concept will satisfy. But if our intuitions about whether a state has the content *that p* are guided by prototypes, or exemplars, or tacit theories, or if the mental structures that determine our intuitive judgments are constructed partly in response to the circumstances in which the judgment is called for, then there will be no such conditions. So if using the method of definition and counterexample is the hallmark of a philosophical theory in this area, and if the commonsense concept of mental representation is like every other concept that has been studied empirically, there is a sense in which *there can be no philosophical theory of content.*

It is important not to read too much into this conclusion, however. For, although the traditional method of philosophical analysis may have to be abandoned, there is no reason why we cannot use other methods in constructing a descriptive theory about the ordinary concept of mental representation. Linguists, cognitive psychologists and cognitive anthropologists have developed a variety of methods for exploring the structure of commonsense concepts, none of which presuppose that these concepts have a classical structure that can be captured by a set of necessary and sufficient conditions. With a bit of ingenuity, one or more of these methods might well be used to probe the mechanisms underlying our intuitive judgments about mental representation.

We began this section by asking what a theory of mental representation was supposed to do. And we now have at least the outlines of one plausible answer. A theory of mental representation is supposed to describe the concept or knowledge structure underlying people's ordinary judgments about the content of beliefs, desires and other intentional states. However, if *this* is the sort of theory that philosophers want when they set out to build a theory of mental representation, then it is a good bet that they will have to give up "doing philosophy" (as traditionally conceived) and start doing cognitive science instead.

4   Mental Representation as a Natural Phenomenon: A Second Family of Projects

The description of commonsense concepts, when not encumbered by a priori philosophical requirements on what such a description must look like, is a perfectly reasonable activity. But it is not the only project that those who seek a theory of mental representation might have in mind. To see what the alternative might be, consider the concept of disease. There is a substantial anthropological literature aimed at describing the concept of disease as it is used in various cultures.[10] And if you are interested in how people conceive of disease, this is the place to look. But if you are interested in what disease is then it is biology or medicine you should be studying, not cognitive anthropology. An entirely analogous point could be made about *gold*, or *space*, or *mass*, or *heredity*. If you want to know how people conceive of them, then the description of commonsense concepts or knowledge structures is the project to pursue. But if you want to know what gold, or space, or mass, or heredity is really like, then you should be studying chemistry or physics or genetics.

Sometimes the relevant science will be pretty explicit about how it conceives of the item of interest. *The Handbook of Physics and Chemistry* will tell you all you want to know about gold, and then some. But in lots of other cases a science will use a concept quite successfully without providing a fully explicit or philosophically satisfying account of that concept. In those cases, philosophers of science often step in and try to mark the notion in question more explicit. In recent years, there have been illuminating studies of *fitness, grammaticality, space-time* and a wide variety of other notions.[11] Part of this work can be viewed as straightforward conceptual description – trying to do for scientific concepts and theories what linguists, cognitive psychologists, and cognitive anthropologists have tried to do for commonsense concepts and theories. Indeed, in recent years a number of philosophers of science have begun using the techniques of cognitive science in the analysis of science, often with intriguing results.[12] Sometimes, however, the concepts philosophers find, and the theories in which they play a role, are uncomfortably vague or poorly developed. And in these cases it is not at all uncommon for philosophers of science to propose improvements in the concepts and theories they are describing. It is often no easy matter to say where description stops and construction begins, and for most purposes it hardly matters.

It looks like we now have the beginnings of second, rather different, answer to the question of what a theory of mental representation is supposed to do. On this second account, a theory of mental representation doesn't much care about the commonsense conception of mental representation. The intuitions and tacit knowledge of the man or woman in the street are quite irrelevant. The theory seeks to say what mental representation really is, not what folk psychology takes it to be. And to do this it must describe, and perhaps patch up, the notion of mental representation as it is used by the best cognitive science we have available. So on this account, a theory of mental representation begins as part of the cognitive psychology of cognitive science, though it may end up contributing to the conceptual foundations of the science it sets out to describe.

In the large literature on mental representation, I know of only one author who explicitly undertakes the project I have been sketching. The author is Robert Cummins, and in his book *Meaning and Mental Representation*[13] he offers a detailed account of a notion of mental representation. But he goes out of his way to stress that the notion he is concerned with is not the folk psychological concept that underlies our ordinary language of intentional characterization (p. 26). Rather, his goal is to give an account of the notion of mental representation that is used in one venerable and still vigorous research tradition in cognitive science – the tradition that seeks to build what Cummins calls "orthodox" computational theories of cognition. This tradition "assumes that cognitive systems are automatic interpreted formal systems" (p. 13), and much of the work on problem solving, planning, language processing and higher level visual processing that has been done during the last two decades falls squarely within the orthodox computational paradigm.

An essential part of Cummins's project is an explication of the explanatory strategy of computational theories of cognition. He offers an account of what these theories are trying to explain, and of what successful explanations in this paradigm must do. This explanatory structure imposes strong constraints on an account of mental representation since the notion of representation used in computational theories must make sense of the explanations being offered. Here's how Cummins characterizes his approach.

> First determine what explanatory role representation plays in some particular representation-invoking scientific theory or theoretical framework; then ask what representation has to be – how it is to be explicated – if it is to play that role. (p. 145)

Though Cummins's target is the notion of representation exploited in computational theories of cognition, he recognizes that this is not the only promising research tradition in cognitive science. "There are a number of different frameworks in the running in cognitive science today" (p. 26), including "orthodox computationalism, connectionism, neuroscience" (p. 12) and a variety of others. Much the same approach could be used on the notions of representation exploited in these other traditions, though the results might well turn out quite different. "[T]o suppose that . . . [these other research traditions] all make use of the same notion of representation seems naive" (p. 12). If we ask what each of these frameworks takes mental representation to be, "we are not likely to get a univocal answer" (p. 26).

This pluralistic picture is one I vigorously endorse. It adds an important dimension to the account of theories of mental representation that I have been sketching in this section. For if different paradigms within cognitive science use different notions of representation, then there isn't going to be *a* theory of mental representation of the sort we have been discussing. There will be *lots* of theories. Moreover, it makes no sense to ask which of these theories is the right one, since they are not in competition with one another. Each theory aims to characterize a notion of representation exploited in some branch of cognitive science. If different branches of cognitive science use different notions of representation, then there will be a variety of correct accounts of mental representation. Of course it might be thought that the various branches of cognitive science are themselves in competition, and that the correct theory of mental representation is the one that describes the notion of mental representation exploited by the correct cognitive science. But I see no reason to suppose that there is a unique correct framework for theories in cognitive science. There are lots of phenomena to explain, and lots of levels at which illuminating and scientifically respectable explanations can be given. Thus I am inclined to be a pluralist in this domain as well.

This is not the place for a detailed discussion of Cummins's account of the notion of mental representation, as it is used in computational theories of cognition. But there are a few themes in Cummins's work that I want to pursue a bit further, since they will lead us back to the question of how theories of mental representation are supposed to function in the debate over eliminativism.

5 Theories of Mental Representation and the Eliminativism Debate[14]

As Cummins sees it, the notion of mental representation that he is trying to describe abstracts from both the history of the system and "the actual items in a system's current environment" (p. 81). "According to computationalism, cognitive systems are individuated by their computational properties" (p. 82). And a pair of systems can have the same computational properties, even though they differ in history, in environment and even in physical make-up. The taxonomy generated by this notion of mental representation is *individualistic* – if a pair of organisms or systems have the same physical make-up, then their representational states represent the same thing. However, following Putnam, Burge and others, Cummins also maintains that the taxonomy of intentional states exploited by folk psychology is *anti-individualistic* – "beliefs and desires cannot be specified in a way that is independent of environment" or history (p. 140). What Cummins concludes from all of this is that beliefs, desires and the rest of the intentional states of commonsense psychology are not among the items recognized by the computational theory of cognition. "What the anti-individualist arguments of Putnam and Burge prove from the point of view of the [computational theory of cognition] is that beliefs and desires aren't psychological states in the sense of 'psychological state' of interest to the CTC" (p. 140).

It looks like what we have here is the beginnings of an argument for eliminativism in which both sorts of theories of mental representation that we have been sketching play a role. In outline, the argument works like this: first describe the notions of mental representation exploited by commonsense psychology and by computational theories of cognition. Next, compare the two. If they are significantly different, then the representational states of commonsense psychology are not part of the ontology of computational theories. Of course, this sort of argument won't make the eliminativist's case if it is restricted to the computational theory of cognition, since, as we've lately noted, contemporary cognitive science is a variegated discipline, and there are lots of other research traditions around. So, to develop a plausible defence of eliminativism, this argument would have to be repeated for each of the viable research traditions in the cognitive science market place. As an alternative to this case-by-case approach, the eliminativist could try to compress the process by showing that there are some features that any scientifically respectable notion of mental representation will have to have, and then arguing that these features are not endorsed by the account of mental representation implicit in folk psychology.[15]

However, even if all this goes well for the eliminativist, it is not clear that he will have made his case. To see why, let's go back to Cummins's contrast between beliefs, as they are construed in commonsense psychology, and the representational states of the computational theory of cognition. According to Cummins, commonsense psychology views beliefs anti-individualistically – they can't be specified in a way that is independent of environment. The psychological states posited by computational theories of cognition, by contrast, are individualistically individuated – they can be specified independent of environment. From this Cummins seems to conclude that the ontology of commonsense psychology is different from the ontology of the computational theory. The two theories are talking about different things. And Cummins is not alone in reasoning in this way. I have myself offered a similar argument in a variety of previous publications, as have some other authors.[16] But despite having such distinguished advocates, it is not at all clear that the premises of the argument support its conclusion. What the premises do entail is that folk theory and computational theories make different and incompatible claims about the states they talk about. But that surely is not sufficient to show that they are talking about different things. If it were it would be all but impossible for theorists to disagree. Could it not be the case that folk psychology and computational theories are talking about exactly the same things, and that folk psychology is just *wrong* about them?

What is really at issue here is the question of what determines the reference of the terms used in a theory. Those with eliminativist sympathies often write as though they accepted some version of the description theory of reference.[17] But this is a doubly dubious doctrine for eliminativists to adopt. One danger is that naive versions of the description theory tend to *trivialize* eliminativism. If minor disagreements between what commonsense says about mental states and what cognitive science says about them are sufficient to show that commonsense and cognitive science are positing different entities, then of course eliminativism is correct. But who cares? No one ever thought that commonsense psychology would turn out to be right about everything. Indeed, if we grant that minor theoretical differences always engender different ontologies, and if we assume that later theories are typically closer to the truth than earlier ones, we end up with a quite mad view – a sort of *pan-eliminativism*. For surely it is very likely that *every* theory we now accept will undergo some improvements during the next century. If that's enough to show that the entities posited by current theories don't exist then *nothing* we now believe in exists!

A second concern about the description theory of reference is that even much more sophisticated versions of the theory may well be wide of the mark. And if they are, then no interesting ontological conclusions can be drawn from the fact that folk psychology and the cognitive sciences disagree about mental states. One philosopher who has seen this point very clearly is William Lycan. Here's how Lycan views the matter:

> I incline away from Lewis's Carnapian and/or Rylean cluster theory of the reference of theoretical terms, and toward Putnam's causal-historical theory. As in Putnam's examples of "water," "tiger," and so on, I think the ordinary work "belief" (qua theoretical term of folk psychology) points dimly toward a natural kind that we have not fully grasped and that only mature psychology will reveal. I expect that "belief" will turn out to refer to some kind of information-bearing inner state of a sentient being, . . . but the kind of state it refers to may have only a few of the properties usually attributed to beliefs by common sense. Thus I think our ordinary way of picking out beliefs and desires succeeds in picking out real entities in nature, but it may not succeed in picking out the entities that common sense suggests that it does. (1988, p. 32)

As Lycan emphasizes, it is a consequence of this view that our commonsense theories may end up having been very wrong about the nature of beliefs and other representational mental states:

> I am entirely willing to give up fairly large chunks of our commonsensical or platitudinous theory of belief or of desire (or of almost anything else) and decide that we were just wrong about a lot of things, without drawing the inference that we are no longer talking about belief or desire. (1988, pp. 31–2)

Unfortunately, when the issue at hand is eliminativism, Lycan's line has much the same defect as naive versions of the description theory – though in the opposite direction. For on Lycan's view it is hard to see how *anything* could show that the posits of folk psychology are not part of the ontology of a given branch of cognitive science. Indeed, on Lycan's view, it is far from clear why we should not say that phlogiston really does exist. It's the stuff we now call "oxygen," and earlier theorists were "just wrong about a lot of things." So it seems that, if we accept either the theory of reference that Lycan favors or the naive description theory, then the eliminativist's claim will be *trivialized*. On the description theory, eliminativism is trivially true; on the causal-historical theory, eliminativism is trivially false.

Where does all this leave us? If we want to construe eliminativism as an *interesting* doctrine, rather than one which is trivially true or trivially false, then our account of reference will have to be less restrictive than the naive description theory, and more restrictive than the causal-historical theory. And plainly we *do* want to construe eliminativism as an interesting doctrine – or so I used to think. Thus, when I first set out the argument that I've just sketched, my initial reaction was to hunt around for a more promising story about reference. However, I now think that was a serious mistake.

The problem is not that alternative accounts of reference are hard to find; quite the opposite. It's relatively easy to construct accounts of reference that appear to do just what we want. They are more restrictive than the causal-historical theory and less restrictive than the description theory. But this raises questions that should by now sound very familiar: Which of these theories of reference is the right one? And what counts as getting the theory right? Moreover, in light of the close connection between the notion of reference and the notion of mental representation, it is pretty clear that much of what was said about the latter notion in sections 3 and 4 could be repeated, with equal plausibility, about the former. If it can, then there isn't going to be any single, correct account of reference. Rather, there will be one account that describes our commonsense notion of reference (or several accounts, if there is more than one commonsense notion in circulation), and other accounts describing reference-like notions that may be of use in one or another project in psychology or linguistics or epistemology, or perhaps in some other discipline.

Now if all of this is right, some surprising conclusions follow. The first is that eliminativism cannot be viewed as a single thesis, nor even as a pair of theses as suggested in section 2. To see the point, consider the weaker of the two eliminativist theses distinguished earlier – the thesis which claims that the posits of commonsense psychology are not part of the ontology of cognitive science. If our recent reflections are on the right track, then this thesis makes no sense – it has no determinate truth conditions – unless it is tied to some specific account of reference. So if there are many perfectly correct accounts of reference, then there are many different readings of the "weak" eliminativist thesis. Moreover, it is plausible to suppose that on some of these readings the eliminativist's claim will turn out to be true, while on others it will turn out to be false. But if this is right, then it is far from clear that any reading of the eliminativist thesis is all that interesting a claim. Before we realized that any intelligible version of the doctrine had to be relativized or indexed to a theory of reference, it was perhaps plausible to claim that, if eliminativism was true, then some grave intellectual catastrophe would ensue. And that, surely, is more than enough to make the doctrine interesting. But once we've seen the need to index the doctrine to some particular theory of reference, things look rather different. For surely no one is prepared to claim that eliminativism, no matter what theory of reference it is relativized to, will bring the intellectual roof down. Of course, one still might maintain that there is some particular theory of reference such that if eliminativism, indexed to that theory, is true, then worrisome consequences will ensue. And for all I know this might be right. But if it is right, it certainly isn't *obvious*; it is a claim that needs an argument. And I haven't a clue how that argument might go. So until we get some enlightenment on the matter, I think it is reasonable to suspect that the interest of eliminativism has been very much exaggerated.

6 Eliminativism and the Naturalism Constraint[18]

Recall that on Fodor's view the "deepest motivation" for eliminativism, or "intentional irrealism," is the suspicion that "the intentional can't be *naturalized*" (1987, p. 97). Presumably the implicit argument for irrealism that Fodor has in mind has the structure sketched in the previous section: to be exploited in a respectable scientific theory a concept must be naturalizable. So if intentional notions can't be naturalized, then they can't be exploited in any respectable scientific theory. Fodor's own theory of content is largely motivated by the hope that this suspicion can be laid to rest. In this last section I want to consider a pair of questions about all of this. First: what would it take to allay the concern that "the intentional can't be naturalized," and how might a theory of mental representation of the sort we have been considering play a role in this process? Second: just how bad would it be if the project fails and we discover that we can't naturalize intentional notions?

The answer to the first question seems clear enough, at least in outline. To put to rest the fear that the intentional can't be naturalized, we have to give a naturalistic account of a notion of mental representation that is (or might be) exploited in cognitive science, and with which the commonsense notion of mental representation may plausibly be identified. However, this answer raises a pair of problems. The first is simply a version of the problem that we were wrestling with in the previous section: what does it take to justify the cross-theoretic identification of a pair of theoretical concepts? On my view, there is no determinate answer to this question. But I have already said my piece on that topic, and won't reopen the issue here. The second problem is one that has been lurking in the shadows since the early pages of this paper, when the issue of "naturalizing" mental representation was first raised: what does it take for an account of mental representation to be *naturalistic*? Though I know of no one who has offered a detailed answer to this question, the literature strongly suggests that those who want a naturalistic account of mental representation want something like a definition – a set of necessary and sufficient conditions

– couched in terms that are unproblematically acceptable in the physical or biological sciences.

Whether an appropriately naturalistic account of mental representation can be given is, of course, very much an open question. My own guess, for what little it's worth, is that the project is quite hopeless. However, in contrast with Fodor and many others, I am inclined to think that very little hangs on the matter. Fodor suggests that, if we can't give a naturalistic account of mental representation, then there will be no place for the notion in serious science. And if that's the case, then the eliminativists will have won a major battle. Indeed, perhaps they will have won the war. But this suggestion strikes me as quite wrong-headed. To see why, we need only consider a few examples. Let's begin with the notion of a phoneme. What is it to be a /p/ or a /b/? If you want a naturalistic answer, one which gives necessary and sufficient conditions in physical or biological terms, then I'm afraid you're going to be disappointed. For, despite many years of sophisticated research, there is currently no naturalistic answer available.[19] Of course that situation might change. Phoneticians may come up with a naturalistic account of what it is for a sound sequence to be a /p/. But then again the current situation might not change. If it does not, this is surely no reason to become a phoneme-eliminativist and deny the existence of phonemes. Much the same point could be made about lots of other notions of unquestionable scientific utility. There is no naturalistic account of *grooming behavior* in primate ethology. Nor is there a naturalistic account of *attack behavior* in stickleback ethology. But surely it would be simply perverse to deny the existence of grooming behavior, simply because we can't define it in the language of physics and biology. Suitably trained observers can detect grooming behavior (or phonemes) with impressively high intersubjective reliability. And that, I would urge, is more than enough to make those notions empirically respectable. To demand more – in particular to demand that the notions in question can be "naturalized" – seems unmotivated and silly. The situation for *mental representation* looks entirely parallel. There may, perhaps, be good reasons to be an eliminativist. But the fact that mental representation can't be naturalized is not one of them.[20]

Notes

"What Is a Theory of Mental Representation?" originally appeared in *Mind*, 101 (1992) and is reprinted here by permission of Oxford University Press.

1   For causal covariation theories, see Dretske (1988), Fodor (1987), and Fodor (1990b). For teleological theories, see Fordor (1990c), Millikan (1984), and Papineau (1987). For functional role theories, see Block (1986), Field (1977), and Loar (1981). For a theory inspired by the causal theory of reference, see Devitt and Sterelny (1987). For a single factor theory, see Harman (1986). For a multiple factor theory, see McGinn (1982). For narrow theories, see Fodor (1987) and Devitt (1990). For a wide theory, see Burge (1979).

2 For some not entirely satisfactory discussion of the point, see Stich (1983), chapter 11, §1.

3 See, for example, Ramsey, Stich and Garon (1990).

4 For a rather different story about the mechanism underlying our ability to attribute mental states by characterizing their content, see Gordon (1986) and Goldman (1989). For an extended critique of the Gordon/Goldman view, see Stich and Nichols (1993).

5 See McCloskey, Caramazza and Green (1980), and McCloskey (1983).

6 See, for example: Block (1986), p. 660; Field (1986a), p. 444; Jones, Mulaire and Stich (1991), §4.2; Loewer (1987), p. 296.

It is worth noting that on several occasions Fodor has claimed that he would be satisfied with sufficient conditions "for one bit of the world to be about (to express, represent, or be true of) another bit," even if they are not necessary (Fodor, 1987, p. 98. See also Fodor, 1990a, p. 52 ff.).

But, as noted in Jones, Mulaire & Stich (1991), if we read him literally, then it is hard to believe that this is what Fodor really wants. For providing conditions that are merely sufficient is just too easy.

> If x is Fodor's most recent utterance of "Maria Callas" (or: if x is the concept that underlies that utterance) then x represents Maria Callas.
> If y is Fodor's most recent utterance of "Meaning Holism is a crazy doctrine" (or the thought that underlies it) then y is about Meaning Holism, and y is true iff Meaning Holism is a crazy doctrine.

There are two sufficient conditions, and for a few pennies each I will be happy to provide indefinitely many more.

7 As Rosch frequently notes, her work in this area was inspired by Wittgenstein's *Philosophical Investigations*.

8 For an excellent review of the literature on prototype and exemplar theories, see Smith and Medin (1981).

9 Murphy and Medin (1985); Barsalou (1987); Rips (1989).

10 See, for example, Murdock (1980).

11 For fitness, see Sober (1984b), for grammaticality, see Fodor (1981c); for space-time see Sklar (1974).

12 See, for example, Giere (1988), Glymour, Kelly, Scheines, and Sprites (1986), Langley, Simon, Bradshaw and Zytkow (1987), Nersessian (1991), Thagard (1988).

13 Cummins (1989a). Page references to Cummins's book will be given in parentheses in the text.

14 Parts of this section were borrowed in Stich (1991).

15 This is, in effect, the strategy I tried in Stich (1978). Still another strategy would be for the eliminativist to argue that one or another of the competing research traditions in cognitive science is not a serious contender, and thus need not be considered.

16 See Stich (1979), (1983), part II, and Stack (unpublished).

17 Lycan (1988) correctly characterizes the "doxastaphobe's" argument as follows:

> Typically their arguments take the form: "Common sense characterizes beliefs [say] as having each of the following properties: F, G, H, . . . But nothing that will be mentioned by any respectable future psychology will

have all or even very many of those properties; therefore, beliefs will not figure in a mature psychology." (p. 4)

18   For a more detailed treatment of the issues discussed in this section, see Stich and Laurence (1994).

19   For useful overviews, see Fry (1979) and Pickett (1980).

20   Earlier versions of this paper have been presented at the Royal Irish Academy, at MIT, at Northwestern University, and at the Universities of Bielefeld, Colorado, Gothenberg, Konstanz, Montreal, South Carolina and Syracuse. Comments and criticism from these audiences have been helpful in more ways than I could possibly record. I am grateful to Eric Margolis for help in tracking down some of the references.

After this paper was written I was delighted to discover that Michael Tye had independently reached very similar conclusions on the basis of very similar arguments. Tye (1992) develops these themes in an extremely interesting way.

References and Bibliography

Adams, F. (1990). "Causal contents," in McLaughlin (1990).

Adams, F. (in preparation). *Mind and Action.*

Adams, F. and Aizawa, K. (1992). " 'X' means X: semantics Fodor-style," *Minds and Machines*, 2, pp. 175–83.

Adams, F. and Aizawa, K. (1993). "Fodorian semantics, pathologies, and Block's problem," *Minds and Machines*, 3, pp. 97–104.

Adams, F. and Aizawa, K. (forthcoming). " 'X', means X: Fodor/Warfield semantics."

Adams, F., Aizawa, K. and Fuller, G. (forthcoming). "A cure for disjunctivitis."

Appiah, A. (1986). "Truth conditions: a causal theory," in Butterfield (1986).

Armstrong, D. (1968). *A Materialist Theory of the Mind.* London: Routledge & Kegan Paul.

Baker, L. (1987). "Content by courtesy," *Journal of Philosophy*, 84, pp. 197–213.

Baker, L. (1989). "On a causal theory of content," *Philosophical Perspectives*, 3, pp. 165–86.

Barsalou, L. (1987). "The instability of graded structure: Implications for the nature of concepts," in *Concepts and Conceptual Development: Ecological and Intellectual Factors in Categorization*, ed. U. Neisser (Cambridge: Cambridge University Press).

Barwise, J. (1984). *The Situation in Logic I.* Technical Report CSLI-84-2. Stanford University.

Barwise, J. and Perry, J. (1983). *Situations and Attitudes.* Cambridge, MA: MIT Press.

Barwise, J. and Perry, J. (1984). *Shifting Situations and Shaken Attitudes.* Research Report CSLI-84-13. Stanford University.

Blakemore, R. P. and Frankel, R. B. (1981). "Magnetic navigation in bacteria," *Scientific American*, 245.

Block, N. (1978). "Troubles with functionalism," *Minnesota Studies in the Philosophy of Science*, 9.

Block, N. (1980). "What intuitions about homunculi do not show," *Behavioral and Brain Sciences*, 3, pp. 425–6.

Block, N. (1981a). *Readings in the Philosophy of Psychology*, 2 vols. Cambridge, MA: Harvard University Press.

Block, N. (1981b). "Psychologism and behaviorism," *Philosophical Review*, 90, pp. 5–43.

Block, N. (1981c). "Introduction: what is functionalism?" in Block, (1981a).

Block, N. (1983). "Mental pictures and cognitive science," *Philosophical Review*, 92, pp. 499–541.

Block, N. (1986). "Advertisement for a semantics for psychology," *Midwest Studies in Philosophy*, 10, pp. 615–78. Reprinted in this volume.

Block, N. and Bromberger, S. (1980). "States' rights," *Behavioral and Brain Sciences*, 3.

Boghossian, P. (1989). "Review of Colin McGinn's *Wittgenstein on Meaning*," *Philosophical Review*, 98, pp. 83–4.

Boyd, R. (1979). "Metaphor and theory change," in *Metaphor and Thought*, ed. A. Ortony (Cambridge: Cambridge University Press).

Brison, S. (unpublished). "Do we think in Mentalese?".

Burge, T. (1979). "Individualism and the mental," *Midwest Studies in Philosophy*, 4, pp. 73–121.

Burge, T. (1986). "Individualism and psychology," *Philosophical Review*, 95, pp. 3–46.

Butterfield, J., ed. (1986). *Language, Mind and Logic*. Cambridge: Cambridge University Press.

Cherniak, C. (1986). *Minimal Rationality*. Cambridge, MA: MIT Press.

Chisholm, R. (1957). *Perceiving a Philosophical Study*. Ithaca, NY: Cornell University Press.

Churchland, P. M. (1979). *Scientific Realism and the Plasticity of Mind*. Cambridge: Cambridge University Press.

Churchland, P. M. (1981). "Eliminative materialism and propositional attitudes," *Journal of Philosophy*, 78, pp. 67–90.

Churchland, P. M. (1984). *Matter and Consciousness*. Cambridge, MA: MIT Press.

Churchland, P. M. and Churchland, P. S. (1983). "Content – semantic and information-theoretic," *Behavioral and Brain Sciences*, 6, pp. 67–8.

Churchland, P. S. (1986). *Neurophilosophy: Toward a Unified Science of the Mind-Brain*. Cambridge, MA: MIT Press.

Crane, T. (1990). "The language of thought: no syntax without semantics," *Mind and Language*, 5, pp. 187–212.

Cummins, R. (1983). *The Nature of Psychological Explanation*. Cambridge, MA: MIT Press.

Cummins, R. (1989a). *Meaning and Mental Representation*. Cambridge, MA: MIT Press.

Cummins, R. (1989b). "Representation and covariation," in Silvers (1989).

Davidson, D. (1967). "Truth and meaning," *Synthese*, 17, pp. 304–23.

Davidson, D. (1984). *Truth and Interpretation*. Oxford: Oxford University Press.

Dennett, D. (1969). *Content and Consciousness*. London: Routledge & Kegan Paul.

Dennett, D. (1971). "Intentional systems," *Journal of Philosophy*, 68, pp. 87–106. Reprinted in Dennett (1978a).

Dennett, D. (1973). "Mechanism and responsibility," Reprinted in Dennett (1978a).

Dennett, D. (1975a). "Why the law of effect won't go away," Reprinted in Dennett (1978a).

Dennett, D. (1975b). "Brain writing and mind reading," *Minnesota Studies in the Philosophy of Science*, 7.

Dennett, D. (1976). "Conditions of personhood," Reprinted in Dennett (1978a).

Dennett, D. (1978a). *Brainstorms*. Cambridge, MA: MIT Press.

Dennett, D. (1978b). "A cure for the common code," in Dennett (1978a).

Dennett, D. (1978c). "Intentional systems," in Dennett (1978a).

Dennett, D. (1978d). "On giving libertarians what they say they want," in Dennett (1978a).

Dennett, D. (1981a). "Making sense of ourselves," *Philosophical Topics*, 12, pp. 63–81.

Dennett, D. (1981b) "Three kinds of intentional psychology," Reprinted in Dennett (1987).

Dennett, D. (1981c). "True believers: the intentional strategy and why it works," in *Scientific Explanations*, ed. A. F. Heath (Oxford: Oxford University Press). Reprinted in this volume.

Dennett, D. (1982a). "How to study consciousness empirically, or nothing comes to mind," *Synthese*, 53, pp. 159–80.

Dennett, D. (1982b). "Beyond belief," reprinted in Dennett (1987).

Dennett, D. (1983a). "The myth of the computer: an exchange," *New York Review of Books* [includes letter from Dennett], 29 (June 24), pp. 56–7.

Dennett, D. (1983b). "Intentional systems in cognitive ethology: the 'Panglossian Paradigm' defended," *Behavioral and Brain Sciences*, 6, pp. 343–90.

Dennett, D. (1984). *Elbow Room: The Varieties of Free Will Worth Wanting*. Cambridge, MA: MIT Press.

Dennett, D. (1987). *The Intentional Stance*. Cambridge, MA: MIT Press.

Devitt, M. (1981). *Designation*. New York: Cambridge University Press.

Devitt, M. (1990). "A narrow representational theory of the mind," in Lycan (1990).

Devitt, M. (1991). *Realism and Truth*, 2nd edn. Oxford: Blackwell.

Devitt, M. and Sterelny, K. (1987). *Language and Reality: An Introduction to the Philosophy of Language*. Cambridge, MA: MIT Press.

Dretske, F. (1981). *Knowledge and the Flow of Information*. Cambridge, MA: MIT Press.

Dretske, F. (1983). "Precis of *Knowledge and the Flow of Information*" (with commentaries and replies), *Behavioral and Brain Sciences*, 6, pp. 55–63.

Dretske, F. (1986). "Misrepresentation," in *Belief: Form, Content and Function*, ed. R. Bogdan (Oxford: Oxford University Press). Reprinted in this volume.

Dretske, F. (1988). *Explaining Behavior*. Cambridge, MA: MIT Press.

Dreyfus, H. (1979). *What Computers Can't Do*. New York: Harper & Row.

Dreyfus, H. and Dreyfus, S. (1985). *Mind over Machine*. New York: Free Press.

Enc, B. (1982). "Intentional states of mechanical devices," *Mind*, 91, pp. 161–82.

Feyerabend, P. (1978). *Science in a Free Society*. London: New Left Books.

Field, H. (1972). "Tarski's theory of truth," *Journal of Philosophy*, 69, pp. 347–75.

Field, H. (1977). "Logic, meaning and conceptual role," *Journal of Philosophy*, 74, pp. 379–409.

Field, H. (1978). "Mental representation," *Erkenntnis*, 13, pp. 9–61. Reprinted in this volume.

Field, H. (1980). *Science without Numbers: A Defense of Nominalism*. Oxford: Oxford University Press.

Field, H. (1986a). "Critical notice: Robert Stalnaker, *Inquiry*," *Philosophy of Science*, 53, pp. 425–8.

Field, H. (1986b). "Stalnaker on intentionality," *Pacific Philosophical Quarterly*, 67, pp. 98–112.

Fodor, J. (1974). "Special sciences," reprinted in Fodor (1981a).

Fodor, J. (1975). *The Language of Thought*. New York: Thomas Y. Crowell.

Fodor, J. (1978). "Tom Swift and his procedural grandmother," reprinted in Fodor (1981a).

Fodor, J. (1981a). *Representations*. Cambridge, MA: MIT Press.

Fodor, J. (1981b). "The mind-body problem," *Scientific American*, 244, pp. 515–31.

Fodor, J. (1981c). "Some notes on what linguistics is about," in Block (1981a).

Fodor, J. (1982). "Cognitive science and the twin earth problem," *Notre Dame Journal of Formal Logic*, 23, pp. 98–118.

Fodor, J. (1983a). "A reply to Brian Loar's 'Must Beliefs be sentences?'," *PSA 1982*, 2 [Ann Arbor].

Fodor, J. (1983b). *The Modularity of Mind*. Cambridge, MA: MIT Press.

Fodor, J. (1984). "Semantics, Wisconsin style," *Synthese*, 59, pp. 231–50. Reprinted in Fodor (1990b).

Fodor, J. (1985). "Fodor's guide to mental representation," *Mind*, 94, pp. 76–100. Reprinted in this volume.

Fodor, J. (1986a). "Banish discontent," in Butterfield (1986).

Fodor, J. (1986b). "Why paramecia don't have mental representations," *Midwest Studies in Philosophy*, 10, pp. 3–23.

Fodor, J. (1987). *Psychosemantics*. Cambridge, MA: MIT Press.

Fodor, J. (1990a). "Information and representation," in *Information, Language and Cognition*, (ed.) P. Hanson (Vancouver: University of British Columbia Press).

Fodor, J. (1990b). *A Theory of Content and Other Essays*. Cambridge, MA: MIT Press.

Fodor, J. (1990c). "Psychosemantics," in Lycan (1990).

Fodor, J. (1990d). "Substitution arguments and the individuation of beliefs," in Fodor (1990b).

Fodor, J. (1991). "Replies," in Loewer and Rey (1991).

Fodor, J. (unpublished). "On there not being an evolutionary theory of content."

Fodor, J. and Lepore, E. (1992). *Holism: A Shopper's Guide*. Oxford: Blackwell.

Fry, D. (1979). *The Physics of Speech*. Cambridge: Cambridge University Press.

Gerhardt, H. C. (1983). "Communication and environment," in Halliday and Slater (1983).

Giere, R. (1988). *Explaining Science: A Cognitive Approach*. Chicago: University of Chicago Press.

Glymour, C. (1987). "Android epistemology and the frame problem," in *The Robot's Dilemma*, ed. Z. Pylyshyn (Norwood, NJ: Ablex).

Glymour, C., Kelly, K., Scheines, R. and Sprites, P. (1986). *Discovering Causal Structure: Artificial Intelligence for Statistical Modelling*. New York: Academic Press.

Godfrey-Smith, P. (1988). "Review of Millikan's *Language Thought and Other Biological Categories*," *Australasian Journal of Philosophy*, 66, pp. 556–60.

Godfrey-Smith, P. (1989). "Misinformation," *Canadian Journal of Philosophy*, 19, pp. 533–50.

Goldman, A. (1976). "Discrimination and perceptual knowledge," *Journal of Philosophy*, 73, pp. 771–91.

Goldman, A. (1989). "Interpretation psychologized," *Mind and Language*, 4, pp. 161–85.

Goodman, N. (1953). *Fact Fiction and Forecast*. Cambridge, MA: Harvard University Press.

Gordon, R. (1986). "Folk psychology as simulation," *Mind and Language*, 1, pp. 158–71.

Gregory, R. (1970). *The Intelligent Eye*. New York: McGraw-Hill.

Grice, P. (1957). "Meaning," *Philosophical Review*, 66, pp. 377–88.

Grünbaum, A. (1968). *Modern Sciences and Zeno's Paradoxes*. London: Allen & Unwin.

Halliday, T. R. (1983). "Information and communication," in Halliday and Slater (1983).

Halliday, T. R. and Slater, P. J. B. eds (1983). *Animal Behavior*, vol. 2: *Communication*. New York: Freeman.

Harman, G. (1968). "Three levels of meaning," *Journal of Philosophy*, 65, pp. 590–602.

Harman, G. (1970). "Language learning," *Nous*, 4, pp. 33–43.

Harman, G. (1973). *Thought*. Princeton, NJ: Princeton University Press.

Harman, G. (1974). "Meaning and semantics," in *Semantics and Philosophy*, ed. M. Munitz and P. Unger (New York: New York University Press).

Harman, G. (1975). "Language, thought, and communication," *Minnesota Studies in the Philosophy of Science*, 7.

Harman, G. (1982). "Conceptual role semantics," *Notre Dame Journal of Formal Logic*, 23, pp. 242–56.

Harman, G. (1986). "Wide functionalism," in *The Representation of Knowledge and Belief*, ed. R. Harnish and M. Brand (Tucson: University of Arizona Press).

Harman, G. (1987). *Change in View*. Cambridge, MA: MIT Press.

Haugeland, J. (1978). "The nature and plausibility of cognitivism," *Behavioral and Brain Sciences*, 2, pp. 215–60.

Haugeland, J. (1980). "Programs, causal role, and intentionality," *Behavioral and Brain Sciences*, 3, pp. 432–3.

Haugeland, J. (1981). "Semantic engines," in *Mind Design*, ed. J. Haugeland (Cambridge, MA: MIT Press).

Haugeland, J. (1982). "The mother of intention," *Nous*, 16, pp. 613–19.

Hayes, P. (1979). "The naive physics manifesto," in *Expert Systems in the Microelectronic Age*, ed. D. Michie (Edinburgh: Edinburgh University Press).

Hills, D. (1981). "Mental representations and languages of thought," in Block (1981a).

Hopkins, C. D. (1983). "Sensory mechanisms in animal communication," in Halliday and Slater (1983).

Horgan, T. (1992). "From cognitive science to folk psychology: computation, mental representation, and belief," *Philosophy and Phenomenological Research*, 52, pp. 449–84.

Horgan, T. (forthcoming). "Naturalism and Intentionality," *Philosophical Studies*.

Horgan, T. and Timmons, M. (1992). "Troubles on moral twin earth: moral queerness revived," *Synthese*, 92, pp. 223–60.

Horwich, P. (1982a). "Three forms of realism," *Synthese*, 51, pp. 181–201.

Horwich, P. (1982b). *Probability and Evidence*. Cambridge: Cambridge University Press.

Israel, D. (1987). *The Role of Propositional Objects of Belief in Action*. CSLI Monograph Report No. CSLI-87-72. Palo Alto: Stanford University Press.

James, W. (1907). *Pragmatism*. Reprinted in James (1975).

James, W. (1909). *The Meaning of Truth*. Reprinted in James (1975).

James, W. (1975). *Pragmatism and The Meaning of Truth*. Cambridge MA: Harvard University Press.

Jech, T. (1973). *The Axiom of Choice*. Amsterdam: North-Holland.

Johnson-Laird, P. (1977). "Procedural semantics," *Cognition*, 5, pp. 189–214.

Johnson-Laird, P. (1978). "What's wrong with grandma's guide to procedural semantics: a reply to Jerry Fodor," *Cognition*, 6, pp. 241–61.

Jones, T., Mulaire, E. and Stich, S. (1991). "Staving off catastrophe: a critical notice of Jerry Fodor's *Psychosemantics*," *Mind and Language*, 6, pp. 58–82.

Kahneman, D., Slovic, P. and Tversky, A. (1982). *Judgement under Uncertainty: Heuristics and Biases*. Cambridge: Cambridge University Press.

Kaplan, D. (unpublished). "Demonstratives."

Katz, J. (1972). *Semantic Theory*. New York: Harper & Row.

Katz, J. (1982). *Language and Other Abstract Objects*. Totowa, NJ: Rowman & Littlefield.

Kolers, P. and Brison, S. (1984). "On pictures, words and their mental representations," *Journal of Verbal Learning and Verbal Behavior*, 23, pp. 105–13.

Krantz, L. (1971). *Suppes and Tversky, Foundations of Measurement*, vol. 1. New York: Academic Press.

Kripke, S. (1972). *Naming and Necessity*. Cambridge, MA: Harvard University Press.

Kripke, S. (1979). "A puzzle about belief," in *Meaning and Use*, ed. A. Margalit (Dordrecht: Kluwer).

Kripke, S. (1982). *Wittgenstein on Rules and Private Language*. Cambridge, MA: Harvard University Press.

Kuhn, T. (1983). "Commensurability, comparability, communicability," *PSA 1982* [Ann Arbor].

Langley, P., Simon, H., Bradshaw, G. and Zytkow, J. (1987). *Scientific Discovery: Computational Explorations of the Creative Process*. Cambridge, MA: MIT Press.

Lewis, D. (1970). "How to define theoretical terms," *Journal of Philosophy*, 67, pp. 427–46.

Lewis, D. (1971). "An argument for the identity theory," in *Materialism and the Mind-Body Problem*, ed. D. Rosenthal Englewood Cliffs, NJ: Prentice-Hall.

Lewis, D. (1972a). "General semantics," in *Semantics of Natural Language*, ed. D. Davidson and G. Harman (Dordrecht: Reidel).

Lewis, D. (1972b). "Psychophysical and theoretical identifications," *Australasian Journal of Philosophy*, 50, pp. 249–58.

Lewis, D. (1974). "Radical interpretation," *Synthese*, 23, pp. 331–44.

Lewis, D. (1975). "Languages and language," *Minnesota Studies in the Philosophy of Science*, 7.

Lloyd, D. (1987). "Mental representation from the bottom up," *Synthese*, 70, pp. 23–78.

Lloyd, D. (1988). *Simple Minds*. Cambridge, MA: MIT Press.

Loar, B. (1981). *Mind and Meaning*. Cambridge: Cambridge University Press.

Loar, B. (1982). "Conceptual role and truth conditions," *Notre Dame Journal of Formal Logic*, 23, pp. 272–83.

Loar, B. (1983). "Must beliefs be sentences?" *PSA 1982* [Ann Arbor].

Loewer, B. (1983). "Information and belief," *Behavioral and Brain Sciences*, 5, pp. 79–80.

Loewer, B. (1987). "From information to intentionality," *Synthese*, 70, pp. 287–317. Excerpted in this volume.

Loewer, B. and Lepore, E. (1986). "Dual aspect semantics," in *New Directions in Semantics*, ed. E. Lepore (New York: Academic Press).

Loewer, B. and Rey, G., eds. (1991). *Meaning in Mind: Fodor and his Critics*. Oxford: Blackwell.

Lycan, W. (unpublished). "Semantic competence and truth condition."

Lycan, W. (1981). "Toward a homuncular theory of believing," *Cognition and Brain Theory*, 4, pp. 139–59.

Lycan, W. (1988). *Judgment and Justification*. Cambridge: Cambridge University Press.

Lycan, W., ed. (1990). *Mind and Cognition*. Oxford: Blackwell.

Maloney, J. C. (1985). "Fred I. Dretske's *Knowledge and the Flow of Information*," *Nous*, 19, pp. 299–306.

Maloney, J. C. (1986). "Sensuous Content," *Philosophical Papers*, 15, pp. 131–54.

Maloney, J. C. (1990). "Mental Misrepresentation," *Philosophy of Science*, 57, pp. 445–58.

Mandler, J. (1983). "Representation," in *Manual of Child Psychology*, ed. P. Mussen (New York: Wiley).

Manfredi, P. and Summerfield, D. (1992). "Robustness without assymetry: a flaw in Fodor's theory of content," *Philosophical Studies*, 66, pp. 261–83.

Marr, D. (1982). *Vision*. San Francisco: W. H. Freeman.

Matthen, M. (1988). "Biological functions and perceptual content," *Journal of Philosophy*, 85, pp. 5–27.

Matthews, R. (1984). "Troubles with representationalism," *Social Research*, 51, pp. 1065–97.

McCarthy, J. (1979). "Ascribing mental qualities to machines," in *Philosophical Perspectives in Artificial Intelligence*, ed. M. Ringle Atlantic Highlands, NJ: Humanities Press.

McCloskey, M. (1983). "Naive theories of motion," in *Mental Models*, ed. D. Gentner and A. L. Stevens (Hillsdale, NJ: Erlbaum).

McCloskey, M., Caramazza, A. and Green, B. (1980). "Curvilinear motion in the absence of external forces: naive beliefs about the motion of objects," *Science*, 210.

McGinn, C. (1982). "The structure of content," in *Though and Object*, ed. A. Woodfield (Oxford: Oxford University Press).

McGinn, C. (1983). *The Subjective View*. Oxford: Oxford University Press.

McGinn, C. (1989). *Mental Content*. Oxford: Blackwell.

McLaughlin, B. (1987). "What is wrong with correlational psychosemantics," *Synthese*, 70, pp. 271–86.

McLaughlin, B. (1990). *Dretske and his Critics*. Oxford: Blackwell.

Mellor, D. H. (1988). "I and now," *Proceedings of the Aristotelian Society*, 89, pp. 79–94.

Miller, G. and Johnson-Laird, P. (1976). *Language and Perception*. Cambridge, MA: MIT Press.

Millikan, R. (1984). *Language, Thought, and Other Biological Categories*. Cambridge, MA: MIT Press.

Millikan, R. (1986). "Thoughts without laws; cognitive science with content," *Philosophical Review*, 95, pp. 47–80.

Millikan, R. (1989). "In defense of proper functions," *Philosophy of Science*, 56, pp. 288–302.

Millikan, R. (1990a). "Truth rules, hoverflies, and the Kripke–Wittgenstein paradox," *Philosophical Review*, 94, pp. 323–53.

Millikan, R. (1990b). "Speaking up for Darwin," in Loewer and Rey (1991).

Murdock, G. (1980). *Theories of Illness*. Pittsburgh: University of Pittsburgh Press.

Murphy, G. and Medin, D. (1985). "The role of theories in conceptual coherence," *Psychological Review*, 92.

Nersessian, N. (1991). "How do scientists think? Capturing the dynamics of conceptual change in science," *Minnesota Studies in the Philosophy of Science*, 15.

Papineau, D. (1987). *Reality and Representation*. Oxford: Blackwell.

Papineau, D. (1990). "Truth and teleology," in *Explanation and its Limits*, ed. D. Knowles (Cambridge: Cambridge University Press).

Parfit, D. (1984). *Reasons and Persons*. Oxford: Oxford University Press.

Peirce, C. S. (1877). "The fixation of belief," reprinted in *Charles S. Peirce: Selected Writings*, ed. P. Weiner (New York: Dover 1966).

Perry, J. (1977). "Frege on demonstratives," *Philosophical Review*, 86, pp. 474–97.

Perry, J. (1979). "The problem of the essential indexical," *Nous*, 13, pp. 3–21.

Perry, R. (1954). *The Thought and Character of William James: Briefer Version*. New York: George Brazziller.

Pickett, J. (1980). *The Sounds of Speech Communication: A Primer of Acoustic Phonetics and Speech Perception*. Austin, TX: Pro-Ed.

Pietroski, P. (forthcoming). "Intentionality and teleological error," *Pacific Philosophical Quarterly*.

Pollock, J. (1987). *Contemporary Theories of Knowledge*. Totowa, NJ: Rowan & Littlefield.

Posner, M. (1978). *Chronometric Explorations of Mind*. Hillsdale, NJ: Erlbaum.

Potter, M., Valian, V. and Faulconer, B. (1977). "Representation of a sentence and its pragmatic implication: verbal, imagistic or abstract?" *Journal of Verbal Learning and Verbal Behavior*, 16, pp. 1–12.

Premack, D. (1983). "The codes of man and beast," *Behavioral and Brain Science*, 6, pp. 125–37.

Putnam, H. (1962). "The analytic and the synthetic," in *Mind Language and Reality* (Cambridge: Cambridge University Press).

Putnam, H. (1975a). "The meaning of meaning," in *Mind Language and Reality* (Cambridge: Cambridge University Press).

Putnam, H. (1975b). "On properties," in *Philosophical Papers*, vol. 1 (Cambridge: Cambridge University Press).

Putnam, H. (1978). *Meaning and the Moral Sciences*. London: Routledge & Kegan Paul.

Putnam, H. (1979). "Reference and understanding," in *Meaning and Understanding*, ed. A. Margalit (Dordrecht: Kluwer).

Putnam, H. (1981). *Reason, Truth and History*. Cambridge: Cambridge University Press.

Putnam, H. (1983). "Computational psychology and interpretation theory," in *Philosophical Papers*, vol. 3: *Realism and Reason* (Cambridge: Cambridge University Press).

Putnam, H. (1986). "Meaning holism," in *The Philosophy of W. V. Quine*, ed. L. Hahn and P. Schilpp (La Salle, IL: Open Court).

Pylyshyn, Z. (1984). *Computation and Cognition*. Cambridge, MA: MIT Press.

Quine, W. V. (1960). *Word and Object*. Cambridge, MA: MIT Press.

Quine, W. V. (1963). "The problem of meaning in linguistics," in *From a Logical Point of View* (New York: Harper & Row).

Quine, W. V. (1970). *Philosophy of Logic*. Englewood Cliffs, NJ: Prentice-Hall.

Ramsey, F. (1927). "Facts and propositions," in *The Foundations of Mathematics and Other Logical Essays*, ed. R. Braithwaite (London: Routledge & Kegan Paul).

Ramsey, W., Stich, S. and Garon, J. (1990). "Connectionism, eliminativism and the future of folk psychology," *Philosophical Perspectives*, 4, pp. 499–533.

Rey, G. (unpublished). "Concepts, stereotypes and individual psychology: sketch of a framework."

Rips, L. (1975). "Inductive judgments about natural categories," *Journal of Verbal Learning and Verbal Behavior*, 8, pp. 240–7.

Rips, L. (1989). "Similarity, typicality, and categorization," in *Similarity, Analogy and Thought*, ed. S. Voisniadou and A. Ortony (New York: Cambridge University Press).

Rorty, R. (1982). *Consequences of Pragmatism*. Minneapolis: University of Minnesota Press.

Rosch, E. (1973). "On the internal structure of perceptual and semantic categories," in *Cognitive Development and the Acquisition of Language*, ed. T. E. Moore (New York: Academic Press).

Rosch, E. (1975). "Cognitive representation of semantic categories," *Journal of Experimental Psychology: General*, 104, pp. 192–233.

Rosch, E. (1978). "Principles of categorization," in *Cognition and Categorization*, ed. E. Rosch and B. Lloyd (Hillsdale, NJ: Erlbaum).

Schiffer, S. (1972). *Meaning*. Oxford: Oxford University Press.

Schiffer, S. (1981). "Truth and the theory of content," in *Meaning and Understanding*, ed. H. Parret (Berlin: De Gruyter).

Schiffer, S. (1982). "Intention based semantics," *Notre Dame Journal of Formal Logic*, 23, pp. 119–59.

Schiffer, S. (1986). "Stalnaker's problem of intentionality," *Pacific Philosophical Quarterly*, 67, pp. 87–97.

Schiffer, S. (1987). *Remnants of Meaning*. Cambridge, MA: MIT Press.

Searle, J. (1980). "Minds, brains and programs," *Behavioral and Brain Sciences*, 3, pp. 417–24.

Searle, J. (1983a). *Intentionality: An Essay in the Philosophy of Mind*. Cambridge: Cambridge University Press.

Searle, J. (1983b). "The myth of the computer," *New York Review of Books* (June 14).

Searle, J. (1984). "Intentionality and its place in nature," *Synthese*, 61, pp. 3–16.

Searle, J. (1992). *The Rediscovery of the Mind*. Cambridge, MA: MIT Press.

Sellars, W. (1963). *Science, Perception and Reality*. London: Routledge & Kegan Paul.

Sellars, W. (1969). "Language as thought and as communication," *Philosophy and Phenomenological Research*, 29, pp. 506–27.

Sellars, W. (1974). "Meaning as functional classification," *Synthese*, 61, pp. 3–16.

Shine, R. (1992). "The lizard of Oz," *Australian Geographic*, 28, pp. 64–79.

Shoemaker, S. (1984). *Identity, Cause and Mind*. Cambridge: Cambridge University Press.

Silvers, S., ed. (1989). *Rerepresentations*. Dordrecht: Kluwer.

Skinner, B. F. (1957). *Verbal Behavior*. New York: Appleton Century Cross.

Sklar, L. (1974). *Space, Time and Space-Time*. Berkeley: University of California Press.

Smith E. and Medin, D. (1981). *Categories and Concepts*. Cambridge, MA: Harvard University Press.

Soames, S. (1984). "What is a theory of truth?" *Journal of Philosophy*, 81, pp. 411–29.

Sober, E., ed. (1984a). *Conceptual Issues in Evolutionary Biology*. Cambridge, MA: MIT Press.

Sober, E. (1984b). *The Nature of Selection*. Cambridge, MA: MIT Press.

Stabler, E. (1983). "How are grammars represented?" *Behavioral and Brain Sciences*, 6, pp. 391–402.

Stack, M. (unpublished). "Why I don't believe in beliefs and you shouldn't," paper delivered at the 1980 meeting of the Society for Philosophy and Psychology.

Stalnaker, R. (1976). "Propositions," in *Issues in the Philosophy of Language*, ed. A. MacKay and D. Merrill (New Haven: Yale University Press).

Stalnaker, R. (1984). *Inquiry*. Cambridge, MA: MIT Press.

Stalnaker, R. (1986). "Replies to Schiffer and Field," *Pacific Philosophical Quarterly*, 67, pp. 113–23.

Stampe, D. (1977). "Towards a causal theory of linguistic representation," *Midwest Studies in Philosophy*, 2, pp. 42–63.

Stampe, D. (1986). "Verificationism and a causal account of meaning," *Synthese*, 69, pp. 107–37.

Sterelny, K. (1985). "Is semantics necessary? Stephen Stich's case against belief," *Australian Journal of Philosophy*, 63, pp. 510–19.

Sterelny, K. (1990). *The Representational Theory of the Mind: An Introduction*. Oxford: Blackwell.

Sternberg, S. (1969). "Memory scanning: mental processes revealed by reaction time experiments," *American Scientist*, 57, pp. 421–57.

Stich, S. (1978). "Autonomous psychology and the belief–desire thesis," *The Monist*, 61, pp. 573–91.

Stich, S. (1982). "On the ascription of content," in *Thought and Object*, ed. A. Woodfield (Oxford: Oxford University Press).

Stich, S. (1983). *From Folk Psychology to Cognitive Science*. Cambridge, MA: MIT Press.

Stich, S. (1990). *The Fragmentation of Reason*. Cambridge, MA: MIT Press.

Stich, S. (1991). "Do true believers exist?" *Proceedings of the Aristotelian Society*, supplementary vol. 65, pp. 229–44.

Stich, S. (1992). "What is a theory of mental representation?" *Mind*, 101, pp. 243–61. Reprinted in this volume.

Stich, S. and Laurence, S. (1994). "Intentionality and naturalism," *Midwest Studies in Philosophy*.

Stich, S. and Nichols, S. (1993). "Folk psychology: simulation or tacit theory?" *Mind and Language*, 7, 1/2, pp. 35–71.

Taylor, K. (1987). "Belief, information and semantic content: a naturalist's lament," *Synthese*, 71, pp. 97–124.

Thagard, P. (1988). *Computational Philosophy of Science*. Cambridge, MA: MIT Press.

Thayer, H. (1981). *Meaning and Action: A Critical History of Pragmatism*, 2nd edn. Indianapolis: Hackett.

Tienson, J. (forthcoming). "The private life of the brain in the vat."

Tolliver, J. (1988). "Disjunctivitis," *Mind and Language*, 3, 1, pp. 64–70.

Turing A. (1950). "Computing machinery and intelligence," *Mind*, 59, pp. 433–60.

Tye, M. (1992). "Naturalism and the mental," *Mind*, 101, pp. 421–41.

Vendler, Z. (1983). *Res Cogitans*. Ithaca, NY: Cornell University Press.

Wagner, S. (unpublished). "Theories of mental representation."

Warfield, T. (forthcoming). "Fodorian semantics: a reply to Adams and Aizawa."

White, S. (1982). "Partial character and the language of thought," *Pacific Philosophical Quarterly*, 63, pp. 347–65.

Whyte, J. (1990). "Success semantics," *Analysis*, 50, pp. 149–57.

Wittgenstein, L. (1922). *Tractatus Logico-Philosophicus*, trans. C. K. Ogden. London: Routledge & Kegan Paul.

Wittgenstein, L. 1958. *Philosophical Investigations*, 3rd edn, trans. G. Anscombe. New York: Macmillan.

Woods, W. (1977). "Meaning and machines," *Proceedings of the International Conference on Computational Linguistics*. Florence.

Woods, W. (1978). *Semantics and Quantification in Natural Language Question Answering*. Technical Report 3687. Cambridge, MA.

Woods, W. (1981). "Procedural semantics as a theory of meaning," in *Elements of Discourse Understanding*, ed. A. Joshi, B. Webber and I. Sag (Cambridge: Cambridge University Press).

Wright, L. (1973). "Functions," *Philosophical Review*, 82, pp. 139–68. Reprinted in Sober (1984a).

Index